Focus on key thinkers

This feature ③ presents you with a summary of the work of a key thinker ④ who has made a significant contribution to an area of sociology. It is followed up by some questions on their work. You may be asked a question about the key thinkers in the examination, so it is important that you know and understand their work.

Activities

Within each topic, you will find a range of activities designed to get you thinking about the material you are studying. There are five types of activity in each chapter: Focus on skills, Focus on theory, Focus on research, Making connections, and Stretch and challenge.

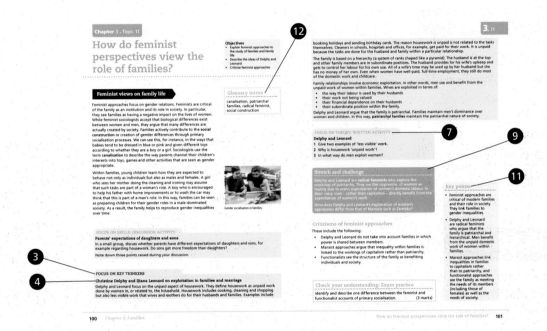

Focus on skills

Focus on skills activities are designed to help you develop the skills that will be assessed in your examination. They may take the form of discussion activities or written activities.

- Discussion activities ⑤ are designed to stimulate discussion and debate on sociological issues. They may be used as the basis of a whole-class or small-group discussion. You may be asked to note down the main points of your discussion or to feed back your ideas to the rest of the class. In this way, you will deepen your understanding of an issue and develop your skills when it comes to evaluation. It is important to appreciate that there may be no 'right' answer to a discussion activity. Everyone's views should be considered equally. This can lead to lively and interesting debates.

- Written activities ⑥ may present you with some statistical data or an extract from a book and you will be asked to answer questions based on this source. This will help you to develop your skills in analysing and making sense of information.

Focus on theory

Focus on theory ⑦ activities are questions designed to get you thinking about the different theories and approaches in sociology.

Focus on research

Some of the Focus on research activities present you with an extract from a piece of sociological research and ask follow-up questions about this research study.

Others are more practical and, for example, might ask you to design your own research. In this way, you will develop your understanding of the different methods of research, as well as your own research skills.

Making connections

As you study the different areas of sociology, it is important to look out for connections **8** or links between them. You could look out for similarities and differences between the different perspectives in sociology (for example, between Marxism and functionalism). Alternatively, you could look out for links between the core areas of sociology (for instance, between Families and Education). The Making connections activities are designed to help you identify and think about these links.

Stretch and challenge

Some Stretch and challenge activities **9** follow on from written activities and others are stand-alone activities. They may ask you to assess arguments and respond using your own ideas or drawing on your experiences. As their name suggests, these activities are designed to encourage you to carefully consider a particular issue or question.

Check your understanding

These questions **10** appear towards the end of each topic. They are designed to enable you to check that you have understood the key ideas in the topic you have been studying. The questions described as 'Exam practice' reflect the types of question you will find in the examination.

Key points

Each topic finishes with a short section on the Key points **11**, which summarise the main learning points of the topic.

Glossary terms

As you read through each topic, you are likely to come across some new terms and concepts **12**. Many of these are explained in the text when they first appear. The more complex terms and concepts also appear in the glossary towards the end of the book, where they are defined for you. All words appearing in the glossary are shown in the Glossary terms box on each spread.

Exam focus

Each chapter ends with a section that looks at examples of examination questions with responses from candidates. An experienced examiner has marked all the candidate responses and detailed comments are provided for you. Some responses have scored full marks and the examiner explains why they have earned full marks. Where answers have not been awarded full marks, the examiner has provided comments to explain how the answer might be developed to score the extra marks. There are also useful tips and advice on areas such as exam technique.

It is worth spending time on these exam focus sections so that you understand:

- why each candidate has been awarded their marks

- the points the examiner is making in the comments

- what the candidate needs to do to develop and improve their answer.

Examination preparation and practice

The Examination preparation and practice section can be found towards the end of the book. The first part provides you with general guidance and is designed to familiarise you with the different types of question that will be asked. The next part gives sample questions on Families, Education, Crime and deviance, and Social stratification, along with advice and tips from an experienced examiner on how to approach these questions.

These questions are ideal to use for revision. Once you have completed the questions, either ask your teacher to mark them or attempt to mark them yourself following the marked examples in the exam focus section of this book.

The AQA GCSE Sociology examination

The examination is made up of two papers:

Paper 1

Section A: Families
Section B: Education

Paper 2

Section A: Crime and deviance
Section B: Social stratification

There will not be a separate section in the examination on the Sociological approach or on Sociological research methods. Instead, these areas will be assessed in the questions on Families, Education, Crime and deviance, and Social stratification.

Sociological knowledge, understanding and skills

This book is designed to help you develop the knowledge, understanding and skills needed to be a competent sociologist at GCSE level. The examination assesses three assessment objectives (AOs). These AOs can be summarised as follows:

AO1 Knowledge and understanding

Can you show that you know and understand the subject matter (the theories, key thinkers, methods, key terms, concepts and evidence) that you have been studying?

AO2 Application of knowledge and understanding

Can you apply your knowledge to the set question? In other words, can you use what you know about an issue in order to address the set question?

AO3 Analysis and evaluation

When writing an extended response:

- Can you examine the different issues raised by the question and show how they are related?
- Can you draw on other relevant topics to show how the core areas of sociology are related to each other?
- Can you assess an explanation or an idea by identifying its strengths and weaknesses?
- Can you evaluate one approach to a question or issue by comparing and contrasting it to other relevant approaches?
- After weighing up the evidence, can you reach a judgment or balanced conclusion?

Do not worry if this looks like a tall order! As you work through the material and activities in this book, you will have lots of opportunities to develop and hone these skills.

Making sense of statistical information

You will come across many examples of statistical tables, graphs and charts in this book and throughout your study of sociology. It is important for you to be able to interpret this information accurately. The following example is included to give you an idea of what you should be looking for when examining statistics.

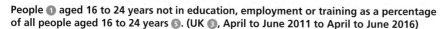

People ❶ aged 16 to 24 years not in education, employment or training as a percentage of all people aged 16 to 24 years ❺. (UK ❸, April to June 2011 to April to June 2016)

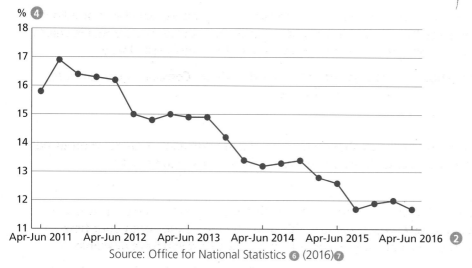

Source: Office for National Statistics ❻ (2016)❼

❶ **Heading**. What general subject is referred to? In the graph above, it is young people aged 16–24 years who are not in education, employment or training (NEETs) as a percentage of all 16- to 24-year-olds.

❷ **Timescale**. Are any dates or years shown? Here, we are looking at April to June 2011 to April to June 2016.

❸ **Where the statistics relate to.** In this case, it is the UK (England, Wales, Scotland and Northern Ireland).

❹ **Units of measurement**. Are the figures shown in percentages? If they are in numbers, is it thousands or millions? Or is it numbers per thousand of the population? Here, the unit of measurement is percentages.

❺ **Relationships in the statistics**. What is being referred to in particular and what is it being related to? Here, the table refers to the proportion of young people who are NEET over a number of years.

❻ **Source of the statistics**. Where are the statistics from? Can this source be relied upon? Is it likely to be biased in any way? Here, the data is from the Office for National Statistics (ONS), which is a major source of government statistics.

❼ **Date**. When were the statistics produced? How up to date are they? Here, the statistics provide information up to April to June 2016 and they were published in 2016.

Identifying trends and changes

In some cases where the statistics span a number of years (for example, 2000, 2005, 2010, 2015), you could be asked to identify or pick out trends in data. A trend refers to the general direction in which statistics on something (such as the divorce rate) move or change over time.

Some statistics present a change between just two points in time, for example between 2007 and 2017. In this case, you may be asked, for example, to identify the percentage change between these two points in time.

Statistics may be presented in a variety of forms, including tables of numbers, bar charts and line graphs (as in the example on page 8), where the rise and fall of a line represents a trend. Pie charts can also be used to represent statistics in the form of percentages in a highly visual way.

The main thing to remember about statistics is not to be afraid of them. Consider them carefully, using the advice given.

Study skills

In addition to the sociological skills outlined above, you should aim to develop a range of other skills to help maximise your chances of success. These are usually referred to as 'study skills'.

Time management

Have you ever felt that you have too much to do and too little time in which to do it? This is a common problem for students. One way to help ease this situation is to think about your time management; in other words, try to make maximum use of the time that you have available.

- The first step is to identify how much time you have available for study in the given week and establish when exactly this is. You will need to consider all of your other commitments and then, in theory, you can use the time left over as study time.
- The next step is to prioritise the tasks you have to complete – perhaps according to when they have to be completed by.
- Once you have done this, you can produce a study plan for the week. This identifies what you will do and when you will do it. All you then have to do is to stick to your plan!

Note taking

In order to develop your sociological knowledge and understanding further, it is often a good idea to read around a topic. You might look at other books or at newspaper articles related to a particular topic you are studying.

As a result of your reading, you may wish to make some notes to use later. While students often have their own approach to taking notes, you may find it useful to read these suggestions for effective note taking.

- ✔ Do skim read the information to get a general understanding first.
- ✔ Do use headings and subheadings to identify key areas.
- ✔ Do use numbers or letters to identify key points.
- ✔ Do use underlining or indentation to help make notes clearer.
- ✔ Do use abbreviations if you prefer, for example, '+' for 'and'.
- ✘ Do not simply produce a slightly shorter version of the material you are making notes on.

The sociological approach

What is sociology?

Sociology is the study of human social life and social relationships. Sociologists investigate and explain the social world and our behaviour in it. This involves examining how people live together in **society** and how they interact with each other in small groups, communities and large organisations. Sociologists try to understand not only the ways in which society influences us in our daily lives but also the ways in which we shape society.

In Britain, people tend to think of themselves as unique individuals who make their own free choices about most aspects of their lives. For example, teenagers make choices about their friends, their clothes and the music they listen to. People also choose whether to marry and what career to pursue. Sociologists are interested in the ways our choices may be constrained (or limited) by factors such as our social class background, **gender** and **ethnicity**. They are also interested in the ways that our choices may be enabled (or helped) by such factors.

Glossary terms

ethnicity, gender, social policies, society, theory

Topics that sociologists study

Sociologists study a wide range of topic areas, as the diagram below shows.

Sociology focuses on the whole range of social life, including big issues (such as poverty and war) and aspects of everyday life. Topics include: The media, Crime, Religions and secularisation, Families and family life, Education, Work, Poverty and wealth, Social class inequality, Gender inequality, Ethnicity and racism, Ageing and ageism, Disability, Health and illness

Making connections

Rather than seeing these topic areas as completely separate, sociologists always look for connections or links between them.

In pairs, choose two of these topics and discuss how they are connected. Then make brief notes to describe the connection.

The sociological approach

Sociology involves a distinctive way of seeing the social world. It focuses on how society influences our behaviour and the choices we make. In doing so, it asks important questions about human social life, groups and society. Here are some examples of these questions:

How do family relationships change over time?

Why are some people obsessed with finding fame through reality TV?

What causes urban riots?

What role do social media play in organising demonstrations?

Why don't all apprentices complete their training programmes?

Why do girls perform better than boys at GCSE?

Do the police and courts treat women and men differently?

Are females more likely to engage in violence today compared to 30 years ago?

When sociologists try to answer such questions, they do not take anything at face value (accept that things are exactly as they appear to be). Instead, they undertake careful investigation to explore what is really going on beneath the surface. In trying to make sense of the social world, sociologists use:

- a body of terms (specialised vocabulary) and concepts (key ideas) that they have built up
- a body of **theories** about the relationship between the individual and society
- a tool kit of research methods such as questionnaires, interviews and observation to gather evidence in an organised and systematic way. As a result, sociology can provide factual information that is more reliable than information from other sources.

Why do girls perform better than boys at GCSE?

However, sociology is not just about carrying out research and contributing to our knowledge of modern society. Many sociologists believe that research should go much further than this by having a practical purpose. They argue that findings from research studies should feed into policy making, shape **social policies** (such as government policies on education) and make a difference to our lives.

FOCUS ON SKILLS: DISCUSSION ACTIVITY

Imagine...

In the 21st century, we take things such as television, computers, mobile phones, the internet, air travel, the education system and the National Health Service for granted. Our lives would probably be very different if we were born in another place or at another time.

1 Imagine that you were born 100 years ago. How would this shape who you are, what you know, what you can do, and the opportunities and choices open to you?
2 In a small group, discuss and compare your ideas.
3 Note down two points arising from your discussion.

Sociology, psychology and journalism

Sociologists study the social influences on human life and focus on group behaviour. Psychologists also study human behaviour but they focus on individuals rather than groups. Journalists sometimes research into social issues, but journalists' research is less thorough than that of sociologists, partly because they often have tight deadlines to meet.

Check your understanding

Identify and describe one possible use of sociological research.

(3 marks)

Key points

- Sociology is the systematic study of human social life, groups and societies.
- Sociologists ask questions about the workings of society; for example, how family relationships change over time.
- Through their research studies, sociologists contribute to our knowledge and understanding of society.

What are social structures, processes and issues?

Social structures and processes

In investigating society and how it is organised, sociologists examine the various parts that make up society. They use the term **'social structures'** to refer to the parts of society such as families, the education system, the political system and the criminal justice system. Sociologists are interested in understanding the connections or relationships between the different structures (or parts) of society. They might study, for instance, the relationship between students' family backgrounds and their achievements at GCSE.

Sociologists are also interested in exploring **social processes** such as socialisation and social control.

The term 'socialisation' refers to the process by which we learn the culture or the way of life of the society we are born into. In exploring how this process operates, sociologists focus on how we learn the culture, who is involved in this learning and what role social structures such as families and schools play in the process.

The term 'social control' refers to the way our behaviour is regulated. In exploring how this process works, sociologists ask questions about:

- how control is exercised
- who exercises control
- how far individuals or groups resist or challenge the processes of social control
- in whose interests social control operates.

By studying these social processes, we can understand more about the workings of society. For example, we learn how such processes take place (the means or mechanisms) and why they take place.

Social issues

Social issues are the issues that affect communities, groups and people's lives. Contemporary social issues relating to education, for example, include academies and grammar schools. Issues relating to families include care of the elderly and forced marriage. Often, social issues are also **social problems**.

Social problems are the problems facing society such as racism, sexism, ageism, **poverty**, domestic violence and hate crime. Social

Glossary terms

poverty, social issue, social problem, social process, social stratification, social structure

Making connections

Choose two social structures from the table on the next page and identify one link or connection between them.

Families are social structures where social processes (such as socialisation) take place. They face social issues (such as care of the elderly).

problems are damaging to society and, as a result, they need to be tackled through social policies.

The table below gives some examples of social structures, social processes and social issues. As you read through the different chapters in this book, you will learn more about these key sociological themes.

Social structures	Social processes	Social issues
Families	Socialisation; Social control; The exercise of power	The quality of parenting; Forced marriage; Care of the elderly; Relationships between parents and children
The education system	Socialisation; Social control; The exercise of power; Labelling; Discrimination	Educational reform; Higher education funding; Academies
The criminal justice system	Social control; Social order; The exercise of power; Discrimination; Labelling	Violent crime; The media coverage of crime; The treatment of young offenders; The prison system
Social stratification systems	Discrimination; The exercise of power; Globalisation	Inequalities linked to class, gender, ethnicity, age, disability and sexuality; Racism, sexism and ageism; Homophobia; Poverty

FOCUS ON SKILLS: WRITTEN ACTIVITY

Government spending on benefits

One way in which governments can try to address social issues such as poverty is through spending on benefits. However, government spending is a controversial issue.

Study the table below, then answer the questions that follow.

Attitudes to government spending on different benefits, 2002–2015

Percentage who would like to see more government spending on benefits for:	2002	2015
People who care for those who are sick or disabled	82%	75%
Parents who work on very low incomes	69%	61%
Disabled people who cannot work	69%	61%
Retired people	73%	49%
Single parents	39%	36%
Unemployed people	21%	17%

Source: adapted from NatCen's British Social Attitudes 33, Welfare. Table 1. p. 5.

1 What percentage of those surveyed in 2015 would like to see more government spending on benefits for single parents?
2 Has this proportion increased or decreased over time?
3 For which group has support for more spending decreased by the biggest percentage?

FOCUS ON SKILLS: DISCUSSION ACTIVITY

Controversial issues

During this course, you will come across social issues such as the quality of parenting, reform of the education system, the causes of teenage crime and the treatment of young offenders.

1 In a small group, discuss why such issues cause public concern and debate.
2 How do you think sociologists could contribute to these debates?
3 Note down three points from your discussion.

Key points

- Sociologists focus on social structures, social processes and social issues.
- Many social issues are also social problems.

Check your understanding

Identify and describe one example of a social structure. (3 marks)

What key concepts do sociologists use?

Objective
• Explain the terms 'culture', 'values' and 'norms'

In Topic 1, you learned that sociologists draw on key concepts (ideas) in their work. These key concepts include **culture**, **values** and **norms**.

Glossary terms

culture, negative sanctions, norms, positive sanctions, sanctions, values

Culture

The term 'culture' refers to the whole way of life of a particular society. It includes the values, norms, customs, beliefs, knowledge, skills and language of a society. Sociologists appreciate that culture is not the same in different societies around the world. It varies according to place (where you are) and time (when). You can see this when looking at food and diet. For example, roast guinea pig is a traditional delicacy in Ecuador, while guinea pigs are often kept as family pets in the UK.

FOCUS ON SKILLS: DISCUSSION ACTIVITY

Living in Britain

The information below is for international students studying at a university in England for the first time. Read through the extract, then answer the questions that follow.

Cafés and bars

Bars and pubs are an important part of British culture, particularly with younger people and students. In the UK, it is quite acceptable for women to use bars, pubs and restaurants without male companions, and there is no pressure on anyone to drink alcohol. Soft drinks are always available.

Smoking

Smoking is prohibited in all enclosed public spaces. It is usual to ask, 'Do you mind if I smoke?' if you are socialising with other people, but do not be offended if you are asked not to.

Source: adapted from http://www.sheffield.ac.uk/polopoly_fs/1.550495!/file/Int-Living-in-Shef-16.pdf, pp. 17, 38.

1 In a small group, discuss how useful this information is in describing aspects of British culture.
2 What advice would your group give to international students on the following: respecting personal space, shaking hands, acceptable topics of conversation, saying 'please' and 'thank you', and humour?
3 Make a note of your ideas.

New students need to learn the expected behaviour associated with university culture.

Values

Values are ideas and beliefs that people have about what is desirable and worth striving for. For example, privacy and respect for human life are highly valued by most people in Britain. Values provide us with general guidelines for conduct.

Not all societies or groups value the same things. Values vary cross-culturally, which means that they differ from one culture to another. In Western societies, for example, wealth and material possessions are often highly valued and considered worth striving for. In contrast, the Apache of North America gave away the property of relatives who died rather than inherit it. They believed that keeping this property might encourage the relatives who inherit it to feel glad when a person died.

Norms

Values provide us with general guidelines for conduct. Norms are more specific to particular situations. For example, we value privacy, and the norms or rules related to this include not reading other people's emails or text messages without permission. Norms tell us what is appropriate and expected behaviour in specific social settings such as classrooms, cinemas, restaurants or aeroplanes. They provide order in society and allow it to function smoothly.

Norms are enforced by **positive sanctions** and **negative sanctions**. This means that people are rewarded for conforming to (or following) the norms, for example, by getting promoted at work. People are punished for deviating from (or breaking) the norms, for example by being 'told off'. Norms and **sanctions** vary depending on time and place. For instance, among the Apache of North America, rule breakers were banished from the group.

FOCUS ON SKILLS: WRITTEN ACTIVITY

Norms

1 Think about the following social settings: a cinema, an aeroplane, a GP's waiting room.
   a Choose one setting and identify two norms related to this setting.
   b Identify two sanctions that might be applied to people who deviate from the norms in this setting.

2 Explain the norms for giving and receiving gifts such as birthday presents.

Check your understanding

Describe what sociologists mean by 'culture'. (3 marks)

Stretch and challenge

Values

Read through the examples of values below, then answer the questions that follow:

- acquiring more and more consumer goods
- honesty and truth
- respect for life
- respect for elders
- privacy
- educational success
- 'getting on' in life at any price
- helping the poor.

1 In your view, which of these values is most important to people in British society today? Briefly explain your answer.

2 Which is least important? Explain your answer.

Key points

- The term 'culture' refers to the whole way of life of a particular society, including its values and norms.

- Values provide general guidelines for conduct and norms define expected behaviour in particular social settings such as in cinemas.

What does the term 'socialisation' mean?

Objective
- Explain the term 'socialisation'

You have seen that culture varies between societies and historically. Sociologists argue that culture is based on learning rather than on instinct – it is not inborn. The term **socialisation** describes the process by which we learn the culture, norms and values of the society we are born into.

Glossary terms

agency of socialisation, established or state church, gender role, gender socialisation, political socialisation, primary socialisation, religion, secondary socialisation, secularisation, socialisation, status

FOCUS ON SKILLS: WRITTEN ACTIVITY

Learning to hunt

The extract below describes an aspect of the socialisation of boys of the Hidatsa people of North America. Read through the extract, then answer the questions that follow.

'Widespread was the practice of boys being taught how to hunt and trap by their fathers, older relatives or a trusted family friend; their roles as hunters were thus conditioned from an early age. Typical are the experiences of the Hidatsa men, Wolf Chief and Goodbird...Wolf Chief told of his early use of the bow and arrow: "I began using a bow, I think, when I was four years of age...I very often went out to hunt birds for so my father bade me do." Armed with blunt arrows and snares, the Hidatsa boys learned skills they would need as hunters and warriors.'

Source: Taylor, C.F. (1996) *Native American Life,* London: Salamander Books, p. 87.

1 Identify one aspect of the Hidatsa culture or way of life.
2 Drawing on this example, explain one way in which the boys were socialised into their culture.

Primary and secondary socialisation

Sociologists distinguish between primary and secondary socialisation and highlight the role of the different **agencies of socialisation**.

Primary socialisation refers to early childhood learning during which, as babies and infants, we learn the basic behaviour patterns, language and skills that we will need in later life. The agencies of primary socialisation are the groups or institutions responsible for primary socialisation. These are usually families and parents. Through interaction within their families, children acquire language and other essential skills.

Secondary socialisation begins later in childhood and continues throughout our adult lives. Through this process, we learn society's norms and values. The agencies of secondary socialisation are the groups or institutions that contribute to this process. Examples include: peer groups, schools, workplaces, religions, mass media.

Peer groups

Peer groups are groups of people who share a similar social **status** and position in society, such as people of a similar age or occupational status. They can exert pressure on their members to conform to group norms and values in settings such as schools or workplaces.

People who do not conform to the group's norms risk being rejected.

Individuals in a peer group may be similar in age and share a group identity.

Schools

During compulsory schooling, students learn how to interact in groups larger than the family. They develop important new skills. They also learn that they are expected to conform to rules and regulations – regarding punctuality and dress, for example. Some students, however, resist the rules and oppose their teachers' authority.

Workplaces

On starting a new job in an office, factory or hospital, for example, newly appointed employees must learn the culture of the workplace. They learn the formal rules regarding dress, punctuality, and health and safety. They may also pick up tips informally from colleagues on things such as how much work is expected and which of the bosses to avoid.

Religions

Religions provide guidelines for behaviour and sanctions when those guidelines are broken. Christianity, for example, provides the Ten Commandments as a guide to how followers should behave. Muslims are expected to put into practice the Five Pillars of Islam, including the alms tax (giving a proportion of one's wealth to the poor). However, some sociologists argue that a process of **secularisation** is taking place and the influence of religion is declining in society. For example, church attendance within the Church of England (the **established or state church**) is falling. If secularisation is occurring, it would suggest that religion has less of a role in the socialisation process today.

Mass media

The mass media, which include television, radio and newspapers, are a powerful source of information and knowledge about the world. Magazines, for example, often give advice on life and relationships. The media sometimes put forward messages about **gender roles** by, for example, showing women advertising washing-up liquid and men advertising cars. In this way, the media contribute to **gender socialisation**. The media (along with families and workplaces) also contribute to **political socialisation**, that is, the process by which people acquire their political views.

FOCUS ON SKILLS: DISCUSSION ACTIVITY

The influence of social groups

We are all members of groups such as families, religious, cultural, friendship or workplace groups.

1 Identify two groups that you are a member of.

2 In pairs, discuss how these groups have influenced you, your behaviour, your beliefs or your identity (how you see yourself).

3 Note down two points arising from your discussion.

Stretch and challenge

How far do you think human behaviour is learned and how far is it instinctive? Explain your thinking.

Key point

In studying society, sociologists draw on the concept of socialisation. This term refers to the process by which we learn the culture, norms and values of the society or group we are born into.

Check your understanding

Describe what sociologists mean by 'socialisation'. (3 marks)

What are the key ideas of Karl Marx?

Objective
- Describe the key ideas of Karl Marx

Three key thinkers – Karl Marx, Emile Durkheim and Max Weber – are seen as the founders of sociology as an academic subject. Marx wrote during the 19th century, while the work of Durkheim and Weber spanned the late 19th and early 20th centuries. They were all writing during times of rapid economic and **social change** (such as the development of **capitalism** and industrialisation) and their work attempts to make sense of these changes. Even today, their ideas are still discussed and debated in sociology.

Glossary terms

bourgeoisie, capitalism, capitalist, class struggle, classless society, communism, lumpenproletariat, Marxism, means of production, petty bourgeoisie, proletariat, social change, theoretical perspective

FOCUS ON KEY THINKERS

Karl Marx (1818–1883)

Place of birth: Germany

Key contribution to the development of sociology: Karl Marx's ideas are linked to an important **theoretical perspective** – the Marxist approach, or **Marxism**. This perspective has inspired a lot of research on social class. Sociologists are still debating Marx's ideas today and many have adapted them to fit contemporary societies.

Karl Marx was writing at an early stage in the development of capitalism (an economic system in which private owners of capital invest money in businesses to make a profit). He wanted to explain the changes taking place in society at that time. In 1849, Marx moved to England and focused on the workings of capitalism in Britain.

People from around the world visit London's Highgate Cemetery to see Karl Marx's grave.

Marx argued that in order to understand the development of societies in the past and today, we must begin by examining production. In other words, it is necessary to examine how people go about producing the things they need in order to subsist. Marx used the term 'mode of production' to describe how people produce the things they need to subsist. One example is the **capitalist** mode of production. Marx identified two key aspects of a mode of production: the means of production and the social relations of production.

- **Means of production**: the materials, such as the raw materials or machinery, that people use in production. Under capitalism, these include capital, big businesses, machinery, factories and land.
- **Social relations of production**: the relations between people as they engage in production. Under capitalism, there are two main social classes: the **bourgeoisie** and the **proletariat**.

Social classes

Marx identified two main social classes under capitalism: the bourgeoisie and the proletariat.

- The bourgeoisie are the capitalist class who own the means of production and private property. Marx saw the bourgeoisie as the ruling class in capitalist society. As owners, they have economic power and this gives them political power.

- The proletariat – the working class – own nothing but their ability to work as wage labourers and Marx saw them as the subject class.

Other classes under capitalism included:

- the **petty bourgeoisie**, who own small businesses
- the **lumpenproletariat**, the 'dropouts' who sometimes sell their services to the bourgeoisie.

Marx saw the relationship between the bourgeoisie and proletariat as based on exploitation. The bourgeoisie exploit the proletariat by profiting from their labour. The bourgeoisie aim to maximise their profits and do this by paying low wages. The proletariat's interests lie in ending exploitation. These different interests lead to conflict between the classes.

Marx argued that the gap in the resources of the bourgeoisie and the proletariat would get much wider over time. Members of the petty bourgeoisie would be unable to compete with bigger companies and would sink into the proletariat.

Over time, society would split more and more 'into two great hostile camps'. In Marx's view, the **class struggle** between the proletariat and the bourgeoisie is the key to bringing about social change. Eventually, members of the proletariat would come to see themselves as a social class with common interests and they would take action to overthrow the capitalist class. This would lead to a period of social revolution and the move to **communism**. Under communism, the means of production would be held communally rather than by a small minority. In this situation, there would be no private ownership, no exploitation and a **classless society**.

Stretch and challenge

Karl Marx argued that philosophers interpret the world but the point is to change it.

What do you think he meant by this?

FOCUS ON THEORY: WRITTEN ACTIVITY

Social classes

Identify and describe two social classes that did not benefit from the capitalist mode of production, according to Karl Marx.

Criticisms of Marx

- Marx analysed class but overlooked other social divisions such as gender and ethnicity.
- He saw social class as based on economic divisions. However, critics argue that class is also based on status (social standing or prestige) differences between groups.

Key points

- Karl Marx developed his ideas during the 19th century, when capitalism was at an early stage of development.

- He identified two main classes under capitalism: the bourgeoisie and the proletariat. The bourgeoisie own the means of production and exploit the proletariat.

- Marx believed that eventually the proletariat would overthrow the bourgeoisie and build a classless, communist society.

Check your understanding

1   Describe what sociologists mean by the term 'bourgeoisie'.
(3 marks)

2   Identify and explain one difference between the bourgeoisie and the proletariat.
(4 marks)

What are the key ideas of Emile Durkheim?

Objective
- Describe the key ideas of Emile Durkheim

Emile Durkheim is one of the founders of sociology as an academic subject. His **worldview** or perspective is very different from that of Marx in important respects.

Glossary terms

function, functionalism, social cohesion, structural approach, worldview

FOCUS ON KEY THINKERS

Emile Durkheim (1858–1917)

Place of birth: France

Key contribution to the development of sociology: Durkheim was a main figure in the origins of **functionalism,** an important perspective in sociology. This approach was popular, particularly among North American sociologists in the mid-20th century. Durkheim made a major contribution to sociologists' understanding of the **functions** of crime, education and religion. He also showed how individual actions such as suicide are shaped by the wider society.

Durkheim was a key thinker behind functionalism.

The functionalist perspective

The functionalist approach explains social institutions (such as families, education systems and social stratification systems) in terms of the functions they perform for the wider society.

To understand functionalism, a biological analogy (or comparison) can be used. In other words, we can compare society to the human body. If we want to understand the human body and how it works, we could start by identifying the vital organs such as the heart, lungs or liver. We might then focus on one organ such as the heart and look at its job or function in pumping blood around the body. Next, we might examine how the heart is connected to other parts of the body such as the blood vessels. Finally, we could look at how the heart contributes to the survival of the body as a whole.

In the same way, functionalism views society as made up of different parts that interlock and fit together. The different social institutions such as the family, education and religion are important organs in the body of society. Functionalism examines these institutions in terms of their functions, that is, the job they perform to help society run smoothly. The different social institutions meet the needs of society by performing functions to ensure its survival.

Durkheim studied crime, religion and education by focusing on the functions they fulfil in meeting the needs of society. For example, he argued that the punishment of criminals has an important

FOCUS ON SKILLS: WRITTEN ACTIVITY

Comparing society to the human body

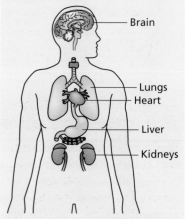

The different parts of the body each have a function.

1 Identify one similarity between society and a human body.

2 How useful do you think it is to compare society to a living body?

function in helping to bring people together. Punishment reinforces the values and beliefs that the majority of people in society hold. By binding people together in this way, crime can contribute to **social cohesion**.

Stretch and challenge

How far do you think that religion binds people together? Explain your ideas.

FOCUS ON THEORY: WRITTEN ACTIVITY

Durkheim and Marx

Durkheim focused on the functions of crime and the way crime can bind people together and contribute to social cohesion.

Did Marx focus more on social cohesion or on conflict between social groups? Write a sentence to explain your thinking.

Similarities between functionalism and Marxism

Although functionalism and Marxism are different in important ways, they are both **structural approaches**. This means that they focus on the structure of society and how this influences and directs human behaviour.

However, not all sociologists agree with structural approaches. Critics argue that these approaches view people as being like puppets who are at the mercy of social forces beyond their control.

FOCUS ON SKILLS: DISCUSSION ACTIVITY

Are people simply puppets?

One debate between sociologists focuses on how far society moulds us and controls our behaviour and how far we create and influence society.

To what extent do you agree that society influences us and directs our behaviour? Can you think of ways in which we can influence, challenge or change society?

Make a note of your ideas.

Criticisms of functionalism

The functionalist approach focuses on the positive functions that things such as crime and religion perform for society. However, critics argue that functionalism overlooks their dysfunctional (or negative) aspects. In reality, crime and religion do not always perform positive functions for society. For example, knife crime can have devastating effects on individual victims and on communities; religion can cause long-term conflicts between different social groups such as Catholics and Protestants in Northern Ireland.

Key points

- Durkheim is one of the founders of sociology and a key figure behind the functionalist perspective.

- Durkheim made an important contribution to sociologists' understanding of the functions of crime, education and religion.

Check your understanding

1 Describe what sociologists mean by the term 'function'. (3 marks)

2 Identify and explain one criticism of functionalism.   (4 marks)

What are the key ideas of Max Weber?

Objective
- Describe the key ideas of Max Weber

Glossary terms

power, social class, social stratification, status

Weber is one of the founders of sociology.

Social class

Both Marx and Weber were interested in issues such as the development of capitalism and social class. Marx saw social class as the key division in society and he defined class in terms of economic factors. Weber agreed with Marx that ownership and non-ownership of property is the most important basis of class divisions. However, Weber argued that class divisions are not just based on economic factors; they are also linked to the skills and qualifications that people have. These skills and qualifications affect the sorts of occupation or job that people get. People with high-level qualifications (such as university degrees) and specialised skills (such as those held by surgeons or architects) are more marketable than people without these qualifications and skills.

Status

Weber identified other aspects of **social stratification** (the way society is structured or divided into strata or layers) in addition to class. One of these is status. Status refers to how much prestige or social standing a group has. There are differences between groups in terms of how much status they have. Some groups, such as surgeons and judges, have high status in the UK today. They also have relatively high incomes. However, Weber argued that status does not always go hand-in-hand with income.

There are groups who earn high incomes but have relatively low status in society. For instance, some second hand car dealers earn much more money than junior doctors, nurses or teachers but have less status. There are other groups, such as religious leaders, who have high status but low incomes.

Power

Weber made a key contribution to the study of power. He argued that an individual or group exercises power when they can get what they want, despite any opposition from other individuals or groups. In Weber's view, people have power in so far as they can get other people to behave as they want them to.

FOCUS ON SKILLS: WRITTEN ACTIVITY

Power

Read through the information below and then answer the questions that follow.

One way of exercising power is through force or coercion. A bully, for example, might use physical force – or the threat of it – to get someone to do what they want. Another way of exercising power is through authority. Politicians, managers, police officers and judges, for instance, are authorised to exercise power over people because of the position they hold within an organisation. The authority of a religious leader might be based on their charisma, that is, the exceptional qualities they have to inspire people.

1 Which form of power (coercion or authority) do you think is likely to be more effective in influencing other people's behaviour? Briefly explain your answer.

2 Choose two groups who have power in the UK today and briefly explain what their power is based on.

FOCUS ON SKILLS: DISCUSSION ACTIVITY

Changing use of language

In the past, Marx, Weber and Durkheim were sometimes referred to as the 'Founding Fathers' of sociology. Some sociologists also used terms such as 'man' or 'mankind' in their writing when referring to people or humankind.

In a small group, discuss why these terms are less likely to be used today. How far does our use of words such as 'man' and 'mankind' matter? Can you think of any similar examples of words that are less likely to be used today compared to the past?

Make a note of the main points arising from your discussion.

Making connections

Weber and Marx focused on class divisions in society but they did not explore inequalities based on gender, ethnicity or age in detail.

How important do you think it is for sociologists today to examine gender, ethnicity and age?

Explain your thinking.

Check your understanding

Identify and explain one similarity between Weber and Marx's approach to social class. (4 marks)

Key points

- Weber agreed with Marx that ownership and non-ownership of property is the most important basis of class divisions.

- However, Weber argued that class divisions are not based just on economic factors; they are also based on people's skills and qualifications.

- Weber also highlighted the importance of status. Groups differ in how much status they have. A particular group may have high status but no wealth and a low income.

What is the consensus versus conflict debate?

Objectives
- Describe the consensus versus conflict debate in sociology
- Describe feminist approaches in sociology

Sociologists disagree about how they see the social world and this means that there are different theoretical perspectives in sociology. A perspective is a particular way of seeing society and explaining how it works. Examples include functionalism, Marxism and **feminism**.

One key difference between these perspectives is whether they see society as based on **consensus** (agreement) or conflict. This is often referred to as the consensus versus conflict debate.

Glossary terms

consensus, discrimination, feminism, feminist perspective, patriarchy, value consensus

The consensus approach

In places such as airports, hospitals and prisons throughout the UK, complex activities take place every day. Much could go wrong. At airports, for example, aeroplanes could be delayed or baggage could go missing. Yet airports are generally ordered places where things usually run smoothly.

Similarly, in wider society, social life is usually ordered and stable. According to the consensus approach, order and stability in society depend on cooperation between individuals and groups who work together for the common good. Generally, this cooperation happens when people believe they have shared interests and goals.

Sociologists who work within the functionalist approach see society as based on **value consensus**. In other words, people agree with society's norms and values. This consensus arises from the process of socialisation (see Topic 4), during which we learn and come to share the norms and values of our society. According to the functionalist perspective, social order is based on consensus and it is maintained over time because most people support the rules and agree to stick to them.

The conflict approach

Some approaches argue that the way society is structured gives power to some groups over others. Marxism and feminism are examples of conflict theories that see society as based on conflicting interests between groups rather than on consensus.

The Marxist perspective sees capitalist societies as based on conflict between two social classes: the bourgeoisie and the proletariat. Marxists focus on class struggle. They argue that there is conflict between powerful and less powerful groups in capitalist society based on their opposing interests. However, social order is maintained over time partly because the bourgeoisie have the power to enforce order. They are able, for instance, to influence the type of laws that are passed and to ensure that the legal system works in their interests.

Feminist perspectives in sociology

Feminist perspectives explore gender inequality and **discrimination** in society. They see sex and gender as different categories. The term 'sex' refers to biological differences between males and females (for example, their roles in reproduction). Gender refers to the different cultural expectations, ideas and practices linked to masculinity and femininity.

Feminists demand an end to male violence against women. The 'Reclaim the Night' marches in London and elsewhere are annual women-only marches against sexual violence and for gender equality.

FOCUS ON SKILLS: WRITTEN ACTIVITY

Masculinity in different cultures

Read through the extract and then answer the questions that follow.

> 'In some cultures, men wear long, flowing garments as a matter of course, but in some the idea of a man in a "dress" is viewed with alarm; in some cultures, men who are good friends walk down the street holding hands, but in others that behaviour is considered a violation of masculinity norms; there was a time in North America when the now-familiar mantra that "pink is for girls, blue is for boys" was reversed and pink was considered a strong, "masculine" colour.'
>
> Source: Lips, H.M. (2013) *Gender: The Basics*. Abingdon: Routledge, p. 14.

1 Identify two examples to show that what is seen as appropriate masculine clothing and behaviour varies between cultures.
2 How far does this information suggest that masculinity is closely linked to biology?

FOCUS ON SKILLS: DISCUSSION ACTIVITY

Nature versus nurture

The nature versus nurture debate concerns how far the differences between men and women are based on biology (nature) and how far they are linked to socialisation and culture (nurture).

In a small group, discuss how far it is possible to separate out the influences of nature and nurture. Note down your ideas.

Gender and power

Some feminist approaches argue that society is patriarchal. In other words, it is based on male power over women. These approaches explore the workings of **patriarchy** within social structures such as families, education, the workplace and the criminal justice system. They see family life, for example, as based on male dominance and this can be seen in men's control of decision-making and in domestic violence.

Check your understanding

Identify and explain one difference between consensus and conflict approaches. (4 marks)

Key points

- The consensus approach is linked to functionalism and argues that society is based on broad agreement about norms and values.

- The Marxist and feminist perspectives view society as based on conflict. Marxism emphasises class conflict and struggle, while feminism emphasises conflict based on gender.

Focus on skills

Using statistical data

You will come across many examples of statistical tables and charts in this book and throughout your study of sociology. It is important for you to be able to make sense of this information.

When you are examining statistical **data**, bear in mind the following checklist:

- What do the statistics refer to?
- What year or years do they refer to?
- Where do they refer to?
- What unit of measurement is used?
- When were they published?
- What is the source of the statistics?

The following activities are designed to give you some practice at making sense of statistical data.

FOCUS ON SKILLS: WRITTEN ACTIVITY

Births outside marriage

Study the information below and then answer the questions that follow.

Live births outside marriage, England and Wales, 1970–2015 (percentages)

1970	1975	1980	1985	1990	1995	2000	2005	2010	2015
8.3%	9.1%	11.8%	19.2%	28.3%	33.9%	39.5%	42.8%	46.8%	47.7%

Source: Office for National Statistics (2016).

1 What percentage of live births were *outside* marriage in 1990?
2 What percentage of live births were *inside* marriage in 2000?
3 Briefly describe the **trend** in the proportion of live births outside marriage between 1970 and 2015.
4 Write down two of your own questions based on these statistics, along with the answers.
5 In pairs, take it in turns to ask each other the questions you have devised.

FOCUS ON SKILLS: WRITTEN ACTIVITY

Attitudes to higher education

As part of the British Social Attitudes survey, the respondents (the people answering the questions) were asked for their views on whether students in higher education (for example, at universities) should get grants to help cover their living costs. Study the pie chart on the next page and then answer the following questions:

1 What percentage of respondents thought that all students should get grants to cover their living costs?
2 Which response received the most support?
3 What response did 5 per cent of respondents give?
4 In which year did this survey take place?

Views on higher education grants, England, 2014

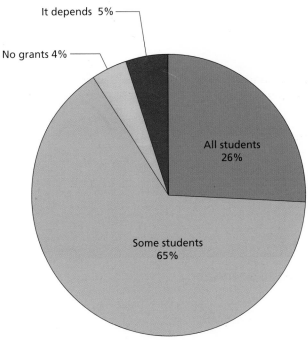

Question: Should students get grants to help cover their living costs?
Source: adapted from NatCen's British Social Attitudes 32, Table 3, p. 7.

FOCUS ON SKILLS: WRITTEN ACTIVITY

Child poverty

Sometimes, statistics are presented within the body of written text rather than in a table or chart. The information below is an extract from a publication produced by the Child Poverty Action Group. Read the extract and then answer the questions that follow.

Child poverty in the UK: a few facts

- There were 3.7 million children living in poverty in the UK in 2013–14. That's 28 per cent of children, or nine in a classroom of 30.
- Work does not provide a guaranteed route out of poverty in the UK. Two-thirds (64 per cent) of children growing up in poverty live in a family where at least one member works.
- Children in large families are at a far greater risk of living in poverty. 35% of children in poverty live in families with three or more children.

Source: Child Poverty Action Group.

1 What percentage of children was living in poverty in the UK in 2013/14?
2 What proportion of children growing up in poverty live in a family where at least one member works?
3 Write down two of your own questions based on the statistics in this extract, along with the answers.
4 In pairs, take it in turns to ask each other the questions you have devised.

Check your understanding

1 Describe what sociologists mean by the term 'data'.   (3 marks)
2 Describe what sociologists mean by the term 'trend' in relation to statistical data.   (3 marks)

Sociological research methods

2

How do sociologists go about their research?

Objectives
- Identify the steps involved in the research process
- Explain the role of the literature review
- Explain the role of the research questions, aims and hypotheses

In the previous chapter, you saw that a key part of sociologists' work involves carrying out **research** in order to collect data (information) in an organised and systematic way. This data provides them with evidence to help explain the social world and to contribute to our knowledge of modern society. Research findings also provide important information for policy makers, government and local authorities.

Glossary terms

hypothesis, literature review, pilot study, research, research aims, research process, sample

The research process

The **research process** in sociology involves several steps or stages. In broad terms, these are:

- reviewing the existing literature
- developing research questions, aims or hypotheses
- choosing a research method or methods
- carrying out a **pilot study**
- selecting a **sample**
- collecting the data
- analysing the data
- evaluating the research.

In practice, research can often be messy and does not always go exactly to plan.

These steps, however, provide a general guide to the research process and show how a study might progress over time.

Reviewing the existing literature

When planning to research a particular topic, a sociologist will read up on the available literature – for example, any studies published in books or journals – relevant to that area. This is known as a **literature review** and it is a key part of the research process.

By doing a literature review, a sociologist:

- becomes familiar with the key concepts that previous researchers have used, the theories they have drawn on, the research methods employed and the findings
- may spot a gap in the literature. If they identify a topic that has not yet been investigated, this will help them to focus their own research on new ground. It will also help if they apply for financial support to cover the costs of their research. This is because funding bodies such as the Economic and Social Research Council (ESRC) expect applicants to show that their research will contribute fresh, original knowledge to the field.
- may be able to identify research questions that have not been addressed yet and to develop new research questions.

Research questions may emerge from a literature review.

Developing research questions, aims and hypotheses

Sociologists ask questions about the social world. During the **research process**, they address these questions in the form of research aims or hypotheses.

- **Research aims** set out what the researcher is planning to investigate and so provide the study with a clear focus.
- A **hypothesis** is a supposition, hunch or informed guess. It is usually written as a statement that can be tested and then either supported by the evidence or refuted (that is, proved wrong).

Sociologists must define what they mean by any key terms or concepts in the research questions, aims or hypotheses. Clear definitions are essential because terms such as 'bullying', 'work' or 'leisure' can be defined in different ways.

FOCUS ON SKILLS: DISCUSSION ACTIVITY

Questions, aims and hypotheses

A research *question* could begin with: 'How?', 'What?', 'To what extent?' or 'Why?'

A research *aim* sets out what the sociologist is planning to investigate.

A **hypothesis** is a statement that can be tested.

1. In pairs, read through the following examples and then decide which one is a research question, which one is a research aim and which one is a hypothesis.
   a. This study will explore British Muslim young women's experiences of education.
   b. Why do some young people join gangs?
   c. Young people are more likely than older people to see themselves as European.
2. Compare your answers with another pair. Once you are sure that your answers are correct, organise them in a table under the headings 'Research question', 'Research aim' and 'Hypothesis'.

Researchers develop their research questions, aims and hypotheses from several sources, including:

- a previous study that they carried out (something may have struck them as interesting, unexpected or puzzling and they go on to explore this in more detail in a later study)
- their review of the existing literature on a particular area
- new developments in technology such as the internet
- their own personal interests or experiences
- a pressing social problem such as poverty, racism or hate crime.

Check your understanding

1. Identify and explain one advantage of carrying out a literature review. (4 marks)
2. Identify and explain one reason why it is important to have clear research questions, aims and hypotheses. (4 marks)

Stretch and challenge

Try to come up with a clear definition of the terms:
a. housework
b. a gang.
Note down your definitions.

FOCUS ON RESEARCH: WRITTEN ACTIVITY

Research and personal life

Read through the information and then answer the question that follows.

Ideas for research can sometimes spring from sociologists' own personal lives and experiences. For example, Sasha Roseneil (2016) has experience of being in a relationship with a partner who lived in another city. However, she realised that LAT relationships ('living apart together' – being part of a couple who live apart) were barely mentioned in books on the sociology of families and relationships. So, with two colleagues, she designed a research study to investigate LAT relationships in Britain.

Identify and describe one source of ideas for sociological research.

Key points

- Sociologists undertake research in order to find answers to the questions they ask.
- The research process involves several stages, from formulating research aims and hypotheses to evaluation.
- Research aims and hypotheses provide the study with a clear focus.

What theoretical factors affect choice of methods?

When sociologists plan a new piece of research, one of the main issues they address is which method or methods to use. There are a range of research methods to choose from, including questionnaires, **observation** and interviews. A researcher's choice of methods is influenced by several factors, including practical issues such as time and money available. One key theoretical issue affecting choice of methods relates to the debates about **positivism** and **interpretivism**.

Glossary terms

in-depth interview, interpretivism, mixed methods approach, observation, participant observation, positivism, qualitative data, qualitative methods, quantitative data, quantitative methods, surveys, triangulation

Positivism

Positivism is based on the idea that the only way to obtain knowledge about the world is through scientific methods. Natural scientists (such as physicists, chemists and biologists) develop hypotheses and test them. This approach allows them to try to discover the laws of nature. Positivists argue that sociologists must use a scientific approach to study the social world. In other words, they should use the methods of the natural sciences to explain human behaviour.

Positivist sociologists focus on behaviour that can be observed and measured rather than on people's feelings or emotions. By generating hypotheses and testing them, sociologists can discover the facts.

Positivists prefer research methods such as large-scale **surveys**. These are known as **quantitative methods** because they are designed to gather facts and figures and to describe society in statistical terms.

Critics of positivism argue that the methods of natural science cannot be applied to the study of the social world. They argue that this is because people – the subject matter of sociology – are completely different from the subject matter of the natural sciences.

Interpretivism

Interpretivist sociologists argue that the subject matter of sociology – people – is completely different from that of the natural sciences. People do not behave like objects or animals. As a result, interpretivists do not believe that sociologists can use scientific research methods to study social life.

The interpretivist approach aims to understand human behaviour and human action by exploring what it means to those involved. So, if we want to understand people's behaviour and motives, we need

FOCUS ON SKILLS: DISCUSSION ACTIVITY

Studying people

In a small group, discuss the similarities and the differences between studying people in society and studying molecules, electrons or chemicals in a laboratory. How different is the subject matter of the natural sciences and sociology? Can they be studied in the same way?

Make a note of your conclusions and your reasons.

to understand the meaning behind their behaviour. The way to do this is by seeing it from that person's point of view.

Interpretivist sociologists prefer methods such as **in-depth interviews** and **participant observation** that collect rich, detailed accounts rather than statistics. These are examples of **qualitative methods**. They are designed to understand what actions mean to the people involved and to see things through their eyes.

FOCUS ON RESEARCH: WRITTEN ACTIVITY

Interpretivism in action

Read through the information below about an interpretivist approach to research and then answer the questions that follow.

> Irene Zempi and Neil Chakraborti (2014) studied the experiences of Muslim women who wear the niqab (a face covering or veil) in public places in Leicester. They adopted an interpretivist approach so that they could see things and experience events through the eyes of the Muslim women. As part of the research, Irene Zempi (who describes herself as a white, Orthodox Christian woman) wore a veil in public places such as on public transport, in shopping centres and on the streets of Leicester for four weeks. This allowed her to understand more fully the women's experiences as victims of Islamophobia (hostility towards Muslims and Islam) in their daily lives.

Research shows that Muslim women who wear the niqab often experience Islamophobia.

1 What do you think the main aim of this research was?
2 Identify one advantage of the method used by Irene Zempi.
3 Drawing on this information, explain briefly what sociologists mean by an 'interpretivist approach'.

Mixed methods approaches

In practice, the division between quantitative and qualitative methods is not so rigid today. Many sociologists now recognise that both are important in building knowledge about society and can be used together. Many studies use **mixed methods approaches** to generate both **quantitative data** and **qualitative data** within one project. By using mixed methods in one study, sociologists can:

- develop a more complete picture of the topic they are investigating
- build on the different strengths of quantitative and qualitative methods (they can get rich insights into people's experiences through qualitative methods and also make connections between variables through quantitative methods)
- cross-check the findings from a qualitative method against the findings from a quantitative method. This is sometimes referred to as **triangulation**.

Check your understanding

1 Describe one difference between a positivist and an interpretivist approach to research. (3 marks)

2 Identify and explain one advantage of using a mixed methods approach in sociological research. (4 marks)

Key points

- Positivists argue that sociologists should try to use the methods of the natural sciences to explain human behaviour. This requires a more quantitative approach.

- Interpretivists seek to understand human behaviour by exploring what it means to those involved. This requires a more qualitative approach.

- A mixed methods approach combines both quantitative and qualitative methods in one study.

What is a pilot study?

Objective
- Explain the role of the pilot study in the research process

Carrying out a pilot study

A pilot study is a small-scale trial run carried out before the main research. It allows the researcher to check whether the main study is likely to generate relevant data that can be used to address the research questions and aims. In this way, a pilot study may save time, money and effort in the long run.

During a pilot study, the researcher can pre-test the proposed research methods to check whether they are appropriate. This helps to identify and overcome potential problems – for example, with the wording or order of questions – so the researcher gets them right in the main study. A pilot interview may, for instance, show that some questions are repetitive. Piloting a **questionnaire** may indicate that it takes far too long to complete.

> **Glossary terms**
>
> anonymity of research participants, questionnaire, respondent, response rate

FOCUS ON RESEARCH: WRITTEN ACTIVITY

Piloting a questionnaire on the Costa del Sol

Karen O'Reilly studied the lifestyles and experiences of British migrants to Spain's Costa del Sol. In the extract below, she discusses her pilot study. Read this extract and answer the questions that follow.

'I designed a questionnaire that asked for background details on household size, age, income, work, class background, and length of stay in Spain. Replies were to be anonymous (those replying did not have to give their names).

I conducted a pilot study, requesting seven individuals of various ages, both men and women, to complete the questionnaire for me so that mistakes or problems might be revealed before it was distributed more widely. Each **respondent** was pleased to do this, but some were not happy about the idea of a survey in general. They worried that people would not want to "be bothered" or would not want to answer personal questions.

One of the men in the pilot study commented: "Why do you have to ask questions on income? As soon as people see questions like that, they are going to think you are from the tax. They think you're a tax inspector or something." He recommended that I ask no questions on name, address, date of birth, income or work, as these could make the questionnaire's anonymity doubtful.

As a result of these concerns, I adapted the questionnaire and added a cover note to make it clear that respondents would remain anonymous.'

Source: adapted from O'Reilly, K. (2000), pp. 154–155 and p. 170

Karen O'Reilly studied the lifestyles of British migrants living on the Costa del Sol.

1 Why did Karen O'Reilly undertake a pilot study?
2 Identify two concerns raised by those who took part in the pilot study.
3 What changes did O'Reilly make to her questionnaire after doing the pilot study?

FOCUS ON RESEARCH: DISCUSSION ACTIVITY

Anonymity in research

In a small group, discuss the following questions about the **anonymity of research participants**.

- If you were taking part in a study, would you want to give your name or other details that might identify you? Why? Why not?
- How important is it that research participants have rights? Are there any other rights they should have?

Make a note of your ideas and be prepared to share them with the class.

FOCUS ON RESEARCH: WRITTEN ACTIVITY

Studying British Muslim converts

Kate Zebiri (2008) studied British Muslim converts and explored what happens after they convert to Islam, and how their attitudes to society and their identities change. Read through the extract and answer the questions that follow.

'When I began this study in early 2005 I was intending to distribute a fairly large number of questionnaires, and then follow up some of the more interesting responses with interviews. However, I soon realised that other researchers in the field (both Muslim and non-Muslim) had experienced considerable difficulty in persuading Muslim converts to fill in questionnaires, citing low **response rates**...Therefore,...I decided to base the study mainly on interviews, and found that on the whole people seemed more willing to engage with a researcher on a personal level.'

Source: Zebiri, K. (2008), p. 8

1 How did Kate Zebiri's plans change over time?
2 Why do you think researchers might find it difficult to persuade some people to fill in a questionnaire?
3 What advantages did interviews have over questionnaires in this context?

FOCUS ON RESEARCH: DISCUSSION ACTIVITY

Piloting a questionnaire

Imagine that you are investigating how far British people see themselves as European. Your hypothesis is that people aged 29 and under are more likely to see themselves as European than people aged 60 and over. Your research method is a social survey.

1 In pairs, work out the first six questions of a draft survey and write these down.
2 Pilot your draft survey by asking four people in your class these questions.
3 Note down any questions that were problematic for your respondents and make any necessary changes to improve these questions.

Check your understanding

1 Describe what is meant by a 'pilot study'. (3 marks)
2 Identify and explain one advantage of using a pilot study. (4 marks)

Key point

A pilot study enables the researcher to trial the chosen research methods and ensure that these are appropriate and cost-effective.

How do sociologists select samples?

Before carrying out surveys or interviews, the researcher must identify the **population** or group they want to study. The population may be made up of people (such as househusbands or students) or institutions (such as families or schools), depending on the focus of the research.

If it is too expensive or time-consuming to question the full population, a sample or subgroup of the population will be studied. A sample is usually selected from a **sampling frame**. This is a full list of all members of the population – for example, school registers or the Royal Mail's list of postcode addresses.

If the sampling frame is inaccurate (for example, incomplete or out of date), the sample drawn from it may not be representative of the population. A **representative sample** is typical of its wider population. In other words, it is a smaller version of the population. An **unrepresentative sample** might, for example, over-represent females or under-represent retired people. If the sample is unrepresentative, it will be difficult to generalise from the findings. **Generalisations** are general statements and conclusions that apply not only to the sample but also to the population.

Glossary terms

generalisations, non-probability sampling, population, probability (or random) sampling, purposive sampling, quota sampling, representative sample, sampling frame, simple random sampling, snowball sampling, stratified random sampling, systematic random sampling, unrepresentative sample

Different sampling techniques

Sociologists can choose between several sampling techniques in order to select a sample. May (2001) divides sampling into two categories:

Probability (or random) sampling	Non-probability sampling
• simple random sampling • systematic random sampling • stratified random sampling	• snowball sampling • quota sampling • purposive sampling

With **probability (or random) sampling**, each member of the sampling frame has a known chance of being selected. If the sample is selected randomly, it is likely that it will mirror the population, so general conclusions can be drawn. **Non-probability sampling** is used where a sampling frame is unavailable.

Probability sampling
- With **simple random sampling**, each member of the population has an equal chance of being included in the sample. Researchers use computers to generate simple random samples.
- **Systematic random sampling** involves taking every 'nth' item from the sampling frame, for example every 10th name from a college register. If the population consists of 1000 students and a sample of 100 is required, the researcher will randomly select a number between 1 and 10. If this was 5, then the 5th, 15th and 25th names – and so on up to the 995th name – would

be selected from the sampling frame to provide the required sample size.

- **Stratified random sampling** may be used if, for example, a sociologist wants the sample to reflect the age and gender characteristics of the population. Stratified random sampling would involve dividing the population into strata (layers or subgroups) – for example: males aged 30 and under; females aged 30 and under; males aged 31 and over; females aged 31 and over. The sociologist then randomly draws a sample from each subgroup in proportion to their numbers in the population. They would, for example, select 15 per cent of their sample from males aged 31 and over.

Non-probability sampling

A sociologist may be interested in studying a population for which there is no sampling frame, for example British Muslim converts or homeless people. In this case, **snowball sampling** may be the only option. Using this technique, the researcher would contact one member of the population, gradually gaining their confidence until they are willing to identify others in the same population who might cooperate. In this way, the researcher can obtain a sample, although it is unlikely to be representative.

Quota sampling is often used by market researchers who interview people on the street. Each interviewer has to interview an exact quota (number) of people from categories such as females or teenagers, in proportion to their numbers in the wider population. So, if the population has 10 per cent white females aged 40 to 49, the interviewer must interview enough white women from this age group to make up 10 per cent of the sample.

With **purposive sampling**, the sample is selected according to a known characteristic (such as being a head teacher or receiving a particular state benefit).

FOCUS ON SKILLS: WRITTEN ACTIVITY

Sampling techniques

Imagine that you are part of a research team investigating students' views on equal opportunities in your school or college. The population consists of 1000 students and you need a sample of 200 students. Study the pie chart and answer the questions that follow.

1 Explain how you would obtain:
   a a stratified random sample of 200 students, stratified according to class, ethnicity and gender
   b a systematic sample of 200 students.

2 Which of these two types of sampling would give you a more representative sample? Explain your view.

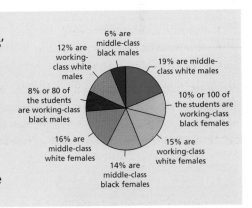

6% are middle-class black males
12% are working-class white males
19% are middle-class white males
8% or 80 of the students are working-class black males
10% or 100 of the students are working-class black females
16% are middle-class white females
15% are working-class white females
14% are middle-class black females

Check your understanding

1 Identify and describe one sampling technique. (4 marks)

2 Identify and describe one reason sociologists may use a non-probability-based sampling method in their research. (4 marks)

Key point

As part of the research process, researchers select a sample (or subgroup) of the population using either probability or non-probability sampling.

How do sociologists collect and analyse data?

Objective
- Explain the role of data collection and analysis in the research process

Once researchers have completed a pilot study and selected a sample, they are ready to begin the **fieldwork**. This involves gathering the raw data that will be used as evidence. Data can be collected by using one or more methods from a range of **research techniques** such as questionnaires, interviews and observation. When data is collected by doing research in this way, it is referred to as **primary data**. When data already exists and was collected by other people, it is known as **secondary data**.

Glossary terms

data analysis, field note diaries, fieldwork, mass media, primary data, research techniques, secondary data, transcript, unstructured interviews

Sources of primary data include:	Sources of secondary data include:
Questionnaires	Existing research by other sociologists
Structured interviews	Official statistics
In-depth or unstructured interviews	Non-official statistics
Participant observation	The mass media (e.g. newspapers)
Non-participant observation	Personal documents (e.g. letters or diaries)

Sociologists may use quantitative or qualitative data (and often a combination of both) from the various primary and secondary sources.

Quantitative data

Quantitative data is presented in numerical form; for example, 48 per cent of respondents visited their local library at least once in the last month. The results are usually displayed in graphs, pie charts, bar charts or tables of statistics that count or measure something.

Sociologists generate quantitative primary data in their own research using standardised, large-scale methods such as questionnaires.

Sources of quantitative secondary data include official statistics on police-recorded crime. Sociologists may also draw on data from existing government surveys such as the census.

Qualitative data

Qualitative data is presented in visual or verbal form, for example as words or quotations, rather than numbers. Researchers gather qualitative primary data, consisting of verbatim (word-for-word) accounts from research participants using less standardised methods such as in-depth or **unstructured interviews**. They might also draw on qualitative primary data in the form of entries in their **field note diaries**.

When sociologists conduct research in places such as schools or in community groups, they usually write about their experiences every day in their field notes.

Sources of qualitative secondary data include the **mass media** (for example, newspapers and TV documentaries) and personal documents such as letters, diaries and photographs.

Keeping field notes

While Marek Korczynski (2014) was studying the role of pop music in a blinds factory, he kept field notes about his experiences. During breaks, he scribbled notes on a notepad in the toilet to remind himself of things he wanted to remember. At the end of the day, he tape-recorded his field notes. When the tapes were transcribed (typed up into a written copy or **transcript**), this created a document of 80 000 words.

Read the excerpt from Korczynski's field notebook and answer the questions that follow.

> '"Come on Eileen" by Dexys Midnight Runners came on the radio. Two or three people sing along to the chorus, changing the words to "Come on Irene" directed at Irene. They're smiling and laughing.'
>
> Source: Korczynski, M. (2014) *Songs of the Factory: Pop Music, Culture, and Resistance.* New York: Cornell University Press, pp. 32–33.

1 Why do you think that Marek Korczynski made notes in the toilet rather than in public?

2 Korczynski worked alongside the factory workers as a participant observer and observed how they interacted together. Identify two advantages of this form of observation compared to interviews with the factory workers.

Sources of data

Copy out the table and add each of the following under the correct heading:

birth rates   unstructured interviews   magazines   questionnaires

Primary and quantitative data sources	Primary and qualitative data sources
• Structured interviews	• Participant observation
Secondary and quantitative data sources	**Secondary and qualitative data sources**
• Police-recorded crime statistics	• Autobiographies

Data analysis

Research produces vast quantities of data, for example, in the form of interview transcripts and completed questionnaires. The researcher now has the task of analysing the data. **Data analysis** involves interpreting or making sense of the information and summarising the main findings or results.

Using computer software packages speeds up the process of analysis. Statistical software packages, for example, can summarise data, examine relationships between factors and present results as graphs and bar charts.

Key points

- As part of the research process, researchers collect raw data and analyse it.

- Sources of data are either primary (collected first hand through methods such as interviews) or secondary (already exists, for example, official statistics or newspaper reports).

- Data may be either quantitative (presented in numerical form) or qualitative (presented in words).

Check your understanding

1 Describe what sociologists mean by 'primary data'. (3 marks)

2 Identify and explain one advantage of using quantitative data in sociological research. (4 marks)

How do sociologists evaluate their research?

Objective
- Explain the role of evaluation in the research process

While they are carrying out a particular study, sociologists present conference papers on their work to their peers (other sociologists). The British Sociological Association's annual conference, for example, provides opportunities for sociologists to present their work and discuss their ideas. Sociologists also submit articles on work in progress to journals such as the British Journal of Sociology of Education.

Once the study is complete, sociologists discuss their research and findings in conference papers and journal articles. At this stage they are also expected to provide the organisation that funded the study (such as the Economic and Social Research Council) with a report on the research.

Sociological research outputs (for example, journal articles and conference papers) are all evaluated by **peer review**. This means that, before sociologists present their work at conferences or before their articles are published in journals, these papers and articles are assessed by experienced sociologists. The journal reviewers provide feedback and, in the case of promising articles, they usually require authors to amend the contents before resubmitting them. In this way, peer review works as a form of quality control.

> **Glossary terms**
>
> data protection, generalisation, peer review, random sample, reliable, representativeness, research ethics, validity

Sociologists present papers on their work at conferences.

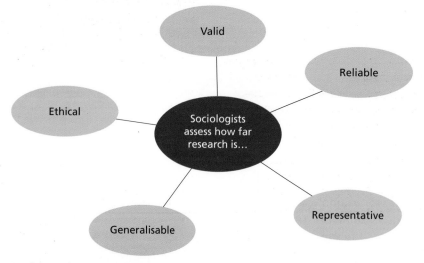

In order to evaluate a piece of research, sociologists focus on a number of key features.

Validity

Research is **valid** if it actually measures or captures what it set out to examine in the first place. To be valid, the data must truly measure or capture what they are supposed to be studying. For example, does an IQ test really measure intelligence or does it measure something else? Do police-recorded crime statistics really measure the extent of crime?

Reliability

Research findings are **reliable** if the same results are obtained a second time using the same methods. If your survey findings are reliable, for example, another sociologist should be able to replicate or repeat your research and get the same results as you got the first time round.

Representativeness

Sociologists usually want the organisation or people they study to represent a larger group so that the findings apply to the wider group. For instance, if we just questioned some of our family members about their leisure activities, the results would apply just to the people we asked. The findings would be unlikely to represent – or be typical of – the wider group. To achieve **representativeness**, you would need to obtain a **random sample**.

Generalisations

Assuming that your research is valid, reliable and representative, you should be able to generalise from your results. A **generalisation** is a general statement or conclusion that applies not only to the sample but also to the broader population that the sample represents.

Research ethics

Research ethics are important in sociology and sociologists are required to carry out their research to a high ethical standard. In other words, they must carry out research in morally acceptable ways. For example, they are expected to respect and safeguard research participants' interests at all times. When they discuss their research in articles, reports or books, they must take into account the interests of research participants. Any personal information about a participant should be kept confidential and should not be reported on in such a way that it reveals the participant's identity. (See Topic 21.) Principles of **data protection** apply to this information, so, for example, it must be stored securely.

Key points

- Peer review operates as a form of quality control.

- In evaluating a piece of research, it is important to ask how far it is valid, reliable, representative, generalisable and ethical.

Check your understanding

Identify and explain one way in which the quality of a piece of sociological research can be assessed. **(4 marks)**

What are social surveys?

Objectives
- Describe the use of social surveys in sociological research
- Outline the main ways of delivering surveys

Social surveys are one of the most popular research methods in sociology. They are also used by opinion pollsters, market researchers and government departments. Social surveys involve collecting information from a large number of people, usually through questionnaires or structured interviews.

A social survey consists of a list of pre-set questions to which the respondent (the person from whom information is sought) supplies the answers. The questions are standardised so each respondent answers an identical set of questions, presented in exactly the same order.

Glossary terms

closed question, interview schedule, leading question, open-ended question, social survey

Ways of carrying out survey research

There are two main ways of carrying out survey research:

1 self-completion questionnaires
2 formal or structured interviews.

Self-completion questionnaires

The respondents answer the questions by filling in the questionnaire themselves. The questionnaires can be delivered in three ways:

- postal questionnaires – the questionnaire is mailed to the respondent, who completes it and sends it back to the researcher
- via email
- hand-delivered questionnaires – the researcher hands a questionnaire to the respondent and returns to collect the completed questionnaire at a later date.

Formal or structured interviews

The interviewer reads the standard questions from the **interview schedule** (the pre-set list of questions) and the respondent gives the answers there and then. This is a formal question-and-answer session. Structured interviews are carried out either face to face or by telephone.

Structured interviews may be undertaken by telephone.

Stretch and challenge

Give two reasons why a researcher might carry out structured interviews by telephone rather than face to face.

Different types of question

Within a questionnaire or structured interview, two types of question may be used: **closed questions** and **open-ended questions**.

Closed (or fixed-choice) questions

These require respondents to choose between a number of given answers. Often, the respondent just has to tick the appropriate box in response to a set question, so it can be answered quite quickly. The question, for example, might be 'Did you vote in the last general election?' and the given answers could simply be 'yes' or 'no'. Other examples include:

a Are you:

Male? ☐   Female? ☐

b How old are you?

Under 21 ☐   21–30 ☐   31–40 ☐   41–50 ☐   51–60 ☐

The responses to closed questions are relatively easy to process by computer and can be presented in numerical form. In a study of voting behaviour, for example, it might be found that 72 per cent of respondents voted in the last general election. However, closed questions would be unsuitable if the researcher was interested in obtaining in-depth, detailed accounts of the reasons for voting in a particular way.

Where closed questions are used, it is essential that all possible answers are anticipated in advance and included in the questionnaire. It is also important that the questions and answers are carefully worded so that their meaning is perfectly clear.

> **Stretch and challenge**
>
> **Processing responses**
> Write a paragraph explaining why the answers to closed questions would be easier and quicker for a researcher to process than the answers to open-ended questions.

> **FOCUS ON SKILLS: WRITTEN ACTIVITY**
>
> **Using social surveys**
> Here are some examples of questions taken from a survey on the topic of 'Work, leisure and family life'. Study the examples and answer the questions that follow.
>
> **1** How long have you been employed in your current post?
>
> **2** Please rate the opportunities for promotion within this company:
>
> Excellent ☐   Good ☐   Fair ☐   Poor ☐   Very poor ☐
>
> **3** How strongly do you agree or disagree with the following statement?
>
> 'Paid work is more important to me than leisure.'
>
> Strongly agree ☐   Agree ☐   Unsure ☐   Disagree ☐   Strongly disagree ☐
>
> **4** How does your job affect your family life outside work?
>
> _____
>
> **1** Which of the above questions are closed?
> **2** A '**leading question**' is a question worded in such a way as to suggest a desired answer. How far do you think question number 4 is a leading question?

Open-ended questions

These enable respondents to put forward their own answers to the set questions rather than choose a response from several pre-set answers. An example of an open-ended question is: 'What are your views on the results of the last general election?' Responses to this type of question are likely to be very varied and so are more difficult to convert into statistics. Open-ended questions, therefore, would be unsuitable if the researcher was only interested in obtaining quantitative data.

> **Check your understanding**
>
> 1 Identify and describe one way of carrying out a social survey.
> (3 marks)
>
> 2 Identify and describe one difference between open-ended and closed questions. (3 marks)

> **Key points**
>
> • Social surveys are a popular way of undertaking social research. Examples include self-completion questionnaires and structured interviews.
>
> • Questions can be open-ended or closed.

What are the advantages and limitations of postal questionnaires?

Objective
- Discuss the strengths and limitations of postal questionnaires in sociological research

Postal questionnaires are an important way of gathering data in survey research. However, like any research method, they have strengths and weaknesses. For example, they can be difficult and time-consuming to design.

Glossary terms

replication, trade union

FOCUS ON SKILLS: DISCUSSION ACTIVITY

Questionnaire design

The following draft postal questionnaire was designed to find out whether domestic tasks are shared equally between partners with children. Study the draft questionnaire and, in a small group, answer the questions that follow.

1 What is your name?

  _____

2 Age

  _____

3 Gender Male / Female

4 Occupation (please state)

  _____

5 Are you:
  Married ☐   Civil partnership ☐   Cohabiting ☐

6 How many young children do you have?
  0 ☐   1–3 ☐   3–4 ☐   4 or more ☐

7 How much housework and childcare does your partner do each week?
  None ☐   1–4 hours ☐   5–9 hours ☐   10+ hours ☐

In your group:

1 Identify any questions that you might not want to include in a questionnaire.
2 Identify the questions that need revising and rewrite them in a more appropriate way.
3 Note down three tips for other students who are designing postal questionnaires.

The advantages of postal questionnaires

✔ Postal questionnaires are a quick and efficient way of obtaining large amounts of information from large samples (for example, of people or households) spread over a wide geographical area.
✔ They are relatively cheap when compared to interviews.
✔ The researcher is not present, so respondents may be more willing to answer potentially embarrassing, personal or sensitive questions, for example about smoking during pregnancy or involvement in crime.

✔ Postal questionnaires ask standardised questions and each respondent answers an identical set of questions. Answers can be compared and any differences highlighted. If respondents answer a particular question differently, this is seen as reflecting real differences of opinion between them.

✔ Closed questions provide quantitative data. With such statistical data, it is possible to measure the strength of a connection between different factors, for example between support for the current government and **trade union** membership.

✔ The questions are standardised, so **replication** is possible. This means that a postal questionnaire can be replicated or repeated by other researchers to check whether the findings are reliable. If a second researcher repeats the questionnaire and obtains the same or consistent results, then these can be seen as reliable.

The limitations of postal questionnaires

✗ The interviewer is not present to clarify the questions, so respondents may misunderstand them and answer incorrectly.

✗ The respondent may not complete all sections of the questionnaire.

✗ You can never be sure that the right person actually completed the questionnaire. For instance, a group of people may work on it together.

✗ Postal questionnaires would be unsuitable for some populations such as homeless people and people with literacy problems.

✗ Postal questionnaires consist of pre-set questions, at least some of which are fixed-choice or closed. In this case, the researcher has already decided the questions and also the possible answers in advance.

✗ Closed questions do not allow respondents to develop their answers. Respondents have no opportunity to explain why they ticked one box rather than another.

✗ The response rate – that is, the number of replies received in proportion to the total number of questionnaires distributed – is usually low. Those who do respond may not be representative or typical of the population under study. It will be impossible, therefore, to generalise from the sample of people surveyed to the population as a whole.

Check your understanding

Imagine that you are investigating how much time women spend on housework and childcare each week compared to their partners. You are considering self-completion postal questionnaires as your research method.

1   Identify and explain one advantage of using postal questionnaires when carrying out this research.   (4 marks)

2   Identify and explain one problem you may face when carrying out this research.   (4 marks)

FOCUS ON SKILLS: DISCUSSION ACTIVITY

Studying people

One way to encourage respondents to complete and return postal questionnaires is by offering them payment (for example, in gift vouchers) or some other incentive, such as entry into a prize draw.

In a small group, discuss whether respondents should be compensated for giving up their time to take part in research.

Note down two reasons for, and two reasons against, compensating respondents in this way.

Stretch and challenge

Write a paragraph to explain why positivist sociologists might be more likely than interpretivists to use social surveys in their research.

Key points

• Postal questionnaires are a cost-effective way of reaching large samples. They ask standardised questions and provide statistical data on differences between respondents. They can be replicated to check the reliability of findings; getting the same or similar results a second time round confirms reliability.

• Postal questionnaires, however, tend to have a low response rate. Respondents cannot develop their answers and may misunderstand or skip questions.

What are the uses, advantages and limitations of structured interviews?

An **interview** may be structured, semi-structured or unstructured, depending on how far the questions are standardised in advance. Structured (or formal) interviews are questionnaires that are delivered in person or by telephone. Computer-assisted interviewing (CAI) is becoming more widespread as an alternative to paper-and-pencil questionnaires.

Glossary terms

computer-assisted personal interviewing (CAPI), computer-assisted self-interviewing (CASI), computer-assisted telephone interviewing (CATI), feminist, interview, interview bias, interviewer bias

FOCUS ON SKILLS: WRITTEN ACTIVITY

Computer-assisted interviewing

Study the table below and answer the questions that follow.

Types of computer-assisted interviewing (CAI)

Computer-assisted personal interviewing (CAPI)	Computer-assisted self-interviewing (CASI)	Computer-assisted telephone interviewing (CATI)
CAPI is used when delivering a questionnaire in a face-to-face structured interview	CASI is used when asking potentially sensitive or embarrassing questions (e.g. about participation in crime) during a face-to-face structured interview	CATI is used when delivering a questionnaire in a structured interview over the telephone
The interviewer is present to read the questions from, and enter answers directly into, a laptop computer or tablet.	The interviewer gives the computer to the respondent so that they can input their own answers to some sections or questions for themselves.	The interviewer reads the questions from, and enters answers into, a computer. The interview takes place via telephone rather than face to face.

1 What is the main difference between **computer-assisted personal interviewing (CAPI)** and **computer-assisted telephone interviewing (CATI)**?

2 Why might researchers prefer to use computer-assisted interviewing (CAI) rather than paper-and-pencil questionnaires?

The advantages of structured interviews

Structured (or formal) interviews and postal questionnaires are both examples of social surveys, so it is not surprising that they have some advantages in common.

✔ As with postal questionnaires, interview questions are standardised. Each respondent responds to the same set of questions, asked in exactly the same order. As a result, any differences between respondents' answers are seen as revealing real differences in their attitudes or opinions.

Stretch and challenge

CASI and validity

One view is that **computer-assisted self-interviewing (CASI)** can increase the validity of responses to sensitive questions.

Write a short paragraph explaining why CASI might increase validity when used to ask questions about sensitive issues.

✔ The researcher is able to compare respondents' answers and measure the strength of a connection between different factors. This provides the researcher with statistical data.

✔ With standardised questions, other researchers can replicate or repeat the structured interview to check the reliability of the findings.

✔ Interviewers are trained in interviewing techniques and are familiar with the interview schedule. Consequently they will be able to clarify the meaning of questions and clear up any misunderstandings.

✔ The interviewer can ensure that all relevant questions and sections are fully completed.

The limitations of structured interviews

✘ Structured (or formal) interviews are usually delivered face to face. The interview situation itself may influence the respondents to give answers that they think are socially acceptable or that show them in a positive light. In this way, respondents might not reveal their true thoughts or behaviour. When this occurs, it is known as **interview bias** or the interview effect.

✘ The age, gender, ethnicity, accent or appearance of the interviewer may also influence the respondents' responses. When this occurs, it is referred to as **interviewer bias** or the interviewer effect. In cases of interview and interviewer bias, the results will be invalid in that they do not provide a true or authentic picture of the topic under study.

✘ Structured interviews (and postal questionnaires) are based on a pre-set list of standardised questions. The wording, order and focus of the questions are all predetermined by the researcher. This assumes that the researcher knows, in advance, exactly what the important and relevant questions are. Critics argue that these techniques impose the researcher's prior assumptions about the topic being studied on the respondent. They also limit opportunities for respondents to express their own views and opinions. In this sense, structured interviews (and postal questionnaires) close off, rather than open up, new and interesting issues and areas.

✘ Some **feminist** researchers see structured interviews as based on unequal power relationships between the interviewer (who asks the questions) and the respondents (who are expected to answer rather than ask questions).

Interview and interviewer bias are potential problems with face-to-face interviews.

Key points

- Structured (or formal) interviews are based on a standardised interview schedule. Interviewers are able to clarify questions. Differences between respondents' answers are seen as reflecting real differences in their attitudes or opinions. Structured interviews can be replicated to check the reliability of the findings.

- The disadvantages of structured interviews include the potential for interview bias and interviewer effect.

Check your understanding

Identify and explain one advantage of using structured interviews when compared to postal or emailed questionnaires. (4 marks)

What types of interview are used in qualitative research?

Using interviews in qualitative research

In qualitative research, sociologists use interviews that are sometimes referred to as **in-depth** or **qualitative interviews**. In this type of interview, the interviewer does not have a standardised interview schedule to follow and each interview is unique.

In-depth interviews are much less structured than those used in survey research and range from completely unstructured to loosely structured.

- In a completely unstructured interview, the interviewer might ask one question to start things off and then the interviewee is free to tell their story or talk about their experiences in their own terms. An unstructured interview is like a conversation with a purpose.
- In a semi-structured interview, the interviewer may work with an interview guide – a list of questions, points or issues they want to cover. The interviewer does not have to cover these points in any particular order and is free to pick up on any issue that the interviewee raises.

Glossary terms

in-depth interview, qualitative interview

FOCUS ON RESEARCH: DISCUSSION ACTIVITY

Researching Islamophobia

Read through the information below and, in pairs, discuss the questions that follow.

Irene Zempi and Neil Chakraborti (2014) carried out research into the experiences of veiled Muslim women who were victims of Islamophobia in public places.

The fieldwork took place in Leicester between 2011 and 2012 (see p. 35). Irene Zempi conducted 60 semi-structured interviews with veiled Muslim women about their experiences as victims of Islamophobia in Leicester. These individual interviews allowed her to collect rich and detailed data.

1 Why do you think the researchers decided to use semi-structured interviews rather than structured interviews to investigate this particular topic?
   Make a note of at least two reasons.
2 Can you think of any disadvantages of using semi-structured interviews in this context?
   Make a note of at least one disadvantage.
3 Now team up with another pair to compare your answers. Write down any points that you have not already noted.

FOCUS ON RESEARCH: DISCUSSION ACTIVITY

Maria Papapolydorou (2013) focused on the ways that sixth form students talk about social class issues in relation to themselves and their friends inside and outside school. She carried out in-depth, semi-structured individual interviews with Year 12 students in four state secondary schools in London.

The extract below is from a transcript of an interview with one of the students.

In a small group, read through the extract and discuss the questions that follow.

'ISABELLA: Most of these people I would say they are about the same but some of them are not as well off as me. Most of them are about the same but...They all call me rich (laughs).

(That is true – from another interview they do consider her rich.)

RESEARCHER: Why do they think that?

ISABELLA: Because I go on holidays with my family a lot so...that's funny.

(laughs)

RESEARCHER: Right. But what do you think? Do you not think you are (rich)?...

ISABELLA: Not really, because family friends outside this school...My mum and dad's friends...their children all go to private schools and are really rich. So I think I'm so poor compared to them. But then compared to my friends here I say I'm not poor, I'm rich.

(Isabella, White British, middle-class student)'

Source: Papapolydorou, M. (2013) 'Direct, Indirect and Relational: Social Class Manifestations in Teenage Students' Accounts', *Youth and Policy*, 111, October, p. 30.

1 Would you describe this extract as containing quantitative or qualitative data? Write one sentence to explain your answer.
2 What particular skills does a researcher need in order to carry out in-depth interviews with young people? Make a note of your group's ideas.

Stretch and challenge

Read through the information below and answer the questions that follow.

The contents of in-depth interviews are usually audio-recorded and transcribed. It can be very time-consuming to transcribe interviews, particularly when the quality of the recording is not very good or there is a lot of background noise. Estimates suggest that it can take five hours to transcribe the contents of an interview that lasted one hour. If research funding is available, researchers may pay someone else to transcribe the interviews, but if there are hours of recordings this can be expensive.

1 Why do you think it is important to record and transcribe in-depth interviews?
2 Can you identify any possible disadvantages or potential problems with recording in-depth interviews? Make a note of at least one possible disadvantage or problem.

How do young people see social class in their everyday lives?

Key points

- In qualitative research, sociologists use in-depth or qualitative interviews.

- In-depth interviews are much less structured than those used in survey research and range from completely unstructured to loosely structured.

- Each interview is unique.

Check your understanding

Identify and describe one difference between structured and unstructured interviews. (3 marks)

What are the strengths and limitations of in-depth interviews?

The advantages of in-depth or qualitative interviews

✔ In-depth interviews are much more flexible than standardised methods. Interviewers can clarify questions and clear up any misunderstandings. They can also prompt, probe and ask follow-up questions.

✔ Interviewees can talk at length in their own words. They can develop their answers and introduce important issues that the researcher had not thought of.

✔ Through in-depth interviews, sociologists can explore how interviewees understand their own experiences and behaviour and so can obtain rich, detailed data. Consequently, in-depth interviews allow researchers to explore more complex issues than standardised methods do.

✔ In-depth interviews are a popular method among feminist sociologists such as Ann Oakley (1974). They prefer in-depth rather than structured interviews because the relationship between interviewer and interviewee is more equal. Using in-depth interviews allows the interviewees to express their ideas and feelings in their own terms.

The limitations of in-depth interviews

✘ In-depth interviews are relatively time-consuming and expensive. For example, interviewers may need to be trained, and their salaries and travel expenses paid.

✘ Even with trained interviewers, in-depth interviews can be difficult to carry out successfully. They require a skilled interviewer who is able to encourage interviewees to open up and keep the conversation flowing. If interviewees are unresponsive, the quality and quantity of the data will be affected.

✘ In-depth interviews may be affected by interview bias. In an interview situation, interviewees may give answers that they think the interviewer wants to hear or that present them in a positive light.

✘ **Interviewer effect** occurs if the interviewer asks leading questions or unconsciously influences the interviewee. If interview or interviewer bias occurs, the findings are likely to be invalid.

✘ Without a standardised schedule of questions to follow, it would be difficult to replicate or repeat an in-depth interview in order to check the **reliability** of the findings.

✘ Compared to survey research, fewer in-depth interviews can be undertaken and the sample is relatively small. With a small sample, it is difficult to claim that the findings apply to the wider population.

Stretch and challenge

The interviewer effect

Factors affecting the quantity and quality of interview data include the interviewer's style and presentation – for example, their clothes, age, gender, ethnicity or accent. In the following extract, Beth, a research participant, comments on the interview styles of two researchers who worked on a project interviewing young people. Read the extract and answer the questions that follow.

Beth on researcher number one, a 30-something female:

'I think young people feel quite comfortable with her because of how she's quite young in feeling, and she dresses quite young, so I think she gets a good response…[and] she sounds more down to earth. She talks more – I won't say common – but like down to earth.'

Beth on researcher number two, a 50-something male:

'He's very soft when he speaks and he sounds quite caring towards them. But I don't think he gets as good responses. I think he's very well-spoken and they may feel threatened by that…I don't know if they feel under pressure to explain things but as they explain, it comes out not completely as they intended. So he's re-explaining it for them and they're going "yes, that's what I mean".'

Source: Robson, E. (2001) 'The Routes Project: Disadvantaged Young People Interviewing Their Peers', p. 48.

1 Identify three factors that could explain why researcher number one gets a better response than researcher number two.

2 Drawing on this information, explain what the term 'interviewer effect' means.

FOCUS ON RESEARCH: WRITTEN ACTIVITY

Violent Night

Simon Winlow and Steve Hall (2006) studied night-time leisure in city-centre bars and alcohol-related violence among young people. In this extract, they discuss their interviews with male victims of violence. Read the extract and answer the questions below.

'There were a number of rather awkward moments during interviews with the victims of violence. They were keenly aware of the impact of being a victim upon their reputations and their masculine identities. All the respondents who spoke about being victims were men and we felt that, in what was basically a conversation between two men, much was left unsaid. Some, for example, gave the impression that they might be playing down the impact of being a victim of violence on their social status. Others seemed to be searching for ways to brush off the incident as unimportant.'

Source: adapted from Winlow, S. and Hall, S. (2006), p. 15.

1 What do you think the authors mean by 'much was left unsaid'?

2 Drawing on this study, explain one problem with using interviews.

Key points

- In-depth interviews are flexible. Interviewers can clarify questions and probe answers. Interviewees have more scope to discuss topics.

- However, in-depth interviews are time-consuming, expensive and need a skilled interviewer. Possible problems include interview and interviewer bias.

Check your understanding

Identify and explain one advantage of using in-depth interviews to study sensitive issues. **(4 marks)**

What are the uses, advantages and limitations of group interviews?

Objectives
- Describe the use of group interviews in sociological research
- Discuss the strengths and limitations of group interviews

Differences between group interviews and focus groups

In a **group interview**, the researcher interviews a number of people at the same time. A group interview covers several areas, themes or topics. It is usually associated with qualitative rather than quantitative research and is often used together with other methods such as individual interviews.

A **focus group** is a group interview that focuses on one particular topic. Some of the main differences between group interviews and focus groups are outlined below.

Group interviews	Focus groups
• are interview situations in which the interviewer asks the questions and the interviewees respond	• explore how people interact within the group and how they respond to each other's views
• often cover a wide range of themes or topics	• explore (or focus on) one particular theme or topic in depth
• may be used in order to save time and money, as the researcher interviews several people together	• are not used to save time and money but to gain extra insights through group interactions

Advantages of group interviews

✔ Group interviews enable researchers to access a wide range of views and experiences and so provide a rich source of information on topics.

✔ By interviewing several people together, the researcher can save time and money.

✔ Individuals may feel more comfortable putting their experiences forward in a group setting because they are supported by others.

✔ Participants may be recruited to take part in follow-up individual interviews.

✔ The group interviews might generate new ideas for the researcher to explore.

Glossary terms

focus group, group interview, research design

FOCUS ON SKILLS: DISCUSSION ACTIVITY

Using focus group interviews

Focus group interviews have been used to study:

- young people's values and moral identities
- how sixth form students understand and talk about social class
- mass media (for example, television and newspaper) messages about AIDS.

In a small group, choose one of these areas and explain why focus group interviews would be an appropriate method to use in this situation. Note down your reasons.

Limitations of group interviews

✗ Group interviews need to be managed carefully by the researcher, particularly when the topics are potentially sensitive.

✗ In a group setting, the interviewees may influence each other. Some may dominate the discussion and, in this case, not everyone's voice will be heard. Others may be less open in a group interview than in a one-to-one setting.

✗ In a group context, a researcher cannot guarantee that what the interviewees said will remain confidential.

✗ If interviewees talk over each other, it becomes difficult to transcribe the contents of the group interview.

Stretch and challenge

Young, free and single?

Sue Heath and Elizabeth Cleaver (2003) studied young adult house sharers and their experiences of living in shared households. As part of their **research design**, they used group interviews. Read through the extract and answer the questions that follow.

'Our sample consisted of 25 shared households, containing a total of 81 individuals. The way shared living routinely worked was explored partly through group interviews with 75 household members, 61 of whom later agreed to be interviewed individually. The group interviews lasted an average of 95 minutes and most were held in a communal space in each household.

The group interviews covered a number of areas including: a discussion of the household's history, different expectations of acceptable behaviour, how shared and private spaces are organised, who does what tasks, household finances, how conflict is addressed, and the pros and cons of shared living. In most group interviews, each major theme was introduced by a video clip from *Friends*, *This Life* or *Shallow Grave* as a way of breaking the ice and stimulating discussion.

Permission was given to record the group interview on minidisc. All but one of these interviews were conducted jointly by both of us, partly for safety reasons, but also to keep track of the order of speech for later transcription. This was very important in single-sex households where it would be difficult to recognise different voices on the recording.'

Source: adapted from Heath, S. and Cleaver, E. (2003), pp. 7, 195–196.

1 Why did the researchers show video clips during the group interviews?
2 Drawing on this information, identify two possible problems with group interviews.
3 Which other method did the researchers use in their study?

Key points

• Group interviews cover a range of relevant areas or themes while focus groups explore one topic.

• Group interviews can access wide-ranging views and experiences, and so provide rich data. Interviewees may feel supported in a group setting and open up more.

• However, in group interviews participants may influence each other, some may dominate discussion, while others may say very little. Confidentiality cannot be guaranteed.

Check your understanding

Identify and explain one disadvantage of using group interviews to study young men's experiences of being victims of violence.   (4 marks)

What are longitudinal studies?

Objectives
- Describe the use of longitudinal studies in sociological research
- Discuss the advantages and limitations of longitudinal studies

In research based on interviews or questionnaires, researchers may use either a **cross-sectional study** or a **longitudinal study**.

- A cross-sectional study questions a sample of the population on the relevant issues on one occasion. This is a one-off approach that gives us a 'snapshot' view. So it only tells us about individuals at one particular point in time. It does not allow researchers to measure changes in values or attitudes over time.
- A longitudinal study follows the same group of people over a period of time. After the initial survey or interview has taken place, follow-up surveys or interviews are carried out at intervals over a number of years.

Alan Bryman (2016) identifies two types of longitudinal design:

- A **panel study** – a sample (usually randomly selected from the full population) is surveyed on two (or more) occasions. For example, the Understanding Society survey is a UK household longitudinal study funded by the ESRC. Each year, the same people in the same households are interviewed to build a picture of how their lives are changing over time.
- A **cohort study** – either an entire **cohort** of people or a random sample of them is selected. Everyone in the cohort shares a certain characteristic or experience – for instance, they were all born in the same week. For example, the 1970 British Cohort Study (BCS) began by collecting information about the births and families of around 17,200 babies born during one particular week in April 1970. Since then, the respondents have been surveyed at intervals (aged 5, 10, 16, 26, 30, 34, 38 and 42 years) to monitor their health, physical development, education and social and economic circumstances. The BCS is a cradle-to-grave study and will track people into old age.

> **Glossary terms**
>
> adolescence, cohort, cohort study, cross-sectional study, longitudinal study, panel study

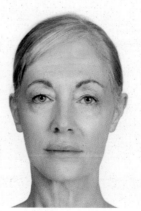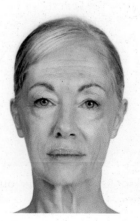

Some longitudinal studies run for decades.

The Millennium Cohort Study (MCS)

Read through the information below, then answer the questions that follow.

The Millennium Cohort Study (MCS), based at University College London, is a major longitudinal study that follows people through time. The first survey gathered information from the parents of 18,818 babies who were all born during a 12-month period (2000–01) and living in selected areas of the UK. It was carried out between June 2001 and January 2003, when the babies were 9 months old. Follow-up surveys were carried out when the children were aged 3, 5, 7 and 11 years old.

Future surveys will provide information on issues such as the respondents' education, employment and health experiences as these unfold over time, as well as changes in the family and gender roles. The MCS plans to follow the children through **adolescence** and into adulthood.

1 Identify two research aims that the MCS researchers could address by using a longitudinal study rather than a one-shot survey.
2 Identify one way in which information from the MCS might be useful to policy makers in government departments such as education or health.

Longitudinal studies are usually associated with quantitative research based on social surveys. However, qualitative longitudinal research is also possible. The Timescapes Initiative, for example, was a major qualitative longitudinal study that was funded by the ESRC and ran from 2007 to 2012. It involved seven different research projects in five UK universities that explored how people's personal and family relationships develop and change over time. Research methods included in-depth interviews, observation, video diaries and photography.

Advantages and limitations of longitudinal studies

Longitudinal studies allow researchers to examine social changes over time. Changes in individuals' daily lives, experiences, behaviour, values and opinions can be identified.

However, longitudinal studies have several limitations. In particular:

- the time scale involved means that longitudinal studies are relatively expensive and time-consuming
- involvement in a longitudinal study may affect the behaviour of the participants – they might behave differently from the way they would have behaved if they had not been involved in the study
- there are problems in maintaining contact with the original sample over time: people leave home, move house, move abroad or otherwise disappear for periods of time
- people may change their minds and decide to withdraw from the study.

Stretch and challenge

Over time, as more and more people become untraceable or withdraw from the study, the sample becomes less representative of the population. Explain why this would make it more difficult to generalise from the findings of a survey.

Key points

- Longitudinal studies follow a group of people over time. Changes in people's social attitudes and experiences can be examined.

- However, they are expensive to conduct and there are practical problems in retaining the original sample.

Check your understanding

Identify and describe one topic for which a researcher might use a longitudinal study.
(4 marks)

How is participant observation used in sociological research?

Objective
- Describe the use of participant observation in sociological research

Participant observation

Much sociological research involves asking questions through surveys or in-depth interviews. Sociologists also conduct research by using observation techniques. These involve watching people in everyday settings, listening to the group under study and recording what is observed over time.

There are two types of observation: **participant observation** (PO) and **non-participant observation**.

In a participant observation (PO) study, the researcher joins a group and participates in its activities as a full member on a daily basis in order to investigate it. The researcher has to decide whether to carry out the study overtly or covertly.

With **overt PO**, the researcher 'comes clean' and so the group is aware of the research activities. One potential problem with overt PO, however, is that the researcher's presence may influence and change the behaviour of the group under study. When this occurs, it is known as the **observer effect**.

> **Glossary terms**
>
> covert participant observation, non-participant observation, observer effect, overt participant observation, participant observation

FOCUS ON RESEARCH: DISCUSSION ACTIVITY

Studying pop music in a factory

Marek Korczynski (2014) studied the role of pop music in a factory in the Midlands that made window blinds (see Topic 5). In pairs, read the extract and answer the questions that follow.

> 'I observed the behaviour of the workers, and I talked with them about their jobs and their feelings about music generally, and particularly about music and work…Because I was not a normal worker (and also because I was not being paid) I had some scope to walk around the shop floor and talk with people.'
>
> Source: adapted from Korczynski, M. (2014) *Songs of the Factory: Pop Music, Culture, and Resistance.* New York: Cornell University Press, pp. 212–213.

1 In pairs, identify two possible reasons why Marek Korczynski might have used overt PO rather than structured interviews.
2 Note down two possible problems with using overt PO in this context.

With **covert PO**, the researcher joins the group without informing its members about conducting research activities. A potential difficulty with covert PO is that researchers may be reluctant to ask too many questions in case they 'blow their cover'. One problem with covert PO is that the people being observed have not been informed that they are involved in a study and are not given the opportunity to consent (or otherwise) to taking part in it. This is considered unacceptable research practice by some because it involves deception and invasion of privacy.

Supporters of covert PO argue that it may sometimes be the only way to study and develop sociological knowledge about topics related to illegal activity. Also, if group members are unaware that they are being observed for research purposes, then they will not change their behaviour. In other words, covert PO avoids any observer effect. Supporters also argue that covert methods are acceptable so long as research participants are not harmed by taking part in the research.

FOCUS ON RESEARCH: WRITTEN ACTIVITY

Researching drug-sellers

Jenni Ward (2008) studied drug-selling within the London rave dance culture during the 1990s. She used semi-covert participant observation as the main method. In doing so, she generated in-depth, rich data. Jenni Ward suggests that sitting down with a drug-seller, pen poised ready to record illegal activities, could have closed down a study before it began.

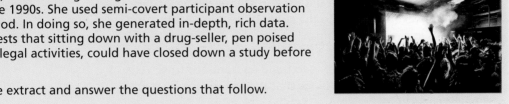

Read through the extract and answer the questions that follow.

'I located myself over a five-year period in London nightclubs, dance parties, bars and pubs and people's houses. I was already a member of the rave dance culture when my study began. I was friends with people whose social lives were embedded within the "clubbing" scene. These people became a focus of my study.

I used a semi-covert style of observation, as while many of the people I was socialising with knew I was undertaking a study of drug-selling, over time they often forgot that I was a researcher. They simply viewed me as a member of the friendship group to which we belonged. The problem with this was that many observations were made in situations where people were not fully aware that their actions were the focus of my research...In my desire not to upset naturally occurring activities, I generally did not announce my research.'

Source: adapted from Ward, J. (2008) 'Researching Drug Sellers: An "Experiential" Account from "The Field"', *Sociological Research Online*, 13.

1 What role did Jenni Ward adopt in order to access the world of the rave dance drugs culture?
2 Why was she able to adopt this role successfully?

Stretch and challenge

1 What does Jenni Ward mean by 'semi-covert style of observation'?
2 Give one reason why Jenni Ward's use of semi-covert PO could be seen as unacceptable research practice.

Check your understanding

1 Describe what is meant by the term 'participant observation'.
(3 marks)

2 Identify and explain one reason why a researcher might decide to use covert participant observation to study the behaviour of 'football hooligans'.
(4 marks)

Key points

- Participant observation (PO) may be conducted overtly or covertly.

- While covert PO can be seen as unethical, supporters argue that it may be the only way to study some topics.

What are the strengths and limitations of participant observation?

Objective
- Discuss the strengths and limitations of participant observation

The advantages of participant observation (PO)

Glossary terms

bias, ethnography, over-involvement

✔ Participant observation allows the researcher to study a group in its natural everyday settings and observe its activities as they occur. Therefore it is seen as less artificial than standardised methods such as surveys. PO is used in ethnographic studies. The term **ethnography** refers to the study of people's culture and practices in everyday settings.

✔ A PO study is usually carried out over an extended period of time. The researcher has time to build up bonds of trust. As a result, they see and hear things that they would not normally have access to.

✔ By participating in its activities, the researcher can see things from the group's perspective and develop a deeper understanding of its behaviour and activities. This helps the researcher to obtain rich, in-depth data about how people experience their social world.

✔ Some groups such as religious cults, violent football supporters or users of illegal drugs may not agree to be interviewed. In this case, PO may be the only method available if a researcher wants to study such groups.

The limitations of participant observation

✘ Entry and trust – at the outset, it may be difficult for the researcher to gain entry to the group under study. After joining the group, they may find it hard to gain acceptance and develop trust.

✘ Taking notes and recording activities as they happen can be challenging. Producing a notepad or a digital recorder would probably arouse suspicion. Often, researchers must rely on memory and make notes after the event (for example, in the toilets). This is particularly an issue with covert PO, where the group is not aware of the researcher's true identity.

✘ PO tends to be a relatively time-consuming and therefore expensive research method. Some researchers have spent over two (and up to eight) years in the field collecting data for a PO study.

✘ The observer effect – with overt PO, the very presence of the researcher may influence the group and its activities. If people do behave differently, the validity of the findings will be affected.

Dr Smith, I think our research into football hooliganism is starting to get to you!

Over-involvement may lead to bias

✗ **Over-involvement** – there is a danger with PO that a researcher may become too involved with a group and its activities. If this happens, the research findings could be biased or one-sided. In this case, over-involvement would invalidate the findings.

✗ Each PO study is unique, a one-off, so it would be virtually impossible to replicate (repeat) it. This means that a second sociologist would find it difficult to check the reliability of the results of the first sociologist's work. Consequently, it is difficult to generalise or draw general conclusions about other similar groups.

FOCUS ON RESEARCH: WRITTEN ACTIVITY

Researching hooligans abroad

Read through the information below, then answer the questions that follow.

John Williams, Eric Dunning and Patrick Murphy (1989) worked together on a project in the Department of Sociology at the University of Leicester that explored football hooliganism among English fans in Europe. John Williams carried out all three of their participant observation studies. This is because he was young enough, street 'savvy' enough and interested enough in football to be able to pass himself off as an 'every day' English football fan.

1 Why do you think it was important for Williams to fit in as an ordinary football fan?

2 Why might a researcher decide to use covert participant observation rather than overt participant observation to study groups who engage in illegal behaviour?

Eileen Barker used overt PO to explore why people joined the Moonies (the Unification Church).

Key points

• Participant observation (PO) enables a researcher to observe naturally occurring events and to gather rich data. However, gaining entry to a group, building trust and recording information may prove difficult.

• PO tends to be relatively time-consuming and expensive. The researcher may become too involved in the group, leading to **bias**. Each PO study is unique and would be almost impossible to replicate in order to check the results. This makes generalisation difficult.

Check your understanding

Imagine that you are undertaking research on the beliefs and experiences of animal rights protesters. You are considering overt participant observation as a possible research method.

1 Identify and explain one advantage of using overt PO when carrying out this investigation. **(4 marks)**

2 Identify and explain one problem you could encounter if you used overt PO in this investigation. **(4 marks)**

How is non-participant observation used in sociological research?

Objectives
- Describe the use of non-participant observation in sociological research
- Discuss the strengths and limitations of non-participant observation

Using non-participant observation in research

With non-participant observation, the researcher is like a 'fly on the wall', observing the group's activities in a natural setting without taking part in them. The observer may be present in the setting while studying behaviour or they may videotape the group instead.

Studies of teachers' and students' behaviour in classrooms, for example, may involve non-participant observation of lessons. Some researchers use structured or systematic observation when studying classroom behaviour. In this case, they use an **observation schedule** to observe and record behaviour and interaction between the teacher and students as it unfolds. For instance, the researcher might observe a classroom during a lesson and, every 10 seconds, log the type of activity that takes place in that 10 second period on a coding sheet. This enables the researcher to generate data on behaviour such as who talks the most, how much silence or confusion there is and how often the teacher gives praise or encouragement. However, if it is to work, the observation schedule must clearly specify which kinds of activity are to be observed.

Glossary term

observation schedule

Studies of teachers' and students' behaviour in classrooms often involve non-participant observation of lessons.

Advantages of non-participant observation
✔ Non-participant observers can actually see for themselves how people behave in natural settings such as classrooms. By contrast, in an interview situation, researchers have to rely on what interviewees tell them about how they behave.
✔ Non-participant observers are less likely than participant observers to get too drawn into the group's activities.
✔ Non-participant observers may be more objective than participant observers. In other words, they may be less influenced by their personal feelings or opinions about the group, its members and activities.

Limitations of non-participant observation
✘ It is more difficult for observers to see the world through the eyes of group members if they do not participate in their social world. A non-participant observer is less likely than a participant observer to understand things in the same way as group members.
✘ The observer effect may come into play with non-participant observation. This means that group members may change their behaviour if they are aware that they are being observed.

PO or non-PO?

Imagine that you are part of a research team studying young people, night-time leisure and alcohol-related violence in a city centre near your home. You have decided to use observation but you are not sure whether to use participant observation (PO) or non-participant observation (non-PO).

In a small group:

1 Discuss the advantages and disadvantages of using PO and non-PO in your study.
2 Reach a decision about whether to use PO or non-PO. Note down your decision and your reasons.

Factors affecting choice of methods

Several factors influence a sociologist's choice of research methods. Some of these factors appear in the table below.

Copy the table. Take each factor in turn and, drawing on what you have learned so far, explain how it could influence a researcher to choose one method rather than another. Try to refer to specific methods in your explanations.

Factor affecting choice of methods	Explanation
Research topic and aims	
How much time is available	
How much money is available	
How easy it is to gain access	

Looking at primary data

Would the data obtained from each of the following research techniques be mainly qualitative or mainly quantitative?

a structured interview
b in-depth interview
c questionnaire
d participant observation.

Check your understanding

1 Identify and explain one advantage of using non-participant observation to investigate the behaviour of Year 6 pupils during lessons in a local primary school. (4 marks)

2 Identify and explain one problem you may encounter when carrying out this research. (4 marks)

Stretch and challenge

Positivism and interpretivism

Another factor that influences sociologists' choice of methods is whether they are more interested in measurement (for example, of attitudes) or in seeing the world through other people's eyes.

Write a paragraph to explain how this could influence choice of methods. Try to refer to the debate on positivism and interpretivism in your answer.

Key points

- Non-participant observers will observe a group's activities – possibly using an observation schedule – without participating in the activities.

- Non-participant observers are less likely than participant observers to be drawn into activities and may be more objective.

- However, it is more difficult for non-participant observers to see the world through group members' eyes.

- Also, the observer effect comes into play if group members change their behaviour.

What are official statistics?

Objective
• Describe some of the official statistics that are available to sociologists

So far, we have examined sources of primary data such as questionnaires, interviews and observation. Secondary data is pre-existing information that has been collected by other people or organisations such as government agencies. It is available to sociologists secondhand.

Secondary data may be either quantitative or qualitative. Quantitative data is presented in statistical form, for example as percentages. Examples of quantitative secondary data include **official statistics** such as:

- birth rates
- marriage rates
- death rates
- suicide rates
- unemployment rates
- crime rates.

Official statistics are compiled by government departments and agencies. Sources include the Office for National Statistics (ONS), the Department for Education (DfE) and NHS England.

The census

The ONS is responsible for the **census** in England and Wales. The census is conducted every 10 years and collects information on the whole of the population. This information allows central and local governments to plan housing, education, health and transport services. It also allows changes to be measured over time, for example in the size of the population.

The census involves mailing a self-completion questionnaire survey to every household in England and Wales during a census year. In 2011, householders could submit their responses either by post or online. Although we are legally required to complete the questionnaire, not everyone does so. The 2011 census had an overall response rate of 94 per cent in England and Wales. The response rate varied by local authority and, for example, in West Devon it was estimated at 98 per cent and in Kensington and Chelsea at 82 per cent. Particular groups within the population, such as students and other young people, are considered less likely to respond.

For the first time in official statistics, the 1991 census asked a direct question on **ethnic group** origin, so providing detailed information on the ethnic composition of the population. The 2001 census included questions on religion for the first time and the 2011 census included nine new topics such as main language and number of bedrooms.

Inevitably, given the massive scale of the census, errors do occur. Incorrect information may be provided on the census forms or coding errors may be introduced when the responses are processed.

Glossary terms

census, ethnic group, non-response rate, official statistics

Questions asked by the 2011 census for England and Wales

The census asked for specific information on the household, such as:

- the type of tenure (for example, rented or owned)
- the number of rooms
- the number of bedrooms
- whether amenities such as central heating are available
- availability of cars or vans.

There were also questions on each person in the household regarding:

- their sex
- their date of birth
- their main language
- their marital or civil partnership status
- their country of birth
- their ethnic group
- their religion (to be answered voluntarily)
- whether they are a schoolchild or student
- their health in general.

There were also work-related questions for household members over the age of 16 years on their:

- qualifications
- employment status
- occupation
- place of work
- usual means of travel to work
- number of hours worked per week.

Other official statistics

The registration of births, marriages and deaths is another source of official statistics. All births, marriages and deaths must be registered with the registrar at the local council offices.

All marriages are officially recorded as statistics.

FOCUS ON SKILLS: WRITTEN ACTIVITY

The Family Resources Survey (FRS)

Other important sources of official statistics used by sociologists include nationwide surveys such as the Family Resources Survey, the Labour Force Survey and the Crime Survey for England and Wales.

Study the information below and answer the questions that follow.

Survey:	Family Resources Survey 2014/15
Topics include:	Respondents' income, caring responsibilities and spending on housing
Frequency:	Continuous
Sampling frame:	Royal Mail's Postcode Address File
Type of respondent:	All adults in the household
Location:	UK
Sample size:	20 000 private households
Response rate:	58%

1 What was the **non-response rate** in 2014/15? (Be careful! The question is not asking for the response rate.)
2 What sampling frame was used in the FRS?
3 How many households were in the sample?

FOCUS ON SKILLS: DISCUSSION ACTIVITY

Reasons for refusing to participate in the FRS

When respondents refuse to participate in the Family Resources Survey (FRS), interviewers record up to three reasons for refusal. In a small group, discuss the possible reasons why people might refuse to participate in the FRS. Make a note of three possible reasons.

Key points

- Secondary data are collected by other people or organisations and may be quantitative or qualitative.

- Official statistics are produced by government departments and agencies such as the ONS.

Check your understanding

1 Describe (with reference to the census) what is meant by a 'large-scale longitudinal survey'. (3 marks)

2 Describe what is meant by the term 'response rate'. (3 marks)

What are the advantages and limitations of official statistics?

The advantages of official statistics

✔ Official statistics save time and money because they have already been collected. They are readily available and cover many aspects of social life.

✔ Official statistics are based on large samples. The census, for example, provides statistical information on the full population of England and Wales. Parallel censuses provide information on the populations of Scotland and Northern Ireland.

✔ They may be the only source of data on a particular topic – on the suicide rate 100 years ago, for instance.

✔ They allow sociologists to do 'before and after' studies. For example, researchers could study the impact of the Divorce Reform Act (1969) by examining official statistics on divorce before and after the Act came into effect.

✔ Official statistics allow sociologists to investigate **trends** over time – that is, the general direction in which statistics on something move or change over time. It is possible to chart the trends in areas such as divorce, crime, **unemployment**, **underemployment** and births by looking at official statistics.

✔ Official statistics may be used in a mixed methods research design combining quantitative and qualitative data. If the researcher was investigating educational achievement and gender, for instance, then official statistics on gender, subject choice and examination results would provide useful quantitative secondary data. Qualitative primary data could be generated through in-depth interviews with teachers and students in order to understand social processes (such as labelling) in schools and classrooms.

The limitations of official statistics

✗ Official statistics are collected by officials, so they might not tell sociologists exactly what they want to know about a particular social issue. Statistics, for example, can provide us with useful information about the number of divorces recorded each year (see Chapter 2 Topic 23). Such data, however, can tell us little about the strength of marriage in modern society. This is because divorce statistics exclude **empty shell marriages** (couples remaining in unhappy marriages) and separations that are arranged informally without going through the courts.

Glossary terms

empty shell marriage, trends, underemployment, unemployment

Stretch and challenge

1 Explain why some official statistics (such as birth rates) are more likely to give a true picture of what they are supposed to be measuring than others (such as crime statistics).

2 How reliable is data from the census likely to be?

FOCUS ON SKILLS: DISCUSSION ACTIVITY

Under-reporting of crime

In a small group, discuss the possible reasons why crimes such as assault, domestic violence and vandalism are likely to be under-reported to the police.

Make a note of three possible reasons.

FOCUS ON SKILLS: WRITTEN ACTIVITY

Ethnicity in England and Wales

The census provides statistical data on the full population of England and Wales. Study the information below from the 2011 census and answer the questions that follow.

Ethnic groups in England and Wales based on the 2011 census

(Percentages)

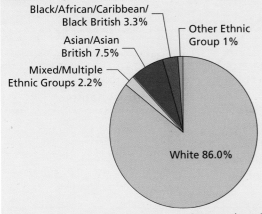

Source: adapted from http://www.ons.gov.uk/peoplepopulationandcommunity/culturalidentity/ethnicity/articles/ethnicityandnationalidentityinenglandandwales/2012-12-11 Accessed 10/07/16.

1 What percentage reported their ethnic group as White?
2 Which was the third largest ethnic group?
3 Which ethnic group comprised 7.5 per cent of the population?

✗ Interpretivist sociologists are interested in understanding what people's experiences, behaviour and actions mean to them. They argue that official statistics on divorce, unemployment or crime tell us nothing about what it means to the individuals involved to be divorced, unemployed or the victim of a crime.

✗ Sociologists cannot check the validity of official statistics. Some statistics are likely to give us a valid or true picture. Official figures on the number of births recorded in a particular year, for example, are likely to provide a true measure of how many babies were born in that year. Statistics on domestic violence or violence in classrooms, however, may be invalid. In other words, they may not actually measure what they are supposed to be measuring.

✗ Interpretivist sociologists argue that official statistics are 'socially constructed'. In other words, the statistics are the outcome of the decisions and choices made by the various people involved in their construction. Crime statistics, for example, are published as statements of fact. They are, however, the outcome of decisions made by people such as victims and police officers. A victim of assault, for instance, might decide not to report this to the police.

These statistics on divorce are all very well, but they tell us nothing about what divorce means to people.

Key points

• Official statistics are cheap and easy to access, cover many topics and are based on large samples. They enable sociologists to study trends, for example in divorce or crime.

• However, interpretivists argue that official statistics tell us nothing about people's lived experiences and that they are socially constructed. Crime statistics, for example, do not provide a true measurement of criminal activity.

Check your understanding

Identify and explain one advantage of using official statistics to study divorce.   (4 marks)

What other sources of quantitative secondary data are available to sociologists?

Objectives
- Outline the difference between official and non-official statistics
- Describe some of the uses of quantitative data collected by other researchers

Non-official statistics

Many non-governmental bodies in the UK (including banks, trade associations, professional associations, charities and market research organisations) produce statistics. These are usually referred to as **non-official statistics**. The British Bankers' Association, for example, produces statistics on household banking such as the number of plastic cards issued to customers.

Glossary term

non-official statistics

FOCUS ON SKILLS: WRITTEN ACTIVITY

Statistics about Childline

Childline is a service that the National Society for the Prevention of Cruelty to Children (the NSPCC) provides for children and young people so that they can talk about the issues affecting their lives. In their annual reviews, the NSPCC (a national charity) produces a range of statistics about Childline. These statistics can be accessed from the Childline website.

childline

ONLINE, ON THE PHONE, ANYTIME
childline.org.uk | 0800 1111

Childline is used by many children and young people.

The following table shows, for example, that 57 per cent of the children aged 11 years and under who contacted Childline in 2014/15 did so by telephone.

Study the information in the table and answer the questions that follow.

How children and young people contacted Childline in 2014/15

Age group	Telephone	Online	Total
11 years and under	57%	43%	100%
12–15 years	32%	68%	100%
16–18 years	39%	61%	100%

Source: adapted from 'Always There When I Need You'. *Childline Review NSPCC*, p. 9.

1 What percentage of the young people aged 12–15 years who contacted Childline did so online?
2 What percentage of young people aged 16–18 years who contacted Childline used the telephone?
3 Which age group was most likely to contact Childline by telephone?
4 Which age group was least likely to contact Childline by telephone?

Using quantitative data collected by other researchers

Rather than collecting primary data themselves, sociologists can analyse data that other researchers have already collected. This existing data may be quantitative (for example, survey data) or qualitative. Statistical data from large, high-quality surveys is available in the UK Data Archive at the University of Essex and can be accessed online. This is an important source of quantitative data for secondary analysis. Sociologists can access it online and use it for their own research purposes.

Other examples of large data sets that can be used for secondary analysis include the 1970 British Cohort Study (BCS) and the Millennium Cohort Study (MCS), which are both based at the Institute of Education, University College London (see Chapter 2 Topic 13).

Advantages of using existing quantitative data for secondary analysis

- Researchers can save time and money by analysing pre-existing data from surveys rather than collecting data from scratch. Data sets can be easily accessed online via the UK Data Archive.
- Many of the data sets (such as the MCS and the BCS) are of a high quality. For example, they are based on large samples that are reasonably representative.
- It is possible to carry out longitudinal analysis of this data.

Limitations of using existing quantitative data

- The researcher has no control over the quality of the data because they did not collect it in the first place.
- The data was collected by other researchers for other purposes, so some key variables may be missing.

Stretch and challenge

Advantages and disadvantages of non-official statistics

Copy and complete the following table. Try to include at least two advantages and two disadvantages of non-official statistics.

Advantages of non-official statistics	Disadvantages of non-official statistics
• •	• •

Check your understanding

1. Describe one difference between official and non-official statistics. (3 marks)

2. Identify and explain one advantage of using quantitative data that has been collected by other researchers. (4 marks)

3. Identify and explain one disadvantage of using quantitative data that has been collected by other researchers. (4 marks)

Stretch and challenge

Access to statistical data

Official statistics and many non-official statistics from organisations such as Childline can be accessed easily via the internet.

Briefly explain one advantage of this ease of access.

Key points

- Non-official statistics are produced by non-government bodies such as banks and charities. Using them can save time and money.

- Pre-existing quantitative data collected by other researchers is readily available, cheap to access and may save time. Many data sets (such as the MCS) are high quality and can be used in longitudinal research.

- There are potential problems with using statistics collected by other researchers or organisations. For example, the researcher has no control over the way the data was collected or the quality of the data, and there is no guarantee that the data will cover all of the variables that the researcher is interested in.

What sources of qualitative secondary data are available to sociologists?

Objectives
- Describe sources of qualitative secondary data that are available to sociologists
- Discuss the value and limitations of qualitative secondary data

Sources of qualitative secondary data

Qualitative secondary data, presented in words or visual form rather than numbers, may be useful to sociologists. Qualitative secondary data already exist and have not been produced by the researcher during the course of their research.

Sources of qualitative secondary data include:

- data from existing research studies carried out by other sociologists
- mass media products such as newspaper articles and television documentaries
- personal documents in written form such as diaries and letters or in visual form such as photographs
- material produced via the internet such as email, Facebook, Twitter and blogs
- autobiographies (an individual's account of their own life, usually written for publication) and biographies (a written account of someone else's life).

Glossary term

content analysis

Stretch and challenge

Sharing qualitative data through the UK Data Archive
Read through the information below and answer the question that follows.

The UK Data Archive gives researchers access to a wide range of secondary data including qualitative studies. Qualitative data collected during research can be shared with others and reused for research purposes in the future. Sociologists can access archived collections of transcripts from qualitative interviews. They can also deposit the data they collected from high-quality research projects funded by the ESRC as well as from other studies. Sharing data in this way can save time and money because researchers do not have to start from scratch. Instead, they can analyse relevant pre-existing data from in-depth interviews.

Identify two possible problems or disadvantages of using qualitative data from the UK Data Archive.

Content analysis

Content analysis is one way of dealing with qualitative secondary sources in a systematic way. It has been used to analyse the contents of personal documents and mass media products such as newspapers, magazine photographs, advertisements on television, and news programmes.

Feminist studies of the representation of gender in television advertisements might use content analysis. In this case, the researcher constructs a set of categories in advance, for example 'takes the lead/follows', 'gives orders/takes orders'. The researcher then works through the advertisements, coding or indexing all sections that show a character taking the lead or taking orders and so on. Once the contents have been coded, the researcher can count up (measure or quantify) the number of times female and male characters do these things.

Strengths of content analysis	Weaknesses of content analysis
✔ Content analysis is one way of dealing systematically with documents and visual images. ✔ It gives an indication of the importance of certain themes by counting the number of times they occur. It generates quantitative data from secondary sources, and the contents of different products (for example, different TV advertisements) can be compared statistically. ✔ The researcher works with a set of categories so the analysis can be replicated to check reliability.	✘ It can be time-consuming and laborious. ✘ It involves subjective judgments which may create quantitative but invalid data.

The advantages and limitations

Written documents may provide useful background information about the organisations, experiences or events they refer to. In researching different school cultures, for example, existing documentary sources such as prospectuses, newsletters and websites may be a valuable source of information. On the other hand, school websites and prospectuses are often put together with a particular purpose in mind (for example to market and promote the school) and might not reflect reality.

Qualitative secondary sources have to be treated with caution.

- Written documents such as diaries, letters or autobiographies may have been forged, in which case they are not genuine. If these documents are genuine, the contents may not actually be true.
- The experiences or events described may have been misinterpreted, for example due to the writer's prejudices.
- Autobiographies are likely to be one-sided and written for a particular audience of readers.
- Similarly, letters are written to a particular person and the contents are likely to be influenced by the writer's views of the recipient.

Check your understanding

1 Identify and explain one disadvantage of using written documents as sources of qualitative secondary data. (4 marks)
2 Identify and explain one advantage of content analysis. (4 marks)

FOCUS ON RESEARCH: WRITTEN ACTIVITY

Using qualitative secondary data

Read through the information, then answer the question that follows.

Nickie Charles et al. (2008) studied families in Swansea (in south Wales) and how they have changed since 1960. Their research took the form of a restudy of the work carried out in 1960 by two other sociologists, Rosser and Harris. So Rosser and Harris's earlier study provided Charles et al. with a source of qualitative secondary data.

Explain one advantage of using qualitative secondary data.

Key points

- Qualitative secondary sources include data from existing studies, personal documents, mass media products and material from the internet.

- Qualitative secondary sources can be analysed systematically using content analysis. This method has advantages and disadvantages.

What sorts of ethical issues arise during the research process?

Ethical issues

In carrying out research with people, sociologists are likely to face ethical issues. Ethical issues relate to morals and, in the context of sociological research, raise questions about how to conduct morally acceptable research. Ethical research practice involves protecting the rights and interests of research participants. It also involves ensuring that the research does not harm participants or have a negative effect on their wellbeing.

In this chapter, we have already touched upon **ethical considerations** such as:

- taking care not to reveal participants' **identities** when discussing or writing about research (see Topic 6)
- survey respondents' **anonymity** (see Topic 3)
- getting **permission** to record group interviews on minidisc (see Topic 12)
- difficulties in promising **confidentiality** in group interviews (see Topic 12)
- the use of semi-covert participant observation (PO) and what this meant for obtaining participants' **informed consent**.

Glossary terms

anonymity, confidentiality, ethical considerations, identity, informed consent, permission

In group interviews, a researcher cannot guarantee confidentiality.

Stretch and challenge

Informed consent

When researchers carry out research with children (for example, educational research or studies of families), they have to think carefully about issues related to informed consent.

1. In your view, at what age is a child able to give informed consent?

2. One option might be to ask parents or guardians to give consent on their children's behalf. To what extent do you think this is a satisfactory solution?

3. Another option is for a parent or guardian to be present when their child is being interviewed or filling in a questionnaire. Is this a satisfactory solution in your view?

FOCUS ON RESEARCH: WRITTEN ACTIVITY

Doing ethical research

In pairs, read through the information below, then answer the question that follows.

When Maria Papapolydorou publishes articles about her research, all real names of people and schools are changed. In her research with sixth form students, the participants were asked to choose their own pseudonym (a fictitious or 'made up' name).

Marek Korczynski (2014) studied the role of pop music in a factory in the Midlands. He negotiated access to the factory through his personal contacts. Before being granted research access, he had to agree to keep the firm anonymous.

Why do you think it is important not to reveal the real names of participants, schools or factories? Note down at least two possible reasons.

FOCUS ON RESEARCH: WRITTEN ACTIVITY

Research ethics

The British Sociological Association has drawn up a set of ethical guidelines to help sociologists in their work. Some of these are outlined in the extract below. Read through the extract and answer the questions that follow.

'**Informed consent**: as far as possible, participation in sociological research should be based on the freely given informed consent of those studied. This means the sociologist should explain, for example, what the research is about and why it is being undertaken. Research participants should be made aware of their right to refuse to participate in the research at any stage and for any reason.

Anonymity, privacy and confidentiality: the anonymity and privacy of research participants should be respected. Personal information should be kept confidential.

Covert research: the use of covert research may be justified in certain circumstances. For example, difficulties arise when research participants change their behaviour because they know they are being studied. However, covert methods act against the principles of informed consent and may invade the privacy of those being studied. They should be resorted to only where it is impossible to use other methods to obtain essential data.'

Source: adapted from BSA (2002) *Statement of Ethical Practice for the British Sociological Association.*

1 Explain what the following terms mean in relation to research ethics:
   - informed consent
   - anonymity
   - confidentiality.
2 According to the extract, under what circumstances might covert research be used?

FOCUS ON RESEARCH: DISCUSSION ACTIVITY

Ethical issues in practice

Ethical guidelines cannot cover every possible issue that researchers may encounter while carrying out research. Often, a researcher must decide how to respond to issues as they arise during interviews or observation.

In a small group, discuss whether you consider the following examples to involve ethical issues and, if so, whether and how you would address them.

1 One of the participants makes a racist comment during a group interview about religious beliefs.
2 It emerges during an interview on leisure activities that the interviewee is being physically abused at home.
3 During an interview, you begin to suspect that the interviewee is not telling you the truth.
4 During a study of a girl gang, you witness a violent attack on a rival gang member.

Note down your decisions and your reasons.

Key points

- Ethical guidelines help sociologists to carry out morally acceptable research that protects the rights of participants, their interests and their wellbeing.

- Guidelines cover issues such as informed consent, anonymity, privacy and confidentiality.

Check your understanding

Identify and explain one reason why ethical guidelines are important in sociological research. **(4 marks)**

What are the links between sociology, social problems and social policies?

Objectives
- Identify ways in which sociology addresses social problems
- Explain ways in which sociology contributes to social policy

The uses of sociology

Social policies are sets of plans and actions that governments, local authorities or other organisations put into place in order to address particular social problems such as poverty or discrimination. Many sociologists carry out research on **social policy** issues. They examine, for example, issues such as welfare and **welfare reform**, ageing and disability, crime, poverty and wealth.

Sociological concepts and research findings may be useful to governments or local authorities in designing and implementing social policies in fields such as welfare, criminal justice and education.

In this way, sociology has practical uses. It has an impact on society by:
- contributing to informed debates on social issues and social problems
- helping to shape social policy in areas such as ageing and poverty. It does this by proposing changes in policy in order to alleviate social problems.

Jane Pilcher (2004) points out that sociological studies in the late 19th and 20th centuries played a significant role in the creation of the **welfare state** by investigating poverty. Pilcher also highlights sociology's practical uses in dealing with social problems today. The inquiry into the murder of Stephen Lawrence (discussed opposite), for instance, is an important example of how sociology has helped to address social problems such as **institutional racism**.

Sociology has also made an important contribution to policy debates within the field of education. Paul Bagguley and Yasmin Hussain (2007), for example, explored young South Asian women's experiences of going to university and barriers to higher education. One of their findings was that some students, particularly those in universities or on courses without large numbers of Asian students, experienced racism from staff and students.

In writing up their research, Bagguley and Hussain discussed the policy implications of their findings and produced recommendations for changes in policy. They suggest that, in order to improve the university experience for South Asian women, some schools, colleges and universities need to ensure that unacceptable behaviour from staff and students is challenged.

> **Glossary terms**
>
> institutional racism, social policy, welfare reform, welfare state

The uses of sociology

Read through the extract below and then answer the questions that follow.

'Stephen Lawrence, a young man of African-Caribbean descent, was killed in 1993 by a group of white men in South London. There was a failure to convict anyone of Stephen's murder and, in 1997, a public enquiry was held into the police handling of the investigation. This resulted in the Macpherson Report, published in 1999. One of the key conclusions of the report was that the police's handling of the investigation into Stephen's murder was hindered by "institutional racism". Sociologists played a key part in this aspect of the report.

Stephen Lawrence.

Individual sociologists submitted evidence to the inquiry in areas such as policing, "race" and community relations. These sociologists were also involved in defining the key term "institutional racism". This concept refers to a process that produces racist outcomes, even when individuals themselves act without racist intent. In other words, unintentional prejudice and discrimination can lead to institutional racism. The inquiry into Stephen Lawrence's death is an example of the ways in which sociologists contribute to public debates and to social policy initiatives.'

Source: adapted from Pilcher (2004), pp. 2–4.

1 Identify two ways in which sociologists contributed to the Macpherson Report.
2 Explain one way in which sociology has contributed to social policy initiatives.

Researching stop and search

Kath Murray investigated the use of stop and search by the police in Scotland. Her findings showed a very high incidence of police stop and search of teenage boys. However, young children were also stopped and searched by the police. In 2010, for example, around 500 children aged 10 years and under were stopped and searched. Based on her findings, Kath Murray argued that it was not clear whether the main aim of stop and search was to deter people from committing crime or to detect crime that had been committed. In her report, she recommended that the main aim of stop and search should be clarified.

Kath Murray's work has made a difference in society. It led the Scottish government to set up a group to review the situation, and this group's recommendations informed a new law on criminal justice in Scotland in 2015.

In a small group, discuss the following questions and note down your ideas.

1 How important is it that the findings of research make a difference in society?
2 Can you think of other areas of social life in which research findings could make a difference?

Check your understanding

1 Describe what is meant by the term 'social policy'.   (3 marks)
2 Identify and explain one way in which sociology can have an impact on society.   (4 marks)

Key points

- Sociological research may be useful to governments and local authorities in formulating social policies in fields such as education and welfare.

- Sociology has a practical use today in addressing social problems such as racism. It has an impact on society by contributing to debates on social issues and helping to shape social policy.

Focus on skills

Making connections: Written activity

Official statistics

As you study the different areas of sociology, try to look for connections or links between them. For example, the topic of official statistics can be linked to many other areas including those shown in this spider diagram.

Choose two of the links in the diagram and, in each case, explain how it is connected to official statistics.

FOCUS ON RESEARCH: WRITTEN ACTIVITY

Planning research

Imagine that you and a colleague have been given a grant to fund your research into one of the following topics:

- young people's use of the internet
- migrants' experiences of racism
- changing attitudes to marriage
- male victims of violence
- males' and females' attitudes to science lessons
- what it means to be a victim of bullying in the workplace.

In pairs, choose one of these topics and answer the questions below.

1 Decide on a title for your study and note it down.
2 Make notes on how you would go about searching for the relevant literature on your chosen topic.
3 Identify two research aims, questions or hypotheses.
4 Identify one primary research method that you would use in your investigation and explain:
   a why you would use this particular method in your study. Try to link your chosen method to your research topic rather than discussing the advantages of this method in general terms.
   b one disadvantage of using this particular method to study your chosen topic.
5 Identify one secondary source of data that you would use in your study and explain why you would use this particular source.
6 Explain how you would select a sample.
7 Identify one ethical issue that could arise during your research and explain how you would deal with this issue.
8 Once you have completed your study, how would you go about publicising your findings among other sociologists and policy makers?

Analysing statistical data

Numerical data is often presented in graphs, particularly when showing trends. A trend refers to the general direction in which statistics on something (such as the number of births or divorces) move. The trend may be upwards, downwards or it may fluctuate (change frequently).

Study the graph and answer the questions that follow.

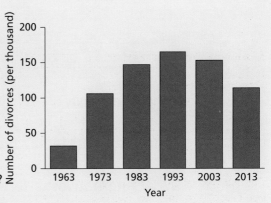

1 In which year was the number of divorces in England and Wales at its lowest?
2 In which year was the number of divorces at its highest?
3 How would you describe the trend in the number of divorces between 1993 and 2013?
4 How would you describe the trend between 1963 and 1993?
5 How would you describe the overall trend between 1963 and 2013?

Stretch and challenge

Differences between quantitative and qualitative methods

The following table is incomplete and your task is to fill in the blanks. Select one word from the list to fill in each blank. Check your answers with your teacher before copying out a complete version of the table.

Official statistics
The meaning of behaviour
Statistical data: numbers and figures
Unstructured interviews

Quantitative methods	Qualitative methods
a)	Rich data: word-for-word quotations
Structured interviews	b)
c)	Written documents such as letters and diaries
Human behaviour	d)

Mixed methods approaches

In Topic 2, you saw that sociologists today are more likely to use a mixed methods approach in order to generate both quantitative and qualitative data within one project. Mixed methods approaches have advantages – for example, they allow sociologists to build a more rounded picture of the topic they are studying.

Imagine that you are investigating first-time fathers and their experiences of fatherhood. Explain briefly how you could combine quantitative and qualitative data within this study.

Practical issues of time, cost and access

1 Explain why it would be quicker and cheaper to use official statistics from the Crime Survey for England and Wales rather than unstructured interviews when investigating people's experiences of crime.
2 John Williams managed to gain access to, and pass himself off as, an ordinary English football fan. Identify two groups who might find this more difficult and, in each case, explain why they might find it difficult.

Stretch and challenge

When sociologists use a mixed methods approach, they collect and analyse both quantitative and qualitative data within one study. There are some practical disadvantages of doing this.

Identify two practical disadvantages of using a mixed methods approach.

Families

3

What is a family?

Studying families

At some stage in our lives, most of us live as part of a **family** unit. However, even though we are likely to have some experience of family life, this does not necessarily mean that it is an easy topic to study. One problem is that it can be difficult to separate the facts about families from our own experiences of them and our beliefs about them.

Here are just a few examples of people's beliefs about families, family life and parenting:

1   There is nothing wrong with a woman who lives on her own choosing to have a baby.
2   It is OK for gay men or lesbian women to adopt children.
3   Mothers with children under the age of 11 should not work in full-time, paid employment.
4   Marriage is still the best form of relationship for partnering and parenting.
5   Family members should take more responsibility for the care of elderly relatives.

Issues such as these can arouse strong feelings because they involve judgments not only about how we live but also about how other people think we should live. These issues are hotly debated by politicians and the media. Through their research, sociologists aim to inform these debates.

Glossary terms

civil partnership, cohabitation, dependent children, family, family diversity

What do we mean by 'family'?

FOCUS ON SKILLS: DISCUSSION ACTIVITY

Beliefs about families, family life and parenting

In pairs, choose one of the above statements and discuss how sociologists might inform the debates in this area. Could the statement be turned into a research question, aim or hypothesis? Make a note of your conclusions.

What do we mean by 'family'?

Initially, answering the question of what we actually mean by 'family' might seem fairly straightforward, as we probably all use this word regularly. However, the problem is that we tend to use it to mean a range of different things. This is illustrated in this extract:

'At times, "my family" can mean my partner and children; at other times, it may include my grandchildren too. Alternatively, it may refer to my own family of birth, that is my parents, brothers and sisters, or it may mean a wider range of relatives including, for instance, aunts and uncles. It may also mean a much smaller group, for example just a married or cohabiting couple living alone. Often, the meaning intended is clear enough from the context in which the term is being used. However, when sociologists study the family, there is a need for greater precision in the use of terms.'

Source: adapted from Allan and Crow (2001) *Families, Households and Society,* p. 2.

FOCUS ON SKILLS: WRITTEN ACTIVITY

Different meanings of the term 'family'

How many different meanings of 'family' are included in the extract from Allan and Crow?

FOCUS ON SKILLS: DISCUSSION ACTIVITY

Defining 'family'

One possible, but very narrow, definition of a family is a group consisting of a married couple and their dependent children who all live together. This definition implies that a family is a group based not only on marriage and blood ties but also on shared residence. It can be criticised because it is not broad enough to include all of the different types of family in the UK today.

In a small group, discuss and note down:

    a   any examples of types of family that are excluded from this definition

    b   your own definition of a family that includes all the possible family types.

When we look more closely at the idea of a family, the picture becomes complicated. It is difficult to come up with a definition that manages to capture the increasing **family diversity** (or variety) that exists in the UK today. One approach is to define family broadly in terms of:

a couple whose relationship is based on marriage, **civil partnership** or **cohabitation**, with or without **dependent children**, or a lone parent and their child or children.

Some sociologists prefer to use the term 'families' rather than 'the family'. This is because they recognise that a range of family types, relationships and household arrangements can be found in the UK today.

Check your understanding: Exam practice

Identify and explain one reason why some sociologists use a broad rather than a narrow definition of family. (4 marks)

What different family types are there in the UK?

Objective
- Describe the different forms of family in the UK today

A range of family forms exists in the UK today. Examples include nuclear, extended, lone-parent and reconstituted families.

Glossary terms

beanpole families, blended families, extended families, lone-parent families, nuclear families, reconstituted families, same-sex families, step-families, step-parent

Nuclear families

A **nuclear family** consists of a father, mother and their dependent child or children. It contains just two generations and the family members live together in the same household. The parents may be married to each other or they may be cohabiting before, or instead of, getting married.

Same-sex families

A **same-sex family** in which a gay or lesbian couple live together with their child or children, is one alternative to the traditional, heterosexual nuclear family. The rise of gay and lesbian families marks a shift towards greater freedom for individuals to make choices about their domestic situations and personal relationships.

Extended families

An **extended family** includes relatives beyond the nuclear family.

- The classic extended family contains three generations who live together under the same roof (Charles et al., 2008b) or who live nearby. In this case, the family is extended vertically.
- Families may also be extended horizontally, for example with the addition of the husband's brother or the wife's cousin. In this case, the family would consist of just two generations who live under the same roof or nearby.
- The term 'modified extended family' is used in relation to extended family groupings whose members live apart geographically but who nonetheless maintain regular contact and provide support for each other. One example is children who leave home to work or study elsewhere but stay in regular contact with their parents.

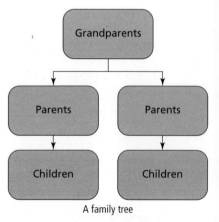

A family tree

Beanpole families

The term **beanpole families** describes families with multiple generations of older people and few children in any one generation. These multigenerational families are long and thin in shape, like a bushy family tree that has been pruned. In four-generation families, the children's parents, grandparents and great-grandparents are all alive at the same time.

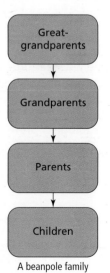

A beanpole family

Lone-parent families

A **lone-parent family** consists of one parent and a dependent child or children who live together. The majority of lone-parent families are headed by women who may be single, divorced, separated or widowed. In 2015, only 10 per cent of lone-parent families with dependent children in the UK were headed by men.

Reconstituted families

Reconstituted families are sometimes referred to as **blended families** or **step-families**. In a reconstituted family, one or both partners have a child or children from a previous relationship living with them. So at least one of the partners is a **step-parent**. Most step-families comprise a step-father, a biological mother and her child or children who live together. This family form might come about when a previously divorced woman with children marries a single childless man. In this case, while the man is the children's social father, in that he helps bring them up, he is not their biological father. However, the couple may go on to have a child or children together.

Most lone-parent families are headed by women.

Stretch and challenge

Have you noticed many advertisements on television or in magazines, for products such as breakfast cereals, which show the nuclear family? Have you noticed many advertisements that show family types other than the nuclear family?

What do you think the idea of the 'cereal packet' family is getting at?

The 'cereal packet' nuclear family: mum, dad and their two children.

FOCUS ON RESEARCH: WRITTEN ACTIVITY

Researching family types

Identify one type of family and explain how you would investigate this family type using questionnaires.

In your explanation, discuss how you would:

- select a sample
- distribute your questionnaires (for example, online or by post)
- obtain informed consent from respondents.

Also, discuss the advantages of using questionnaires to investigate the family type that you have identified.

When answering questions like this, try to link the research topic (in this case, the family type you identified) to the specific research method (in this case, questionnaires).

Check your understanding: Exam practice

Describe what sociologists mean by the term 'lone-parent family'.
(3 marks)

Key point

Many different types of family exist in the UK today.

What alternatives to families exist in the UK today?

Objective
- Describe the alternatives to families that can be found in the UK today

Many people do not live with their families. Instead, they might live alone, with friends or in communal establishments. We will now examine these different alternatives to family living.

Glossary terms

household, kin

Households and family households

A **household** consists of either one person who lives alone or a group of people who live at the same address and who share at least one meal a day or facilities such as a living room. A household could consist of a nuclear or a same-sex family. It could also consist of someone who lives on their own in a flat or a group of students who live in a shared house.

People in households are not necessarily related to one another by blood ties or marriage. A 'family household', however, is one in which family members live together in the same home.

Not everyone lives in traditional families.

The increase in one-person households

Over the last 30 years, the number of one-person households in the UK has increased significantly. In 1996, there were 6.6 million one-person households in the UK and by 2015 there were 7.7 million (29 per cent of UK households).

This increase is partly due to the changing age structure of the population. People are living longer, so there are more elderly, one-person households that typically contain older women whose partners have died.

However, the growth in one-person households is also linked to the increase in solo living among younger people. These households may consist of people who:

- remain single and childless throughout their lives
- are divorced
- are international migrants, including students, who have moved to Britain from abroad
- live alone before marrying or cohabiting
- choose to live apart from their partner.

Are friends becoming the new family?

One view is that families are less central in our lives and are increasingly being replaced by friends. For example, our friends rather than our family may provide us with emotional support and nurture.

In their research, Sasha Roseneil and Shelley Budgeon (2006) found that, among people who did not live with a partner, friends more than biological **kin** offered support to those who suffered mental health problems or emotional distress. Friends more than kin also picked up the pieces when love relationships came to an end.

However, not everyone agrees that friends are replacing families. Some researchers argue that many people turn first to their family members rather than to friends when they need help or support with a problem. It may be that friends are becoming more like family, rather than replacing them, and family members are becoming more like friends.

Singletons in the UK

Study the table and answer the questions that follow.

People living alone in the UK, by age group: 2005 and 2015 (millions)

	16–24	25–44	45–64	65–74	75+	Total
2005	0.2	1.77	2.0	1.27	1.99	7.23
2015	0.19	1.45	2.47	1.55	2.08	7.74

Source: adapted from ONS (2015) *Statistical Bulletin Families and Households.*

1 How many people in total lived alone in 2015?
2 Which age group had the biggest increase in solo living between 2005 and 2015?
3 In which age groups did the numbers fall?

Looked-after children and residential care

- In the UK today, some children do not live with their families. In March 2015, local authorities looked after 69 540 children in England. Of these, around 60 per cent were looked after due to neglect or abuse.
- Around 75 per cent of looked-after children are placed with foster carers, who provide them with a home on a short-term or long-term basis. Many other looked-after children are placed in children's homes or secure units.
- Children's homes provide children and young people with accommodation and care. Some homes specialise in looking after children with behavioural or emotional difficulties or who are dependent on drugs or alcohol.
- Secure units are homes that accommodate children who have committed an offence, and these homes can restrict children's liberty or freedom.
- Some older people live in institutions such as residential care and nursing homes. In 2011, 3.2 per cent of people aged 65 and over lived in care homes in England and Wales.

Researching looked-after children

What sort of ethical issues would you need to consider when investigating looked-after teenagers' experiences of foster care? Make a note of three possible issues that could arise during your research.

Choose one of these issues and explain how you would address it in your research.

Check your understanding: Exam practice

Identify and describe one example of an alternative to families in the UK today.   (3 marks)

Key point

Alternatives to families include one-person households, children's homes and residential care homes.

How might an individual's family and household settings change over the course of their life?

Changing household settings over the course of life

At any one time, most people live in a particular household setting. Individuals are likely to move between different family and household settings during their lifetime, as their relationships and situations change. This idea that our family and household settings will change over the course of our life is illustrated in the following pictures. They focus on the example of one female as she passes through the stages of childhood, youth and adulthood into older age.

4 A student household

1 A nuclear family

2 A lone-parent family

3 A reconstituted family

5 Solo living

6 Newly wed

7 A nuclear family

8 An empty nest family

The individual, families and households over time

Examine the pictures on the previous page.

1 Starting from the top-left picture, when this female was a baby, how many different types of family does she experience over the course of her life?

2 In each case, note down briefly what may have triggered the change in her family or household setting.

3 Note down any family types that are not included as examples in the pictures.

4 In what ways might this female's interests, leisure activities and the issues she has to deal with at the newly wed stage be different from those at the nuclear family stage (stage seven)?

5 In what ways might her interests, leisure activities and the issues she has to deal with at stage seven be different from those at stage eight (**empty nest family**)?

6 People now live longer than they did 50 years ago. How might this affect the length of time people spend in empty nest families?

When an individual is born, she may live with her parents and older siblings in a nuclear family. Her parents may later separate, marking a turning point in family life. After the separation, the girl may live with her mother in a lone-parent family. Her mother may go on to meet a new partner who comes to live with them. This marks another turning point, as the girl now lives in a reconstituted or blended family.

As a young adult, she may leave home to go to university or take up a job in a different city. During this period, she is likely to live alone or in a shared house with friends. After three years at university, she may return to live at home temporarily until she pays off her bank loan and saves to buy a flat. By this time, her mother may have remarried and had another baby.

Significant events such as the birth of a child, marriage, separation, **divorce** and remarriage may mark important turning points in a person's life. Such turning points often lead to changes in an individual's family and household settings. It is likely that such changes will continue over the course of people's lives.

Researching changes in people's families and households over the life course

Imagine that you work as part of a research team looking at the changes that people experience in their family and household settings over the course of their life.

1 In pairs, decide on an appropriate method of research and discuss the strengths and weaknesses of your method for this particular piece of research.

2 What ethical issues might you experience during this research? How might you address these issues?

Note down the key points of your discussion.

Check your understanding: Exam practice

Identify and explain how one turning point in an individual's life might lead to change in their family or household situation.

(4 marks)

Key point

Individuals will live in different family and household settings during their lifetime.

What are the links between families, households, ethnicity and social class?

Objective
- Describe the links between families, households, ethnicity and social class

Families, households and ethnicity

As a culturally diverse society, Britain is home to a rich mix of cultural, ethnic and religious groups. For example, in London over 300 languages are spoken. People have been migrating to Britain for centuries. In the 19th century, for instance, migrants came from Ireland, and after World War II there was **migration** from former colonies such as India and Pakistan, and parts of the Caribbean. This **immigration** takes place alongside **emigration** as people leave Britain to settle abroad.

Charles et al. (2008a) note that **cultural diversity** in Britain is associated with different patterns of family formation. For example, among people of African-Caribbean heritage, becoming a mother is not necessarily associated with stopping full-time paid work. By contrast, among Asian heritage families, there is still some emphasis on being a full-time mother. However, these patterns do appear to be changing among second-generation migrants.

Glossary terms

cultural diversity, egalitarian, emigration, immigration, migration

FOCUS ON SKILLS: WRITTEN ACTIVITY

Solo living by ethnic group

The bar chart below presents data on people who lived alone in England and Wales in 2011 according to their ethnicity. For example, 16.4 per cent of White British people lived alone.

Study the information and then answer the questions that follow.

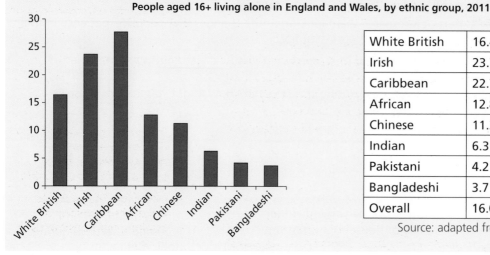

People aged 16+ living alone in England and Wales, by ethnic group, 2011

White British	16.4
Irish	23.7
Caribbean	22.7
African	12.8
Chinese	11.3
Indian	6.3
Pakistani	4.2
Bangladeshi	3.7
Overall	16.0

Source: adapted from ONS (2014).

1 From which ethnic group were people most likely to live alone in 2011?
2 What percentage of people from Chinese ethnicity lived alone?
3 Which ethnic group had the smallest proportion of people living alone?
4 These figures are based on data from the 2011 census of the population. Identify and explain one strength of this source of data.

Data on households containing three or more generations in England and Wales in 2001 show that 10 per cent of Bangladeshi and Pakistani households contained a multigenerational extended family, compared with 2 per cent of White British and Mixed households and 3 per cent of Black Caribbean households.

Qureshi et al. (2015) point out that British Asians are often seen as committed to traditional, old-fashioned family life with low rates of divorce and a low proportion of lone-parent families. Qureshi et al. question this image and argue that British Asian families are changing. This is reflected in changing patterns of lone-parent families (see page 118).

(see page 118)

Stretch and challenge

How far is the information in the bar chart likely to give a true picture of what it is supposed to be measuring? Explain your thinking.

FOCUS ON SKILLS: DISCUSSION ACTIVITY

Multigenerational extended family households

1 In a small group, discuss the possible advantages and disadvantages of living in a multigenerational extended family household. In your discussion, you should consider both social and economic factors.
2 Note down two advantages and two disadvantages.

Family relationships, ethnicity and social class

Popular beliefs suggest that British Asian families are based on unequal, male-dominated relationships. Westwood and Bhachu (1988) challenge such beliefs, suggesting that popular images of 'the Asian family' are often based on prejudice (or prejudgments). In reality, there are ethnic differences between people of Asian heritage in Britain, for example according to their religion and social class. This makes it difficult to generalise about 'the Asian family'. Westwood and Bhachu point out that 'Asian families' are, in fact, British families and are a major source of strength and resistance against the racism of British society.

Some sociologists argue that relationships within families vary according to social class. Popular images suggest that working-class families are male-dominated. There is some evidence to suggest that, in general terms, middle-class role relationships are more **egalitarian** or equal than working-class ones. Other evidence, however, seems to suggest that working-class fathers are more involved in childcare than middle-class fathers.

Migration has added to the overall diversity of families in Britain.

Key points

- Britain is a culturally diverse society and immigration has been taking place for centuries.

- Migration has added to the overall diversity of families and households in Britain.

Check your understanding: Exam practice

Describe what sociologists mean by 'cultural diversity'.   (3 marks)

What types of family diversity are there?

Objectives
- Understand the different aspects of family diversity
- Describe Rapoport and Rapoport's account of family diversity

Family diversity

We have already examined some aspects of family diversity, for example in terms of ethnicity and social class. Rapoport and Rapoport (1982) explore the issue of diversity in detail. They argue that families in Britain are undergoing a process of change. In the past, there was one dominant norm in society regarding what family life should be like. Today, a wider range of options is available and people value their freedom to choose the pattern of family life that suits them. The contemporary situation is one of diversity of families and this reflects the variety of needs and wishes in society.

Glossary terms

childrearing, domestic division of labour, dual-worker families, gender roles, life course, lifestyles, social network, stigma

FOCUS ON KEY THINKERS

Rapoport and Rapoport: Dimensions of family diversity

Rapoport and Rapoport (1982) identify five types of diversity in families in Britain: organisational, cultural, social class, **life course** and cohort.

Organisational diversity: there are differences between families in their structures, the ways they organise their **domestic division of labour** (how tasks within the home are divided) and their **social networks** such as their links to their extended family. Examples of family structures that illustrate this sort of diversity include:

- conventional (nuclear) families
- **dual-worker families**
- one-parent families
- reconstituted families.

Cultural diversity: families differ in their cultural values and beliefs. Different minority ethnic groups such as those of Cypriot, South Asian and African-Caribbean heritage illustrate this diversity in beliefs and values. There are also differences in values between Catholics and Protestants.

These differences between families in their beliefs and values affect their **lifestyles** and ideas about **gender roles**, the domestic division of labour and **childrearing**. They also affect families' attitudes to education and paid work.

Social class diversity: a family's social class position affects the resources available to it. Working-class families tend to favour more conventional role relationships between husbands and wives. On the other hand, in some middle-class families, roles may be unequal because of the demands of the husband's career even when the couple value more equal roles. Social class also affects childrearing practices such as the way parents discipline their children. For example, discipline is more physical among working-class parents.

Life-course diversity: this relates to the stage in the family life-cycle that a particular family has reached. Newlyweds without children are at a different stage to retired couples whose adult children have left home. Families at a specific stage in the life-cycle develop lifestyles that reflect their circumstances. For instance, families with young children often have similar concerns and issues to deal with. Their concerns are not the same as those of families at other stages in the family life-cycle such as retired couples.

Cohort diversity: this refers to the particular period in which a family passes through different stages of the family life-cycle. For example, the **stigma** attached to divorce has reduced over time, so younger couples may find it easier to get divorced today.

Secondary analysis

Rapoport and Rapoport's account of the five aspects of family diversity is based on their review of the existing literature on families in Britain. In other words, their analysis is based on secondary sources such as the research carried out by Bott (see Topic 12) rather than on primary data that they collected themselves during the course of research.

1 Identify and explain one advantage of Rapoport and Rapoport's approach.

2 Identify and explain one disadvantage of their approach.

Can you think of other examples of the way cohort can affect the life experiences of family members? For example, how might living through a global recession affect young people within families?

Make a note of your ideas.

Unequal roles

In a small group, discuss how the demands of the husband's career in some middle-class families might affect the roles of the husband and wife, even though they value more equal roles.

Note down your ideas.

Since Rapoport and Rapoport first examined family diversity in the 1980s, diversity has increased. For instance, there are more same-sex families headed by a lesbian or gay couple. This increase is due to factors such as changes in social attitudes, changes in the law (for example, the introduction of civil partnerships and gay marriage) and developments in reproductive technology (for instance, IVF or surrogacy).

Family diversity has increased since the 1980s and there are now more same-sex families in the UK.

Key points

- Rapoport and Rapoport identified five aspects of family diversity.

- Families are changing and people now have more freedom to choose the pattern of family life that suits them.

Identify one aspect of family diversity and explain how you would investigate this aspect using unstructured interviews.   (4 marks)

How do families differ within a global context?

The traditional nuclear family is often seen as normal and natural compared to other family types. Yet if we examine families and households around the world, we will find a range of household organisations and personal relationships. Not all of these are based on the nuclear family. Childrearing, for example, is organised in various ways. **Communes** and kibbutzim (plural of **kibbutz**) are examples of alternatives to nuclear family households.

Communes

Communes were popular during the 1960s and 1970s, especially in the USA, and some still exist today. In broad terms, a commune is a group of people who share living accommodation, possessions, wealth and property. It is difficult to generalise about communes because they vary, but usually each adult has their own room and young children share a room.

Members of the commune often make decisions together and try to achieve equality in the status of women and men, adults and children. Kanter (1979) describes one commune in the USA that named its cat as head of household on official forms rather than singling out a particular individual.

Communal households may be based on shared political beliefs or environmental principles. For example, members might avoid activities or products that exhaust the earth's natural resources.

Kibbutzim

The original kibbutzim were agricultural settlements set up by Jewish settlers in Palestine around a century ago. Over 2 per cent of Israel's population now live in kibbutzim. A kibbutz consists of a group of people who live together communally and value equality and cooperation between members.

Originally, all children lived and slept separately from their parents in the children's quarters. They were looked after by 'kibbutz mothers' and saw their biological parents for a few hours every day. This has changed, however, and on some kibbutzim children now live with their biological parents up to the age of 15 years, when they move to the teenagers' houses.

Each family has its own apartment but meals are usually eaten in the communal dining hall. All children born in the same year are raised and educated together, spending the day in the children's houses. In longer-established kibbutzim, multigenerational families exist.

A kibbutz consists of a group of people who live together communally and value equality and cooperation between members.

Researching communes

1 Identify and explain one advantage of using overt participant observation to investigate relationships between members of a commune.

2 Identify and explain one disadvantage of using overt participant observation in this context.

One-child family policy in China

Within a global context, government policies on families can differ markedly. In an attempt by the Chinese authorities to control population growth, couples in China who lived in cities were by law allowed to have just one child. If the couple did have a second child, they could face fines, demotion or dismissal from work. This policy, introduced in 1979, was seen as cruel and unfair by people in many countries.

In January 2016, this controversial policy came to an end. Although families still need government-issued birth permits, or face the sanction of a forced abortion, married couples in China can now request to have two children.

China's **ageing population**, together with one of the lowest **birth rates** in the world, prompted the change in policy. China now needs more young people to provide the workforce of the future and to look after ageing relatives.

Stretch and challenge

Why is it important for sociologists to study social structures such as families across different societies and cultures rather than in just one society?

Researching changes to government policy on families

Imagine that you are part of a research team that is investigating people's views on proposed changes to government policy on a family-related issue such as cuts in child benefit payments, changes in the law on abortion or plans to make divorce more difficult. You want to gather rich and detailed data on people's views.

In pairs, decide which research method you would use.`

Make a note of your decision and your reasons.

Key point

Cross-cultural studies show that different family forms, household arrangements and personal relationships exist in different cultures.

Check your understanding: Exam practice

Identify and describe one alternative to nuclear family households.

(3 marks)

How does the functionalist perspective view families?

Objective
- Explain the functionalist theory of the nuclear family's functions

There are a number of different sociological perspectives or approaches to the study of families and family life. These include the **functionalist**, **Marxist** and **feminist** approaches.

During the 1940s and 1950s, functionalists viewed the nuclear family in positive terms as a necessary part of society.

Functionalism focuses on the role and functions of the nuclear family in industrial society. It sees the nuclear family as a key social structure because it performs several essential functions for individuals and for society as a whole. This view starts off from the assumption that individuals and society have basic needs that must be met if society is to function smoothly.

Glossary terms

economic function, feminism, functionalism, Marxism, sexual division of labour, socialisation

---

FOCUS ON SKILLS: DISCUSSION ACTIVITY

Individuals' needs

1 In a small group, discuss what sorts of things individuals need in order to survive. You could, for example, consider people's physical, emotional or financial needs. Note down three things.

2 Does the nuclear family meet any of the needs you have identified? If so, make a note of how the nuclear family meets them. If not, note down how they are met.

Murdock's four functions of the nuclear family

G.P. Murdock (1949) argues that the nuclear family carries out four vital functions that are essential for society and for individuals. These are the sexual, reproductive, economic and educational functions.

The sexual function

Society needs a way of regulating sexual activity. In a nuclear family, the husband and wife live together and have a sexual relationship that is approved of in society. The nuclear family regulates the sexual behaviour of the married couple, helps to maintain their relationship and binds them together.

The reproductive function

Society needs new members if it is to survive over time. The nuclear family has an important role in this through procreation and childbearing. It has the main responsibility for bearing, rearing and caring for children.

The economic function

Society needs to ensure that there is a way of providing people with economic support (for instance, shelter, food and clothes) and the nuclear family fulfils this **economic function** or need. Murdock argues that economic cooperation is based on a division of labour between the husband and wife within a nuclear family. In his view, all known societies have developed a **sexual division of labour** because it has definite advantages. For instance, the husband can undertake the most strenuous tasks such as house building, while the wife can perform the lighter tasks such as preparing food or making clothes.

The educational function

Society needs to ensure that new members learn its culture. Through the **socialisation** process within the nuclear family, parents have the main role in teaching and disciplining their children.

Murdock argues that the nuclear family is universal – it exists in every known society. No society has found an alternative structure that could perform these four functions so well. From this, Murdock concludes that the nuclear family is an inevitable part of society – it is bound to occur.

According to Murdock, the nuclear family is universal and inevitable.

FOCUS ON THEORY: DISCUSSION ACTIVITY

Evaluating Murdock's account of the nuclear family

Since the 1950s, Murdock's ideas about the nuclear family and its functions have been criticised as outdated and unrealistic.

1 In a small group, discuss the four functions and, for each, suggest two reasons why the ideas presented could be seen as outdated or unrealistic.

2 On what grounds might feminists criticise Murdock's theory?

3 Make a note of your ideas.

Stretch and challenge

Murdock developed his theory about the functions of the nuclear family from information he gathered about families in 250 different societies across continents such as Africa, Asia and South America. In his research, he used secondary sources including information from books and articles.

1 What are the advantages of using these data?

2 What are the possible limitations of using these data?

Check your understanding: Exam practice

Identify and explain one of Murdock's four functions of the family.

(4 marks)

Key points

- There are different sociological approaches to the study of families, one of which is the functionalist perspective.

- Murdock argues that the nuclear family performs four essential functions for individuals and society.

- Critics of Murdock see his ideas as outdated, unrealistic and sexist.

How does Parsons view the functions of the nuclear family?

Objectives
- Describe Parsons' ideas on the functions of the nuclear family
- Criticise his views on these functions

FOCUS ON KEY THINKERS

Talcott Parsons and the main functions of the nuclear family

Talcott Parsons (1902–1979), an American sociologist, was one of the key contributors to functionalist views on the family. He examined the family in the USA and argues that the nuclear family has become more **isolated** or separated from the wider family.

Glossary terms

agency of socialisation, dysfunctional families, ethnic diversity, idealisation, isolation

Parsons and the loss of functions

Parsons (1956) argues that, over time, the family has gradually lost some of its functions. Several functions (such as education and economic production) have transferred from the family to other structures in society. Many needs – such as for clothing, food and recreation – are now met by agencies outside the family.

Parsons argues that the nuclear family is now almost functionless in terms of the functions it performs for society. However, this does not mean that it has become less important. According to Parsons, the nuclear family is still important because society depends on it to perform certain vital functions related to the formation of personality.

In Parsons' view, human personalities are not born. Instead, they are made through the primary socialisation process. Nuclear families are necessary because they are factories that produce human personalities. Once human personalities are produced, nuclear families keep them stable.

FOCUS ON THEORY: DISCUSSION ACTIVITY

Made or born?

How far do you agree that our personalities are made through socialisation rather than being inborn?

Note down three main points from your discussion.

The basic and vital functions of the nuclear family

Parsons identifies two basic and vital functions that all families perform in all societies: primary socialisation and stabilisation of adult personalities.

Primary socialisation of children

The nuclear family functions as an **agency of socialisation**. Through the process of primary socialisation in families, children learn the culture of their society. By absorbing this culture, they become members of society. The family is so important because it socialises children so that they learn and accept society's shared values and roles. This helps to maintain the stability of society.

Stabilisation of adult personalities

The nuclear family functions as an agency of personality stabilisation. Everyday life outside the family can be stressful for adults and can put them under pressure. However, the husband and wife support each other emotionally and this relieves the pressure. In this way, the family plays a key role in maintaining the emotional stability of adults. It is a safe haven, a counterweight to balance out the stresses of daily life.

Furthermore, by living with children, parents can express and act out the childish elements of their own personality. This also helps to keep adult personalities stable.

Criticisms of Parsons

Critics argue that:

- Parsons focuses on American middle-class families and ignores **ethnic diversity** as well as diversity linked to social class and religion.
- Parsons ignores alternatives to the nuclear family (such as communes or kibbutzim) that could fulfil the two functions.
- Parsons gives an idealised view of families. His **idealisation** ignores **dysfunctional families** in which, for example, child abuse and domestic violence occur. The picture he paints does not match the reality of family life.

Leach (1967) argues that the nuclear family intensifies the emotional stress between spouses and between parents and children. Members of nuclear families demand too much of each other and this leads to conflict, with parents fighting and children rebelling. This situation becomes like an overloaded electrical circuit in which the fuses blow.

Unlike functionalists, Marxists are critical of the nuclear family and see it as functional for capitalist society. For example, one of its functions is to socialise children into accepting the values of capitalism. In this way, it serves the interests of capitalism.

Many feminists see the family as a major source of female oppression. They argue that nuclear families imprison women in their own homes, tied to children and housework.

Stretch and challenge

Alternatives to the family

How far do you agree that primary socialisation and stabilisation of adult personality are basic and vital functions? Can you think of any alternative ways of fulfilling these two functions? Could these functions be carried out by social structures other than the nuclear family?

Note down your ideas.

The nuclear family may increase rather than relieve stress.

Key points

- Parsons is a key thinker in the sociology of the family. From a functionalist perspective, he argues that the nuclear family performs two vital functions: primary socialisation and stabilisation of adult personalities.

- Critics of Parsons argue that he presents an idealised and unrealistic account of families and ignores diversity.

> ### Check your understanding: Exam practice
>
> Identify and explain one criticism of Parsons's view of the nuclear family. (4 marks)

How does the Marxist perspective view the role of families?

Objectives
- Explain the Marxist approach to the study of families and family life
- Describe the ideas of Eli Zaretsky
- Criticise the Marxist approach

The Marxist approach

Unlike functionalism, the Marxist perspective is critical of the nuclear family as an institution and the role it plays in capitalist society. Rather than viewing the family as meeting the needs of individuals and society, Marxists see it as serving the interests of capitalism.

The Marxist approach argues that the family is one of the key institutions through which social inequalities continue from one generation to the next.

- The bourgeoisie (the owners of the means of production such as land and factories) are able to pass on their wealth to family members. In this way, the social class system is re-created over time.
- Educational advantages are passed down through families. For instance, only people from wealthy backgrounds can afford to send their children to expensive public schools.
- Through the socialisation processes within the family, working-class people may learn to accept their subordinate (inferior) position in capitalist society and to see the system as fair.

FOCUS ON KEY THINKERS

Eli Zaretsky on capitalism, the family and personal life

Eli Zaretsky (1976) is interested in understanding the family and family relationships under capitalism. He argues that the family was a unit of production before the early 19th century. For example, during the early stages of the textile industry, all members of the family were involved in the production of cloth in the home.

The rise of industrial capitalism and production in factories led to a split between family life and work. As a result, the family and the **economy** are now seen as two **separate spheres**: the private sphere and the public sphere.

With the separation of home and work, women became responsible for personal relationships within the family and for family members' emotional wellbeing. Women now had to maintain the home as a private refuge from a brutal society. However, Zaretsky believes that the family is not able to meet people's emotional and social needs. It can do no more than cushion them from the harsh effects of capitalism.

According to Zaretsky, the family serves the interests of capitalism in several ways.

Glossary terms

economic function, economy, patriarchy, separate spheres, socialism

Capitalism led to a split between home and workplace.

- The family has an **economic function** under capitalism. Women, as housewives and mothers, carry out unpaid labour within the home such as childrearing, cleaning and cooking. The system of wage labour at work relies on this unpaid domestic labour getting done. This is because women's labour within the home maintains daily life. However, it is devalued because it is seen as separate from the production of commodities and profits in the public world of the economy.
- Through the family, each social class reproduces itself over time. The bourgeois family preserves its private property and transmits it from one generation to the next. The proletarian family reproduces the labour force by producing future generations of workers.
- Zaretsky sees the family as a vital unit of consumption for capitalism. Families buy and consume the products of the capitalist system and, in doing so, enable the bourgeoisie to make their profits.

Zaretsky believes that only **socialism** (a society without social classes) can end the artificial separation of family life and public life and make it possible for people to be personally fulfilled.

FOCUS ON SKILLS: DISCUSSION ACTIVITY

The family as a unit of consumption

In a small group, discuss how far you agree that the family is a unit of consumption. What sort of products and services do families buy or consume? How does this benefit capitalism?

Make a note of your ideas.

Criticisms of the Marxist approach to families

There are several key criticisms of the Marxist approach to families:

- Marxists tend to ignore the fact that many individuals are satisfied with family life. Many people see marriage and having children as a central goal in life.
- Feminists point out that Marxists tend to work with the traditional model of the nuclear family – that of the male breadwinner and female housewife. In this way, Marxists ignore the diversity of families today.
- Some feminists see female oppression as linked to **patriarchy** rather than to capitalism. They question the Marxist view that female oppression will simply disappear in a socialist society.
- Functionalists view the nuclear family in positive terms as meeting the needs of individuals and industrial society.

Key points

- Marxists link families to social class inequalities in capitalist societies.

- Zaretsky is a key thinker in the sociology of the family. From a Marxist perspective, he argues that the nuclear family serves the interests of capitalism. Women carry out unpaid domestic labour and are responsible for personal life within the private sphere of the family.

- Critics argue that Marxists ignore family diversity and do not address patriarchy.

Check your understanding: Exam practice

Identify and explain one function of the nuclear family from a Marxist perspective.   (4 marks)

How do feminist perspectives view the role of families?

Feminist views on family life

Feminist approaches focus on gender relations. Feminists are critical of the family as an institution and its role in society. In particular, they see families as having a negative impact on the lives of women. While feminist sociologists accept that biological differences exist between women and men, they argue that many differences are actually created by society. Families actively contribute to the **social construction** or creation of gender differences through primary socialisation processes. We can see this, for instance, in the ways that babies tend to be dressed in blue or pink and given different toys according to whether they are a boy or a girl. Sociologists use the term **canalisation** to describe the way parents channel their children's interests into toys, games and other activities that are seen as gender appropriate.

Within families, young children learn how they are expected to behave not only as individuals but also as males and females. A girl who sees her mother doing the cleaning and ironing may assume that such tasks are part of a woman's role. A boy who is encouraged to help his father with home improvements or to wash the car may think that this is part of a man's role. In this way, families can be seen as preparing children for their gender roles in a male-dominated society. As a result, the family helps to reproduce gender inequalities over time.

Gender socialisation in families.

FOCUS ON SKILLS: DISCUSSION ACTIVITY

Parents' expectations of daughters and sons

In a small group, discuss whether parents have different expectations of daughters and sons, for example regarding housework. Do sons get more freedom than daughters?

Note down three points raised during your discussion.

FOCUS ON KEY THINKERS

Christine Delphy and Diana Leonard on exploitation in families and marriage

Delphy and Leonard focus on the unpaid aspect of housework. They define housework as unpaid work done by women in, or related to, the household. Housework includes cooking, cleaning and shopping but also less visible work that wives and mothers do for their husbands and families. Examples include booking holidays and sending birthday cards. The reason housework is unpaid is not related to the tasks themselves. Cleaners in schools, hospitals and offices, for example, get paid for their work. It is unpaid because the tasks are done for the husband and family within a particular relationship.

The family is based on a hierarchy (a system of ranks shaped like a pyramid). The husband is at the top and other family members are in subordinate positions. The husband provides for his wife's upkeep and gets to control her labour for his own use. All of a wife's time may be used up by her husband but she has no money of her own. Even when women have well-paid, full-time employment, they still do most of the domestic work and childcare.

Family relationships involve economic exploitation. In other words, men use and benefit from the unpaid work of women within families. Wives are exploited in terms of:

- the way their labour is used by their husbands
- their work not being valued
- their financial dependence on their husbands
- their subordinate position within the family.

Delphy and Leonard argue that the family is patriarchal. Families maintain men's dominance over women and children. In this way, **patriarchal families** maintain the patriarchal nature of society.

FOCUS ON THEORY: WRITTEN ACTIVITY

Delphy and Leonard

1 Give two examples of 'less visible' work.
2 Why is housework 'unpaid work'?
3 In what way do men exploit women?

Stretch and challenge

Delphy and Leonard are **radical feminists** who explore the workings of patriarchy. They see the oppression of women as mainly due to men's exploitation of women's domestic labour. In their view, men – rather than capitalism – directly benefit from the exploitation of women's work.

How does Delphy and Leonard's explanation of women's oppression differ from that of Marxists such as Zaretsky?

Criticisms of feminist approaches

These include the following:

- Delphy and Leonard do not take into account families in which power is shared between members.
- Marxist approaches argue that inequality within families is linked to the workings of capitalism rather than patriarchy.
- Functionalists see the structure of the family as benefiting individuals and society.

Check your understanding: Exam practice

Identify and describe one difference between the feminist and functionalist accounts of primary socialisation. (3 marks)

Key points

- Feminist approaches are critical of modern families and their role in society. They link families to gender inequalities.

- Delphy and Leonard are radical feminists who argue that the family is patriarchal and hierarchical. Men benefit from the unpaid domestic work of women within families.

- Marxist approaches link inequalities in families to capitalism rather than to patriarchy, and functionalist approaches see the family as meeting the needs of its members (including those of females) as well as the needs of society.

What were conjugal roles and relationships like in the past?

Objective
• Describe gender roles and relationships between adult partners in the past

Conjugal roles in the past

Conjugal roles refers to the domestic roles of married or cohabiting partners (who does what) and **conjugal relationships** refers to the relationships between married or cohabiting partners.

Elizabeth Bott (1971) identifies two different types of conjugal roles: **segregated conjugal roles** and **joint conjugal roles**.

Segregated conjugal roles and relationships	Joint conjugal roles and relationships
• There is a clear division of labour in the household, with tasks divided into male and female tasks.	• The husband and wife do not have a rigid division of household tasks, and share many tasks.
• The husband and wife spend little of their leisure time together. They have separate interests and their own friends outside the home.	• The husband and wife spend much of their leisure time together. They have few separate interests.

Stretch and challenge

Bott studied families in the 1950s. Her methods included qualitative interviews with husbands and wives in 20 London-based families with children aged under 10 years. She did not claim that these families were a random or representative sample of a wider population of families and she did not try to make any generalisations.

Why do you think:

a Bott's sample cannot be seen as a representative sample?

b She did not try to generalise?

Some sociologists argue that one important change within families is the move towards equality in conjugal roles and relationships. According to this view, conjugal roles within the home are becoming more joint (**integrated conjugal roles**) rather than segregated.

Segregated conjugal roles in the past

During the early part of the 20th century, conjugal roles were segregated. In other words, they were separate and unequal: there was a clear-cut division of labour within the home based on gender. In general, married women were expected to take the main responsibility for housework and childcare. Their husbands were expected to be the main breadwinner (**wage** earner).

Segregated conjugal roles during the early 20th century.

However, women's roles differed according to their social class. In addition to housework and childcare, many working-class women also had to go out to work or take on paid work from home, such as taking in laundry, in order to survive. Among the **middle class**, on the other hand, the wife was not expected to undertake paid employment. Her role was to supervise the work of the household employees such as the maid, the governess and the nanny. Families were male dominated and both working-class and middle-class husbands were expected to provide for their family.

FOCUS ON RESEARCH: DISCUSSION ACTIVITY

Planning research on conjugal roles

Imagine that you are investigating the division of housework and childcare among married and cohabiting couples today. Your main method of research is questionnaires. In pairs, answer the following questions and note down your answers.

1 Identify two research aims or hypotheses.
2 Who would your population consist of (for example, couples or one partner only) and why?
3 Which sampling technique would you use?
4 How would you obtain informed consent from respondents?
5 Explain one advantage of using questionnaires to investigate conjugal roles.

FOCUS ON SKILLS: WRITTEN ACTIVITY

Parsons on instrumental and expressive roles

Read through the following account and answer the questions below.

From a functionalist perspective, Parsons (1956) links sex roles within the American family to its functions. In the nuclear family, the man takes the more **instrumental role** in the world of paid work as breadwinner of the family. The woman takes the more **expressive role** as housewife and mother, with responsibility for the household and for providing emotional support.

Parsons explains the allocation of roles in terms of biological differences between the sexes. Women bear children and this sets up a strong relationship between a mother and her child. Men specialise in the instrumental direction within the workplace. The different roles of the parents are important to the primary socialisation process.

1 What does the term 'expressive role' mean?
2 According to Parsons, why do women have the expressive role?
3 How could you criticise Parsons' account from a feminist perspective?

Key points

- Conjugal roles can be seen as either segregated or joint.

- It can be argued that, in the early part of the 20th century, conjugal roles were segregated, or separate and unequal.

Check your understanding: Exam practice

1 Describe what is meant by 'joint conjugal roles'. (3 marks)
2 Describe what is meant by 'segregated conjugal roles'. (3 marks)

What is the symmetrical family?

Objectives
- Explain the term 'symmetrical family'
- Describe Young and Willmott's ideas on the symmetrical family

FOCUS ON KEY THINKERS

Young and Willmott on the symmetrical family

Young and Willmott (1973) are influenced by the functionalist perspective. They published research findings that suggested the **'symmetrical family'** had become the typical family form in Britain.

In a symmetrical family:

- The roles of husband and wife were less segregated than in the past and there was more equality between the spouses. Symmetrical relationships are opposite but similar. Although the husband and wife carry out different (opposite) tasks, they each made a similar contribution to the home. So while women still took the main responsibility for housework and childcare, men spent an equivalent amount of time on home-related tasks such as DIY and were more likely to help with housework and childcare.
- The couple and their children were more home-centred than in the past. They spent much of their leisure time together and, with developments in technology, more of their entertainment was home-based. Also, relationships between spouses were warmer and more caring.
- The extended family counted for less and the nuclear family for more. The nuclear family became more separated from the extended family.
- The husband and wife had more of a financial partnership. Decision-making, including decisions on how money was spent, was more shared.

The principle of stratified diffusion

Young and Willmott (1973) examined changes in family life since the second half of the 19th century. They developed the **principle of stratified diffusion** as a general guide to these changes. According to this principle, many social changes (for example, in values and attitudes) start at the top of the social class system and work downwards. Changes in family life, for instance, filter down from the middle class into the **working class**.

Glossary terms

principle of stratified diffusion, symmetrical family, working class

Explaining the move to symmetry

Some sociologists have pointed to wider social changes to explain the move towards symmetry. In particular, they highlight the following:

- The rise of feminism since the 1960s has had an impact on gender roles. Feminism has influenced women's attitudes towards education and work and has led them to reject the traditional housewife role.

- More effective forms of contraception mean that women can decide whether to have children, when and how many. Women can combine motherhood with paid employment and a career.
- As a result of their increased participation in paid employment, many women are financially independent and now have more freedom, equality and status, both inside and outside the home.
- People's interest in home life has increased, for example in DIY and home improvements. Technological developments have created opportunities for home-based leisure pursuits linked, for example, to computer games, DVDs and satellite television. Consequently, men are now more likely to spend time at home and to become more involved with their family.

FOCUS ON SKILLS: WRITTEN ACTIVITY

Changing attitudes to gender roles

Study the following information from the British Social Attitudes (BSA) survey and then answer the questions below.

Attitudes to male and female roles in the workplace and home, 1989–2012

	1989	2012
Agree that a man's job is to earn money; a woman's job is to look after the home and family	28%	13%
Agree that a job is all right, but what most women really want is a home and children	31%	26%
Agree that a pre-school child is likely to suffer if his or her mother works	46%	30%

Source: adapted from Scott, J. and Clery, E., in NatCen (2013) *British Social Attitudes 30*, p. 137.

1 What percentage of people agreed that 'a man's job is to earn money; a woman's job is to look after the home and family' in 1989?

2 Did this figure increase or decrease during the period shown?

3 What percentage agreed that 'a job is all right, but what most women really want is a home and children' in 2012?

4 What percentage agreed that 'a pre-school child is likely to suffer if his or her mother works' in 1989?

Stretch and challenge

Drawing on evidence from the information in the 'Attitudes to male and female roles in the workplace and home' table above, write a short paragraph to show how far people's attitudes to gender roles changed between 1989 and 2012.

Key points

- Young and Willmott (1973) suggested that the symmetrical family – in which there was greater equality between spouses – was typical in Britain.

- The rise of the symmetrical family is linked to feminism, effective contraception, changes in the social position of women and increased interest in home life.

Check your understanding: Exam practice

Identify and explain one factor that may have led to an increase in the number of symmetrical families. **(4 marks)**

Is the symmetrical family reality or a myth?

Objective
- Evaluate the idea of the 'symmetrical family'

Criticisms of the 'symmetrical family'

Feminists such as Ann Oakley (1974) reject the idea of the symmetrical family. Oakley is not convinced by the quality of Young and Willmott's evidence. For example, they regard a husband who washes up at least once a week as 'helpful in the home'. They also regard occasional help from a husband, such as ironing his own trousers on a Saturday, as a sign of a 'good' husband. In her own research on housework, Oakley found little evidence of symmetry. In fact, even women in paid employment still had the major responsibility for the housework.

Although people's attitudes to gender roles may have changed, their actual behaviour has not necessarily altered significantly. Scott and Clery (2013) argue that, in most cases, women usually still do the laundry and men usually still do the small repairs around the house. Women continue to feel that they do more than their fair share of housework and caring for family members.

Scott and Clery also note a marked increase in women's participation in the labour market over the past 30 years. Among couple families today, both partners tend to work and there are far more **dual-earner households** in Britain than **male-breadwinner households**. Many women now work a **double shift** by doing a paid job as well as most of the housework and caring for the family.

Scott and Clery argue that gender inequalities in the home make it difficult to achieve equality in the workplace. Women's responsibilities for domestic work and caring mean that, in practice, many of them do not compete on equal terms with men in paid employment.

Glossary terms

double shift, dual-earner household, male-breadwinner household, new man

FOCUS ON SKILLS: WRITTEN ACTIVITY

Hours spent on housework and caring for family members

The BSA survey asked respondents to report how many hours they and their partner spent on housework and caring for family members per week. The results show, for example, that men said they spent 8.3 hours per week on housework in 2012 but their partners said they only spent 5.7 hours on housework.

Study the information in the table below and then answer the questions that follow.

Average reported hours spent by men and women in couples per week, 2012

	Housework	Looking after family members
Male (self-reported)	8.3	10.4
Male (reported by partner)	5.7	12.1
Female (self-reported)	13.3	22.7
Female (reported by partner)	14.1	15.3

Source: adapted from Scott, J. and Clery, E., in NatCen (2013) *British Social Attitudes* 30, p. 127.

1 How many hours did women report that they spent on average per week on housework?
2 How many hours did men report spending on looking after family members?
3 Is it possible to tell whether men over-reported their share of household work?

FOCUS ON SKILLS: DISCUSSION ACTIVITY

It's a chore!

Since the 1990s, commentators have reported on the emergence of the '**new man**', a caring, sharing man who gets fully involved in the housework and childcare. However, Charter (2007) suggests that the 'new man' is nowhere to be seen when the cleaning needs doing.

1 In a small group, discuss the possible reasons why men with female partners tend not to do the ironing or cleaning.
2 Note down three points raised during your discussion.

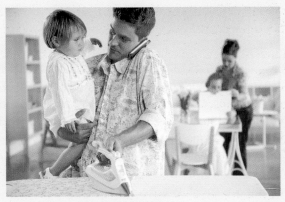

The 'new man': reality or wishful thinking?

The changing role of fathers in families

Caroline Gatrell (2008) studied heterosexual dual-worker couples and found that many fathers today play a greater role in their children's lives than fathers did in the past. In some cases, these men had fathers who were not involved as parents and so they sought to do things differently with their own children.

However, Gatrell notes that, among some married or cohabiting couples, the idea of the father's increased involvement in childcare causes tension. Some women do not want their traditional maternal role to be eroded. Other women are unenthusiastic about father – child relationships because they think fathers tend to 'cherry-pick' the most rewarding jobs and avoid boring domestic tasks such as ironing. Mothers might resist the enhanced role of fathers because they think that, if men want to divide 'parenting time' more equally, they should also divide housework equally.

Stretch and challenge

Why might fathers' increased involvement in childcare cause tension between partners?

Check your understanding: Exam practice

Discuss how far sociologists agree that feminism has led to a change in gender roles within families. (12 marks)

Key points

- Feminists reject the idea that conjugal roles and relationships are symmetrical.

- Attitudes to gender roles have changed and there is evidence that fathers are becoming more involved as parents. This may, however, lead to tension between partners.

How is power distributed between partners in relationships?

Objective
- Understand the distribution of power in relationships between partners

Power and decision-making in families

Glossary term

power

Sociologists are interested in the issue of who holds **power** in family relationships. One way of studying power is to look at decision-making and to examine who decides how money is spent.

One aspect of the symmetrical family that Young and Willmott (1973) identified was the growth of a financial partnership between husband and wife. Decision-making, including decisions on how money was spent, was becoming more of a shared activity. Feminists such as Delphy and Leonard (1992), however, argue that the family is hierarchical and patriarchal. Family life is still based on male power and dominance over women.

Jan Pahl (1989), in her study of power and money in marriages, interviewed 102 married couples with dependent children in Kent. She found that husbands are more likely than wives to be dominant in decision-making. As such, they can be seen as wielding more power in the relationship. Pahl argues that, compared with 30 years ago, more couples share decisions about how the household income is spent. She points out, however, that there are still many marriages in which the husband controls the finances and the wife's access to money is very limited. Women and children can sometimes live in poverty, even though the man with whom they live has a good income.

Power and domestic violence within families

Domestic violence can be seen as a form of power and control in which one family member attempts to dominate others. Domestic violence includes violence by men against women within the home, and violence by women against their male partners. It also includes the physical, psychological or sexual abuse of children, violence between brothers and sisters, and the neglect and abuse of the elderly (Clarke, 1997).

How widespread is domestic violence?

There is some disagreement about the extent of domestic violence. Victim surveys such as the Crime Survey for England and Wales (see Chapter 5 Topic 11) indicate that domestic violence is often not reported to the police. Some male victims, for example, may be reluctant to report that their female partners have been violent towards them. Victims may also not report domestic violence because they consider it to be a private matter, they fear the consequences or they believe that the police can do nothing about it. So an increase in the recorded incidence of domestic violence may be due to increased reporting rather than to any increase in its actual occurrence.

Some critics of functionalism highlight the apparent increase in violence within the home in order to show that families are not necessarily safe havens for their members. These critics argue that family life does not always function in ways that contribute to members' wellbeing.

FOCUS ON SKILLS: WRITTEN ACTIVITY

Refuge from domestic violence

Refuge opened the first safe house in the world for women and children who were escaping domestic violence. This safe house was opened in London in 1971. Since then, Refuge has campaigned against domestic violence. Read the information below from Refuge's website and complete the task that follows.

'Who does domestic violence happen to?

Anyone can be abused, regardless of their social background, age, gender, religion, sexuality or ethnicity.

Although men can be abused too, the statistics show that in most cases it is women who are abused.

- One in four women is abused during her lifetime.
- One in nine is severely physically abused each year.
- Two are killed each week.'

Source: Refuge, http://www.refuge.org.uk/about-domestic-violence/. Accessed 31/07/2016.

We have seen that functionalist approaches view the family as a safe haven that provides its members with emotional support and fulfils important functions for individuals and society.

Drawing on the information above, write a short paragraph to show that these functions are not always fulfilled.

Stretch and challenge

Some sociologists have strong views on the issues they investigate.

1 How far do you think it is possible for sociologists to set aside their own personal views when researching issues such as gender roles and relationships or domestic violence?

2 How far do you think they should be expected to set aside their own views?

Key point

Sociologists are interested in studying the distribution of power in relationships between partners. They focus on issues such as financial decision-making and domestic violence.

Check your understanding: Exam practice

Identify and describe one way in which power can be measured in families.   (3 marks)

What are conventional families?

FOCUS ON KEY THINKERS

Oakley's feminist approach to the study of families and family life

Ann Oakley (1982, p. 124) focuses on **conventional families** and defines them as:

> 'nuclear families composed of legally married couples, voluntarily choosing the parenthood of one or more (but not too many) children (otherwise they become another category, "large families"). Parents and children reside together as a distinct domestic unit.'

Glossary term

conventional family

FOCUS ON SKILLS: WRITTEN ACTIVITY

Defining conventional families

Read through Oakley's definition of conventional families and answer the following questions:

1 What type of family is a conventional family?
2 What is the relationship between the adults in a conventional family?
3 Would a childless couple be included in this definition?
4 Would a separated couple with children be included in this definition?

Oakley points out that the conventional family is no longer the norm in statistical terms. Despite this, the idea of conventional family life is a powerful one in society. The following are central to the idea of the conventional family:

• family members have different roles based on their age, occupation and gender
• women are expected to work inside the home without pay, while men are expected to work for pay outside the home.

Oakley identifies social class differences in people's views on gender roles. Working-class couples are more likely to hold a traditional view of gender roles than middle-class couples. Some families do not conform fully to the conventional pattern, for example when men carry out domestic tasks such as playing with children.

Stretch and challenge

An ideology is a set of ideas about how something should be. Oakley argues that more married women are in paid employment but this has not brought about significant change in male domestic roles. This is because sex role ideology remains conventional.

What do you think Oakley means by the term 'sex role ideology'?

The strains of conventional family life

In Oakley's view, people expect conventional family life to bring them happiness. However, beneath the surface, there are strains. For example, mothers based in the home may experience depression, or dissatisfaction with housework. Men may experience health problems linked to the stress of being the family breadwinner.

The strains beneath the surface

In pairs, discuss how far you agree that living in conventional families can create stress and health problems for people today.

Note down your ideas.

Financial inequality in conventional families

Oakley argues that, in a conventional family, one aspect of inequality is the woman's dependence on the man's wages. The man's economic power is linked to his income from paid work. This power increases when children are young and mothers care for them full time. During this period, women lack income and often lack control over their husbands' income; they are dependent on men's economic power.

When married women work outside the home, they tend to be concentrated in low-paid, part-time jobs. Their wages may be spent on household bills, while men keep a greater proportion of their wages for themselves.

Signs of limited change

According to Oakley, some groups, particularly among the educated middle classes, are exploring other ways of living – both in families and without them. There is an increase in dual-worker families and lone-parent families. However, norms are not changing across all social groups. One reason is that conventional families are self-perpetuating over time – they set the pattern for the next generation of parents.

Using secondary sources of data

In her analysis of conventional families, Oakley draws on research carried out by other sociologists.

1 Identify one advantage of using the research of other sociologists in this way.
2 Identify one disadvantage of drawing on other sociologists' research in this way.

Stretch and challenge

1 Identify and explain one source of male power over women in conventional families.
2 Is the balance of power necessarily more equal when women work in paid employment?
3 Identify one difference between Oakley's account of the conventional nuclear family and that of functionalism.

Key points

- Oakley is a key thinker in the sociology of family life. She examines conventional families, which – although not the norm in terms of numbers – have power as an idea.

- Conventional families are based on traditional gender roles and the husband holds the economic power. In practice, conventional family life can be stressful.

Check your understanding: Exam practice

Identify and explain what Oakley means by the term 'conventional families.'   (4 marks)

How have relationships between parents and their children changed?

Objective
- Outline changes in authority relationships between parents and children

Relationships between parents and their children have changed over time. During the 19th century, children's experiences varied according to their age, gender and social class. Middle-class children were often looked after by a paid employee such as a nanny. Working-class children, especially boys, were expected to work in paid employment from an early age.

Glossary terms

childhood, democratic relationships, immigrant

Parent–child relationships in the past

Details from the 1841 census show that in towns around Lancaster, more boys than girls aged 10–14 years were employed in paid work. The Lancashire textile industry provided the greatest number of jobs for children, who were employed as cotton mill workers, spinners and weavers.

Few children under the age of 10 years worked in paid employment. According to census figures for England and Wales, in 1851, 36.6 per cent of boys and 19.9 per cent of girls aged 10–14 worked. Many girls were involved in unpaid work at home, for example in housework and childminding, but this was not officially recorded in the statistics.

Poverty may have prevented many parents from sending their children to school. Well into the 20th century, many working-class parents seem to have viewed education as a barrier to their children's paid employment. Many working-class parents sent their children out to work as soon as they could and relied on their children's income.

However, following the introduction of the Education Act of 1918, all children had to attend school until the age of 14 years. Young and Willmott argue that only then did **childhood** come to be officially recognised as a separate stage in human life.

Children at work in the 19th century.

Contemporary parent–child relationships

Some sociologists argue that relationships between parents and children are becoming less authoritarian. There is less emphasis on discipline, obedience and parental authority and more emphasis on individual freedom. Children are seen as important members of the family. They are listened to and their views are taken seriously. It is increasingly recognised that children have rights and are able to contribute to decisions about parental separation and divorce.

Children's rights in families

In a small group, discuss how far you agree that children have rights in families today. Should their rights be extended?

Should children be encouraged to contribute to decisions about issues such as moving house, which school they will attend or where to go on holiday?

Note down three points raised during your discussion.

Pryor and Trinder (2004) identify class differences in the relationships between parents and children. Middle-class families are more likely to have **democratic relationships**, whereby parents consult their children and involve them in decision-making.

Today, relationships between parents and children are generally more child-centred and focus on the interests and needs of the child. Parent–child relationships are emotionally closer and warmer. The average family size is smaller than it was 100 years ago, so individual children are likely to get more attention from their parents. At the same time, for many parents, full-time parenting is not seen as an option, due to either financial necessity or choice. As a result, many young children are regularly separated from their parents, sometimes for most of the working week.

Childrearing is no longer dominated by economic factors. The minimum school-leaving age was raised to 18 years in 2015 and, although young people may have part-time jobs before they are 16, their working hours are restricted by law. This means that young people are financially dependent on their family for longer, particularly if they go to university. Youth unemployment also makes it more difficult for young people to achieve independence. This can potentially lead to conflict and stress within families.

Sociologists such as Scott (2004) question how far children should be seen as dependent. Children may contribute to childcare and housework, and help out in family businesses. They may also provide emotional support to their parents. Children of **immigrant** parents may be asked to translate for their parents. As a result, it is misleading to see children solely as dependants who contribute nothing within families (see also page 131 on young carers).

Stretch and challenge

Identify one way in which children are dependent on their families and one way in which they may make a contribution to their families.

Key points

- Relationships between parents and their children have changed over time. One view is that there is now less emphasis on discipline and more emphasis on individual freedom.

- Children may contribute to childcare and domestic tasks within families.

Check your understanding: Exam practice

Identify and explain one factor that may have led to changes in the relationships between parents and children over the last 100 years. (4 marks)

How have people's relationships with their wider family changed?

Young and Willmott (1957) studied family life in Bethnal Green in the East End of London during the mid-1950s. Among their working-class sample, they found that the extended family flourished. For example, many young couples began their married life living with one set of parents. Family ties were strong and 43 per cent of daughters had seen their mothers within the last 24 hours. In later research, however, Young and Willmott (1973) found that the nuclear family had become more separated from the extended family.

One view is that increasing **geographical mobility** (moving to live in another area, region or country) and women's involvement in full-time paid work have meant that family members see each other less often. As a result, the wider family in the UK is becoming less important in people's lives and family ties are weakening.

Other approaches, however, believe that family members continue to depend on each other. In their study of changing families in Swansea between 1960 and 2002, Charles et al. (2008b) found that mothers and their daughters were still central to **kinship relationships** (see Chapter 2 Topic 20). High rates of face-to-face contact between family members were found. For example:

- Grandmothers, and sometimes grandfathers, were regularly involved in caring for their grandchildren. This enabled younger women to return to work after maternity leave.
- Fathers often helped their adult children with home improvements.
- Adult children (particularly women) were involved in caring for their parents.
- Older grandchildren were sometimes involved in caring for their grandparents.

In 2002, over two-thirds of married children lived close enough to their parents to see them at least every week. Frequency of contact between brothers and sisters, however, fell significantly between 1960 and 2002.

Charles et al. (2008a) found that geographical distance affects the type of support between family members but does not eliminate it altogether. For example, support at a distance took the form of visits, telephone calls and financial help. Other studies have found that middle-aged parents may provide financial support to their children and grandchildren, for instance loans when they are buying a house. However, this transfer of money may not be possible among families without savings.

Grandparents may be involved in caring for their grandchildren.

Life expectancy, beanpole families and the sandwich generation

Life expectancy at birth (the average number of years a newborn baby may be expected to live) has increased. According to Denscombe (1997), life expectancy in the UK in the fifth century was around 33 years for men and 27 years for women. Data from the Office for National Statistics (ONS) shows that life expectancy in the UK was 79.3 years for men and 83 years for women in 2014. Increased life expectancy is linked to factors such as NHS provisions, developments in medicine and improvements in nutrition.

The UK has an ageing population. There is a smaller proportion of children and young people in the population and an increasing proportion of older people.

Longer life expectancy and an ageing population may lead to an increase in families with three or more generations. In beanpole families, women who are mothers, grandmothers and daughters are likely to be under pressure. This is because they have the burden of caring for family members from different generations. These women are described as part of the **sandwich generation**, because they are sandwiched between younger and older generations. Some grandmothers in the sandwich generation may provide childcare for their grandchildren and also look after their frail elderly parents.

Boomerang children

Boomerang children are young people who leave home (for example, to go to university) and return to live at home with their parents before leaving permanently. Young adults may be more likely to leave home and then return during a global financial crisis or because affordable housing is not available.

FOCUS ON SKILLS: WRITTEN ACTIVITY

Researching boomerang children
Identify and explain one advantage of using a longitudinal study to investigate boomerang children.

Key points

- Some sociological approaches suggest that the wider family is becoming less important to people living in Britain.
- Other sociologists emphasise the continuing importance of family ties in Britain.

Check your understanding: Exam practice

Discuss how far sociologists agree that in Britain today the wider family is becoming less important in people's lives. (12 marks)

What changes are taking place in family structures?

We have already identified the diverse forms of families in Britain today. Examples include nuclear, lone-parent and reconstituted families. Since the mid-1970s, there have been important changes in these family structures.

Glossary term

dual-career families

FOCUS ON SKILLS: WRITTEN ACTIVITY

Dependent children in families

Look at the information in the table and then answer the questions.

Percentage of dependent* children: by family type, 2005, 2010 and 2015, UK

	2005	2010	2015
Married couple (same-sex and opposite-sex) family	66%	63%	62%
Cohabiting couple (same-sex and opposite-sex) family	11%	13%	15%
Lone-parent family	23%	24%	23%
Totals	100%	100%	100%

Source: adapted from ONS (2015) *Statistical Bulletin: Families and Households.*

* Dependent children are those aged 0–15 years or those aged 16–18 years in full-time education and living with their parents.

1 By how many percentage points did the proportion of children living in a married couple family decline between 2005 and 2015?
2 What percentage of children lived in cohabiting couple families in 2015?
3 In which type of family did the proportion of children increase between 2005 and 2015?
4 In which type of family did the largest proportion of children live in 2015?
5 Write a paragraph to describe the trends shown in the table.

Reconstituted families

Reconstituted families may come about as a result of remarriage or cohabitation. When parents separate, children often stay with their mother and so the majority of step-families comprise a biological mother and a step-father.

Stretch and challenge

The statistics in the table above are based on official statistics. How reliable are these statistics likely to be? Explain your thinking.

FOCUS ON SKILLS: WRITTEN ACTIVITY

Reconstituted families in Britain in 2011
- 85 per cent of step-families comprise a step-father, a biological mother and her child or children.
- 11 per cent comprise a step-mother, a biological father and his child or children.
- 4 per cent comprise children from both partners' previous relationships.

1 In 2011, what percentage of reconstituted families contained children from both partners' previous relationships?

2 Which type of reconstituted family was most common?

4% comprise children from both partners' previous relationships

85% of step-families comprise a step-father, a biological mother and her child or children

11% comprise a step-mother, a biological father and his child or children

Source: adapted from ONS (2014).

According to data from the census, the number of reconstituted families in England and Wales fell from 631 000 to 544 000 between 2001 and 2011. Possible reasons for the decrease include:

- The average age at which women have their first baby is increasing. Children are now more likely to be born to older couples, who are less likely to split up. This may reduce the chances that children will become step-children later on.
- Lone parents may be more likely than in the past to be one half of a couple who live apart. The lone parent's partner may be a step-parent to their children while living somewhere else. This example of a 'living apart together' relationship (see Chapter 2 Topic 1) would not be counted as a reconstituted family in the census data.

Dual-worker families

In 2013, 72 per cent of married or cohabiting mothers with dependent children in the UK were in paid employment. As a result of the increasing proportion of married or cohabiting women in employment, there has been an increase in dual-worker and **dual-career families**.

FOCUS ON SKILLS: DISCUSSION ACTIVITY

Working mothers

Some people believe that women with young children should not work in paid employment.

In a small group, discuss what evidence you would need in order to identify the effects on young children of their mothers going out to work.

Note down three important points that were raised during your discussion.

Check your understanding: Exam practice

1 Identify and explain one advantage of using official statistics to study families.   (4 marks)

2 Identify and describe one reason why the majority of reconstituted families have a biological mother and a step-father.   (3 marks)

Key point

Since the mid-1970s, there have been significant changes in families. These changes include a decline in the proportion of children living in families headed by a married couple and an increase in dual-worker families.

What are the trends in lone-parent families?

Objectives
- Describe the increase in the number of lone-parent families
- Explain this increase

The proportion of dependent children living with one parent in the UK has increased markedly since the 1970s. More recently, the proportion has remained fairly stable. In 2005, 23 per cent of dependent children lived in lone-parent families. This rose to 24 per cent in 2012 but dropped back to 23 per cent in 2015.

Some lone-parent families come about because a couple separates or divorces, or one of the partners dies. Others form when a single woman has a baby and brings up the child on her own.

The vast majority of children in lone-parent families live with their mothers rather than their fathers. When relationships break down, women are more likely than men to take responsibility for caring for the children. As a result, they are more likely than men to become lone parents.

Jewson (1994) indicates that there is evidence that African Caribbean communities have a higher than average proportion of lone-parent families, and Asian communities a lower than average proportion. More recently, Williams (2008) notes that Black Caribbeans and Black Africans are more likely than other ethnic groups to head lone-parent households with dependent children. He points out, however, that these numbers appear to have fallen between the 1991 and 2001 censuses.

Qureshi et al. (2015) point out that the proportion of lone-parent families among British Asians is rising. In 1991, lone parents made up 5 per cent of British Indian families with dependent children and 10 per cent of British Pakistani and Bangladeshi families. By 2011, these figures were 11 per cent for British Indian families, 17 per cent for British Pakistani families and 16 per cent for British Bangladeshi families. The figures indicate a rise in long-term separation and divorce. They also highlight differences between British Asian groups.

Glossary term

underclass

Explanations for the increase in lone-parent families

- The increase in divorce: The majority of lone-parent families come about as a result of parental divorce (see page 126). Many lone-parent families are headed by divorced women. Each year, however, many lone mothers will form new partnerships and, with their children, become part of blended families.
- Changing attitudes: Social attitudes towards lone parents have changed. It is now more socially acceptable for single women to have children without a partner. Single and divorced women can use new technologies to become single mothers by choice without the need for a male partner.

- Some commentators explain the increase in fatherless families in terms of the decline in moral standards in society. In this view, many single-parent families are part of an **underclass** – that is, a group in society who depend on welfare benefits.
- Other approaches see the rise in lone-parent families as part of the changes in how people view the family, marriage and intimate relationships. According to this view, the family and marriage are less important in society and people now have more freedom of choice in the relationships they have with others.

FOCUS ON SKILLS: DISCUSSION ACTIVITY

The consequences of lone-parent families

As we have seen, the number of lone-parent families has increased since the 1970s.

1 In a small group, discuss the possible consequences of this increase for:

a marriage

b family life

c demands on the welfare state.

2 Note down three of the possible consequences that you identified during your discussion.

FOCUS ON RESEARCH: WRITTEN ACTIVITY

Writing survey questions

The British Social Attitudes survey examines changing attitudes over time (see Chapter 3 Topic 13).

1 Devise three closed questions that could be used in a survey on attitudes to births outside marriage. Remember to supply all of the possible answers.

2 Test your questions out on another member of your class. Is the wording clear? If not, make any necessary changes to your questions.

3 Identify one advantage and one disadvantage of using closed questions in surveys.

Stretch and challenge

Sociologists' role in informing debates

Some politicians and media reports see the increase in lone-parent families in negative terms, as a social problem. How might sociologists inform the debates about lone-parent families? Make a note of one way in which sociologists could inform these debates.

Check your understanding: Exam practice

Identify and explain one factor that may have led to the increase in the number of lone-parent families since the 1970s. (4 marks)

Key points

- Since the mid-1970s, there has been an increase in lone-parent families. This rise is linked to factors such as the increase in divorce, changing social attitudes and increased freedom of choice in intimate relationships.

- Some commentators see the increase as reflecting a decline in moral standards.

What changes are taking place in fertility?

Objective
- Outline and explain changing patterns of fertility

Falling fertility, smaller family size and having children later

Glossary terms

fertility, fertility rate

The term **fertility** refers to the average number of children that women of child-bearing age (usually 15–44 years) have in a society. Women born in the UK are having fewer children than 30 years ago and there is a trend towards a smaller family size.

Among women born in England and Wales in 1920, the average number of children was 2.0 per woman. This peaked at 2.42 children for women born in 1935, and contributed to the 'baby boom' of the 1960s. Since then, however, family size has fallen. Among women born in England and Wales in 1967, the average number of children was 1.91.

Women born in the UK are not only having fewer children, they are also having them later in life. In 1970, the average age of mothers at childbirth in England and Wales was 26.7; in 2000, it was 28.5; and in 2014, it was 30.2.

FOCUS ON SKILLS: WRITTEN ACTIVITY

Changes in the fertility rates

The **fertility rate** is the number of live births per 1000 women of child-bearing age (usually aged 15–44 years).

The following information shows the trend in fertility rates from 1960 to 2015 in England and Wales. Study this information, then answer the questions that follow.

1 What was the fertility rate in 1970?
2 In which year was the fertility rate at its highest?
3 In which year was it at its lowest?

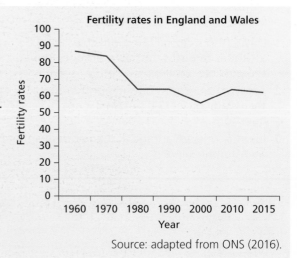

Source: adapted from ONS (2016).

FOCUS ON SKILLS: DISCUSSION ACTIVITY

Having children later in life

Before you read on, work in a small group and discuss the possible reasons why UK-born women are having children later in life than they were in the 1970s.

Note down two possible reasons.

Explanations for the changing patterns of fertility

Stretch and challenge

Write a paragraph to describe the trends in fertility rates between 1960 and 2015 shown on the graph on the previous page.

- Economic factors: During the 19th century, childrearing among poor families was motivated partly by economic factors (see Chapter 3 Topic 17). Many parents relied on their children's income and so tended to have larger families. By the 1920s, factory legislation and the raising of the school leaving age to 14 years made it more difficult for children to contribute to the family income through paid employment. Today, there is little financial incentive in having children. On the contrary, bringing up children is expensive. Estimates suggest that parents in the UK spend an average of around £3 760 per year just on essentials (such as food and drink, babysitting costs and entertainment) for one child. By the time the child is 18 years old, the total figure would be approximately £67 680.

- Labour market uncertainty: During global economic recessions when there is uncertainty about the job market, people may delay having children.

- Later marriage: The trend since the 1970s is for people to get married at a later age. This means that some women who marry later will also delay having children until later in life.

- Women's increased participation in higher education and paid employment: One impact of feminism is that many women have rejected the idea that a woman's main role should centre on motherhood and childcare. Increased opportunities in education and employment over the last 35 years, backed by laws on equal pay and sex discrimination, have given women a wider range of options.

- The increased use of effective birth control methods: The introduction of the contraceptive pill in the 1960s means that women have much greater control over their fertility, including whether and when to become pregnant. Also, the availability of legal abortion means that women can choose whether to continue with a pregnancy.

FOCUS ON RESEARCH: WRITTEN ACTIVITY

Longitudinal research on childbirth

In the 1970s, Ann Oakley (1986) interviewed 55 women several times about their experiences of having their first baby. Years later, she was part of a research team that traced 36 of these women and interviewed them again.

1 Identify one problem researchers might face in trying to trace interviewees.

2 Identify and explain one disadvantage of using interviews to investigate women's experiences of childbirth.

Key points

- Women are not only having fewer children; they are having them later in life.

- There is a trend towards a smaller family size. Reasons include economic factors, women's increased participation in higher education and the availability of contraception.

Check your understanding: Exam practice

Identify and explain one factor that may have led to changes in the patterns of fertility in the UK over the last 30 years.   (4 marks)

How do marriages differ in a global context?

Objective
- Describe the diverse forms of marriage in different cultures

In the United Kingdom, marriage is based on **monogamy**. This means being married to just one person at any one time. In order to remarry, it is necessary to divorce first. Monogamy is the accepted form of marriage in the UK. It is backed by the law and supported by the Christian religion. **Bigamy** (marrying when already married to another person) is a criminal offence.

Serial monogamy occurs when a divorced person enters into a second marriage, then divorces, remarries, divorces, remarries and so on. In this case, marriage is not necessarily considered a lifelong commitment.

Glossary terms

arranged marriage, bigamy, forced marriage, monogamy, polyandry, polygamy, polygyny, rural, serial monogamy

Different forms of marriage

Polygamy

Polygamy occurs when a person has more than one husband or wife at the same time. Although polygamy is illegal in Britain, it has been accepted elsewhere. There are two forms of polygamy: polygyny and polyandry.

Polygyny occurs when a man has two or more wives at the same time. This was acceptable within the Mormon religion in Utah, in the USA, during the 19th century. Mormons believed that polygyny had been ordained by God. Brigham Young, a Mormon leader, had 27 wives and 56 children. In practice, however, only a minority of Mormon men practised polygyny. It was officially outlawed by the Mormon General Conference of 1890.

In some societies, Muslim men are allowed to marry up to four wives, but only under strict conditions. The first wife, for example, has to give her consent and all wives must be treated equally and fairly. A woman may have it written into her marriage contract that she should remain the only wife. Only a minority of Muslims practise polygyny.

Polyandry occurs when a woman has more than one husband at the same time. It is less common than polygyny. Polyandry was practised, for example, in Tibet and, although officially illegal there today, it is said to take place in **rural** areas.

Polyandry – where one woman has more than one husband at the same time – is practised in some remote rural areas in Tibet.

Views on serial monogamy and polygyny

In a small group, discuss the following questions and note down your ideas.

1 How do you think the functionalist approach might view serial monogamy?

2 How do you think feminist approaches might view polygyny?

Arranged marriages

Marriage may be based on romantic love and mutual attraction between the partners and it may also be arranged. Garrod (2005) notes that **arranged marriages** are traditional in many communities. In an arranged marriage, the parents or other family members find partners that they consider to be suitable for their children. In countries such as India, Pakistan and Bangladesh, some young people have arranged marriages.

It is important not to confuse arranged and **forced marriage**. Arranged marriages are based on consent and the right to choose. The families of the prospective partners play a key role in finding a partner and making the arrangements. The individuals decide whether to accept the partner and consent to the marriage.

In a forced marriage, one or both partners do not give their consent but the wedding goes ahead anyway against their will. Forced marriages are illegal in Britain and forcing someone to marry can result in a maximum prison sentence of seven years.

Advantages and disadvantages of arranged marriage

In a small group, discuss the possible advantages and disadvantages of arranged marriage. You should focus in particular on social and economic factors. Make a list of these advantages and disadvantages.

Researching arranged marriage

1 Identify and explain one advantage of using focus groups to investigate arranged marriage in the UK.

2 Identify one ethical issue that you may face in researching arranged marriage in the UK and explain how you would address this issue.

Stretch and challenge

Why do you think sociologists are interested in exploring marriage in different cultures?

Key points

- Different forms of marriage (such as monogamy and polygamy) are found in different cultures.

- In the UK, marriage is based on monogamy and polygamy is illegal.

Check your understanding: Exam practice

Describe what is meant by 'serial monogamy'. (3 marks)

What are the changing patterns of marriage?

Objective
- Outline the changing patterns of marriage in Britain

Major changes are taking place in the patterns of marriage and cohabitation. Official statistics provide a useful source of data about these changes.

The decline in the number of marriages

The number of marriages in the UK peaked in 1972 at 480 000. Since then, the overall number of marriages has fallen, and in 2011 there were just over 286 600 marriages.

People are getting married later

Compared with the early 1970s, people are now putting off marriage until they are older. This is linked to increased educational and employment opportunities, particularly for women. It is also related to changing attitudes towards premarital sex, which in general is now considered more acceptable.

FOCUS ON SKILLS: WRITTEN ACTIVITY

Getting married later

Look at the data below and then answer the questions.

Average age of first marriage (England and Wales)

	1971	2004	2013
Men	24.6	31.4	32.5
Women	22.6	29.1	30.6

Source: adapted from ONS (2016) Tables 6 and 7.

1 What was the average age of first marriage for men in 2013?
2 By how many years did the average age of first marriage among women increase between 1971 and 2013?

FOCUS ON SKILLS: DISCUSSION ACTIVITY

Changing patterns in marriage

1 In a small group, discuss the possible reasons why:
   a   there are fewer marriages
   b   more people are cohabiting
   c   more couples are having children outside marriage.

2 Make a note of the possible reasons you discussed.

Civil partnerships and same-sex marriages

Since the Civil Partnership Act came into effect in the UK in December 2005, same-sex couples aged 16 years and over can have their relationships legally recognised in the form of a civil partnership. In 2006, 16 106 civil partnerships were formed in the UK and in 2013, 6 276 were formed.

Marriages of same-sex couples were introduced in March 2014. After this, the number of civil partnerships formed in England and Wales fell by 70 per cent from 5 646 in 2013 to 1 683 in 2014.

The increase in cohabitation

Official statistics show that the proportion of people cohabiting (living with a partner outside marriage or civil partnership) in Britain has more or less doubled over the last 20 years. Cohabiting couples with children tend to be much younger than married couples with children. In 2001, cohabiting couple families were more common in households headed by someone from a white or a mixed ethnic group.

Some people cohabit without expecting the relationship to develop into a long-term one. For others, cohabitation is a long-term alternative to marriage. Cohabitation may also lead to marriage and for example, during times of global recession, a couple may live together while saving up to get married. The high cost of weddings and the difficulty in saving up for a deposit to get a mortgage may also put people off marriage.

The increase in cohabitation is linked partly to changes in social attitudes towards sex outside marriage since the mid-1960s. Before then, it was considered unacceptable for unmarried women to be sexually active.

The increase in births outside marriage

During the 1960s and 1970s in the UK, births outside marriage became more commonplace. In 1988, 25.2 per cent of all births in the UK were outside marriage and, by 2006, this proportion stood at 43.7 per cent. Compared to the situation before and during the 1950s, births outside marriage are no longer stigmatised or disapproved of. This is reflected in the use of language around non-marital births. Allan and Crow (2001) note, for example, that terms such as 'shot-gun wedding' and 'illegitimacy' are no longer common.

Much of the increase in births outside marriage results from rising numbers of babies born to cohabiting partners. In other words, a high proportion of unmarried mothers are living with their child's father at the time of birth. In 1986, around one in ten babies in England and Wales were born to unmarried parents who lived together. By 2014, this proportion had increased to around one in three babies.

Stretch and challenge

How might legal changes (such as changes in the law on divorce, abortion, same-sex marriages or sex discrimination) impact on families?

Key points

- The number of marriages is declining, people are getting married later, and cohabitation and the proportion of births outside marriage have increased.
- Civil partnerships were introduced in the UK in 2005, and marriages of same-sex couples in 2014.

Check your understanding: Exam practice

1 Identify and explain one reason why the average age at which people get married in Britain has increased during the last 30 years. (4 marks)

2 Identify and explain one factor that may have led to the increase in cohabitation during the last 20 years. (4 marks)

What are the changing patterns of divorce?

We have seen that patterns of family life are changing. One of the most significant changes relates to divorce. A divorce is the legal ending of a marriage. In general, the number of divorces per year has risen since 1945 in England and Wales, although there have also been decreases.

FOCUS ON SKILLS: WRITTEN ACTIVITY

Trends in the number of divorces and marriages

Study the graph and then answer the questions that follow.

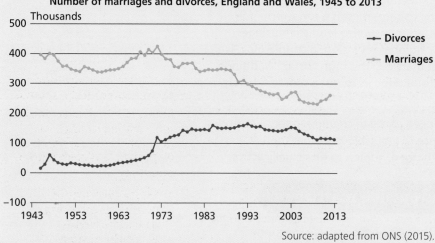

Number of marriages and divorces, England and Wales, 1945 to 2013

Source: adapted from ONS (2015).

1 Describe the trends in the number of divorces between 1945 and 2013.
2 Describe the trends in the number of marriages between 1945 and 2013.

Explaining the increase in the divorce rates

Several factors help to explain the increase in divorce since 1945.

Changes in the law

Legal changes have made divorce easier, quicker and cheaper to obtain. The Divorce Reform Act (1969) in England and Wales came into effect in 1971. Following this, an individual could petition for divorce on the grounds of 'irretrievable breakdown of marriage' as a result of separation, desertion, adultery or unreasonable behaviour.

Legislation in 1984 allowed couples to request or petition for divorce after only one year of marriage, rather than three years as previously. Legal aid facilities became available, which made divorce cheaper to obtain. However, changes to legal aid funding in 2013 limited the availability of legal aid in England and Wales.

Changing social attitudes and values

The 1960s can be seen as marking a shift towards more liberal attitudes to issues such as divorce. As a result of changing attitudes, divorce has become less stigmatised and more socially acceptable. Some members of the Royal Family, for example, have divorced and we regularly hear about celebrity divorces in the media.

The impact of the secularisation process

The term **secularisation** refers to the idea that religion is losing its influence in society. Statistics suggest that the Christian churches, in particular, are attracting fewer members today compared with 20 years ago. Rather than a church wedding, many people now choose to have a civil ceremony in a registry office or elsewhere. This means that fewer people take sacred vows before God to stay together 'till death us do part'. Consequently, the religious barrier to divorce is weaker today than in the past.

Changes in the status of women in society

In the 1950s, many women in **empty shell marriages** were tied to their husbands through economic dependence. Today, more married women participate in the labour market. This means that they are less economically dependent on their husbands and have more financial security than before. Also, with the availability of welfare benefits, mothers with young children will not be left without money as a result of divorce. They may be entitled to a number of state benefits to help support their family.

Despite these social changes, however, women with young children and few qualifications may still experience financial hardship after divorce. In addition, it is still much easier for the male partner to walk away from his marriage and family than it is for the female.

The influence of the media

The popular media (such as pop music, magazines and soap operas) tend to emphasise the importance of mutual attraction and 'romantic love' in relationships. As a result, individuals may have high **expectations** of marriage. These expectations may not match the daily realities of married life. As an increasing number of marriages do not fulfil such hopes over the long term, more people are getting divorced.

FOCUS ON RESEARCH: WRITTEN ACTIVITY

Using a mixed methods approach to study divorce

Many sociologists use mixed methods approaches to generate both quantitative and qualitative data within one study.

1 Explain one way in which you could use a mixed methods approach to study divorce.

2 Identify one disadvantage of using a mixed methods approach to study divorce.

Key point

The number of divorces peaked in 1993 in England and Wales. Several factors explain the increase in divorce. These include changing social attitudes, legal changes, changes in the status of women and secularisation.

Check your understanding: Exam practice

Discuss how far sociologists agree that changing gender roles in society are responsible for the increase in divorce since the 1960s.

(12 marks)

What are the consequences of divorce?

Divorce has consequences for family members including the children and the extended family as well as the husband and wife. It also has consequences for the structure of the family. Rising divorce rates are linked to the increases in the numbers of lone-parent families (see Topic 20), reconstituted families and one-person households.

Changes to family structures

As a result of rising divorce rates, there are now more reconstituted families. Some children may have full siblings (brothers and sisters), half-siblings and step-siblings. Full siblings share both biological parents and half-siblings share just one. Step-siblings are unrelated by blood but each has a biological parent in a relationship together.

Living in a reconstituted family may cause problems for some family members, who have to adjust to different expectations of behaviour. On the other hand, it may result in more people being there to provide attention, emotional support and love.

After their parents' divorce, most children live with their mother and visit their father. However, it is common for children to lose daily contact with their father and estimates suggest that between one third and one half of divorced fathers lose all contact with their children over time.

Relationship breakdown and emotional distress

Conflict between the former husband and wife may continue after divorce due to disputes over issues such as parenting and property (houses, money and so on). A breakdown in the relationship between the parents may mean that the children's relationship with their father suffers if they are living with their mother. Pressure groups such as Fathers4Justice (F4J) aim to draw attention to the cause of fathers and their treatment following separation and divorce. For example, F4J point out that fathers do not have a legal right to contact with their children. In fact, F4J argue that there are more laws to protect animals than there are to protect fathers.

Before, during and after divorce, people may experience emotional distress. This can be worse if it is linked to changes in people's social networks. Men in particular may lose sources of emotional support after divorce if their friends and kinship networks change. Women, on the other hand, are more likely to have their own support networks (Pryor and Trinder, 2004).

Some members of the extended family may lose contact with, or see less of, the children. For example, the father's parents may see less of any grandchildren who live with the mother in a reconstituted family.

F4J believe that fathers should have equal rights to see their children after separation.

Financial hardship

Divorce often leads to changes in people's financial circumstances such as loss of income for the former partners after assets (such as property and money) are divided. Lone-parent families with dependent children are at risk of poverty and, after divorce, single parents may experience financial hardship. They can also face difficulty in juggling the demands of paid employment and home life.

Remarriage

Remarriage seems to be declining in England and Wales. For example, between 1995 and 2000, 19 per cent of all marriages were remarriages for both partners. In 2013, this figure was 15 per cent.

Reasons why divorced people remarry

- One view is that people who divorce are rejecting their spouse rather than the institution of marriage itself. In other words, they are not against marriage in general but do not want to stay married to that particular person. People still value a happy marriage and hope to succeed in a relationship the second time round.
- Divorcees with young children may want a partner to help them raise their children.
- People may remarry for companionship and love.
- In the past, marriage was a source of status, particularly for women. While this is not true today, in many ways marriage remains the norm.

FOCUS ON SKILLS: DISCUSSION ACTIVITY

Support networks

Why might women be more likely than men to have their own support networks?

Note down your ideas.

Stretch and challenge

How do pressure groups such as Fathers4Justice generate publicity for their cause? How effective do you think campaigns and protests can be in bringing about social change?

Make a note of your ideas.

FOCUS ON SKILLS: WRITTEN ACTIVITY

Changing patterns in households, families, marriage and divorce

We have examined changing patterns in households, families, marriage and divorce, such as the increasing number of one-person households and the declining birth rate. Summarise these changes by copying out and completing the table below. Two examples are included to get you started. Add at least two changes under each heading.

Increase in	Decrease in
• Number of one-person households	• The birth rate among UK-born women

Key points

- Divorce has consequences for individuals and society.

- One consequence of divorce is an increase in lone-parent and blended families.

- Other possible consequences of divorce include loss of contact between children, their fathers and grandparents; conflict over parenting and property issues; financial hardship and loss of emotional support, particularly for divorced men.

Check your understanding: Exam practice

Discuss how far sociologists agree that there is a 'typical British family' today.   (12 marks)

What contemporary social issues relate to families?

Contemporary issues related to children and families include:
- the quality of parenting
- relationships between teenagers and adults
- care of disabled and elderly people.

Such issues cause concern in the media and among politicians and policy makers. One of sociology's key roles is to challenge our everyday understandings of issues from a sociological perspective.

The quality of parenting

Policy makers and government often see teenage motherhood as a serious problem, not only for the young mothers and their children but also for society. However, sociologists do not simply accept such judgments and views at face value. Instead, they undertake research and gather evidence in order to explore what is really going on. Ideally, such research evidence should inform the debates and contribute to social policy.

Simon Duncan (2006) researched teenage parenthood and found that having a baby is usually not a disaster for young mothers. On the contrary, the research evidence suggests that becoming a teenage parent can be more of an opportunity than a disaster. For example, having a baby could make young mothers feel more responsible or encourage them to take up education, training and employment.

Duncan's work provides a good example of the way in which social research can inform debates on issues that are viewed as social problems. It also highlights an area in which research on families might contribute to social policy.

Stretch and challenge

Everyday understandings of arranged marriage

People sometimes confuse arranged and forced marriages, and treat them as the same thing. How would you go about challenging everyday understandings of arranged marriage from a sociological perspective?

FOCUS ON RESEARCH: WRITTEN ACTIVITY

Parent–child relationships

The quality of parenting is one of the main factors affecting children's wellbeing. Childhood obesity, for example, is seen by some as evidence of poor parenting.

The Joseph Rowntree Foundation (2007) commissioned several reviews of the existing research literature on parenting. One review examined the literature on the link between parenting and outcomes for children. This review concluded that the quality of parent–child relationships is associated with:
- **Children's educational achievements** – children's reading ability is linked to the reading environment around them. Evidence suggests that parental involvement with school is associated with their children's achievements.
- **Children's social skills and relationships with peers** – parental warmth, lack of conflict, and control seem important in developing children's social skills.

1 What source of data did the Joseph Rowntree Foundation reviewers draw on?
2 Identify and explain one disadvantage of using a longitudinal study to investigate the quality of parenting.

Young carers in families

In some families, children and young people provide unpaid care for relatives who are disabled or sick. According to data from the 2011 census, there were over 177 900 unpaid carers aged 5 to 17 in England and Wales in 2011. Over half of these were girls. Most young carers provide between 1 and 19 hours of unpaid care per week. Providing care in this way can affect the young people's general health, their social lives and educational opportunities.

One view is that the 2011 census figures underestimate the number of young carers. The Children's Society, for example, believes that many young carers are hidden from the official statistics. Reasons for this include family loyalty and not knowing where to go for support.

Census data may not provide a true picture of the number of young carers.

1 Drawing on this information, identify one problem with using data from the 2011 census to investigate young carers.

2 Identify one ethical issue you might face when studying young carers and explain how you might address this issue.

Relationships between teenagers and adults

Relationships between parents and their teenage children is an issue that can cause concern. For example, one view is that some parents cannot control their teenage children. A related view is that delinquent teenagers have not been socialised adequately by their parents into society's norms and values. Another concern is that a minority of teenagers are themselves parents.

Care of elderly people

Older people of all ages are generally fitter and healthier than ever before. They may themselves provide care within their families, for example by caring for a spouse with physical disabilities.

Everyday understandings of older people can see them all as frail and dependent on others. However, research by Ginn and Arber (1992) challenges this view by highlighting diversity in later life. They point out that an individual's social class, gender and ethnicity influence their chances of having resources such as savings, good health and access to care in their own home. As a result, class, gender and ethnicity affect an older individual's independence, well-being and social life.

Key points

- Issues related to families and children cause concern in the media and among politicians and policy makers.

- Sociological research findings can challenge our everyday understandings of social issues, inform the debates on them and influence social policy.

Check your understanding: Exam practice

1 Identify and describe one contemporary social issue related to the family. (3 marks)

2 Identify and explain one way in which sociology could contribute to our understanding of relationships between adults and young people. (4 marks)

What methods are used to research families?

Objectives
- Describe some of the methods used to research families
- Evaluate these methods

FOCUS ON RESEARCH: WRITTEN ACTIVITY

The BSA survey: researching hours spent on housework and caring for family members

The British Social Attitudes (BSA) survey (see Topic 14) is an **attitude survey** based on structured interviews. Interviewers ask around 3000 people each year about what it is like to live in Britain and how Britain is run. The BSA survey is based on random sampling, so everyone has an equal chance of being picked to participate. This means that the results are representative of the British population. Many of the questions are repeated over time, so it is possible to measure real changes in social attitudes over time.

1 Examine one strength of the BSA research.
2 Identify and explain one disadvantage of delivering the BSA survey through face-to-face interviews.

Glossary terms

attitude survey, time budget diaries, time budget study

FOCUS ON RESEARCH: WRITTEN ACTIVITY

Delphy and Leonard: researching exploitation in families and marriage

Delphy and Leonard (see Topic 11) drew on information from existing research on families, including three research studies of factory workers' families in Britain.

Read through the extract and then answer the questions that follow.

'There are a few studies which provide good information, and we shall discuss in this chapter an influential sociological study of affluent workers in car assembly in Luton in the mid 1960s; a study of 25 couples where the husbands were production foremen, shop stewards and rank and file production workers in a firm making cardboard packing cases in Bristol in the early 1970s; and a study of steel workers in Port Talbot in South Wales who were all made redundant in the 1980s.'

Source: adapted from Delphy and Leonard (1992) p. 166.

1 Identify the research method used by Delphy and Leonard.
2 Identify and explain one disadvantage of using this method.

Young and Willmott: researching the symmetrical family

Young and Willmott (1973) attempted to trace the development of the family from pre-industrial Britain to the present using a combination of historical research, a social survey and a **time budget study** (see Topic 13).

For their main questionnaire survey, Young and Willmott selected a sample of places in the London Metropolitan Region and then a sample of people from these places. This gave them 3000 names, but the response rate was low (533 people refused to take part) and they only interviewed 1928 people in the main survey.

The main survey questionnaire took the form of a structured interview, consisting of questions on the house, car, occupation, work, leisure, home and family life. The results provided quantitative data.

A time budget study is a record of a person's use of time over a particular period and aims to give a systematic account of how people spend their time. The informants completed a diary to provide information on the sequence, times and duration of their activities. When **time budget diaries** generate new information in this way, they provide a source of primary data.

By getting a record of the duration of activities, the researchers had a useful measure of the significance of different activities. This allowed them to compare the time spent by husbands and wives on work in the home.

The sample for the time budget study was drawn from respondents who had completed the main questionnaire, who were married and aged 30–49 years. A total of 699 people from the general survey sample were eligible but only 411 respondents completed the diaries.

Young and Willmott also questioned middle-class managing directors. The sample of managing directors was selected from male members of the Institute of Directors.

1 How far was Young and Willmott's survey sample representative of the population under study?

2 How far could they make general statements about all families in Britain on the basis of this London-based study?

3 Time budget studies measure the time spent on activities only. What might this leave out concerning the involvement of many women within the home?

4 Drawing on this information, explain what sociologists mean by the term 'mixed methods research'.

Stretch and challenge

Young and Willmott and the BSA survey examined people's use of time within the home.

Identify one difference in the way they researched people's use of time.

Check your understanding: Exam practice

Identify and explain one strength of the survey questionnaire used by Young and Willmott to research the symmetrical family.

(4 marks)

Focus on skills

Making connections: Written activity

The functions of families

As you study the different areas and topics within sociology, it is important to look for connections or links between them. For example, the topic of 'the functions of families' can be linked to each of the different sociological perspectives such as functionalism, feminism and Marxism.

Study the diagram and answer the question below.

Choose two of the links in the diagram and, in each case, explain how it is connected to the topic of 'the functions of families'.

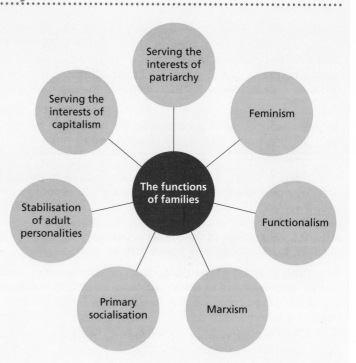

FOCUS ON SKILLS: DISCUSSION ACTIVITY

Different criticisms of families

As you revise the topics in this chapter on families, an important area to focus on is the different criticisms of families. One way to approach this is to think about the views of the different perspectives such as feminism and Marxism. How would the feminist and Marxist approaches criticise the role and functions of families in society? You could draw on the key ideas of the sociologists we have examined in this chapter to help you. For instance, how would Zaretsky or Delphy and Leonard criticise the role and functions of the family in society?

When trying to organise your ideas or revising topics, it can help to use mind maps. An example is shown here.

In pairs, choose one branch and discuss how each of the three items can be seen as a criticism of families.

Then team up with another pair, who have selected a different branch, and share your ideas. Make a note of your ideas.

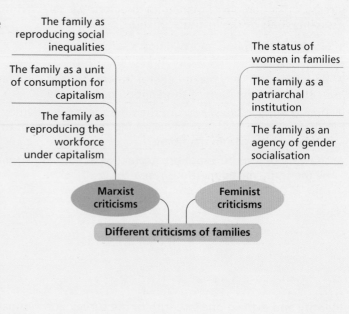

Stretch and challenge

Factors affecting families, marriage and family life

Copy and complete the following table to explain how each of these factors might have an impact on families, marriage or family life.

Factors affecting families, marriage or family life	Explanation
The ageing population	
The global recession	
Changing norms	
Secularisation	
The impact of feminism	
Developments in new reproductive technology	
Developments in birth control	
Immigration	
Developments in home-based leisure activities	

Check your understanding

Aspects of diversity in families and marriage

Copy the following table and complete it to explain each aspect of diversity.

Diversity in families and marriage

Aspect of diversity	Explanation
Diversity in types of family	
Social class diversity	
Cultural diversity	
Cohort diversity	
Life-course diversity	
Organisational diversity	
Global diversity in marriages	

Families (Paper 1)

In this section we look at what the Families section of Paper 1 will look like, with some possible questions and marked candidate responses.*

*Please be aware that marks are advisory, based on sample AQA materials. Examination grade boundaries and marking guidance change annually – please visit the official AQA website for more information.

01 Which term is commonly used by sociologists to describe a marriage where domestic roles are not shared? **[1 mark]**

A Traditional conjugal roles ◯

B Modern conjugal roles ◯

C Joint conjugal roles ◯

D Segregated conjugal roles ☑ 1/1

> Tip: Read these questions carefully! Often, in the hurry to get started, candidates can misread the question and lose what is essentially an easy mark.

> Tip: In the exam you will simply need to tick whichever you think is the correct answer.

02 Identify and describe how economic dependency can affect the power relationship within families. **[3 marks]**

Economic dependency is sometimes referred to as covert power and is where one or more members of a family are financially dependent on another family member. Traditionally, women have been economically dependent on men in families, as traditional views have meant that men have worked to earn money and women took on work in the home.

> Examiner comment: This is a good example of a 'partial description'. Although the candidate shows an understanding of what economic dependence is and how it might look within a family, they do not say how economic dependence affects the 'power balance' within a family – for example, by giving the breadwinner more of a say in what they buy. 2/3

Item A

This bulletin (from the Office for National Statistics) presents annual statistics for 1996 to 2015 on the number of families by type, people in families by type and children in families by type.

- In 2015 there were 18.7 million families in the UK.
- The most common family type in 2015 was the married or civil partner couple family with or without dependent children, at 12.5 million.
- The cohabiting couple family continues to be the fastest growing family type in the UK in 2015, reaching 3.2 million cohabiting couple families.
- In 2015 around 40 per cent of young adults aged 15 to 34 in the UK were living with their parents.
- There were 27.0 million households in the UK in 2015; 35 per cent of all households were two-person households.
- In 2015 there were 7.7 million people in UK households who were living alone.

Source: Office for National Statistics (2015), November.

> Tip: Be sure to study items carefully. Pay extra attention to things such as dates and who conducted the research, as this will be crucial to answering the next couple of questions, which will test how well you have read the item. You could be asked about the type of research methods that the researcher has used, strengths or weaknesses of the research, or even to identify trends, patterns or make observations.

> Tip: The three questions that follow in the actual exam will expect you to have the 'context' of this item in mind. Try to refer to it whenever you can!

03 From **Item A**, examine **one** weakness of the research. **[2 marks]**

The research in item A is quantitative research conducted by a government body 'the Office for National Statistics'. Such research does not tell sociologists anything about the experience of individuals in their families, only what family types

> Tip: This question is testing how well you can read and analyse Item A!

are common or not in the UK. For example, sociologists might be interested in the reasons why 35 per cent of all households are two-person households in 2015 but this research does not provide anything other than the statistics.

04 Identify and explain **one** factor that may have led to the growth in cohabiting couple families referred to in **Item A**. **[4 marks]**

Item A shows that cohabiting couples are the fastest growing family type in the UK, reaching over 3 million in 2015. One factor that may have led to this is secularisation in UK society; this refers to the fact that religion (for example, the Church) is now less influential over people's lives and in forming social attitudes in society (research in 2015 revealed that 28 per cent of the UK had no religious beliefs and that this was increasing yearly). The Church has tended to see sex outside marriage and having children 'out of wedlock' as unacceptable.

05 Discuss how far sociologists agree that families are the main agent of socialisation. **[12 marks]**

Sociologists would have differing views about the importance of family in socialising individuals; while some would argue that they are the main agent of socialisation, others might say other agencies of socialisation such as the media are more influential.

Socialisation refers to the process through which individuals learn the norms and values of society, such as how to behave in public and how to use a knife and fork. Families are an agent of 'primary' socialisation; this means they are often the main or only agent for individuals in the early stages of their lives. As they are the first part of socialisation and the only agent present through our whole lives, some sociologists may say this makes them the main agent.

However, there are lots of other 'secondary' agents of socialisation such as the media, school and our peers/friends. Schools play a large part in our socialisation, teaching us things about the world and enforcing standards and expectations such as punctuality through the hidden curriculum so we behave the way society expects us to when we go to work. As you get older, you may even spend more time at school than with your family, so although school is not a primary agent of socialisation it takes over as the main agent. Despite this, your family are often involved in your school life and have a choice in what school you attend; they may only choose schools that support their own values (for example, a faith school). This would mean family remains the main agent of socialisation, as they have control over where and how you are educated.

Some sociologists would argue that the media is the main agent of socialisation; you are exposed to the media from a very young age (such as children's TV programmes).

Examiner comment: This response scores full marks. 1 mark is awarded for successfully analysing the item: the candidate has spotted that the research is quantitative data from the Office for National Statistics and has given an appropriate weakness of such data. The second mark is awarded as the candidate has successfully evaluated the reason they have given (sociologists may want to know reasons behind statistics.) 2/2

Examiner comment: This is a good response where the candidate has successfully identified a factor (secularisation) and given a brief explanation. To score the missing mark, the candidate would need to have explicitly linked secularisation to the context of the item, e.g. because the Church's attitude may no longer be accepted, people are now comfortable to cohabit and so this could be causing the increase in this family type we see in Item A. 3/4

Tip: In the essays, you are being assessed on four things: 1. Sociological knowledge (A01: 4 marks); 2. Your ability to apply knowledge of theories, research and methods (AO2: 4 marks); 3. Your ability to evaluate sociological theories and concepts (AO3: 4 marks); 4. Your ability to write clearly and coherently, spelling well and using specialist terms accurately will affect the total mark you receive. If your response is not well structured (for example, in bullet points), even if you have demonstrated knowledge, application and evaluation, you will be unable to go beyond 7–9 marks.

Examiner comment: The candidate shows a good understanding of the concept of socialisation and some of the agents involved. They have mentioned peers but this point is not developed. The response is relevant to the question; note how the candidate refers back to family as an agent of socialisation in *every paragraph* in comparison to the other agents of socialisation. To raise the mark, the candidate could reach a conclusion that explicitly addresses the issue of 'how far'. 9/12

Education

Topic 1:   What are the economic and selective roles of education?

Topic 2:   What are the socialisation, social control and political roles of education?

Topic 3:   What is learned through formal and informal education?

Topic 4:   How does the functionalist perspective view the role of the education system?

Topic 5:   How does Parsons view the role of the education system?

Topic 6:   What is the Marxist view on the role of education for a capitalist society?

Topic 7:   What have been the key historical changes in Britain's education system?

Topic 8:   How is the education system organised in contemporary Britain?

Topic 9:   Should education be provided by the state or by the independent sector?

Topic 10:   What are vocational education and alternative forms of provision?

Topic 11:   What key changes were introduced through the 1988 Education Act?

Topic 12:   How else has marketisation influenced education?

Topic 13:   How did New Labour develop educational policy after 1997?

Topic 14:   What are academies, free schools and selection by ability?

Topic 15:   How can social class affect achievement?

What are the economic and selective roles of education?

Objectives
- Describe the role that education plays in society: economic and selective roles
- Understand functionalist and Marxist views on education

Initially, we need to examine the role that education plays in society. There is a lot of disagreement among sociologists over this question.

Functionalist perspectives examine institutions in terms of the positive role they play in society as a whole. So, for functionalists, education is seen as performing a beneficial role in society.

Marxist perspectives, on the other hand, examine society in terms of the struggle between powerful and less powerful groups. They argue that the powerful groups in society (the ruling classes) use the education system to impose their own beliefs and values on the rest of society. From this point of view, education would be seen as having a beneficial role only for certain groups.

According to these different viewpoints, what, then, is the role of education?

Glossary terms

meritocratic, social mobility

Is this what education is for?

The economic role – teaching skills for work

For functionalists, schools and colleges teach the skills and knowledge necessary for work in a modern, technical, industrial society, for example literacy, numeracy and computer technology. Vocational courses aim to train young people for the world of work. In this way, education prepares young people for their future occupational roles and benefits the economy.

For Marxists, education is seen as reinforcing the class system. Thus children from less powerful groups (the working classes) learn the skills necessary for lower-status occupations, while children from more powerful groups (the middle and upper classes) gain the qualifications needed for higher-status occupations.

FOCUS ON SKILLS: DISCUSSION ACTIVITY

Thinking about the future

Think about all the subjects you are studying.

1 For each subject, explain how it could be useful in preparing you for your future working life.

2 Do you think the education system teaches the skills and knowledge necessary for work in a modern industrial society? Explain your answer.

The selective role – choosing the most able people for the most important jobs

Functionalists see the education system as a sieve, grading students according to their ability and placing individuals in occupational roles best suited to their talents and abilities. This process is based on the functionalist belief that all individuals have equal opportunities in their school career. In this way, those who achieve high qualifications are seen as the most able and are therefore rewarded with higher pay levels and higher status in society. This is known as a **meritocratic** system.

One result of this process is **social mobility**: by receiving qualifications through the education system, students can progress to a higher position in society than they started from.

Marxists, on the other hand, do not believe that the education system provides equal opportunities for everyone. They argue that it is designed to benefit the powerful groups. They claim that both teachers and schools reject working-class children and that working-class children therefore underperform.

From the Marxist point of view, the education system is not seen as meritocratic, because it does not offer an equal opportunity to all groups in society.

FOCUS ON SKILLS: WRITTEN ACTIVITY

Looking at occupations

This list of occupations has been ranked in terms of qualifications required.

1 doctor
2 lawyer
3 bank manager
4 teacher
5 nurse
6 typist
7 supermarket cashier
8 pop singer
9 refuse collector

1 Identify what qualifications each of these occupations would require. Do the jobs requiring more qualifications pay more than those requiring fewer qualifications?

2 How else could we rank occupations, other than by qualifications needed? Rewrite the list using another method. Explain which you think is the best method of deciding on the importance of occupations.

3 Do you think people who get high qualifications always gain the more skilled, better-paid jobs? Explain your thinking.

Check your understanding: Exam practice

Identify and explain one function of education for society.
(4 marks)

Key points

- Education can be seen to play an economic and selective role in society.

- Functionalist perspectives see education as positive and of benefit to the whole society. Marxist perspectives see education as having a beneficial role for privileged groups in society and reinforcing existing inequalities.

What are the socialisation, social control and political roles of education?

Objectives
- Describe the roles that education plays in society: socialisation, social control and political roles
- Understand functionalist and Marxist views on education

For functionalists, education also plays a role in teaching the values and norms of society to each new generation. School is seen as an agent of **secondary socialisation**, through which young people learn a common culture, beliefs and expectations. The education system 'knits' children from different backgrounds into a flexible whole.

Marxists, on the other hand, see education as socialising individuals into accepting the values of the powerful groups. For example, the stress placed on the importance of hard work in schools and colleges is seen as preparing the future workforce for accepting hard work as normal when it enters the workplace.

Glossary terms

agent of social control, secondary socialisation, social cohesion

FOCUS ON RESEARCH: DISCUSSION ACTIVITY

Are schools an effective agency of socialisation?

You are going to carry out some research on how effective the education system is as an agency of socialisation that teaches a common culture, values and expectations.

1 What research method would you suggest using in order to do this?

2 Why might this be a useful method to use?

3 What sorts of problems might you expect to encounter in carrying out this research?

Social control – teaching acceptance of rules and authority

Functionalists argue that for society to run smoothly there must be some means of regulating people's behaviour and activities. Schools act as an **agent of social control** by teaching rules such as obedience and punctuality.

Social control operates at two levels: the formal and the informal. In this way, people learn to conform to rules and authority in later life.

Social control

Formal	Informal
• discipline of staff (e.g. during lessons) • punishments • school rules	• through general school life (e.g. peer-group pressure) • learning to live and work with others

For Marxists, social control in schools and colleges is seen as reflecting social control in the wider society, which benefits those groups in power. For example, the importance of obeying a teacher in school is seen as preparation for obeying a boss in the workplace.

The political role – teaching people to be effective citizens and creating social cohesion

The development of Citizenship as a subject in schools has been linked to the belief that it is important to create **social cohesion** in society. This relates to the idea that education has a role in teaching the norms and values of British culture, as well as helping individuals to identify themselves as part of that wider culture. This is sometimes called developing a sense of 'Britishness'. This may involve teaching students about the voting system in Britain, the legal system or asking them to consider what it means to be 'British'.

According to functionalists, people learn about society through education. In this way, they accept the political system and, for example, they are able to exercise their voting rights wisely at election time.

Marxists disagree, suggesting that only certain political opinions and ideas are tolerated in education – radical ideas are rejected or ridiculed. In this way, the political ideas of the powerful groups come to be accepted by individuals.

FOCUS ON SKILLS: DISCUSSION ACTIVITY

Should education have a political role?

1 Do you think education has a role in teaching students about the political system and the law? What benefits and problems might there be in doing this?

2 What do you think 'Britishness' means? Is it the role of the school to teach this to students? What benefits and problems might there be in doing this?

3 Would you agree with the functionalist or the Marxist view on the political role of education?

Making connections

Social control in society

1 How effective do you think schools and colleges are in formally and informally socially controlling students? Give some examples to support your views.

2 How else are we socially controlled in society? Think about the other topics you have studied and how people may be formally and informally controlled.

Stretch and challenge

Functionalist vs Marxist

Consider functionalist and Marxist views of the role of the education system.

Make a list of arguments for and against each point of view.

Key points

- The education system has a role in socialising, controlling and politically educating people in society.

- Functionalist perspectives see these roles of the education system as positive and of benefit to the whole society.

- Marxist perspectives see education as having a beneficial role for privileged groups in society and reinforcing existing inequalities.

Check your understanding: Exam practice

Identify and explain one way in which schools teach children to become part of society.   (4 marks)

What is learned through formal and informal education?

Objectives
- Understand the differences between formal and informal education
- Identify the role of the 'hidden curriculum' in schools and colleges

It is important to note that the education system, consisting of schools, colleges and universities, is not the only source of learning. Learning also takes place informally through the socialisation process.

The education system provides students with **formal learning** through the **official curriculum**, which includes all those subjects studied in lessons, for example maths, history and so on. However, students also learn through the **hidden curriculum**, which refers to the learning that takes place outside particular subjects or lessons as part of general school or college life. The hidden curriculum of a school may be very different from that of a college, but it will generally involve learning rules, routines and regulations. Students may learn such things without explicit teaching and without necessarily realising they are learning them. This is known as **informal learning.**

Glossary terms

formal learning, hidden curriculum, informal learning, official curriculum

Stretch and challenge

Applying theory to the hidden curriculum

How might the following theories view the role of the hidden curriculum?
- Functionalism
- Marxism
- Feminism

What is the importance of the hidden curriculum?

The hidden curriculum reflects society's values and prepares students for their place in society and their future work role, in the following ways.

Hierarchy

Schools are hierarchical institutions. Any hierarchy can be illustrated in the shape of a pyramid: each layer of the pyramid is smaller than – and has more power than – the one below it, with the layer at the top having the most power of all. So, in a school, the head teacher is at the very top of the pyramid and the students are at the bottom. Students may also see themselves in a hierarchy, with older students at the top. Teachers may also see themselves in a hierarchy based on which subjects are seen as most important.

The hierarchy in school can be seen to reflect the hierarchical structure of society at large. In the workplace, for example, a hierarchy may exist between a manager and a trainee.

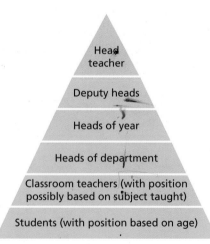

The school hierarchy.

Competition

Schools encourage competition between students for example in sport or for exam results. Society is also based on competition, for example for jobs, material possessions or status. So schools reflect the value that society places on competition and prepare students for their place in a competitive society.

Social control

The hidden curriculum – of rules, regulations, obedience and respect for authority – is one mechanism of social control that reflects those social controls operating in society at large. In effect, students learn to accept society's social controls while they are in the education system.

Gender role allocation

There is a link between expectations, subject choice and gender in school and gender role allocation in the wider society. Job segregation begins at school. For example, teachers may still expect girls to be less good at science than boys; this may discourage girls from entering science-based careers. Equally, girls may learn that the playground is a space that boys may seek to dominate, for example through taking up space with football games. This may prepare girls for the idea that men may seek to dominate other aspects of the social world as adults.

Lack of satisfaction

Critics of schools claim that much of the schoolday is taken up with boring and meaningless activities. Students have little say in the content of the subjects they study or in the overall organisation of the day. Equally, following the same timetable, week in week out, may lead to a sense of boredom and powerlessness.

Schools, it is argued, prepare students for boring, meaningless and repetitive jobs. In this way, there is a link between students' experience of school and many employees' experience of work.

The playground is a space that boys tend to dominate.

FOCUS ON SKILLS: WRITTEN ACTIVITY

The hidden curriculum

For each aspect of the hidden curriculum described (hierarchy, competition, social control, gender role allocation, lack of satisfaction):

1 Note down whether this happens in your school or college and give an example.
2 Note down two other things that students may learn through the hidden curriculum.
3 Identify two ways in which the hidden curriculum in a college may be different to that of a school.

FOCUS ON RESEARCH: WRITTEN ACTIVITY

Researching the hidden curriculum

Informal learning, which takes place through the hidden curriculum, is often thought to occur without people realising it is happening to them.

1 What problems might this create for researching the hidden curriculum?
2 What method(s) might you use to research the effects of the hidden curriculum?

Check your understanding: Exam practice

1 Describe what sociologists mean by the 'hidden curriculum'.
(3 marks)

2 Identify and describe one way in which the hidden curriculum socialises children.
(3 marks)

Key point

The education system provides both formal and informal learning to students. This learning takes place through the official curriculum and the hidden curriculum.

How does the functionalist perspective view the role of the education system?

Objectives
- Describe the views of Durkheim on the role of education for society
- Evaluate Durkheim's views on the role of education

As we saw previously, functionalists see the education system as performing a range of key roles for society. These are seen as beneficial and necessary for a society to perform effectively.

The following sections look at key functionalist thinkers and their views on the role of education.

Glossary term

social solidarity

FOCUS ON KEY THINKERS

Emile Durkheim – social solidarity and skills for work

The French sociologist Emile Durkheim (1858–1917) is often seen as the founder of functionalist sociology.

Social solidarity

Durkheim saw the main function of education as the transmission of society's norms and values to individuals. He argued that in order to function, societies must be able to ensure that all their members are united together behind a shared set of values. This creates **social solidarity**, where the individual sees themselves as part of the wider community and no longer simply as an isolated individual focused on their own selfish aims. Durkheim argued that it wasn't simply through teaching shared values via the hidden curriculum (see Topic 3) that this could happen, but subjects like history could also instil a sense of a shared past and a commitment to the wider society.

Society in miniature

Durkheim also argued that schools were 'society in miniature'. Schools prepare us for the wider society where we have to cooperate with people who are neither family nor friends. They provide us with a set of rules to guide our interactions with others and this in turn prepares us for following society's rules in dealing with people that we don't have a personal connection with.

Skills for work

Durkheim believed that in complex industrial societies the production of goods and services involves cooperation between a number of different specialists. This cooperation promotes social solidarity, but also requires individuals to have developed specialist skills. He argues that one function of an education system was to provide these skills.

Rules and punishment

'It is by respecting the school rules that the child learns to respect rules in general, that he develops the habit of self-control and restraint simply because he should restrain and control himself.'

Source: Durkheim (1961) *Moral Education. Glencoe:* The Free Press.

Durkheim believed that punishments should reflect the seriousness of the damage done to the wider social group or society. He also believed that this would lead to people being self-disciplined, as they would come to realise that their behaviour damaged society as a whole.

To what extent do you agree with Durkheim's ideas on punishment and its effects?

Is history important?

Think about Durkheim's ideas about the importance of history in creating social solidarity.

How far would you agree? Could learning the history of a country have the opposite effect?

Criticisms of Durkheim

Durkheim's ideas have been criticised in the following ways:

- Durkheim seems to be assuming that there is a shared culture that can be transmitted through education and the hidden curriculum. In a multicultural society, there may not be one single culture to be transmitted. This can be linked to the debate about what we mean by 'British values'.
- The education system may not adequately teach specialised skills useful in the workplace.
- Marxists would argue that the culture being transmitted through the education system is one that benefits the ruling class and not society as a whole.
- Feminists would argue that the culture being transmitted is patriarchal, or male dominated.
- Durkheim assumes that students in education will come to accept the values of society that are being taught. This may not be the case for all students.

Schoolchildren learn to see themselves as part of a larger society.

Key point

Durkheim is a key functionalist thinker who argues that the education system has a vital role in creating a unified society. It transmits norms and values, creates social solidarity and teaches specialised skills needed for the workplace.

Check your understanding: Exam practice

Identify and explain one criticism of Durkheim's view of the role of the education system. **(4 marks)**

How does Parsons view the role of the education system?

Objectives
- Describe Parsons' views on the role of the education system
- Evaluate Parsons' views

The American functionalist Talcott Parsons (1902–1979) further developed functionalist ideas about the role of education in society.

Universalistic values

Parsons argued that schools prepare children for entry into the wider society by treating everyone according to the same **universalistic standards.** This is different to the **particularistic standards** that apply in the family. Parents treat and judge their child in line with the values and standards of their particular family, which may be different to those of other families. The child's status in the family is an **ascribed status** – it is given to them (daughter, eldest and so on) and they are judged as 'good' or 'bad' depending on the values of the family.

However, in the wider society, people are judged according to universalistic standards (for example, the school rules or the laws), which are applied in the same way to everyone. People's status in society is **achieved status**, for example as a result of educational qualifications and hard work. The education system prepares people for this transition.

Value consensus

Parsons believed that schools promote two key values – the importance of achievement and the value of equality of opportunity.

- Students are encouraged to value high achievement and the rewards that this brings and so aim to achieve more as a result. In this way they are encouraged to maximise their potential, which will benefit the wider society.
- Students are also encouraged to believe that they are competing with each other on equal terms in the classroom. As a result, the higher achievers are seen as deserving their success and the lower achievers accept their lower status as fair.

Meritocracy

Parsons saw the education system as being a **meritocracy** (or a meritocratic system). Students' achievements are based on their abilities and efforts and not on social class, gender or ethnicity. The education system is seen as treating everyone equally with status being based on merit alone. In this way, Parsons saw education as

Glossary terms

achieved status, ascribed status, meritocracy, particularistic standards, role allocation, universalistic standards

FOCUS ON KEY THINKERS

Talcott Parsons: values, meritocracy and roles

Writing in 1961, Parsons argued that the education system was the key socialising agency in modern society, acting as the bridge between the family and society, where children are prepared for their adult roles.

FOCUS ON SKILLS: WRITTEN ACTIVITY

Different standards?

1 Make a list of the particularistic standards that apply in your family or a family you are familiar with.

2 Make a list of the universalistic standards that apply in your school or college.

3 To what extent are these standards similar or different?

4 Do you always accept the standards you have listed?

5 What conclusions do you draw about Parsons' ideas from completing this exercise?

mirroring the wider society, which he felt was increasingly based on achieved status, based on merit and universalistic standards applied equally to all.

Role allocation

Parsons argued that the education system is an effective device for sorting people out so that they are matched to the correct job for their abilities. This is known as **role allocation**. Based on their qualifications, the most able should reach the top jobs in society. Again, this is seen as fair, as the system is meritocratic.

Education functions to allocate people to their future work roles.

Criticisms of Parsons

- Like Durkheim, Parsons is accused of not fully considering whose values are being transmitted via the education system. Marxists, for example, would see these as the values of the dominant groups in society.
- Many sociologists have questioned the idea that the education system is meritocratic. Feminists, for example, argue that gender can have an influence on achievement and subject choice and that the system does not provide equality of opportunity.
- Role allocation has also been criticised on the basis that those with the best qualifications don't always get the top jobs and many of the highest financially achieving individuals in society left school with few qualifications.

Stretch and challenge

Meritocracy?

1 Think about your own experiences in the education system – does it seem to have been meritocratic? Why/why not?
2 How might a Marxist or a feminist sociologist view the idea of meritocracy in education? Explain your answer.

Key points

- Parsons developed functionalist thinking on the role of education for society.
- He identified a range of functions, such as role allocation and teaching universalistic values as a bridge between the family and the wider society.
- He also saw the system as meritocratic and effective at allocating people to future work roles.

Check your understanding: Exam practice

Identify and explain one function of the education system according to Parsons.   (4 marks)

What is the Marxist view on the role of education for a capitalist society?

Objectives
- Describe Bowles and Gintis' Marxist view of education
- Evaluate the Marxist view of education

Marxists take a critical view of the role of education in society, seeing it as a form of social control that creates obedient and passive workers for the capitalist economy, teaching ruling-class values rather than the shared values that functionalists claim. Marxists also argue that education reproduces the existing social class structure by ensuring that working-class students are less likely to achieve good qualifications compared to students from the dominant groups.

Glossary term

correspondence principle

FOCUS ON KEY THINKERS

Bowles and Gintis: Schooling in capitalist America

The American Marxists Bowles and Gintis (1976) see the key role of the education system as creating and reproducing a workforce with the correct characteristics to meet the needs of the capitalist economy. These characteristics include being hard working, disciplined, submissive, obedient and willing not to question low wages and poor conditions.

Bowles and Gintis based their findings on their own study of 237 New York high school students, as well as the findings of other studies. They found that schools reward students who display the above characteristics, while students who show greater independence and creative thinking are more likely to gain lower grades. Bowles and Gintis concluded that the schools were producing an unimaginative and unquestioning workforce.

The correspondence principle

Bowles and Gintis argue that there is a close link, or correspondence, between the relationships and interactions expected and valued in schools and those expected and valued in the workplace. They describe this as the **correspondence principle**. For Bowles and Gintis, the needs of the economy influence what happens in the education system.

The correspondence principle operates through the hidden curriculum (see Topic 3) by teaching the values required by the capitalist system in the following ways:

- Students learn to obey rules and not to question them.
- Students learn to accept the hierarchy in schools, which prepares them for the workplace, where the manager or supervisor will have authority over them.
- Students learn to be motivated by external rewards in the form of exam results and grades, rather than enjoying the subject

Bowles and Gintis concluded that the education system produces an obedient workforce for capitalism.

matter and gaining intrinsic satisfaction from it. This prepares them for the workplace, where work is also likely not to be intrinsically satisfying, and therefore motivation comes in the form of the extrinsic rewards of pay and bonuses.

- Students learn that the knowledge they cover in school is fragmented – there are few connections made between subjects studied, and knowledge is broken down into isolated chunks. This prepares them for many jobs in which tasks are very specific and separate to the tasks being carried out by other workers. The worker is denied knowledge of the overall process at work.
- Students learn to be competitive in schools through tests, grades, setting and so on. This prepares them to compete in the workplace for promotions and higher pay. This benefits capitalism as it produces a more motivated workforce.

The myth of meritocracy

Unlike functionalists, Bowles and Gintis reject the idea that the education system is meritocratic. Instead, they argue that we are led to believe that it treats people fairly and equally, as this prevents people questioning the system. Bowles and Gintis describe this as 'the myth of meritocracy'. They argue that social class background, and not intelligence or educational achievement, is the main factor affecting someone's income. However, the system disguises this fact and leads us to believe that those with the highest incomes deserve to be in this position as a result of their ability and qualifications.

Criticisms of Bowles and Gintis' Marxist approach

Bowles and Gintis are accused of taking a deterministic view – they assume that students have no free will and passively accept the values taught via the hidden curriculum. However, many students reject the values of the school.

Modern economies and businesses can be seen as requiring a different kind of workforce to the one Bowles and Gintis describe. Instead of passive and unthinking workers, businesses require creative and independent workers capable of taking on responsibility and developing new ideas as part of a team.

Check your understanding: Exam practice

Identify and describe one feature of the correspondence principle. (3 marks)

What have been the key historical changes in Britain's education system?

Objectives
- Assess the impact of the tripartite system
- Assess the impact of the comprehensive system

There have been a number of major changes and developments in Britain's education system over the years. We will look here at the most significant ones.

The 1944 Butler Education Act

The aims

The 1944 Education Act aimed to give all students an equal chance to develop their talents and abilities in a system of free, state-run education. The main changes were in the organisation of the secondary sector. The aim here was to introduce a meritocratic system where children would receive an education based on their own academic ability, rather than on the ability of their parents to pay. The result was the **tripartite system**.

Children's ability was tested at the age of 11 years by the **11-plus exam**. Based on the results of this exam, children went to one of three types of school (see table below), each of which was designed to meet their needs. The 11-plus exam still exists in some areas of the country where grammar schools still exist, and much of the private sector uses entry tests.

Glossary terms

11-plus exam, comprehensive system, mixed-ability groups, tripartite system

FOCUS ON SKILLS: DISCUSSION ACTIVITY

Testing ability

In the tripartite system, school allocation was based on the 11-plus exam.

1 What arguments can you make to suggest that students may not have shown their true abilities in the 11-plus test?

2 Do these arguments raise any issues for the use of testing in schools today, for example SATs or entrance exams in the private sector?

The tripartite system

11-plus exam		
(taken at age 11 years; designed to test ability and potential of student)		
Based on this, students were placed in either:		
SECONDARY MODERN	**SECONDARY TECHNICAL**	**GRAMMAR**
general education for less academic	practical education, e.g. crafts, skills	academic education for more academic
(approximately 75% of students)	(approximately 5% of all students)	(approximately 20% of all students)

FOCUS ON RESEARCH: RESEARCH ACTIVITY

What was it like?

Carry out an unstructured or informal interview with a relative or friend who might have experienced the tripartite system.

You might like to ask them questions such as:

- which type of school they attended
- how it felt to do an 11-plus exam
- whether they became separated from friends as a result of the exam and so on.

1965: the start of the comprehensive system

In 1965, the then Labour government asked Local Education Authorities (LEAs) to reorganise secondary education so that all students, regardless of academic ability, attended the same type of school. This became known as a 'comprehensive' school, and still exists in this form today.

Comprehensive schools were introduced in response to what some saw as the failings of the tripartite system, which often simply reflected social class backgrounds.

Why are comprehensives thought to be a good idea?

The **comprehensive system** is based on the principle of one type of school for everyone.

- Social reasons: As children of all abilities and from different social classes attend the same school and mix, so social barriers are broken down.
- Educational reasons: Comprehensive schools are designed to cater for children of all abilities. There is no entrance examination or selection, so no child is labelled as a 'failure'. This is seen to be fairer to many, and particularly to late developers.
- Geographical reasons: Each school has a specific 'catchment area' – a particular area or neighbourhood from which students are drawn. This has established the principle of local schools enrolling local children of all abilities and providing them with the same opportunities.

What are the problems with the comprehensive system?

- It is argued that in practice comprehensives limit parental choice. Each student is expected to go to the nearest school in the area, no matter how good or bad that school's reputation.
- It is also argued that the more academically able students are held back by the less able, particularly in **mixed-ability groups** (that is, where children of all abilities are taught in the same classroom).
- Some see comprehensive schools as accepting lower standards, as comprehensives contain a mixture of social classes with a range of values and attitudes. The grammar school, on the other hand, was largely middle class and so would reflect middle-class standards only.

Do comprehensives break down class barriers?

- Comprehensives are not really of mixed social class, as they are based on a local neighbourhood – for example, inner-city comprehensives are usually working class and suburban ones are usually middle class.
- Some argue that most comprehensives are not really comprehensive at all because, for instance, they stream or band students within the school according to ability. Critics claim that streams reflect social class differences.

> ## Check your understanding: Exam practice
>
> Identify and explain one disadvantage of the comprehensive system.
>
> (4 marks)

Key points

- The tripartite system aimed to create a meritocratic system where ability determined the type of school attended.

- The comprehensive system was introduced to allow all students, regardless of academic ability, equality of opportunity by attending the same type of school. However, it can be questioned whether this has been achieved in every case.

How is the education system organised in contemporary Britain?

There is a range of different types of schools and colleges in Britain. However, we can broadly describe educational provision in the following ways.

Pre-school education

This refers to the care and education of children under the age of 5 years. It may take a variety of forms, such as:

• day nurseries, which may be provided through the local authority (LA) or by voluntary or private means
• playgroups, which provide care and learning experiences mainly for 3- to 5-year-olds
• nursery education, which may be provided in nursery schools or in nursery classes attached to primary schools for children up to 5 years old.

Primary education

This refers to infant and junior schools, which are usually co-educational (that is, they take both girls and boys) and tend to take any student from a particular area from age 5 to 11 years. Most primary education is provided by the state (or public sector) through the LA. However, some schools at this level are private and fees must be paid.

Secondary education

This refers to schools that take students from the ages of 11 to 16 years, although many may also provide sixth form education up to the age of 18. Most secondary education is provided by the state in comprehensive schools, where no fees are paid. However, private fee-paying schools, grammar schools and independent faith schools provide some secondary education.

Further and higher education

This refers to education outside schools, beyond the compulsory age of 16 years. From 16 to 18 years, students can study for a range of qualifications (for example, A levels and Scottish Highers) at sixth form colleges or further education colleges, or they can take skills training courses and apprenticeships. At 18 years, students may then

FOCUS ON RESEARCH: RESEARCH ACTIVITY

Secondary provision in my area

Find out about the range of secondary schools in your area.

• Are there only comprehensives?

• Are there any private, fee-paying schools?

• Are there any faith schools or other types of secondary provision?

• Are there any academies or Free schools?

You could look on your Local Authority's website and/ or ask your school's careers adviser.

qualify to go on to higher education and study at higher levels, including at universities.

Developments in further education

At 16 years, young people must decide whether to:

- remain in full-time education
- go into apprenticeships; or traineeships
- seek employment with training.

In recent years:

- Governments have been committed to raising the number of young people remaining in full-time education or training after the age of 16 years. This is because, in order for Britain to remain competitive and prosperous in a global economy, it needs a highly educated and well-trained workforce.
- Competition has been encouraged in the further and higher education sectors.
- Colleges' performances are monitored against targets set for recruitment, exam performance, and so on. In this way, as with schools, supporters hope that these measures will result in improved quality of provision in the sector.

The independent sector

The **independent sector** refers to schools that charge fees. This sector is made up of:

- **private schools** – all schools that charge fees
- **public schools** – these are the older and more famous independent secondary schools, such as Eton, Harrow and Rugby.

Around 7 per cent of all schoolchildren attend independent schools. These are not subject to the same rules as the state sector schools – for example, they do not have to teach the National Curriculum.

Because of the high tuition fees paid (for example £37 062 per academic year at Eton in 2016)), critics have claimed that they allow the children of the rich to receive a separate and particular kind of education that gives them certain advantages over state-educated children. For example, ex-independent school pupils made up around 40 per cent of accepted places at Oxford University in 2016, even though only around 7 per cent of all children are educated at independent schools.

FOCUS ON RESEARCH: RESEARCH ACTIVITY

Would you like to go to public school?

Carry out some research on a famous public school, such as Eton, Charterhouse or Harrow.

Draw up a table to show some advantages and disadvantages of attending this school.

Key points

- In contemporary Britain, most primary education is provided by the state through LAs. Most secondary education comes through state comprehensive schools.

- There is also provision through the independent sector, where fees are paid.

- A range of provision exists beyond compulsory education and there is an emphasis on remaining in education or training after the age of 16 years.

Check your understanding: Exam practice

1. Identify and describe one form of pre-school educational provision. (3 marks)

2. Describe what is meant by a 'faith school'. (3 marks)

Should education be provided by the state or by the independent sector?

Why are independent schools favoured by some?

- They generally have a lower teacher–student ratio than state schools, which means that classes are smaller and students receive more attention from the teacher.
- Resources and facilities are often better than in some state comprehensive schools.
- Many independent schools have an academic culture, in which academic achievement is emphasised and examination results tend to be significantly higher than the national average. Students are said to be highly motivated and most go on to university.
- Parental input is high in terms of fees, support and expectations.
- Independent boarding schools are said to benefit from the full immersion of staff and students in school life.

Why are state schools favoured by others?

- State schools are free – they are not based on the ability of parents to pay the high fees of private schools. Some critics argue that it is not morally right to have a private education system to which only the rich have access, as this reinforces inequalities in society based on wealth.
- State schools are more socially mixed. Independent schools are seen as elitist and socially divisive.
- State schools may provide a route of upward social mobility for students from poor families. Fee-paying schools are less likely to do so, as the fees may not be affordable.
- Students do not have to travel so far on a daily basis if they attend a local state school. Private school students may have to travel relatively long distances or live away from home altogether at a boarding school.

A state school and an independent school. Independent schools may have their own theatres, swimming pools, squash courts, cricket pavilions and hockey pitches on site; by contrast, state schools' facilities are limited dependent on the level of state funding available to them.

The pros and cons of the independent sector

Read the following summaries of the main arguments for and against the independent sector:

- Independent schooling maintains privilege based on social class position; that is, only the rich can afford it. The rich use it to give their children a head start. Education should only be provided through a properly funded state system, to ensure that everyone has access to the same levels and quality of education.

- Independent schooling is similar to private healthcare in that people should be able to spend their money however they choose. If they can afford to send their children to an independent school, then, in a free society, this option should be available to them.

Using these summaries and other information in this topic, discuss arguments for and against the following statement: 'Education should be provided only by the state.'

Private schools still best route to top jobs

Examine the following figures and then answer the questions.

'The research looked at the educational backgrounds of 1,200 people working in high positions and showed the following:

- 67 per cent of British Oscar winners were privately educated.

- 74 per cent of the UK's top judges went to a fee-paying school, with 78 per cent also going to Oxford or Cambridge Universities.

- 71 per cent of the top military personnel went to private schools.

- 51 per cent of the leading print journalists attended fee-paying schools.

- 50 per cent of the cabinet under David Cameron were privately educated.

- 61 per cent of top doctors were educated at independent schools with only 16 per cent educated at comprehensives.'

Source: the Sutton Trust (2016).

1 People from which of the professions in the table are most likely to have gone to a private school?
2 Which professions have the lowest proportions of people from private schools occupying the top jobs?
3 In what ways might attendance at a private school give students an advantage?

Key points

- Currently, the UK has a mixture of state and independent provision, with the majority of children (approximately 93 per cent) attending state schools.

- Both forms of provision can be seen to have advantages and disadvantages.

Check your understanding: Exam practice

1 Identify and explain one argument in favour of private education. (4 marks)

2 Describe what is meant by an 'independent school'. (3 marks)

What are vocational education and alternative forms of provision?

Objectives
- Explain the role of vocational education
- Describe and assess some alternative forms of educational provision

Vocational education and training

In recent years, governments have placed much emphasis on providing **vocational education** – work-related qualifications and training for students aged 14 to 18 years. Although this trend has been developing since the mid-to late 1970s, it is still sometimes known as 'the new vocationalism'. This development reflects the importance of functionalist views that the education system has to provide the skills and expertise needed by industry and the economy in the modern world far more effectively than it used to.

'The new vocationalism' has resulted in an expansion of post-16 education and training related to work, with National Vocational Qualifications (NVQs), Applied A-level qualifications and Diploma qualifications linked to specific work areas such as health and social care and engineering. There are also work experience programmes in schools and colleges and, linked to this, government has sought to ensure that skills training is targeted at school leavers by placing 16-year-olds on training programmes for vocational skills or work experience – that is, unless they have a job to go to or are continuing in education.

Arguments for and against vocational education

- Supporters of these changes argue that they will lead to a more skilled, better-qualified workforce that will allow Britain to be more competitive.
- Critics argue that the emphasis on skills training disguises the fact that the problem is not that young people lack the necessary skills for work, but rather that there is no work for skilled young people to do. In effect, vocational education and training is seen as reducing the numbers of 16-to 18-year-olds that are NEET (that is, Not in Education, Employment or Training).
- Marxists argue that vocational education is viewed as lower status compared to purely academic qualifications and that it is aimed at working-class children to prepare them to be workers for a capitalist society.
- Vocational qualifications are also seen by critics as being similar to the ideas of the tripartite system, in that students who are not seen to be academic are considered failures and are pushed into what some see as lower-status vocational training.

Glossary terms

co-educational, de-schooling, home education, vocational education

FOCUS ON SKILLS: DISCUSSION ACTIVITY

Ivan Illich – de-schooling

Illich (1995) argues that schools repress children and promote passive conformity rather than developing creative individuals able to think for themselves. He argues that the school fails those who don't conform or who question the role of education. He argues for **de-schooling**, suggesting that education in its current form should be abolished, with people instead encouraged to pursue knowledge and skills in smaller networks with like-minded individuals rather than attending schools.

1 Do you agree with Illich that schools create passive conformists and that those who challenge the school are failed? Explain your answer.

2 Identify some advantages and some potential problems with Illich's ideas about abolishing schools altogether.

Alternative forms of educational provision

There are a number of examples of alternatives to mainstream, formal education. One such example is that of **home education** (also called home schooling or home learning). This involves teaching children at home rather than in a state or independent school. Parents or professional tutors usually carry out home education. It is a legal option for people who wish to provide a different learning environment and ethos to local schools; however, more recently, concerns have been raised about the standards of this form of education and its impact on the social development of children.

Another form of alternative provision comes in the way in which a school is organised and the types of values it teaches students. A.S. Neill's Summerhill school is one example. This **co-educational** (for boys and girls) boarding school, set up in 1921 in Suffolk, has been seen by some as a model for progressive education. Another example is the Sands school (see below).

Self-directed study is an alternative form of education. Illich proposed 'learning webs', where people get together to study topics of interest.

FOCUS ON SKILLS: WRITTEN ACTIVITY

Sands School an alternative approach

Read the following details about Sands School and then answer the questions that follow.

> 'We value people as individuals. Students are free to be themselves and to explore their own paths through education. There are no uniforms, no petty rules resulting in detention and everyone is on first name terms.
>
> No one has more power than anyone else, the teachers and students are equal and there is no headteacher. The school is democratic with everyone having their say and an equal vote in the weekly school meetings. It is the students who have the real power and this encourages a real sense of responsibility.
>
> Sands has timetabled lessons…if a student chooses not to study a subject, leaving a gap in their timetable, they are encouraged to find a constructive activity to fill that time…It seems foolhardy to put every child through the same program of study hoping that at the end individuals will surface…(as in other schools)…(it is) better to teach children how to make wise choices relative to their own needs and interests.'
>
> Source: adapted from www.sands-school.co.uk

1 Make a list of the ways in which you think Sands School might be different to your school or college.

2 Outline the advantages and disadvantages that there might be in attending a school like this.

Check your understanding: Exam practice

1 Identify and explain one criticism of vocational education.

(4 marks)

2 Describe what sociologists mean by 'de-schooling'. (3 marks)

Key points

- Over the years, vocational education has been seen by governments as an increasingly important way of ensuring a more effective workforce to meet the needs of the economy.

- Some alternative forms of educational provision do exist in the UK such as home schooling and 'progressive' education such as at Sands School.

What key changes were introduced through the 1988 Education Act?

Objectives
- Describe what is meant by 'marketisation' in education
- Describe and assess the impact of the National Curriculum and testing

The 1988 Education Act brought in by the Conservative government introduced many changes that are still fundamental to the contemporary education system.

Glossary terms

core subjects, marketisation, National Curriculum

Marketisation in education

Marketisation refers to the idea that the forces of the market such as consumer choice and competition have been introduced into education. The focus on parental choice, funding based on student numbers and more freedom for schools have reflected this process.

FOCUS ON SKILLS: WRITTEN ACTIVITY

Marketisation in education

Read the following extract and then answer the questions.

'Schools need to create an "image" that is attractive to parents and students. They do this through school policy, documentation, the building, name and their students. Newly developed schools need to create instant "traditions" through logos and uniforms. Most schools had new reception areas with a "business-like feel". School documentation had to fit with "school style". Values of hard work and discipline were emphasised. School prospectuses were better produced and glossy.

'The concern was to give schools a more middle-class flavour in order to attract the high-achieving child of ambitious parents. The term "able" had become code for students who were "middle class", female, white or Indian. Unattractive intakes consisted of less able, emotionally damaged children with learning disabilities. Integration was resisted for children with special educational needs in some schools, not for educational reasons, but because of the possible perceptions of parents. Image making is turning schools into organisations that value certain children above others. The market does not ensure equality of access for all if schools only desire the custom of certain groups at the expense of others.'

Source: adapted from Gewirtz, Ball and Bowe (1995). 'Markets, Choice and Equity in Education', in J. Blundell and J. Griffiths (2002) *Sociology Since 1995*.

1 Identify two effects of marketisation in schools.
2 Which social groups may face inequality as a result of marketisation in schools?

The National Curriculum and testing

The **National Curriculum** was introduced in September 1989 in all state schools in England and Wales. It established a number of **core subjects** (English, maths, sciences), which all students aged 5 to 16 must study. In addition, students' progress was to be assessed formally by their teachers and by national tests in the core subjects at the end of key stages. Sixteen-year-olds are assessed by means of the GCSE examination.

The aim of the National Curriculum was to measure students' performance against national targets so that parents and schools can be informed as to whether a child is performing above or below the expected level for their age. Measures can then be taken to improve the performance of children who are below the expected level, as well as the performance of schools whose students fall below the national targets.

One aim of the National Curriculum has been to provide greater equality of education for all by ensuring that all students take the same subjects. Science, for example, has traditionally been a boys' subject but it is now compulsory for *all* pupils up to GCSE level.

The National Curriculum made science compulsory for all students up to 16 years (GCSE level).

FOCUS ON SKILLS: WRITTEN ACTIVITY

Assessing students' progress

'I think we're now trapped in an education system driven by testing…we have too much testing now. Assessment actually goes on all the time in school. Teachers will say: "Well done", "That's right", every day to their pupils – but 99% of this school assessment is low stakes and informal. Only 1% of assessment is high stakes and formal, and it is this 1% – SATs, GCSEs, A levels, AS levels – on which everything rests.'

Source: interview with Ted Wragg (2003) *Sociology Review*, 13, November.

1 Make a list of the possible benefits and problems of testing primary school children and using the results as a measure of their ability.

2 What might be better ways of assessing students' progress?

3 Note down your views on the usefulness of testing as a way of assessing progress.

Key points

- Market forces have become part of the education system, for example through parental choice and competition.

- The National Curriculum has resulted in compulsory core subjects for all and testing at different key stages.

Check your understanding: Exam practice

1 Identify and explain one effect of the introduction of the National Curriculum. (4 marks)

2 Describe what is meant by 'marketisation' in education. (3 marks)

How else has marketisation influenced education?

The 1988 Act introduced the principles of choice and diversity in educational provision linked to the idea of marketisation. These policies have been central to much of educational policy since.

Features of marketisation

- Parents should be able to choose the type of school they prefer for their children from a range of options.
- Schools must now produce a prospectus and hold open days.
- **League tables** are published showing exam results and National Curriculum test results, as well as a comparison between the school and national (average) results.
- Businesses can sponsor schools, for example by providing extra funds, work experience opportunities or offering their expertise to governing bodies.
- Open enrolment has been introduced, whereby schools can recruit students from outside their immediate area and parents can apply to send their children to schools outside their local area. This allows successful schools to recruit more pupils. Those with better positions in league tables may be able to select students who are more able or seen as 'ideal' students.
- There is a wider range of types of school for parents to choose from, such as **academies** and **Free schools**.
- Formula funding means schools are funded based on the numbers of students they attract. Popular schools get more funds as a result and can therefore attract better teachers and pay for better facilities.
- The rise of a **parentocracy** (rule by parents): As parents become consumers of education they have greater power; for example, in choosing a school, asking questions at open days and through providing parent feedback.

Those who support these policies believe that standards will improve as schools compete with each other for students.

FOCUS ON SKILLS: WRITTEN ACTIVITY

Parental choice?

Read the following extracts:

'The aim of introducing market forces into education was justified in two ways: as an extension of personal freedom and also to improve schools as they compete to attract parents – who are effectively "customers" for education.

'The researchers have identified parents as belonging to broad categories of choice-making:

- **Privileged/skilled choosers** were generally middle class...These parents arrange for their children to attend the correct primaries and then use negotiating skills and training of their children to ensure that they are accepted by the selected schools.
- **Semi-skilled choosers** were a mixed class group of aspirant working-class parents. They were highly motivated for their children, but were less aware of some of the...insider knowledge of the system necessary in order to privilege their children. They were more open to media reports of the schools and they relied on the judgments of others. Many did not fully understand the significance of the open evenings and brochures and so they relied on reputation and rumour in their selection processes.
- **Disconnected choosers** who were less able to make choices, often viewed parental choice as being of little significance and viewed all schools as being "much the same". They usually made their selections on geography or on the current "happiness" of the child rather than in terms of job prospects.

Source: adapted from Gewirtz, Ball and Bowe (1995) 'Markets, Choice and Equity in Education', in Blundell and Griffiths (2002) *Sociology Since 1995.*

1 Explain why the idea of schools competing for parents would lead to them improving their standards.
2 According to the research, what factors may affect parents' ability to make choices about which school to send their children to?
3 How might some parents be more able to get their children into the 'correct' primary schools for the secondary school of their choice?
4 Note down two arguments for the idea of parental choice in education and two arguments against this.

FOCUS ON KEY THINKERS

Ball, Bowe and Gewirtz: Market forces, parental choice and competition between schools (1994)

This research looked at 15 schools in 3 neighbouring LEAs and focused on the effects that parental choice and competition between schools was having on the education system, in particular on whether it was leading to greater inequality.

Ball, Bowe and Gewirtz found that the publication of league tables led schools to focus on recruiting more academically able students who could boost the school's position in the tables. Some schools reintroduced streaming and setting in order to focus resources on students who were more likely to be successful in examinations. Students were seen as 'commodities' by some schools: they could do something for the school rather than the school doing something for them. Less able students were neglected and this also applied to those with special educational needs.

Ball et al. argued that marketisation policies had made education less equal and that schools were now more concerned with selecting the gifted and advantaged than helping the disadvantaged.

Open days allow schools and colleges to market themselves.

Key points

- Marketisation has led to greater choice and competition in education.
- Supporters of marketisation believe it will increase educational standards and achievement levels.
- However, critics argue that marketisation has made education less equal, leading schools to see students as commodities and giving advantages to middle-class parents.

Check your understanding: Exam practice

Identify and explain one effect of marketisation on education in Britain.   (4 marks)

How did New Labour develop educational policy after 1997?

Objective
• Describe and assess government educational policies since 1997

From 1997, Labour governments viewed education as a key area of policy. A number of themes have been addressed.

Raising Standards

This involved a range of policies such as:

- providing nursery places for all 3- and 4-year-olds
- reducing class sizes in primary schools
- national literacy and numeracy schemes
- looking at league tables in value-added terms – that is, providing a measure of how well a child has progressed in a school academically, rather than simply relying on their final results; this is thought to give a clearer measure of the performance of the school
- placing failing schools in 'special measures'
- identifying 'Beacon schools', which are seen as being of an outstanding standard and therefore able to pass on good practice to other schools or colleges in a local area.

Reducing inequality

This involved bringing in policies aimed at reducing inequalities in achievement and widening the range of people participating in post-16 education. These policies were aimed, in particular, at disadvantaged groups in society with the aim of combating social exclusion.

Policies included:

- Educational Maintenance Allowances (EMAs) – payments for students from disadvantaged backgrounds designed to encourage them to carry on into post-16 education (this has been cut since 2010).
- Excellence in cities, which led to the development of the use of learning mentors and a focus on helping students designated as gifted and talented, regardless of social background.
- The Aim Higher programme, designed to raise aspirations for students from disadvantaged backgrounds and to encourage them to go on to higher education.
- The Sure Start programme to support families with preschool children (this has been cut since 2010).
- The Connexions service – introduced to offer personal support to young people, particularly those at risk of social exclusion. It brought together a range of services such as careers and youth services.

Critics of these policies argue that although they were designed to support students from disadvantaged backgrounds, they have,

Glossary terms

academy, faith school, specialist school

There are nursery school places for all 3- and 4-year-olds.

in fact, been used by a range of students and thus have also been beneficial to the middle classes. In addition, Labour has been accused of double standards through the introduction of tuition fees for higher education, which may deter some students from disadvantaged backgrounds from applying to go to university

Promoting diversity and choice

Education policy was also linked to the idea of better meeting the diverse needs of individual students in 21st century Britain. Critics have argued that these policies have continued the policy of marketisation started in 1988. Examples of this include:

- The promotion of **specialist schools** allowed schools to build on their strengths (for example, in technology or languages) and so raise standards of achievement. Specialist schools were also allowed to select up to 10 per cent of their students based on their ability in the school's specialism.
- The promotion of **faith schools** is one example of how greater choice and diversity are provided in a competitive schools market.
- New Labour introduced the idea of **academies**. These were originally former comprehensives in urban areas that were failing, taken out of local authority control and funded by government and private sponsors in order to raise achievement levels. These schools were allowed to select part of their intake and were known as city academies.

FOCUS ON SKILLS: WRITTEN ACTIVITY

The original academies

Read the information below and then answer the questions that follow.

Academies were often former failing comprehensive schools that have been taken out of LA control. The aim was to reinvest in them to regenerate education in their local area. Their social profile began to change with a reduction in the numbers of students eligible for free school meals, as well as increased demand for places as a result of new facilities. However, the proportion of students receiving free school meals in academies was still higher than that for secondary schools.

1 What were academies set up to do?
2 Why is the number of students entitled to free school meals an indicator of social background?
3 a Identify one piece of evidence to suggest that academies have provided diversity in education to meet the needs of individuals.
  b Identify one piece of evidence to suggest that this may increasingly not be the case.

Check your understanding: Exam practice

Identify and describe one educational reform from the last 25 years aimed at reducing inequality in education.   (3 marks)

FOCUS ON SKILLS: DISCUSSION ACTIVITY

A post-comprehensive era?

In a small group, discuss whether you think promoting a range of different school types such as specialist schools, faith schools and academies is a useful idea. Would it be better to have no diversity or choice, with all schools being of one type? Explain your thinking.

Key point

A wide range of New Labour government educational policies since 1997 focused on raising standards, reducing inequalities and promoting diversity and choice in education.

What are academies, free schools and selection by ability?

Objectives
- Describe some key changes in educational policy since 2010
- Evaluate these policies

Since 2010, educational policy has continued to be influenced by marketisation. In particular, more policies have been introduced aimed at reducing the influence of the state on education.

Glossary terms

academy, Free school

New-style academies

Old-style **academies** under New Labour were introduced to target schools in disadvantaged areas. However, since 2010, all schools have been encouraged to become academies and to leave the control of their local authority, with their funding coming direct from government. They are also free from having to follow the National Curriculum, can increase their student numbers should they wish to, and have more control over teachers' pay, term times and the length of the school day.

- Sponsored academies are those that had been low performing schools before converting to academy status.
- Converter academies are usually already high performing schools that have chosen to convert to academy status.

Academies are run through an academy trust or through an academy chain. Academy chains are private businesses that have taken over the running of large numbers of schools across the country.

Free schools

These schools are funded by government, but can be set up and run by groups of parents, teachers, businesses and religious groups, rather than the local authority. They have to submit a business plan, identify a site for the school, are free from the National Curriculum, have control over teachers' pay and can set their own term times.

- Supporters argue that **Free schools** create further choice and provide an option for people unhappy with school provision in their local area.
- Critics argue that they will appeal to middle-class parents who may not want their children to attend a local comprehensive school, and therefore they will produce further inequality in education.

FOCUS ON SKILLS: RESEARCH ACTIVITY

Might selection by ability create more opportunity?

One area under consideration is the introduction of new grammar schools. These schools would select students on entry based on ability. It is argued that this might allow greater numbers of more able children to have access to a better standard of education.

Carry out some research on this proposal using news websites and other sources of news on education such as *Schools Week* and the *TES*.

Are Free schools a good idea?

Read the following extract and discuss the points that follow.

> **'Fears of "free for all" as government opens up free school bid criteria**
>
> New free schools will be allowed to open if they can demonstrate a significant social need or significant demand from parents. Applicants previously had to demonstrate that there was a need for their new school, caused either by a general shortage of places or because of low standards in existing schools.
>
> The New Schools Network said the changes showed the government's commitment to ensuring that the free schools program offers a real opportunity to create the new schools that parents, pupils and local communities so sorely want and need.'
>
> Source: *Schools Week*, 17/9/2016.

1 What change has taken place in the criteria for opening a Free school?

2 Is it a good idea to allow people to set up and run their own school?

3 If you could do this, what sort of school might you want to create?

(Go to www.newschoolsnetwork.org for more details and examples of existing Free schools.)

The pupil premium

This policy was designed to provide extra money for each student that a school takes who is from a poorer home. This money should then be spent on improving the school's provision to support these students. This could include extra one-to-one support, more teaching assistants or helping to fund music lessons and school trips for these students. The policy was intended to encourage higher-performing schools to admit more disadvantaged children.

Critics argue that the money may not be spent on provision that affects these students' experience in the school and may be used instead to cover cuts to budgets in other areas.

Effects of changes

- Critics argue that marketisation and the increased range of school types available has created a chaotic system. Accountability for educational provision is less clear and has been passed to individual schools, academy chains and parents and businesses through Free schools.
- Supporters of these changes argue that they have increased choice and diversity in education in order to meet the needs of individuals.

Key points

- Recent policy in education has led to greater diversity in educational provision, with the development of new-style academies and Free schools.

- Some recent educational policies, such as the pupil premium, have also attempted to address inequality in education.

Check your understanding: Exam practice

Identify and explain one criticism of the introduction of greater choice in educational provision.　　(4 marks)

How can social class affect achievement?

Objectives
- Explain the nature/nurture debate
- Examine patterns of achievement based on social class

Certain groups (such as working-class pupils, boys and some ethnic minorities) appear to perform relatively badly within the educational system, for instance when measured in terms of examination results and entry to higher education. Such groups are said to underachieve educationally.

Glossary terms

nature, nurture, social class

Nature: This theory suggests that the explanation for educational success and failure lies with natural intelligence. The more extreme view sees intelligence as largely inherited; that is, as genetic. Educational successes and failures are seen as reflecting the different ability levels we are born with.

The nature – nurture debate: is it our genes or is it our social environment?

Nurture: This theory suggests that the explanation for educational success and failure lies with the social environment. Educational achievement is related to social factors such as class, gender, ethnicity, peer groups, family and school organisation.

Sociological explanations for different levels of attainment

Research into educational attainment has gone through various stages.

- During the 1960s and 1970s, **social class** was seen as an important influence on people's lives, so much of the research examined social class and how it could affect achievement levels. Although many of the studies carried out seem dated now, their findings still have relevance for today.
- Later research, in the 1980s and 1990s, focused on a growing interest in the importance of gender and ethnicity as influences on people's lives. Consequently, research into educational achievement has reflected this.
- Many of the areas of importance identified during research on social class, such as parental encouragement and teachers' attitudes, have been re-examined from the point of view of gender and ethnicity. For example, differences in teachers' treatment of male and female students have been examined.
- More recently, researchers have noted the ways in which class, gender and ethnicity combine to influence a person's educational achievement.

Stretch and challenge

Social class, gender, ethnic background and achievement

Researchers have looked at the ways in which different factors may combine to influence achievement.

In what ways do you think social class, gender and ethnic background combine to influence achievement?

Speak to some students and ask them what has influenced their achievement in school – do they think social class, ethnicity or gender have been important?

What do the statistics tell us about social class and achievement?

The term 'social class' is one way of describing a person's position in society (see Chapter 6). An individual's social class is usually determined by looking at their occupation or their parents' occupation. In addition, whether or not a child has access to free school meals can be seen as linked to lower income and thus to social class background. Statistics tend to show that the higher a student's social class background, the greater the chance of that student achieving high educational qualifications.

Sociologists have put forward a number of explanations for the relative underachievement of working-class pupils. Such explanations can be divided into:

- the influence of home environment/background
- the influence of the school environment.

FOCUS ON SKILLS: WRITTEN ACTIVITY

Social class and achievement

Look at the information in the table and then answer the questions below.

Percentage of free school meal (FSM) eligible pupils compared to all other pupils achieving 5 or more A*–C grades at GCSE, including English and Maths

	2014	2015
Free school meals	33.5	33.1
All other pupils	60.5	60.9
Gap	27.0	27.8

Source: Department for Education (2016).

1 Identify the patterns in the table.
2 Make a list of factors or ideas that might explain these patterns in achievement.

FOCUS ON SKILLS: DISCUSSION ACTIVITY

Nature vs nurture

Read over the information about nature and nurture. Identify any evidence or arguments that support the idea of nature influencing achievement, and do the same for nurture.

Which do you feel is the most important influence – nature or nurture? Explain your views.

Key points

- Sociological explanations for differences in achievement mainly focus on the social environment.

- Social class is a key factor here, with students from higher social class backgrounds having a greater chance of achieving higher qualifications.

Check your understanding: Exam practice

Identify and describe one way in which an individual's social environment could influence their achievement. (3 marks)

How can material factors affect achievement?

One question that sociologists ask is: how can the home environment affect educational achievement? A range of explanations has been put forward in answer to this question, based on individuals' home backgrounds or environments. One set of explanations relate to **material deprivation**, which refers to a lack of financial resources, or poverty.

Glossary term

material deprivation

The material environment/material deprivation

In spite of 'free schooling', there is still an obvious connection between the material conditions of the home and educational achievement.

- The Child Poverty Action Group has stressed the costs of school uniforms, sports kits and special materials, for example, which may result in poorer children being kept away from school or being sent home. There is a stigma attached to children who are treated in this way.
- Living conditions: poor housing, overcrowding, lack of privacy or quiet places to do homework adversely affect performance at school (Douglas, 1967). These conditions are more likely to apply to working-class children. In addition, research has revealed that absenteeism (absence from school) is higher among such children.
- Many working-class areas, especially in inner cities, may lack pre-school facilities, such as nursery schools and playgroups. While the introduction of the Sure Start programme may have had some impact here, it has been the victim of government cuts since 2010.

FOCUS ON KEY THINKERS

Halsey, Heath and Ridge (1980): Social class inequality

Halsey, Heath and Ridge's research was based on a sample of 8529 males born between 1913 and 1952 and educated in England and Wales. The social class of participants was based on father's occupation and was divided into three groups:

1 Service class – working as professionals, administrators and managers.
2 Intermediate class – clerical or sales workers, the self-employed and lower-grade technicians and foremen.
3 Working class – including manual workers in industry and agriculture.

Their key finding showed that a boy from the service class, compared to a boy from the working class, had four times as great a chance of being at school at 16, eight times the chance at 17 and ten times the chance at 18. His chance of going to university was eleven times greater than a boy from the working class.

Halsey, Heath and Ridge (1980)

1 What problems can you identify with the sample chosen in this research?

2 Can you think of any criticisms of Halsey, Heath and Ridge's method for deciding on the social class of the participants?

3 This research is now very dated. Do some research of your own to see how these figures may have changed.

Halsey, Heath and Ridge showed that a higher percentage of working-class children than middle-class children left school at the first possible opportunity. Many of the policies introduced by New Labour (see Topic 13) to combat social exclusion, such as the EMA and Aim Higher, were designed to change this situation.

On the other hand, middle-class children may have a head start, as their higher social class position and income may lead to better-quality housing and a greater availability of books and study facilities at home, such as their own room, access to the internet or the ability of their parents to afford private tuition.

What is the influence of material deprivation on achievement?

What causes underachievement?

For each of the factors listed, explain how they could lead to educational underachievement:

- lack of new school uniform or sports kit

- lack of privacy or quiet place in the home

- poor diet, for example no breakfast before arriving in school

- poor attendance through illness

- not having attended a nursery school.

Key points

- Statistics show that the higher a student's social class background, the greater his or her chance of achieving high educational qualifications.

- Children from more privileged backgrounds in general have better material facilities in the home.

Check your understanding: Exam practice

Identify and explain one way in which material deprivation could influence educational achievement. (4 marks)

How can parental attitudes affect achievement?

While material conditions seem to be of great importance in a working-class area, parental attitudes seem to be a more important factor in more prosperous areas. The government Plowden Report (1967) and sociological research by Douglas in the same year both stressed the importance of parental attitudes in determining educational success.

Glossary terms

cultural deprivation, middle-class values, social capital, working-class values

Middle class vs working class

Middle-class values	Working-class values
Desire for control over their lives.	A more passive attitude with a fatalistic acceptance of other people being in control.
Emphasis on future planning.	Emphasis upon present or past.
'Deferred gratification' – being prepared to make sacrifices now in order to fulfil future ambitions; investing for the future. Sacrificing money and time now to ensure a better future (for example, staying on at school or going to college/university).	'Present gratification' – living for the moment with little attempt to plan for the future or get a job.
Individual achievement stressed – by their own efforts, individuals will improve their position.	Collective action stressed – working people will achieve improvements by sticking together (for example, trade union activities).

Some researchers have suggested that middle-class parents and working-class parents socialise their children into different sets of values. It has been suggested that **middle-class values** contribute to the development of ambition, disciplined study and individual striving for success among middle-class children. These values are highly thought of by teachers in school. This may be due to the mainly middle-class backgrounds of teachers. **Working-class values** are less likely to lead to such success, as there is an emphasis upon present gratification and a tendency to accept one's position fatalistically. Thus, middle-class parents are more likely than working-class parents to provide their children with attitudes that contribute to educational success.

Middle-class parents' knowledge of how to 'work the system' may also be an important factor in their children's success. Middle-class parents are more aware of how to hold their own in disagreements with teachers about the teaching of their children and how to fight sexual discrimination; they know what books and periodicals to buy and have the money to buy them. It can be argued that middle-class parents expect more from their children and are more interested in their progress, for example as measured in the frequency and use made of school visits.

Stretch and challenge

The involvement of parents
Consider the following points:

1 Are school visits and parents' evenings a useful way to measure parents' interest in their children's education? List reasons why this might be a good method and also any possible problems with this approach.

2 What method(s) would you use to measure whether or not parents were encouraging their children's education? Make a note of the method(s) chosen and list any possible problems with your approach.

The role of cultural deprivation

Working-class children and those from some ethnic minority groups may suffer as a result of **cultural deprivation.**

It is suggested that schools are based on white middle-class values and assumptions and therefore white middle-class culture dominates. Children from middle-class homes will be advantaged in schools, as their upbringing will provide them with a better opportunity for academic success. For example, family visits to a library or museum will encourage interest in learning and introduce children to key elements of general knowledge and research skills more quickly. The middle-class home is seen as a place where books, educational toys and electronic media are the norm. The working-class child, it is argued, is less likely to receive this kind of upbringing.

FOCUS ON SKILLS: DISCUSSION ACTIVITY

What is 'white, middle-class culture'?

1 Explain what is meant by the idea that, in school, 'white, middle-class culture dominates'.
2 Describe how this idea could explain working-class underachievement.
3 Do you think schools are middle-class environments? Do you think it's possible to generalise about social class culture? Explain your thinking.

FOCUS ON SKILLS: WRITTEN ACTIVITY

Social capital

Read the following comments from a middle-class student that might demonstrate their **social capital** – that is, the social advantages and contacts that they may have access to.

'Well, I know some GPs [General Practitioners are doctors in a local medical practice] who sort of teach there [at university]. I know one who teaches at Imperial and one who teaches at UCL [University College London] and they both recommended it. And then we went to the open days and I really liked them both. I really liked UCL – and I went to a "women in maths" day at UCL and that was really good as well...Then there's the teacher whose daughter went to Cambridge [University] and so I spoke to her about it, her course...And then on my work experience I got to speak to about four or five different GPs, because I was spending time with lots of them, so they all told me which one they would recommend.'

Source: Ball, S. (2003) 'Education and Social Capital, *Sociology Review,* 13, November.

1 List the people this student knew who were useful in helping her to find out more about her chosen university course.
2 What type of social background are they likely to be from?
3 Explain what advantage middle-class students might have as a result of their social background.

Check your understanding: Exam practice

Identify and explain one way in which parents' values and attitudes could influence educational achievement. (4 marks)

Key points

- It can be argued that middle-class and working-class parents have different values and expectations towards education.

- Middle-class values may lead middle-class children to fit in better with the school environment, while working-class children may be culturally deprived.

How might the school affect achievement?

Objectives
- Describe the interactionist approach to studying education
- Examine the influence of labelling and the self-fulfilling prophecy on educational achievement

Interactionist perspectives on education

Interactionists study small-scale interactions between individuals, such as those between teachers and students in the classroom. They are interested in understanding these interactions rather than creating a theory about the role of education in society.

Teachers are unavoidably involved in making judgments and classifying students. These judgments often affect a child's chances of educational achievement.

The 'halo effect'

Some teachers may judge children who are well behaved as 'bright', while they tend to be more questioning about the good performance of those children who are less well behaved. This is known as the **'halo effect'**: students may be typecast on the basis of early impressions based upon their appearance, clothing, manners, speech and school records about their homes. Teachers, in effect, are **labelling** students.

Many sociologists suggest that some teachers' assessments of students tend to reflect the teachers' views of what middle-class and working-class pupils should be capable of, rather than their actual performance. However, Gillborn and Youdell (2000) take this a step further by linking the labelling process to the pressure on schools to appear successful in league tables. This pressure, they argue, influences teachers' existing ideas about which students have the ability to achieve five A*–C grades at GCSE. The result is that 'able' students are seen as middle class. The 'less able' are placed in lower sets and entered for lower-tier exams. In this way, pressure from the education system as a whole and the marketisation of education may lead some teachers to act on these labels.

The 'halo effect'.

Glossary terms

interactionists, labelling, self-fulfilling prophecy

FOCUS ON SKILLS: DISCUSSION ACTIVITY

Labelling students

1 Describe four ways in which teachers give labels to students.

2 For each of the four ways you choose, explain why working-class students may be more likely to receive negative labels.

3 Some students may try to 'reject' the label they are given. Identify and explain one way in which this might happen.

4 How might you go about carrying out research on labelling by teachers? What problems might you encounter?

If teachers have low expectations of working-class children, they may see the student as only being capable of reaching a certain level of academic achievement and may see no point in trying to develop the student's performance any further. This is known as a **self-fulfilling prophecy**.

Testing the self-fulfilling prophecy

Read the following details of a study by Rosenthal and Jacobson, called *Pygmalion in the Classroom* (1968). The study was designed to test the theory of the self-fulfilling prophecy.

'Teachers in an elementary school in California were told by the researchers that they had identified a number of students – the "spurters" – who were likely to make rapid academic progress. The teachers were led to believe that the spurters had been identified as a result of high scores in IQ tests.

In reality, the spurters had simply been selected randomly by the researchers and did not display any greater ability than their classmates. However, a year later it became clear that the spurters had, indeed, made significantly greater progress than the other students.

Rosenthal and Jacobson concluded that the progress of the spurters was a result of the teachers' expectations of them. These higher expectations had been communicated to the students and they had come to believe in the teachers' 'prophecy' about them.'

Source: Rosenthal, R. and Jacobson, L. (1968), *Pygmalion in the Classroom.*

Make a note of your answers to the following questions:

1 In what ways could the teachers have communicated their high expectations to the spurters?
2 What do you think happened to the other students who were not labelled as spurters?
3 If you were a parent of a child at that school, how would you have felt about the research?
4 Can you think of any other factors that could have influenced the spurters' achievements, other than the teachers' 'prophecy'?
5 Having considered the study by Rosenthal and Jacobson, do you think the self-fulfilling prophecy is a useful theory in trying to explain educational underachievement? Explain your answer.

The idea of a self-fulfilling prophecy may put students under pressure to bring their own 'self-image' into line with the teacher's judgment of them. What is the point in trying to improve your maths if the teacher has told you that you are hopeless in the subject? In effect, the student is forced to accept the teacher's 'prophecy' about them.

Again, it is thought that working-class students are more likely to receive a negative 'prophecy' from teachers, whereas middle-class students will receive a more positive one.

Stretch and challenge

Ethics in Rosenthal and Jacobson's research

Note down some reasons why this study may be considered unethical. Was this the only way to research the self-fulfilling prophecy? Explain your answer.

Key points

- Processes within the school may be influential on students' achievements. Teachers may develop labels of students and this may lead to a self-fulfilling prophecy.

- Labels can be positive or negative and students can accept them or attempt to reject them.

Check your understanding: Exam practice

1 Identify and explain one possible effect of teachers labelling students. (4 marks)

2 Describe what sociologists studying education mean by the 'self-fulfilling prophecy'. (3 marks)

What is the influence of streaming and subcultures on achievement?

Objective
- Examine the influence of streaming and the counter-school subculture on educational achievement

Effects of streaming

Streaming into groups, based upon an assessment of general ability, can be seen as an ideal way in which to meet the educational needs of individual students. For example, students will receive a level of work that is appropriate to their needs and abilities, and will be working alongside students of similar ability. Equally, teachers will be able to produce materials and lessons that meet the needs of the students more effectively, as they know what ability range they are to teach.

However, streaming may have undesirable effects, similar to the self-fulfilling prophecy described in Topic 18. For example:

- Students in the lower streams tend to have their confidence damaged and this may result in them not trying to improve their position.
- Even when students are not disheartened, teachers may devote less attention to the students in the lower stream than to those in the higher stream.
- Streaming is often linked to social class, with a disproportionately higher number of lower-stream students being drawn from the working class.
- Transfers between streams are rare in practice.

Glossary terms

counter-school subculture, mixed-ability groups, streaming, subject setting

FOCUS ON KEY THINKERS

Stephen Ball – banding and teacher expectations

In his book *Beachside Comprehensive* (1981), Ball examined the internal organisation of a comprehensive school. He carried out participant observation in the school over three years and looked at the process of moving from banding (a type of streaming) to mixed-ability classes.

In the banding system, students were placed into one of three bands, with the first band containing the most able and the third band containing the least able. Although this was supposed to be based on test scores, Ball found that children from higher social classes were more likely to be placed in the top band.

During his observations, Ball noticed that students' behaviour changed as a result of the bands they were placed in. Ball linked this to the expectations that the teachers had of each band. For example, Band One was expected to be well behaved and hard working, while Band Two students were expected to be difficult and uncooperative. This led to a change in the behaviour of Band Two students to mirror the teachers' expectations and to reflect differences in how they were taught and the exams they were entered for.

With the introduction of mixed-ability classes, pupils were less obviously polarised within the school; however, teachers continued to label middle-class students as the most able and cooperative. Ball noted that this labelling was reflected in exam results.

Some schools have sought to overcome the known problems of streaming by having **mixed-ability groups**, or else they have sought a compromise by having **subject setting**, whereby students are placed into ability groups for each individual subject they study.

The school 'counter-culture' and peer-group pressure

Studies by Hargreaves (1967) of an English boys' secondary modern school, and by Lacey (1970) of a grammar school, suggest that one of the effects of streaming is to lead to the development of a **counter-school subculture** that is opposed to the learning objectives of the school.

The lower-stream students tended to reject the academic values and standards of behaviour expected by the school, which had labelled them as 'failures'. Instead, they evolved a counter-school subculture that stressed defiance of teachers and other uncooperative acts, which provided an alternative form of status for the students, for example being held in high regard by their peers for their actions.

Counter-school subculture stresses defiance of teachers and other uncooperative acts.

FOCUS ON SKILLS: WRITTEN ACTIVITY

Home vs school

1 Create two lists of relevant factors: one headed 'home factors', the other headed 'school factors'.

2 For each set of factors, rank them in order of 'most important' or 'most useful idea', to 'least important' or 'least useful idea'. Be prepared to explain your choices.

3 Do you consider home factors or school factors to be the most important influence on achievement levels between social classes? Make a note of the reasons for your choice.

Check your understanding: Exam practice

Identify and explain one possible effect of streaming in schools.

(4 marks)

FOCUS ON THEORY

Stephen Ball – banding and teacher expectations

1 Why do you think Ball chose to use participant observation rather than methods such as questionnaires and interviews?

2 Outline some of the problems of using participant observation to carry out research in schools.

Stretch and challenge: Discussion activity

Researching counter-school subcultures

In a small group, produce a proposal for how you would go about researching counter-school subcultures.

Consider: the pros and cons of different research approaches in relation to validity, reliability and the ability to generalise.

Key points

- Streaming in schools can have both a positive and a negative influence on students' achievements.

- Some students may become part of a counter-school subculture, which may affect their achievement.

How does Willis view the counter-school culture?

Objectives
- Describe Willis' views on the counter-school culture
- Evaluate Willis' research

FOCUS ON KEY THINKERS

Paul Willis – *Learning to Labour* (1977)

Combining two theories

Willis' research combines both a Marxist and an Interactionist approach to the study of the counter-school subculture (also known as **anti-school subculture**). Willis agrees with the Marxist view that education serves capitalism, but he also shows that working-class students are not simply indoctrinated into ruling-class values without question, but rather are able to resist these values through a counter-school subculture. Willis takes an interactionist approach to attempt to understand the students' experiences of school from their own point of view.

Willis' research approach

Willis studied a school in the Midlands situated in a working-class housing estate. He took an interactionist approach to his research by using observations and participant observation in class and around the school; he recorded regular group discussions; carried out unstructured interviews; and he used diaries. The main focus of his study was a group of 12 working-class boys whom he followed over their last 18 months at school and then over their first few months at work. The group were friends and formed their own distinctive attitude to school – their own counter-school subculture. Willis called them 'the lads'.

Glossary term

anti-school subculture

The counter-school subculture

The counter-school subculture had the following features.

- The lads felt superior to the teachers and to the conformist students, who they called 'the ear 'oles'. They saw no value in the academic or other work of the school and aimed instead to 'have a laff', avoiding lessons, doing as little work as possible and generally rejecting the values of the school.
- Willis argued that the lads were able to see through the myth of meritocracy and sought to go through the process of schooling on their own terms. They were focused instead on entering the world of work as soon as possible and this meant the shop-floor culture of male manual workers.

FOCUS ON RESEARCH: DISCUSSION ACTIVITY

Researching the counter-school subculture

1 For each of the methods used by Willis, discuss what might be their strengths and weaknesses. Can you suggest an alternative approach to this research?

2 What might the benefits and problems of an Interactionist approach be?

Willis' conclusions

Willis tried to show that by rejecting school and not accepting the values taught, the lads actually prepared themselves for their future roles as manual workers in the capitalist economy. The lads chose to do this through their creation of a counter-school subculture, rather than the education system socialising them into their role. In this way, Willis shows that the education system does lead working-class pupils into working-class jobs, but that this is partly a result of the students' own actions and not simply due to the effectiveness of schools as agents of socialisation. In this way, Willis' work represents a challenge to the ideas of Bowles and Gintis (1976; see Topic 6).

Willis argues that by rejecting the values of the school, students prepare themselves for their role in a capitalist economy.

FOCUS ON RESEARCH: WRITTEN ACTIVITY

Evaluating Willis' study

1 How would you criticise Willis' sample?

2 Think about your experiences of counter-school cultures. Would you agree that there is only one type of counter-school culture, similar to the lads, or could it take a variety of forms?

3 In what way does Willis' work represent a challenge to Bowles and Gintis' Marxist view? Explain your thinking.

FOCUS ON THEORY: WRITTEN ACTIVITY

Comparing views on the role of the school

Consider the different ideas covered on the role of the school in achievement – labelling, self-fulfilling prophecy, streaming, counter-school subcultures.

For each idea, write a brief paragraph on how each of the following theories might view it: functionalism, Marxism, feminism.

Check your understanding: Exam practice

Identify the research method used by Willis and explain one disadvantage of using this method. (4 marks)

Key point

Willis combines a Marxist and interactionist approach in his study. He shows how the school may not be effective in simply creating workers for capitalism, but rather that working-class students' rejection of the values of the school leads them into working-class jobs.

Why has achievement for females improved?

Objectives
- Describe different patterns of achievement for students by gender
- Explain reasons for improvements in the educational performance of girls

Differences in male and female achievement

Glossary terms

feminism, patriarchy

Official statistics reveal some differences in educational achievement based on gender.

FOCUS ON SKILLS: WRITTEN ACTIVITY

Looking at gender and achievement

Examine the following statistics on gender and achievement:

Percentage achieving 5+ A*–C grades at GCSE including English and Maths

	Girls	Boys	Gap
2014	58.9	48.2	10.7
2015	58.9	49.0	9.9

Source: Adapted from DfE (2014/15).

Percentage achieving A*–C grades at A level by subject, June 2016 (all UK candidates)

	Males	Females
Chemistry	76.9	77.1
Physics	70.6	74.2
Maths	79.8	80.8
History	81.2	85.1
Sociology	68.8	76.3
Art and design	77.6	85.4
English	77.6	81.9

Source: adapted from JCQ (2016).

1 Outline the differences in achievement levels between female and male students at GCSE and A level.

2 Make a list of factors or ideas that might explain these differences in achievement.

At university level the following patterns exist:
- Women in the UK are 35 per cent more likely than men to go to university.
- In 1990, 34 000 women graduated from universities compared to 43 000 men. By 2000 the reverse was true, with 133 000 women graduating compared to 110 000 men.

Source: Hillman, N. and Robinson, N., 'Boys to Men: The Underachievement of Young Men in Higher Education and How to Start Tackling it.' Higher Education Policy Institute.

How can we explain these differences?

The feminist movement

Feminism has led to changes in attitudes towards women's roles and expectations. In the past, boys were usually expected to go on to work and support a family. Girls were expected to make marriage and motherhood their primary concerns. Feminism has helped to challenge these ideas and to give girls greater confidence in their abilities.

Sharpe's research (1994) compared the attitudes of girls in the 1970s to those of the 1990s. Rather than valuing marriage, love and husbands, as had been the case in the 1970s, attitudes had changed and girls valued careers and being able to support themselves most highly. This change is also reflected in Fuller's study (2011), which showed that educational success and the ability to have a professional career were key elements of girl's identity.

Liberal feminists argue that further progress can be made by developing more policies to improve equality, as well as challenging sexist attitudes and stereotypes. Radical feminists argue the system still remains **patriarchal** despite improved achievement for girls. Girls still experience sexism in schools; subject areas still under-represent women's achievements; and male teachers are still more likely to become the heads of secondary schools.

Changing job opportunities

In the future, it is predicted that more women than men will be working. It is also predicted that there will be further decreases in traditionally 'male' jobs in manufacturing and engineering, but a continued increase in 'female' jobs in service industries.

Legal changes and equal opportunities policies

The Sex Discrimination Act (1975) makes sex discrimination in education illegal. It has raised awareness of equal opportunities policies in schools and colleges. For example, Kelly's research (1981) demonstrated that science was a 'male' subject as a result of textbook images, male role models and the dominance in the classroom of male teachers and male students. As a result, national projects such as GIST (Girls into Science and Technology) and GATE (Girls And Technology Education) were set up to try to encourage girls' participation and success in science and technical subjects.

The introduction of the National Curriculum

The National Curriculum has meant that girls and boys in both primary and secondary schools have equal access to the same subjects, and some subjects are compulsory for all students, such as science.

Check your understanding: Exam practice

Identify and explain one reason why female students may achieve better grades in school than in the 1970s.   (4 marks)

Sharpe's research (1994) showed that women are aiming for the top jobs.

Key points

- Although achievement levels for both males and females have improved, female achievement levels are higher overall.

- A range of factors in both the education system and the wider society can be identified to help explain this pattern.

How can we explain differences in subject choice between males and females?

Murphy and Elwood (1999) argue that children learn their gender roles within the home. This relates to how parents treat their children and the expectations they have of them. These early experiences may lead to children associating themselves with certain broad subject areas later on. For example, boys may have more experience of science-related equipment outside of school and this familiarity helps them to see science as a 'male' subject.

For other researchers, such as Mitsos and Browne (1998), factors within the school are also important. These might include:

- gender stereotyping in textbooks
- the continued absence of female role models in science and maths textbooks
- continued stereotyping by teachers
- male domination of equipment in the science classroom.

Glossary term

single-sex schools

FOCUS ON SKILLS: WRITTEN ACTIVITY

Patterns in subject choices at A level

Examine the following statistics on gender and subject choice.

Entries by subject at A level, 2016

	Males	**Females**
Chemistry	25 937	25 874
Physics	27 699	7 645
Mathematics	56 535	35 628
History	25 252	29 497
Sociology	7 848	26 132
Art and design	10 315	32 927
English	22 980	61 730

Source: adapted from JCQ (2016).

1. Identify which subjects seem to be most strongly dominated by males and which by females. Calculate the differences in entries for each subject.
2. Note down some ways in which you might explain these patterns, bearing in mind that female students outperform males in each of these areas at GCSE level (A–C grades).
3. What effects might these patterns have on future career choices?

FOCUS ON RESEARCH: RESEARCH ACTIVITY

Making a choice of subjects

Carry out some research on student subject choices.

1. Select a sample of students who either have made, or will be making, choices about subjects for GCSE, A level or university degree.
2. Use questionnaires or unstructured interviews to find out what factors may influence their choices.
3. Try to use your results to explain differences in subject choice between male and female students at both A level and degree level.
4. How useful do you think your research approach was?

Single-sex or mixed schools?

Some researchers have seen **single-sex schools** as benefiting female students' achievement levels. In particular, they are thought to help to improve girls' performance in traditionally 'male' subject areas such as maths. This may also then have an influence on subject choices made at GCSE level and post-16.

Another theory that has been tried out in a small number of mixed-sex schools is that of single-sex classrooms. The idea here is that female and male students are taught separately for certain subjects in an attempt to remove the disruptive influence of the opposite sex.

FOCUS ON SKILLS: DISCUSSION ACTIVITY

Are single-sex schools and classrooms best?

Read the extract and consider the following questions.

'Teaching girls in single-sex schools, long an obsession of many parents worried about their daughters being distracted by boys, makes no difference to their attainment according to a comprehensive study by Alan Smithers, Professor of Education at Buckingham University and one of Britain's most respected school experts.

…"the reason people think single-sex schools are better is because they do well in league tables', said Smithers. "But they are generally independent, grammar or former grammar schools and they do well because of the ability and the social background of the pupils."

…a growing movement in the US suggests that boys' and girls' brains develop differently, so they benefit from separate teaching styles. In Britain, more and more mixed schools are using single-sex classes because of concerns over boys' results.

…this study comes after research published last month in Scotland showed that even in a co-educational school, separating pupils into single-sex classes failed to improve boys' performance. Rather…the move led to greater indiscipline.'

Source: article by A. Asthana, in *Observer*, 25/06 2006.

Using the extract and your own ideas, discuss the possible benefits and problems of both single-sex schools and classrooms in the following areas:

- raising achievement levels
- students' making subject choices
- students' social development.

Check your understanding: Exam practice

Identify and explain one reason why male and female students often choose different subjects in higher education.   (4 marks)

Key points

- Differences exist in subject choices between males and females – particularly in post-16 education.
- These differences may be related to influences from home, the wider society or from within the education system.
- Single-sex schools and classrooms have been identified as a possible way of addressing these differences and to raise achievement generally.

Why is the performance of female students improving faster than that of male students?

Statistics suggest that the achievement levels of males, although improving, are not doing so at the same rate as that of females. A number of explanations have been suggested for this trend.

Harris's (Harris et al., 1993) research into the attitudes of 16-year-olds from mainly working-class backgrounds has shown that:

- Boys are thought to be suffering increasingly from low self-esteem and poor motivation.
- Boys seem to be less willing to struggle to overcome difficulties in understanding their work.
- Boys are less likely to work consistently hard than girls and are more easily distracted. In areas such as coursework, boys found it more difficult to organise their time effectively.
- Girls are more willing to do homework and also to spend more time on it.
- Girls give more thought to their futures and to the importance of qualifications in this, whereas boys do not seem as concerned.

Although things may have changed since Harris's study was carried out, more recent research has identified some further explanations:

- Moir and Moir (1998) suggest that schools have become too 'girl friendly' and boys are now forced to learn in ways that don't suit them. This may include an emphasis on verbal skills and a non-competitive environment.
- Katz (2000) argues that peer pressure, the fear of ridicule and the need to fit in all contribute to boys not being seen to 'try'.
- Katz also argues that low self-esteem in boys may be linked to images of incompetent men found in advertising, sitcoms, soaps and so on. Low self-esteem may also be linked to the decline in traditional male jobs, leaving boys uncertain about their futures and lacking motivation.
- James (2000) suggests that women have reassessed their role in society and recognise that work and a career (and thus education) is very much a part of their role. Boys, however, are now going through this process of reassessment of what is 'masculine' in society. At present, being a 'geek' is not part of masculinity and this may be a barrier to some boys taking education seriously.

Do girls try harder than boys?

Are girls less distracted than boys?

Why do some male students underachieve?

In a small group, discuss the explanations given for male underachievement in relation to females.

1 Which ones do you agree or disagree with? Make a note of these.

2 Discuss and make a note of at least two other possible explanations.

3 Take each explanation in turn and try to suggest why it is happening.

Stretch and challenge

Changing patterns according to gender

We have examined the changes in patterns of achievement according to gender. While female students still seem to choose 'female' subjects at A level and degree level, it is clear that they are now outperforming males in all areas and that this may lead to some important changes.

Using the information in this section, describe three possible consequences of the changing patterns in attainment according to gender.

Unstructured interviews

Arrange to carry out unstructured interviews with a small number of male and female students. Try to find out their views on the factors that may be leading to different levels of performance.

Evaluate how useful using an unstructured interview proved to be.

Key points

- Although achievement levels for males are increasing overall, male students appear to be underperforming compared to female students.

- A number of factors have been linked to this pattern. These relate to the influence of males' own attitudes to studying, changes within schools and the education system, and changes in the wider society in terms of traditional male roles.

Check your understanding: Exam practice

Identify and explain one reason why male students often achieve lower grades than female students. (4 marks)

What are the patterns of educational attainment for ethnicity and achievement?

Objective
- Identify differences in achievement levels for different ethnic groups

What do the statistics tell us?

Statistics show that educational achievement is, to some extent, related to ethnicity. Students from some ethnic backgrounds tend to underachieve educationally (that is, they do not achieve their full potential and tend to perform relatively poorly in exams), while others over achieve.

FOCUS ON SKILLS: WRITTEN ACTIVITY

Educational attainment among ethnic groups

Examine the following statistics on ethnicity and achievement, then answer the questions that follow.

Percentage of pupils achieving 5+ A*–C GCSE grades including English and Maths, England, state-funded schools, 2015 (including national figure for comparison)

Chinese	76.6
Asian	61.1
Mixed	58.1
National	**57.1**
White	56.8
Black	52.0

Source: DfE (2016).

Percentage of pupils achieving 5+ A*–C GCSE grades including English and Maths, England, 2013–14

Chinese	74.4
Indian	72.9
White and Asian parentage	67.2
Irish	65.9
Bangladeshi	61.3
Any other mixed background	60.6
White and Black African parentage	56.8
Black African	56.8
National	**56.6**
White British	56.4
Pakistani	51.4
White and Black Caribbean parentage	49.0
Black Caribbean	47.0
Gypsy/Roma	8.2

Source: DfE (2015).

1 Identify the patterns in educational attainment for different ethnic groups.
2 Identify how far above or below the national figure each group is.
3 What differences do you notice in the ways people's ethnic backgrounds have been categorised in the two tables?

Are there any problems with using such statistics?

- Note that many studies use categories to classify ethnic groups that are too general. For example, studies that use the term 'Asian' would not allow us to see differences in achievement levels between Indian, Pakistani and Bangladeshi students.
- Most of the statistics produced do not allow us to examine the possible influence of social class background in relation to ethnicity.

Explaining the relationship between ethnicity and educational achievement

As with social class and gender, it is clear that factors other than nature or genetically inherited abilities may be more important in explaining the relative success or failure of different ethnic groups. Indeed, the Swann Committee, which was appointed by the government in 1985 to examine the position of ethnic minorities in the education system, ruled out IQ as a cause of differences in attainment.

FOCUS ON SKILLS: DISCUSSION ACTIVITY

Researching ethnicity and achievement

What sort of issues might a researcher need to consider when looking at reasons for differences in achievement levels for different ethnic groups?

You might consider:

- ethical issues, such as confidentiality or the potentially sensitive nature of looking at the achievement levels of groups

- the ways in which the characteristics of the researcher may affect the research – for example, the age or ethnicity of the researcher

- decisions about appropriate methods to use, for example whether it may be better to carry out questionnaires or to use unstructured interviews. How might a particular method be more or less appropriate for researching this topic?

Be ready to explain your ideas and how they relate to the specific topic of researching ethnicity and achievement.

Check your understanding: Exam practice

Identify and describe one problem in using official statistics to examine the educational achievement of different ethnic groups. (3 marks)

Making connections

Read over the sections on social class and achievement, and gender and achievement.

Identify the key factors influencing achievement from these sections, for example material deprivation or labelling.

Now identify how you think each of these factors might have an effect on the achievement of students from different ethnic backgrounds.

When you have done this, try to write a paragraph to explain how ethnicity, social class and gender may combine to influence students' achievement levels.

Making connections

Think about each of the other topics you have covered, on the course, such as Families.

For each topic, produce a concept map showing how it might be related to ethnicity and educational achievement.

Key points

- Statistics show different levels of achievement for different ethnic groups.

- Research shows that IQ is not a major factor and that other factors relating to social background may be more influential.

Are social class and cultural factors influential?

The home and social class background

These explanations stress the importance of social class and culture to educational success.

Reid (1996) pointed out that differences in achievement may be due to class factors or class in combination with ethnicity. Class position may also be influenced by the types of work offered to groups coming to Britain, as well as the class background and resources that people had prior to arriving in Britain. In this way, many of the factors affecting the attainment of working-class and middle-class students may also affect some ethnic minority students. In other words, there is a kind of 'doubling up' of factors. Thus, some of the differences in achievement between ethnic groups may simply reflect social class differences.

FOCUS ON SKILLS: DISCUSSION ACTIVITY

Ethnicity, class and achievement

Examine the following extract:

'Minority ethnic pupils are more likely to experience deprivation than White British pupils, especially Pakistani, Bangladeshi, Black African and Black Caribbean pupils. For example, 70% of Bangladeshi pupils and almost 60% of Pakistani and Black African pupils live in the 20% most deprived postcode areas (as defined by the Index of Multiple Deprivation) compared to less than 20% of White British pupils.'

Source: 'Ethnicity and Education: The Evidence on Minority Ethnic Pupils Aged 5–16', DFES research paper (2006).

Explain how the information in the extract supports the idea that social class may be a key influence in explaining differences in achievement between different ethnic groups.

Cultural differences

This view suggests that the cultural norms and values of some ethnic minority groups may be different to 'mainstream' cultural norms and values. This may affect students' achievement because schools are seen to be institutions where white, 'mainstream' norms and values dominate.

It has been argued that the language spoken at home may also be an important factor affecting achievement. Some children who have only recently arrived in the UK may speak English as a second language and, as a result, they may be disadvantaged at school.

However, as Clarke (1997) points out, the issue of language may be more complex than at first appears. Some students from various parts of India, Pakistan or Bangladesh may speak up to eight languages. This may lead to some confusion when English is introduced as an additional language or, alternatively, may demonstrate an ability to quickly absorb and use a new language. The fact that students from an Indian background are such high achievers at present perhaps demonstrates that language may not be an important factor.

Parental expectations

Some sociologists have argued that the level of encouragement that children receive from their parents or guardians can explain educational success and failure. From this point of view, it has been argued that parents from some ethnic minority groups are less interested in their children's education than parents from other groups. However, there is plenty of evidence to suggest that this view is inaccurate.

A study by the Inner London Education Authority in 1987 reported that Indian families put pressure on their children to succeed and that this affected their performance in a positive way. In a number of areas, African Caribbean parents established Saturday schools because they were worried about their children's under achievement. Indeed, Ken Pryce's study of the African-Caribbean community in Bristol in 1979 showed that parents had very high academic aspirations for their children.

Bhatti (1999) found that for some Asian parents, who were often poorly educated themselves, there was a strong desire to help their children's education more. However, the parents in her sample felt a sense of frustration at their lack of knowledge of school and the education system—the school's lack of interest in them and the gap between their own experiences and their children's, which led to a difficulty in understanding their children's daily lives.

FOCUS ON SKILLS: DISCUSSION ACTIVITY

Is school dominated by a white, mainstream culture?

Discuss how the following aspects of school life may affect the achievements of some ethnic minority students.

- Expectations about clothing may not take into account some minority cultures' norms and values.
- Teaching staff may not be from minority ethnic groups.
- The holidays celebrated may not be those of some minority ethnic groups.
- The types of food available may not meet the needs of all minority cultures.

Check your understanding: Exam practice

Identify and explain one home factor that may affect attainment levels for some ethnic groups. (4 marks)

Key points

- Various explanations have been given relating to cultural differences.
- Social class background and gender seem influential, suggesting that explanations relating to these two factors are also relevant.

What is the role of the school in ethnicity and achievement?

Objective
- Explain how the school and processes such as labelling may affect achievement

The following explanations stress the importance of the school environment to educational success for ethnic minorities.

Glossary terms

biased, ethnocentric curriculum, stereotype

The type of school attended

Some research suggests that the main factor in explaining differences in educational attainment is not a student's ethnic background or culture but the school attended.

Smith and Tomlinson (1989), in a study of 18 comprehensive schools, identified a range of important influences within the school, including the quality of teaching and the resources available, as well as the attitudes and policies relating to providing equal opportunities within the school. They concluded that ethnic minority students who went to good schools would do as well as white students in these schools.

Stretch and challenge

Were Smith and Tomlinson correct?

Smith and Tomlinson's research has been criticised in a number of ways:

- the size of the sample
- the failure to include a mix of schools with both large and small numbers of students
- the sample was not nationally representative
- some schools had large numbers of African-Caribbean students, while some had small numbers.

1 Explain how the points listed may affect the value of the research of Smith and Tomlinson into the influence exerted by the type of school attended.

2 Note down some other possible problems associated with research into this area.

Labelling and teacher expectation

Some sociologists argue that some teachers have **stereotyped** views and expectations of students, which are influenced by the child's ethnic origin. These stereotypes may also reflect social class and gender. For example, some teachers may have higher expectations of Asian students – they are considered to be capable and hard working – with Asian girls seen as quiet and passive.

Research also shows that some teachers believe that children from an African-Caribbean background are less academic than those from other ethnic backgrounds, with African-Caribbean boys being seen as more disruptive. Teachers expect less, so these students do not receive as much encouragement as other students. However, as Mirza (1997) notes, there is evidence that young African-Caribbean girls have a strong desire and motivation to succeed, which may allow them to reject the negative labels given to them. In this way, the teachers' labels may lead to a self-fulfilling prophecy through which the students' educational achievement is affected, but this may depend on a variety of factors such as gender.

The hidden curriculum

Some sociologists explain the underachievement of some ethnic groups in terms of the hidden curriculum. For example, it is argued that subjects that students study (for instance, history) are **biased** towards a white European culture. Some books may present stereotypical images of some minority groups, or they may ignore ethnic minorities altogether. This may lead, for example, to a sense of not being valued for some students, which may, in turn, lead to underachievement. This is known as the **ethnocentric curriculum.**

FOCUS ON SKILLS: WRITTEN ACTIVITY

Teachers' labels and stereotypes

Mac an Ghaill (1992) found in interviews with Asian and African-Caribbean students that teachers might label students in terms of subject ability, with African-Caribbean girls encouraged to do music and sport. For some Asian students, whether they were seen as 'bad' depended on whether they were the main minority ethnic group in a school. Stereotypes included assumptions about arranged marriage and that Asian female students would be neat and know little about football.

1 What do the comments of the students tell us about the usefulness of the general term 'ethnic minority' when looking at teachers' labels and stereotypes?

2 One African-Caribbean girl states that she was encouraged to do music and sports. Why do you think teachers selected these particular subjects?

3 One girl states that teachers stereotyped Asians as 'bad' in her school if they were the main minority ethnic group. What might this tell us about the attitudes of some teachers?

4 What points do the students make about the different stereotypical labels given to female students?

Check your understanding: Exam practice

Identify and explain one way in which teachers might influence the educational achievement of ethnic minority students. (4 marks)

Key points

• The concept of labelling can explain some teachers' attitudes to different ethnic groups. This is made more complex by differences in labels relating to gender, and labels may vary between ethnic groups.

• The hidden curriculum may also present stereotypical images of some groups.

What methods are used to research education?

Objectives
- Describe some of the methods used to research education
- Evaluate these methods

FOCUS ON RESEARCH: WRITTEN ACTIVITY

Stephen Ball, Richard Bowe and Sharon Gewirtz – Parental choice

This research was conducted between 1991 and 1994 in 15 secondary schools. The schools were of different types and the students came from a range of backgrounds. The researchers visited the schools, attended meetings, examined documents and interviewed a sample of teachers. They also interviewed about 150 parents of primary school children who were choosing their secondary schools. In addition, they interviewed some primary head teachers and looked at local authority documents about patterns of choice over a period of time.

1 What type of research approach did this study take overall?
2 What sorts of problems might Ball, Bowe and Gewirtz have encountered when interviewing the teachers?
3 Can you think of any practical problems they may have encountered when interviewing parents?

FOCUS ON RESEARCH: WRITTEN ACTIVITY

Influences on league tables: David Gillborn and Deborah Youdell – the A–C economy

Read the following extract:

'Schools have become dominated by a need to appear in a good position in league tables, of which the principal measure of success is the number of pupils achieving five A–C passes…[a school's] position in these tables can attract parents to send their children to certain schools. Income is generated by pupil numbers. This creates an ethos … which the research team call *the A–C economy.*

Schools are also pressured into tackling that small group of pupils who are on the borderline between achieving five A–Cs and failing to gain that target. Already teachers focus on those who will improve the A–C rate for the whole school by gaining more than five passes, but now the borderliners are brought into policy planning. This leaves those who are not entered or predicted to fail in a position of increasing inequality of provision and attention.'

Source: adapted from Gillborn and Youdell (2000) 'Rationing Education: Policy, Practice, Reform and Equity', in Blundell and Griffiths (2002) Sociology since 1995.

Gillborn and Youdell carried out their research in two secondary schools in London. They used a qualitative approach, carrying out interviews and observations with teachers and with pupils between the ages of 13 and 16 years.

1 Summarise the findings from this piece of research.
2 How might teachers react to being interviewed about the practices described in the research?
3 How might students respond when interviewed by researchers who have come into their school?
4 What comments might you make about the sample in this piece of research?

Do we need more teachers from ethnic minority groups? Cecile Wright – multi racial primary school classrooms

Wright (1992) carried out an ethnographic study of four inner-city primary schools. This involved classroom observation; observations outside of the classroom; informal interviews with teachers; interviews with parents; and an examination of test results.

Read the following extract:

'Experiences such as these led African-Caribbean boys to identify their relationships with teachers as a special difficulty. Samuel, a 7-year-old African-Caribbean child at school B, talked of what he perceived to be the teachers' unfair treatment of other African-Caribbean pupils:

Samuel:	I always get done and always get picked on...I want to go to a black school with all black teachers, it's better. I want to go to a school with just black people.
Researcher:	Why?
Samuel:	Because when you go to a school with white people they give you horrible food and you're always picked on when you don't do nothing. When it's white people, they just say stop that and stop doing this.
Researcher:	Are you saying that you would like some black teachers here [in the school]?
Samuel:	Yes.'

Source: Wright, C. (1992) 'Multi-racial primary school classrooms', in D. Gill, B. Mayor and M. Blair (eds), *Racism and Education – Structures and Strategies.* London: Sage.

1 How easy do you think it might be to gain access to a school to carry out observations?
2 What ethical issues might there be when observing in a primary school?
3 Cecile Wright found that her African-Caribbean ethnicity had an impact on the research. Explain how this might have had an impact.

Are teachers good research subjects? Are schools easy places in which to carry out research?

Check your understanding: Exam practice

1   Identify and describe one ethical issue that sociologists may face when carrying out research in schools.   (3 marks)

2   Identify and explain one disadvantage of using overt observation when carrying out research in schools.   (4 marks)

Key points

• A range of research methods may be suitable for studying different aspects of education.

• However, researchers need to consider the difficulties presented in studying students, teachers and parents, as well as in gaining access to educational settings in the first place.

Focus on skills

FOCUS ON SKILLS: WRITTEN ACTIVITY

Home vs school

When considering the different influences on educational achievement, it is sometimes useful to consider them in terms of home and school influences.

For each topic linked to achievement, produce a table like the one below, to show the home and school influences.

	Home	School
Social class		
Gender		
Female achievement		
Male underachievement		
Ethnicity		

Making connections: Written activity

Factors affecting achievement

It is important to recognise that class, gender and ethnicity do not influence students in completely separate ways. Instead, they are connected and intertwined. For example, working-class girls do not all underachieve; ethnic background can also be a factor that combines with gender and class.

Look at the table and then answer the questions.

Percentage of FSM-eligible pupils achieving 5+ A*–C grades including English and Maths for selected ethnic groups by gender (where FSM is free school meals), England, state-funded schools, 2015

White British FSM boys	24.0
Black Caribbean FSM boys	24.4
White British FSM girls	32.0
Black Caribbean FSM girls	40.9
National average	**57.1**
Indian FSM girls	58.2
Bangladeshi FSM girls	59.6
Chinese FSM boys	67.6
Chinese FSM girls	80.6

Source: DfE (2016).

1 Which groups perform above the national average?

2 Which is the lowest-performing group overall?

3 Can you suggest any explanations for this, using the knowledge you have from education and other topic areas?

4 Which groups' achievement seems not to be affected by social class differences?

5 How would you explain the gender differences in these tables, using the knowledge you have from education and other topic areas?

Researching education

When considering carrying out research into education, a number of factors may need to be considered.

For each factor in the following list, discuss how it might influence the research process:

- researching inside classrooms
- researching students
- researching parents
- researching schools.

What things might a researcher have to consider? You might explore issues such as access, time, validity of the findings, ethical considerations and so on.

Making connections: Discussion activity

Socialisation

It is important to be able to see how ideas learned from other topic areas can link together; in this case, how socialisation may take place in society and how it may impact upon an individual's educational experiences.

In a small group:

1 Identify two other ways in which socialisation may take place in society.
2 Discuss how the values learned through both of the ways you have identified may affect an individual's experience of education.

As part of your preparation for the exam, it is important to think about how the theories you have studied might link to specific topic areas.

Complete a table similar to the one below by explaining what the view of each theory might be on the topics listed.

	Functionalism	Marxism
Social policy on education		
Differences in achievement		

Research methods in education

Developing your ability to apply your knowledge of research methods to education is a key skill to work on.

Read over the following information and then plan an answer to the question that follows:

Many students experience material deprivation in the home, which can include a lack of income, poor housing conditions and poor diet. This may be a difficult position for both the students and their parents and can have an impact on the achievement levels of students from poorer backgrounds.

How useful do you think it would be to use questionnaires to research this topic area?

In your planning, think about the strengths and weaknesses of questionnaires, but also think about how useful they would be for researching this particular topic area.

Education (Paper 1)

In this section we look at what the Education section of Paper 1 will look like, with some possible questions and marked candidate responses.*

*Please be aware that marks are advisory, based on sample AQA materials. Examination grade boundaries and marking guidance change annually – please visit the official AQA website for more information.

01 Which of the following is a term commonly used by sociologists to describe schools that charge fees for pupils to attend? **[1 mark]**

A Grammar school ◯

B Academy ◯

C Comprehensive school ◯

D Independent school ✔ 1/1

Tip: Read these questions carefully! Often, in the hurry to get started, candidates can misread the question and lose what is essentially an easy mark.

Tip: In the exam, you will simply need to tick whichever you think is the correct answer.

02 Describe the hidden curriculum. **[3 marks]**

The hidden curriculum refers to things students may be taught outside of their normal lessons in school. For example, students are taught in school to turn up to lessons on time and wear uniform and punishments may be used if students don't do these things. This means that when students finish school they know the norms and values of society like turning up to work on time.

Examiner comment: The candidate has given a coherent description of the hidden curriculum with examples. They have also used really good language such as 'norms and values'. 3/3

Item A

Attainment of 5 or more GCSE grades A*–C in Year 11 (2003–2006), percentages

Parental occupation	2003	2006
Higher professional	76	81
Lower professional	65	73
Intermediate	53	59
Lower supervisory	41	46
Routine	33	42
Other/not classified (e.g. no occupation)	34	34

Academic achievement in Year 11 GCSE (2006), percentages

Free school meals	5+	8+	5–7	1–4	5+	1–4	none
	A*–C	A*–C	A*–C	A*–C	D–G	D–G	
No	60	45	15	22	11	4	3
Yes	31	18	13	27	20	14	8

Source: Youth Cohort Study (2008).

Tip: Be sure to study items carefully. Pay extra attention to things such as dates and who conducted the research, as this will be crucial to answering the next couple of questions, which will test how well you have read the item. You could be asked about the type of research methods that the researcher has used, strengths or weaknesses of the research, or even to identify trends, patterns or make observations.

Tip: The three questions that follow in the actual exam will expect you to have the 'context' of this item in mind. Try to refer to it whenever you can!

03 From **Item A**, examine **one** strength of the research. **[2 marks]**

The research in item A is quantitative research; while such research may lack some depth (for example, if someone fits the criteria for being in the routine class they may not see themselves as in this class) it does allow sociologists to spot patterns and trends easily.

Examiner comment: The first lines of this response are not relevant as the candidate is essentially explaining a weakness of quantitative research; the underlined part of the response is enough to score one mark as it is one strength of quantitative research, but this part of the answer needed more development for the second mark. 1/2

04 Identify and explain **one** factor that may have led to the increases in the attainment of five or more GCSEs grade A*–C between 2003 and 2006 shown in **Item A**. **[4 marks]**

Item A shows that the number of students who achieved 5 A*–C GCSEs increased among all parental occupation groups except other/non classified. The biggest increase in achievement was seen among children whose parents had routine occupations; where 9% more children achieved 5 A*–Cs in 2006 when compared to 2003. One factor that may have led to these increases could be the government's Academy programme.

Examiner comment: The candidate has identified one possible factor that could have led to the increase in attainment (which is underlined), but the rest of the response is largely irrelevant to the question (although it does prove that the candidate is able to read the item correctly). To gain more marks, this response needed to explain how or why the academy programme may have led to these increases in attainment. 2/4

05 Identify and describe **one** consequence of streaming pupils in schools. **[4 marks]**

One consequence of streaming in schools could be that students do less well because of labelling. Teachers may label students in lower sets as 'less able' and then reflect this in the way they teach them, perhaps setting them low targets such as '2' grades at GCSE. The students in these lower sets may then begin to believe that they are not very clever.

Examiner comment: The candidate has shown a limited knowledge of labelling and indicated how negative labels could affect students (e.g. they achieve less well). To score more marks, this answer needs to be further developed, perhaps referring to the self-fulfilling prophecy with an example. 2/4

06 Discuss how far sociologists agree that a pupil's gender is the main reason for differences in educational achievement. **[12 marks]**

Sociologists would have differing views about the importance of gender on the achievement of students at school. Research suggests that in most subjects and at most stages of education girls achieve better than boys.

Moir and Moir argue that changes to schools in recent years, such as the introduction of the national curriculum and coursework, have made schools more girl friendly. As girls have more of a bedroom culture than boys (meaning they are watched more and tend to spend more time at home) they are better at doing homework and studying for tests; this means that gender may explain the differences in achievement between boys and girls.

However, there are other factors that could explain differences in educational achievement. For example, Item A shows that students whose parents have 'higher' professional occupations are more likely to achieve 5 A*–C at GCSE. Some sociologists would argue that this is evidence that social class is the most important factor in educational achievement, as students in higher social classes are more likely to do well.

Tip: In the essays, you are being assessed on four things: 1. Sociological knowledge (A01: 4 marks); 2. Your ability to apply knowledge of theories, research and methods (AO2: 4 marks); 3. Your ability to evaluate sociological theories and concepts (AO3: 4 marks); 4. Your ability to write clearly and coherently, spelling well and using specialist terms accurately will affect the total mark you receive. If your response is not well structured (e.g. in bullet points), even if you have demonstrated knowledge, application and evaluation, you will be unable to go beyond 7–9 marks.

Examiner comment: The candidate has presented simple arguments to both agree and disagree with the statement. The general lack of development of the arguments and the heavy reliance on the item (as well as the lack of a clear conclusion) prevent this essay scoring higher marks. 4/12

Crime and deviance

5

What is meant by crime and deviance?

Objective
- Explain the difference between crime and deviance

Many of us are likely to have experienced **crime** at some point in our lives. Some of us, for example, may have committed a crime or been the victim of one. Even if we have not had direct experience of crime, we will almost certainly have come across it secondhand in the mass media, for instance in the press, TV news broadcasts and reality-based crime programmes such as *Crimewatch*.

Issues related to crime are controversial and cause heated discussions within the media and among politicians. Crime is also a major focus of public concern and debate. These debates focus on wide-ranging issues such as violent crime, sentencing, the treatment of young offenders, overcrowding in prisons, cybercrime and **identity theft**, **terrorism**, human trafficking and illegal immigration.

Sociologists are interested in studying criminal behaviour, but they also explore the role of **deviance** in society. The distinction between crime and deviance is an important one in sociology.

- A crime is an illegal act punishable by **law**. Crime involves actions such as robbery, fraud or shoplifting that break the criminal law and, if detected, can result in criminal proceedings.
- Deviance refers to behaviour that does not conform to a society's rules and norms. It is disapproved of by most people in that particular society and, if detected, is likely to lead to **negative sanctions**.

....
Glossary terms

crime, deviance, identity theft, law, negative sanctions, terrorism
....

Body modification as extreme deviance or art?

FOCUS ON SKILLS: DISCUSSION ACTIVITY

Deviant behaviour

1 In a small group, discuss the following actions and decide whether you would class any of them as deviant behaviour:
   - using a fake ID to get into a club
   - sitting next to a stranger on an empty bus
   - stealing a jumper from a charity shop
   - reading a partner's text messages
   - smoking cannabis in the cinema
   - helping a friend to commit suicide.

2 Of those acts that you have classed as deviant, decide which one is the most serious and which is the least serious. Note down your decisions and your reasons.

Goode (2008) argues that deviance may be mild or it may be more extreme. In the case of mild deviance, such as telling a little lie or parking illegally, the penalties imposed might involve harsh words or a small fine. However, we would not think of a person who tells a lie or parks on double yellow lines as a deviant. Extreme deviance includes behaviour or beliefs that are so far outside the norms that they generate very strong negative reactions from others. Examples include people who are extremely heavily tattooed or pierced and people who claim they have been abducted by aliens (Goode, 2008).

Is all deviance necessarily illegal?

We have seen that a crime is an illegal act and deviance breaks society's norms or social rules. Some, but not all, deviant acts are also against the law. This means that deviant behaviour includes both legal and illegal activities. Legal deviance is behaviour that is considered 'abnormal' in some way by most people in a society. Illegal deviance is criminal behaviour that is punishable by the state.

Is all crime necessarily seen as deviant?

Some acts are illegal, but they are not necessarily always considered deviant by everyone. It is a criminal offence, for example, to use a hand-held mobile phone while driving or supervising a learner driver (except to call 999 or 112 in an emergency when it is unsafe to stop). Despite this, some people still use their mobile phone when driving. However, attitudes and behaviour may be changing here.

Stretch and challenge

How far do you agree with Goode (2008) that body modification is an example of extreme deviance? Explain your thinking.

> **FOCUS ON SKILLS: WRITTEN ACTIVITY**
>
> **Deviance and the law**
>
> Consider the following examples:
>
> * murder
> * alcohol dependency
> * smoking at the office
> * parking on double yellow lines
> * shoplifting.
>
> List those acts which:
>
> a are both deviant and illegal
>
> b are deviant but legal
>
> c are illegal but would not usually be considered as deviant.

Key points

* A crime is an illegal act that is punishable by law.

* Deviance is behaviour that the majority of people disagree with, or which goes against the rules and norms of a society.

* Deviant acts can be – but are not always – illegal. Illegal acts are not necessarily considered deviant.

Check your understanding: Exam practice

1 Describe one example of deviant behaviour.   (3 marks)

2 Identify and explain one difference between crime and deviance.   (4 marks)

When is an act seen as deviant?

Objectives
- Explain the view that deviance is socially defined
- Explain historical and cultural variations in what is classed as crime and deviance

Many sociologists argue that, while crime involves legally defined behaviour, deviance involves **socially defined behaviour**. According to this view, whether an act is seen as deviant or not depends on the particular social setting in which it takes place. For instance, there is nothing deviant about nudity in itself. In the shower, bedroom or sauna, for example, nudity is generally seen as perfectly acceptable. By contrast, in a supermarket or on a football pitch, nudity would be seen as deviant. In certain social contexts and settings, therefore, nudity is seen as appropriate and fitting. In other situations, however, it would be seen as deviant and might also be illegal.

Sociologists argue that what is considered 'deviant' does not depend on the act itself but on how other people react to it; how they see, define and label the act. Selling drugs, for example, is likely to be seen as a deviant act if done by a drug dealer on a street corner but not if done by a pharmacist at the local chemist's. Deviance, therefore, is defined according to the social setting in which it takes place – it is socially defined.

Glossary terms

social stigma, socially defined behaviour

FOCUS ON SKILLS: DISCUSSION ACTIVITY

Is the same act always deviant?

1 In a small group, look at the following examples and discuss whether there are any circumstances in which they might be seen as acceptable:
- spraying CS gas in someone's face
- setting fire to someone's pudding
- breaking someone's nose
- claiming to be Elvis Presley
- carrying a gun
- executing a person.

2 Make a note of three important points arising from your discussion.

3 Write a short paragraph to explain the idea that what is considered as deviant can depend on who does it and the setting in which it takes place.

What does the historical evidence tell us about deviance?

Historical evidence suggests that beliefs about what is seen as normal and as deviant can change over time.

- In the past, several cultures carried out human sacrifice. During the 15th century, the Aztec civilisation in Mexico, for instance, offered captive warriors as sacrifices in order to keep the sun alive.
- Attitudes towards suicide have varied over time. During World War II, Japanese Kamikaze pilots dive-bombed and deliberately crashed their planes into enemy ships, resulting in their own deaths. This was considered to be an heroic act.
- Since World War II, social attitudes to issues such as sex outside marriage, divorce, abortion, homosexuality and smoking have changed in the UK. The **social stigma** or disgrace that was attached to extra-marital births during the 1950s, for example, has now almost disappeared.

Making connections

Write a sentence to link the point about social stigma to material you covered in Chapter 3, Families.

What does the cross-cultural evidence tell us about deviance?

Evidence suggests that behaviour classified as deviant can vary from one culture to another. This is because norms and social rules vary cross-culturally.

- Cultures differ in their expectations regarding what is appropriate dress for men, women and children.
- In the USA, it is acceptable for police officers and members of the public (within limits) to carry guns.
- Some countries have the death penalty. According to Amnesty International, at least 1634 people were executed across 25 countries (excluding China) in 2015.
- In Switzerland, assisting someone to die is not a criminal offence if it is done for honourable motives. There are clinics, used by Swiss people and increasingly by people from abroad, that help people to end their lives.

Norms vary between social groups, and this is reflected in particular expectations surrounding appropriate dress within the Amish religion.

What does the evidence tell us about crime?

What is classified as criminal behaviour can also change over time and vary between cultures. For example:

- In the 1920s, it was illegal to produce and drink alcohol in the USA.
- In Saudi Arabia, there are laws against the interaction of women with men other than their husbands in public spaces.

Key points

- Deviance is defined according to the social setting in which it takes place. Behaviour classed as 'deviant' can vary according to who performs the act and where they do so.

- What is classified as deviant also varies between cultures and over time.

Check your understanding: Exam practice

1 Describe one example of an act that breaks the law but which is not usually seen as deviant. (3 marks)

2 Describe one example of a deviant act that is not against the law. (3 marks)

What are social order and social control?

Social order

For people to live and work together, a certain amount of order and predictability is needed. It could be argued that social order and predictability are essential if society is to run smoothly. In studying **social order**, sociologists focus on the many aspects of social life that are stable and ordered.

Sociologists are interested in exploring how social order is achieved and maintained over time. There are two main approaches to explaining social order: the consensus and conflict approaches.

> **Glossary terms**
>
> methods of social control, negative sanctions, positive sanctions, sanctions, social control, social order

Social order is necessary if society is to run smoothly.

The consensus approach to social order

Functionalism argues that modern society is based on value consensus (see Chapter 1 Topic 8). In other words, there is broad agreement among people regarding norms and values. This consensus arises from the process of socialisation (see Chapter 1 Topic 4), during which we learn and come to share the norms and values of our society. Functionalists argue that social order is maintained over time because most people support the rules and agree to abide by them.

The conflict approach to social order

The Marxist approach sees capitalist society as based on conflicting interests between social classes (see Chapter 1 Topic 5). There are two main social classes: the bourgeoisie and the proletariat. The bourgeoisie are the ruling class who own the means of production

> **FOCUS ON THEORY: WRITTEN ACTIVITY**
>
> **Differences between the Marxist and functionalist approaches**
>
> Explain one difference between the functionalist and Marxist approaches to social order.

(the businesses and companies) and employ the proletariat (the working class). Class conflict occurs between these two groups because they have opposing interests. Social order is maintained over time because the bourgeoisie have the power to enforce order. They are able, for example, to influence the type of laws that get passed in society.

Social control

Much of everyday life is subject to rules, and sociologists are interested in understanding why most people conform to (follow or go along with) most of these rules most of the time. In addressing this issue, sociologists point out that people's actions and their behaviour are controlled or constrained by the social groups they mix with (such as families and peer groups) and by the wider society in which they live. In other words, much of our behaviour is socially controlled.

Methods of social control

The term '**methods of social control**' refers to the processes by which people are encouraged or persuaded to conform to the rules. It also refers to the ways that social groups or societies deal with behaviour that violates or breaks these rules. **Social control** methods may involve **sanctions** that aim to limit or reduce the frequency of deviant acts. For example, a promotion at work is a **positive sanction** and a prison sentence is a **negative sanction**.

FOCUS ON SKILLS: DISCUSSION ACTIVITY

The processes of social control

In a small group, choose one setting that you are all familiar with, for example a football match, a shopping centre or your home. Discuss the following questions and make a note of your group's responses.

1 Choose three rules that apply in your chosen setting.
2 Why do you think people stick to each of these rules?
3 If you broke the rules, what would the consequences be:
   a For you?
   b For other people?

Stretch and challenge

Social groups, rules and laws

How far do you agree that the rules and laws are applied in a fair way to people from different social groups? For example, are the laws and rules enforced more strictly against some groups (such as young men) rather than other groups (such as older women)? Explain your thinking.

Key points

- Social order is necessary for society to run smoothly. The functionalist approach argues that social order is based on consensus or agreement on shared values. The Marxist approach argues that it is based on the power of the ruling class to enforce social control.

- Much of our behaviour is controlled by social groups such as families and peers, and by the wider society.

Check your understanding: Exam practice

1 Identify and describe one reason why some degree of social order is necessary in a society.   **(3 marks)**

2 Describe what sociologists mean by 'methods of social control'.   **(3 marks)**

What is the difference between formal and informal social control?

In exploring how social control operates, sociologists highlight the important role of the **agencies of social control**. These are the groups and organisations in society that ensure that most people comply with, or stick to, the rules most of the time. Sociologists have identified two types of control: formal and informal social control.

Methods of formal social control

Glossary terms

agencies of social control, formal social control, informal social control, judiciary, legislature, magistrate, prison service, probation service, right to appeal, unwritten rules

Formal social control is based on written rules and laws. It is usually associated with the ways in which the state regulates and controls people's actions and behaviour. The 'agencies of formal social control' are the bodies in society that make the laws, enforce them or punish people who break them.

- The Houses of Parliament consist of the House of Commons and the House of Lords. They are known as the **legislature** and their role is to legislate; that is, to make the laws that regulate our behaviour.
- The role of the police force as an agency of formal social control is to maintain order, enforce the law, investigate crime and apprehend offenders.
- The role of the **judiciary** (judges and magistrates in the courts) is to deal with alleged offenders and to convict and sentence those found guilty of a crime. Sentences include a fine or a term of imprisonment. These sanctions are official and are backed by the state.
- **Magistrates** are volunteers who hear cases in the Magistrates' Court. They deal with most criminal offences including minor assaults and theft. They pass more serious offences to the Crown Court.
- The Crown Court deals with all indictable (serious) criminal offences such as murder or robbery, and the trial is held before a judge and jury. The jury decides whether the defendant is guilty and the judge passes sentence on those found guilty. If a person is found guilty and disagrees with this verdict, they have the **right to appeal** against the conviction. They also have the right to appeal against their sentence. Appeals are heard before the Court of Appeal.
- The role of the **prison service** is to keep convicted offenders who have received a prison sentence in custody. As an agency of social control, prisons punish convicted lawbreakers, rehabilitate them and deter them and others from committing crime. The role of the **probation service** is to supervise offenders who have been released into the community.

Agencies of formal social control

Study these four photographs and, for each one, identify which agency of formal social control is shown.

Middlesex Guildhall Crown Court

Santa Fu prison, Germany

Stoke Newington Police Station, London

The Houses of Parliament

Methods of informal social control

Informal social control is based on **unwritten rules** and processes such as the approval or disapproval of other people. It is enforced via social pressure – by the reactions of agencies of informal social control such as family members, peers, teachers or work colleagues. These reactions to behaviour may be in the form of positive or negative sanctions. Positive sanctions reward individuals who comply with or behave according to the group's expectations by, for example, praising them or giving them a gift. Negative sanctions punish those who do not conform by, for instance, ridiculing them, ignoring them, playing practical jokes on them, gossiping about them, smacking them or arguing to try to persuade them to change their behaviour.

Making connections

1. Agencies of informal social control include families, peer groups, education, workplaces, religions and the mass media. What other key social process are these groups and social structures linked to?
2. How do formal and informal social controls operate at school?

Informal processes of social control

Informal social control operates through positive and negative sanctions.

In a small group, identify two ways in which positive and/or negative sanctions may work in each of the following examples:

- a school pupil who is seen as hard working and dedicated
- a neighbour who works as a prostitute
- a married MP who is caught having an affair
- a teenager who rescues a drowning child.

Make a note of your suggestions.

Key points

- Formal social control is based on laws and written rules.

- Laws are enforced through agencies of the state, such as the police and the courts.

- Informal social control is based on informal social processes and is enforced through social pressure.

Check your understanding: Exam practice

1 Identify one agency of formal social control and describe how it controls people's behaviour. **(3 marks)**

2 Identify and explain one way in which peer groups may encourage members to conform to their rules. **(4 marks)**

What is the difference between formal and informal rules?

Formal rules

The idea of rules is central to the study of crime and deviance. Sociologists distinguish between formal and informal rules. Formal rules are written down, for example in the form of laws or codes of conduct.

Formal rules guide people's behaviour in many social settings such as schools, workplaces, police stations, motorways and on public transport. Road users such as pedestrians, cyclists and car drivers, for example, each have different rules to follow and these are listed in the Highway Code. In the workplace, people are expected to follow the rules governing health and safety.

These formal, written rules have official status, and official sanctions (formal punishments or penalties) are usually imposed on those caught breaking them. These include imprisonment, electronic tagging or getting sacked.

Glossary terms

formal rules, informal rules

Stretch and challenge

In your view, why is the idea of rules central to the study of crime and deviance?

FOCUS ON SKILLS: DISCUSSION ACTIVITY
Formal rules at school

In a small group, discuss the following questions and note down your responses.

1 Why might it be necessary to have formal, written rules about teacher and student behaviour in a school or college?

2 Pick three of the formal rules in your school or college and, for each, discuss why the rule is either necessary or unnecessary.

Informal rules

We do not usually give much thought to the **informal rules** that guide many aspects of social life. They are 'taken-for-granted' or unwritten rules or guidelines on how we are expected to behave in particular social settings. We would probably not be expected, for example, to get permission before making ourselves a drink, using the toilet or taking a shower at home. At the house of a distant relative who we have only just met for the first time, however, we probably would not wander into the kitchen and help ourselves to a glass of orange juice or a biscuit.

Even though we may not always consciously think about the informal or unwritten rules that govern social life, they can still have a powerful influence over how we behave in particular situations.

Making connections

How might aspects of a school's organisation (for example, streaming) affect students' behaviour?

These informal, unwritten rules do not have official status. Friends, family members and workmates may apply negative sanctions (such as playing practical jokes on someone or ridiculing them) to those caught breaking unwritten rules.

FOCUS ON SKILLS: WRITTEN ACTIVITY

Breaking the informal rules

Look at the following cartoons, which illustrate examples of informal or taken-for-granted rules being ignored or broken.

1 Note down two informal rules that guide how we are expected to:
   a behave in a supermarket checkout queue
   b dress for a job interview.

2 What is likely to happen if we break these rules?

3 List three informal rules that you have obeyed today. Explain briefly why you obeyed each of these rules.

4 Do you think the informal rules apply to everyone in the same way? For example, are children and adults expected to behave in the same way in a supermarket checkout queue? Do we have different expectations about how men and women should dress for a job interview? Explain your thinking.

FOCUS ON SKILLS: DISCUSSION ACTIVITY

Life without rules

1 In a small group, discuss what our lives would be like if there were no rules, or if most people ignored the rules. Does society need rules? Which rules? Why? Who benefits from the rules? Does anyone lose out?

2 Note down three key points that were made during your discussion.

Check your understanding: Exam practice

Identify and explain one difference between formal and informal rules.   (4 marks)

Key points

- Some rules are formal; that is, written down as laws or codes of conduct.

- Other rules are informal; that is, unwritten and taken for granted.

How does functionalism explain crime and deviance?

Objectives
- Explain the functionalist approach to crime and deviance
- Describe Durkheim's account of the functions of crime
- Criticise Durkheim's account

Sociologists explain involvement in crime and deviance in terms of social rather than biological or psychological factors. Beyond this, however, they disagree on how to explain crime and deviance. Some sociological approaches focus on the functions of crime for society, for example, while others explain crime and deviance in terms of **criminal subcultures** or the availability of both legal and illegal opportunities.

Glossary terms

criminal subculture, popular press, quality press, social cohesion

FOCUS ON SKILLS: DISCUSSION ACTIVITY

Is crime always bad news?

In general, we think of crime in negative terms as a bad thing. For example, crime is harmful to individual victims and damaging to communities. But is all crime necessarily always a bad thing?

In a small group, discuss the following questions and note down your responses.

1 Can you think of any ways in which a certain amount of crime could be beneficial to society? Explain your answer.
2 Most of us are probably familiar with the idea that the police and courts are necessary to keep crime under control and to maintain social order. To what extent do you agree with the idea that someone who breaks the law might also have an important role to play in society?

Functionalism examines social institutions in terms of their functions or purposes. Durkheim focused on the functions of crime.

Durkheim (1858–1917) on the functions of crime

Durkheim points out that crime exists in all societies. Despite this, he does not think it is possible to define crimes simply as all actions that are harmful to society. If this were the case, then exactly the same acts would be seen as crimes in each and every society. There would be no variation in what gets defined as a crime over time or between cultures. In Durkheim's view, there is a wide variation in what different societies see as criminal.

Durkheim argues that all crimes have just one thing in common: they are all acts that are disapproved of by the members of the society in which they take place.

Durkheim argues that crime is a vital and necessary part of all healthy societies. This is because it performs key functions in society. Some crimes (particularly violent crimes where the victims are young children or elderly/disabled people) produce a deep sense of shock and outrage among the vast majority of people. This reaction helps to remind everyone of the boundaries between acceptable and unacceptable behaviour.

Stretch and challenge

Do you think Durkheim would agree or disagree with the view that crime is socially defined? Write a sentence to explain your answer.

Although society was very different when Durkheim was studying it, his ideas can be applied to contemporary society. When a serious crime is committed today, for example, it gets a lot of publicity in the media. Immediately afterwards, we read about it in both the **quality press** and the **popular press**. We also see news reports about it on TV. When the case goes to court, the media report on the trial. When the offender is punished, the moral boundaries of society – the boundaries between good and bad behaviour – are laid out for everyone else.

The publicity surrounding some serious crimes can help to bring people together.

The publicity surrounding crimes and the punishment of offenders both have an important role in helping to bring people together. They reinforce the values and beliefs that the majority of people in society hold. By binding people together in this way, crime can contribute to **social cohesion**. For this reason, Durkheim believed that criminals play a definite role in society. He pointed out, however, that crime becomes dysfunctional or harmful to society when there is too much of it or not enough.

FOCUS ON RESEARCH: WRITTEN ACTIVITY

Researching attitudes to crime and punishment

Explain *how* you would investigate people's attitudes to crime and punishment using questionnaires.

In your explanation, discuss how you would:

- select a sample
- distribute your questionnaires (for example, by post)
- obtain informed consent from respondents.

Also, discuss the advantages of using questionnaires to investigate attitudes to crime and punishment.

Criticisms of Durkheim

1 Critics argue that Durkheim's account of the functions of crime is more relevant to small-scale societies than to large-scale, modern, industrial societies.
2 Many crimes harm the victims and damage communities. They are unlikely to reinforce shared values and beliefs.
3 Some Marxists argue that Durkheim ignores the issue of power in society. They point out that the law functions in the interests of powerful groups (the bourgeoisie) rather than in everyone's interests.

Key points

- Sociologists focus on social factors when explaining crime and deviance.

- Durkheim argued that the reaction to crime helps to bind people together. In this way, he believed, crime can contribute to social cohesion.

Check your understanding: Exam practice

Identify and explain one function of crime that Durkheim identified. (4 marks)

How does Merton explain crime and deviance?

FOCUS ON KEY THINKERS

Robert K. Merton on anomie

Merton (1938) examined the causes of criminal and deviant behaviour from a functionalist perspective. He explains crime and deviance in terms of the structure and culture of society. In other words, he puts forward a **structural theory** rather than focusing on people's genes or personalities.

Culturally defined goals

Merton argues that people's aspirations and goals (what they see as worth striving for) are largely determined by the values of their culture. In the USA, for example, people are socialised to believe in, and to strive for, the 'American dream'. This is the idea that, regardless of their background, anyone who works hard can make it, for example by passing exams at school and getting promoted at work.

Limited opportunities to access the means

The problem is that some individuals and groups accept the goal of achieving economic success but lack opportunities to succeed through legitimate (or socially acceptable) means. There is little chance, for example, that many working-class people would be able to go to university and climb the ladder to a high-flying job and a huge salary.

Strain and anomie

Some people end up experiencing strain between the goals they have been socialised to strive for and the means of achieving them. Working-class youths, for example, are taught to believe in the American dream but are held back because society gives them fewer opportunities to succeed through legitimate means such as education. In this situation, where there is a mismatch between goals and means, a condition of **anomie** (or normlessness) develops. In other words, the norms that regulate behaviour break down and people turn to whatever means work for them to achieve material success. When anomie develops, anything goes and high rates of crime and **delinquency** are likely.

> **Glossary terms**
>
> anomie, delinquency, structural theory

Well, we can't all get rich through a college education or get to be President.

According to Merton, when anomie develops, anything goes and high rates of crime are likely.

Merton identifies five possible ways that individuals respond to the goals of success in society. Some of these involve crime and deviance.

Merton's five responses

Responses	Culturally defined goals	Approved or socially acceptable means of achieving the goals
1. **Conformity** to the goals and means, e.g. an ambitious student from a privileged background works hard to qualify as a doctor.	Individuals accept the goals of success.	They accept the legitimate means.
2. **Innovation**, e.g. theft, fraud, organised crime.	Individuals accept the goals of success.	They lack opportunities to succeed through legitimate means and turn to crime.
3. **Ritualism**, e.g. an office worker who rigidly follows the rules but loses sight of the point of the rules.	Individuals reject or abandon the goals.	They accept the legitimate means and stick rigidly to them.
4. **Retreatism**, e.g. people who 'drop out' or escape through dependency on alcohol or drugs.	Individuals reject or abandon the goals.	They reject or abandon the legitimate means.
5. **Rebellion**, e.g. people who set up a new social order or join a radical social group that aims to change society.	Individuals reject the conventional success goals and replace them with alternative goals.	They reject the legitimate means and replace them with other means.

Source: adapted from Merton (1938a)

FOCUS ON SKILLS: WRITTEN ACTIVITY

Merton's five responses

1 Which response involves accepting the goals but not the means?
2 Which response involves rejecting both the goals and the means?
3 Which response involves neither crime nor deviance?

Criticisms of Merton

1 Albert Cohen (see Topic 21) argues that much juvenile delinquency such as gang violence and vandalism is not motivated by money or consumer goods.
2 It is not clear why some individuals faced with anomie break the rules, while others conform.
3 Many sociologists reject the idea that society is based on consensus or agreement about shared values and goals. They argue instead that society is based on conflict between powerful and subordinate groups.
4 Some Marxists argue that Merton, like Durkheim, does not consider power relations in society or examine who makes the laws and who benefits from them.

Stretch and challenge

1 Which of Merton's responses applies when a top athlete takes performance-enhancing drugs before an international event to win the gold medal?
2 How many of the five responses involve some form of deviance? Explain your reasoning.

Key points

- According to Merton, crime occurs when people accept society's success goals (for example, to get rich) but because of their position in society they lack the opportunities to achieve this success legally (for example, through a well-paid job.)

- Merton links crime to anomie (the breakdown of norms), which develops when there is a mismatch between goals and means, leading people to turn to crime as a means to achieve their goals.

Check your understanding: Exam practice

Describe what Merton means by 'anomie'.   (3 marks)

How does Marxism explain crime and deviance?

Objectives
- Describe Marxist theories of crime and deviance
- Criticise Marxist approaches

Marxist approaches (like functionalist approaches) are based on structural theories or explanations in that they explain crime and deviance in terms of the way society is structured rather than in terms of the characteristics of individuals.

Marxists explain crime by examining the type of society we live in and who has power within it. They relate crime to the class structure of capitalist societies in which a small group of very wealthy and powerful people – the bourgeoisie – own the means of production, such as the land, factories and big businesses. Marxists argue that the bourgeoisie exploit poorer working-class people – the proletariat – in order to make as much profit as possible.

Capitalist society is based on values such as:

- materialism (valuing material possessions)
- consumerism (wanting the latest consumer goods such as mobile phones and designer clothes)
- competition between individuals to obtain these products (keeping up with the neighbours).

Marxists argue that the media continually reinforce these values through advertising in magazines, some reality TV shows and Hollywood films based on the lives of the super-rich.

In an unequal society, not everyone can earn enough to consume the products of capitalism. It is likely that some people will try to get material goods through any means possible including illegal means. In this view, crime is seen as a by-product of the way capitalist society is organised.

Marxist views of law enforcement

Marxists are critical of the laws that are enforced in a capitalist society. Criminal law, they argue, is made by, and in the interests of, those who own property. Consequently, it is not surprising that so many laws relate to the protection of private property. Marxists argue that, given this legal system, it is likely that working-class people will be caught breaking the law while crimes committed by the powerful bourgeoisie may often go undetected. For example, benefit fraud (such as when someone lies in order to get a state benefit that they are not really entitled to) is generally seen as being more serious and costly than tax evasion (such as when someone does not declare their income in order to avoid paying tax on it), even though far more revenue is lost through tax evasion.

Glossary term

white-collar crime

Making connections

Power is a key concept in sociology. How does it link to the topic of families?

Stretch and challenge

How far do you agree that the media reinforce values such as materialism and consumerism?

The agencies of social control such as the police and courts operate in the interests of the powerful and against the proletariat. This happens in two ways:

1 Certain types of crime are likely to be targeted – street crime, for example, is policed more rigorously than **white-collar crime**. White-collar crime such as tax evasion is significant in monetary terms. However, it is not seen as such a serious social problem as benefit fraud and frequently goes unnoticed.

2 Certain groups are more likely to be targeted – groups such as black people, inner-city youth and working-class people are more likely to be on the receiving end of law enforcement.

Black Lives Matter UK is part of a global movement that campaigns against racism. It protests against discrimination within the criminal justice system and the deaths of black people in police custody.

FOCUS ON RESEARCH: WRITTEN ACTIVITY

Researching organised crime

Chambliss (1978) studied the relationship between legal corporations and organised crime in Seattle between 1962 and 1972. He defines organised crime as illegal activities organised to make money from vice (for example, crimes involving drugs, gambling and prostitution) and from racketeering (obtaining money by the use of threats or force). He interviewed professional thieves, racketeers, police and government officials.

1 Identify and explain one disadvantage of using interviews to investigate the links between organised crime and legal corporations.

2 Identify one ethical problem researchers might face when investigating people's involvement in crime and explain how they might address this problem.

Criticisms of Marxist approaches

- Not every criminal law supports the interests of the dominant class. Many laws rest on genuine agreement. Pluralists see society as composed of a plurality or range of competing interest groups. The law reflects the interests of many groups rather than just one.
- Functionalists argue that society is based on value consensus rather than conflict.
- Some feminists argue that Marxist approaches focus on issues of social class in capitalist society and ignore issues of gender in patriarchal society.

Key points

- Marxist theories, like functionalist theories, are structural theories in that they explain crime and deviance in terms of the way that society is structured.

- Marxists explain crime as resulting from the way capitalist society is structured and the inequalities within capitalism.

Check your understanding: Exam practice

1 Identify and describe one similarity between Marxist and functionalist explanations of crime and deviance. **(3 marks)**

2 Identify and describe one difference between the Marxist and functionalist explanations of crime and deviance. **(3 marks)**

How does Marxism explain crime and deviance?   215

How does feminism explain crime and deviance?

Objectives
- Describe feminist theories of crime and deviance
- Describe the key ideas of Frances Heidensohn

Until the 1970s, many sociologists neglected women when studying crime and deviance. Instead, they examined crime and delinquency committed by men and boys. More recently, feminist approaches have focused on issues of gender and crime.

Feminist sociologists examine how female offenders are treated within the **criminal justice system** (CJS) including the police and the courts. One view, known as the '**chivalry thesis**', suggests that female offenders are treated more leniently than men, for example when sentenced in court. Another view, the **double deviance thesis**, suggests that the CJS treats some women (including those who do not conform to traditional feminine **stereotypes**) more harshly than others. Female offenders are treated and punished as double deviants because they have broken two sets of rules: first, the law, and second, the norms governing gender behaviour.

Feminist perspectives also examine the ways women are victimised in society. They investigate issues such as domestic violence and sex crimes, and question why these crimes are under-reported to the police.

> **Glossary terms**
>
> chivalry thesis, conformity, control theory, criminal justice system, criminality, double deviance thesis, sexuality, stereotypes

FOCUS ON KEY THINKERS

Frances Heidensohn: Women and crime

Frances Heidensohn (1985, 1996) explores the area of women and crime from a feminist perspective. Women have a lower rate of officially recorded crime than men and commit fewer serious crimes. Heidensohn uses **control theory** to explain this.

Control theory emphasises the social bonds between people (for example, the bonds between family members and peers). By attaching people to families and friends, social bonds can prevent them from turning to crime. In this way, social bonds act as a mechanism of social control to reduce crime and delinquency.

Heidensohn examines the structure of patriarchal society, which has separate spheres for men and women. The sphere of public life is seen as appropriate for men and the home is seen as a woman's place. This concept of separate spheres helps to explain the roles of women and men in social control.

Heidensohn's views on the role of women in social control

According to Heidensohn, women have an important role in controlling other people within the home. As wives and mothers, they are involved in the socialisation process, which is crucial to maintaining order in society. Women also have a role in controlling others informally in their local community. However, women are not usually allowed to exercise control over men.

Carrying out these tasks can act as a constraint on women. For example, a mother with a young child in a pram would find it more difficult than a man to burgle a house. Women's behaviour is constrained by their role in controlling other people.

Heidensohn's views on the control of women

When studying female **criminality**, Heidensohn examines female **conformity** and the control of women. Patriarchal society controls women more effectively than it controls men, so it is harder for women to break the law. Women are constrained and controlled at home, in public and at work.

The control of women in the home

Heidensohn argues that domestic life and marriage are means of controlling women to ensure that they conform. Women's opportunities to commit crime are limited by their housewife role. Their time is taken up in housework and monitoring others.

Daughters and sons are allowed different degrees of freedom, especially as adolescents. Daughters are expected to stay closer to home than sons. Working-class girls in particular are expected to spend time on housework and childcare.

The control of women in public

Women's behaviour in public is controlled by male violence. Although women are no more at risk of street violence than other social groups, they fear crime and sexual assault. This fear acts as a control on their behaviour, for example by preventing them from going out after dark.

Women's behaviour in public places is also controlled by the fear that they could get a bad reputation. Men control women's reputations, for example by describing them in terms of their **sexuality**.

The control of women at work

In the workplace, men hold power and authority over women, for example as managers or supervisors. Sexual harassment at work is a form of male control over women, which limits their freedom in the workplace.

Women's role as mothers can constrain their behaviour.

Making connections

Think about how you could link Heidensohn's ideas on domestic life and marriage to the topic of families. How could you link her ideas to socialisation in families?

Stretch and challenge

How far would functionalist sociologists such as Parsons agree with Heidensohn's arguments?

Key point

Heidensohn, from a feminist perspective, looks at family life, male dominance (patriarchy) and separate spheres to explain female crime. She argues that women have fewer opportunities to commit crime than men and experience social control in public and in private.

FOCUS ON THEORY: DISCUSSION ACTIVITY

The social control of women

In a small group, discuss how far you agree with Heidensohn that:
- domestic life and marriage control women
- the fear of violence controls women's behaviour in public
- the fear of getting a bad reputation controls women.

Make a note of your group's ideas.

Check your understanding: Exam practice

Identify and explain one way in which women may be controlled in public.

(4 marks)

How does interactionism explain crime and deviance?

Objectives
* Describe the ideas of Becker on the causes of crime and deviance
* Criticise the interactionist approach

FOCUS ON KEY THINKERS

Howard Becker: the interactionist theory of deviance

Becker (1997) argues that there is no such thing as a deviant act *per se* (that is, in and of itself). We cannot understand deviance by focusing on acts that people commit. Instead, we must explore the interaction between the person who commits an act and those who react to it. Behaviour only becomes deviant when other people (such as police officers and teachers) define it as such.

Glossary terms

deviant career, interactionism, labelling, master status, self-fulfilling prophecy

Labelling

In Becker's view, deviance is created by society. By this he means that social groups create deviance by making rules, applying these rules to particular people and **labelling** them as 'outsiders.' A 'deviant' is a person who has been labelled as such, and 'deviant behaviour' is behaviour that people label as such. A label is like a sticky tag that, once attached to someone, is difficult to remove.

Becker argues that whether or not a particular act is seen as deviant depends on how others react to it. This varies according to factors such as:

* Time and place: the same behaviour may break the rules at one time or in one place but not another.
* Who commits the act and who feels harmed by it: the same behaviour may break the rules when committed by one person but not by another.

Stretch and challenge

Labelling theory is also referred to as the social reaction approach to deviance. Why do you think it is described in this way?

Who makes the rules?

According to Becker, some groups have the power to make rules and apply them to others. Groups whose social position gives them power are best able to make rules and enforce them. Power is related to age, gender, ethnicity and class. For example, adults make many important rules for young people, such as those regarding school attendance.

Deviant careers

Becker is interested in the process by which people develop **deviant careers** over time and make deviance a way of life. He identifies several steps in this process.

- A young woman starts using illegal drugs.
- She is caught and publicly labelled as a deviant.
- This label changes how others see her – she is now 'the local junkie' or a 'smackhead'. This new status becomes a **master status**. It overrides all her other statuses, for instance as a daughter, sister, friend or employee.
- She now gets treated as though she is likely to break other important rules. People at work, for example, assume that she will steal money from their wallets to feed her habit. Her parents reject her; she loses her home, her friends and her job. She can no longer earn an income through paid employment.
- She may now resort to other criminal and deviant activities, such as shoplifting or robbery, to support her habit.
- Finally, she moves into an organised deviant group whose members are all in the same boat. A deviant subculture develops with its own ideas about what the world is like and how to deal with it, and its own routine activities based on these ideas. The young woman now identifies with the group and comes to see herself as one of them – as a drug addict. She meets older, more experienced group members and through them learns, for example, how to avoid trouble and how to sell stolen goods without getting caught.

Becker argues that labelling may produce a **self-fulfilling prophecy** – the person labelled may come to fit the image people have of them. However, he points out that not everyone labelled as deviant will necessarily move to greater deviance; the prophecies do not always confirm themselves.

Criticisms of the interactionist approach

- Critics argue that **interactionism** does not explain why individuals commit deviant acts in the first place.
- The interactionist approach sees criminals as victims of labelling and ignores the fact that some people choose to break the law.
- Structural approaches argue that interactionism focuses on interactions between people and does not pay attention to the influence of the social structure on behaviour. Marxists, for example, argue that interactionism does not focus enough on power inequalities between social classes.

Making connections

Education

How do sociologists use labelling theory to explain the underachievement of some groups in schools?

FOCUS ON RESEARCH: WRITTEN ACTIVITY

Researching deviant groups

Interactionist approaches to the study of crime and deviance often use participant observation as a research method.

Identify and explain one advantage of using participant observation to investigate deviant groups.

Key points

- Becker's interactionist theory of deviance explores the interaction between the person who commits an act and the social reaction to it.
- Labelling may produce a self-fulfilling prophecy.

Check your understanding: Exam practice

Describe what sociologists mean by the term 'master status'.

(3 marks)

What are the main sources of statistical data on crime?

Objectives
- Identify the main sources of statistical data on crime
- Describe victim surveys and self-report studies

There are two main sources of data that measure the extent of crime:
- surveys of the public, such as **victim surveys** and **self-report studies**
- official statistics of crimes recorded by the police.

Glossary terms

anti-social behaviour, recorded crime, self-report study, victim survey

Victim surveys

Victim surveys ask people about their experiences of crime. The Crime Survey for England and Wales (CSEW), for example, is a large-scale survey run by the Office for National Statistics (ONS) and is carried out every year. The CSEW measures crime through questionnaire surveys, with a sample of 35 000 households in England and Wales. It interviews people aged 16 years and over in their homes. It also interviews around 3000 young people aged 10 to 15 years, who are selected from the same households as the older group. Trained interviewers use a laptop to deliver the questionnaire.

The survey asks respondents whether they have experienced particular crimes during the previous 12 months. If so, it asks which crimes they or their households have been victim of and whether they reported them to the police. It also asks for their views on crime-related issues such as attitudes to the police and courts.

FOCUS ON SKILLS: WRITTEN ACTIVITY

Crime Survey for England and Wales

The table below shows the number of crimes in England and Wales (April 2015–March 2016) disclosed by CSEW respondents. Study this information, then answer the questions that follow.

April 2015–March 2016, adults aged 16 years and over in households, England and Wales

Offence group	Number of incidents (thousands)
Violence	1 268
Robbery	154
Theft offences, e.g. housebreaking, car theft	3 704
Criminal damage	1 209
All CSEW Crime	6 334

Source: adapted from ONS (2016) *Statistical Bulletin: Crime in England and Wales: Year Ending March 2016*

1 According to this information, how many incidents of criminal damage were there between April 2015 and March 2016?
2 Which type of crime had the lowest incidence?
3 Were there more incidents of violence or criminal damage?

Uses and limitations of the CSEW

The CSEW is an important source of data on crime because:

- it includes unreported crime, so it gives information on offences that are not included in statistics on police-**recorded crime**
- it allows trends in particular crimes (for example, domestic burglary) to be identified
- the results help policy makers to devise policies to tackle crime, such as designing programmes to reduce crime against young people.

The CSEW has some limitations.

1 It does not cover the full range of crimes recorded by the police. For example, it excludes:
   - murder (where the victim is dead)
   - so-called victimless crimes (such as possession of drugs)
   - crimes such as shoplifting, where the victim is a business rather than a person or household.
2 Respondents' memories may be inaccurate, they may not mention trivial crimes or they may lie about having reported a crime to the police.

Self-report studies

Self-report studies ask people about their offending. The Offending, Crime and Justice Survey (OCJS), for example, was commissioned by the Home Office and carried out annually between 2003 and 2006. It measured the extent of self-reported offending, drug use and **anti-social behaviour** in England and Wales, particularly among those aged 10 to 15 years. By asking people about their offending, it provided information on offenders and offences that were not necessarily dealt with by the police or courts.

FOCUS ON SKILLS: WRITTEN ACTIVITY

Problems with the OCJS

Like the CSEW, the OCJS was a household survey and did not question homeless people or those living in communal establishments such as prisons, student halls or care homes. Nor did it cover all types of crime.

Identify and explain one limitation of the OCJS as a source of data on crime.

FOCUS ON SKILLS: DISCUSSION ACTIVITY

Young people and the CSEW

In a small group, discuss the following questions and note down your ideas.

1 Since 2009, the CSEW has included a shorter survey of 10-to 15-year-olds. Why do you think it is important to include their views?

2 Why must researchers ask permission from parents or guardians before interviewing 10-to 15-year-olds?

3 One section of the young people's survey covers truanting, alcohol and drugs, street gangs, carrying knives and cyberbullying. Why do you think the interviewers ask respondents to type their answers to these questions into a laptop?

Key points

- Victim surveys and self-report studies provide statistical data on the extent of crime.

- However, they are based on questionnaires, which give rise to possible problems.

Check your understanding: Exam practice

Identify and explain one advantage of using structured interviews to investigate people's experiences of crime. (4 marks)

How useful are statistics on crimes recorded by the police?

Objectives
- Describe official statistics of crimes recorded by the police
- Discuss the usefulness of these statistics

Official statistics of crimes recorded by police forces in England and Wales are reported to the Home Office and published by the Office for National Statistics (ONS). They include serious crimes but exclude offences such as speeding that are dealt with by the Magistrates' Court.

Although statistics on recorded crime may appear to be a straightforward measure of the extent of crime in any one year, they have limitations. Critics argue that they do not provide an accurate picture of the total amount of crime committed.

Discovery and witnessing crime

If a crime has not been discovered or witnessed in the first place, it cannot be reported to the police. It will not, therefore, be counted in official statistics on recorded crime. For example, it is possible that much petty theft in the workplace goes undiscovered. Similarly, a victim must recognise and define an incident such as a smashed window as criminal rather than accidental damage if there is any chance of it being reported.

Reporting crime

Many less serious offences are not reported to the police and so cannot be recorded by them. Victim surveys such as the CSEW suggest that many people who have been victims of crime do not report the crime to the police. This under-reporting helps to explain why the recorded crime figure is lower than CSEW estimates of crime.

> **Glossary terms**
>
> 'dark figure' of crime, reported crime, white-collar workers

Criminal or accidental damage?

FOCUS ON SKILLS: DISCUSSION ACTIVITY

Reporting crime to the police

The CSEW suggests that most thefts of motor vehicles are reported to the police. Burglaries that involve loss are also more likely than some other crimes to be reported. Offences such as vandalism, assault without injury and theft from the person are least likely to be reported.

In pairs, discuss why the likelihood of reporting crime to the police varies according to the type of offence. Note down your ideas.

FOCUS ON SKILLS: WRITTEN ACTIVITY

The table below shows trends in CSEW estimates of crime and police-recorded crime for England and Wales in 1981, 1991 and 2015. Study this information and then answer the questions.

Trends in overall crime for England and Wales

	No. of offences		
	Jan–Dec 1981	**Jan–Dec 1991**	**Jan–Dec 2015**
Total CSEW crime	11 066	15 111	6432
Total police-recorded crime	2964	5276	4435

Source: adapted from ONS (2016) *Statistical Bulletin: Crime in England and Wales: Year Ending December 2015*

1 How many offences were recorded by the police in 2015?
2 How many incidents of crime were shown by the CSEW in 1981?
3 Of the two sources of statistics, which shows higher rates of crime?
4 Has the gap between the two sets of statistics narrowed or widened over time?

Victims might not report a crime to the police if they:

- see the crime as too trivial, for example petty vandalism
- think the police cannot – or will not – do anything about it, for example hate crime
- suffered no loss
- believe that the police will not handle it sensitively – this is a possibility with crimes such as rape
- are afraid of the consequences of reporting it, for example in cases of domestic violence
- feel embarrassed because they think they will be seen as stupid or naive, for example victims of online fraud such as dating or inheritance scams.

Where crime is discovered in the workplace, employers may be reluctant to make public the fact that they have a dishonest person on their staff. They may dismiss the employee rather than involve the police. The term 'white-collar crime' refers to crime committed by **white-collar workers** (broadly, those in relatively high-status positions, such as managers, accountants or lawyers) in the course of their employment. It includes theft from an employer or 'fiddling' travel expenses and is under-represented in crime statistics.

Recording crime

The police may not necessarily record a crime that is reported to them. They may, for example, consider the **reported crime** to be too trivial or doubt the honesty or accuracy of the complainant's report. The police may decide that there is not enough evidence that an offence has been committed to justify recording it as a crime (see also Topic 13).

Sociologists argue that official statistics ignore the hidden or **'dark figure' of crime**, which includes unreported and unrecorded crime. As a result, they tend to treat official statistics on recorded crime with caution.

Check your understanding: Exam practice

Identify and explain one reason why the recorded rate of crime may not include all crimes committed. (4 marks)

Key point

Not all crime is discovered, witnessed, reported or recorded, so official statistics on police-recorded crime do not tell the whole story.

What other problems are there with police-recorded crime statistics?

Objective
- Outline the view that official crime statistics are socially constructed

Police-recorded crime statistics enable researchers to compare the **crime rate** in different areas and to identify trends in crime over time. These statistics indicate that the overall volume of crime in England and Wales has been falling. It is possible to take the statistics at face value and conclude that crime is declining. However, the police-recorded crime statistics may not provide an accurate measurement of crime rates or trends. If the levels of particular crimes such as violent incidents vary over time, this variation may be linked to changes in how much money is spent on CCTV **surveillance**. This will affect the reliability of the crime statistics.

The trends can also be affected by changes in the way crimes are recorded by the police. For example, the rules about police recording practice were changed in 1998 and again in 2003. So it is difficult to make comparisons over time. An increase in police-recorded crime might be linked to improved crime recording by the police rather than to a genuine increase in crime.

> **Glossary terms**
>
> crime rate, social construct, surveillance

FOCUS ON SKILLS: WRITTEN ACTIVITY

Can we count on crime statistics?

The Public Administration Select Committee (PASC), a committee of MPs in the House of Commons, conducted an enquiry into crime statistics in 2013. It investigated whether checks were in place to ensure that the police recorded crimes properly and whether we could have confidence in crime statistics. Its report in 2014 concluded that we couldn't count on police-recorded crime statistics.

One reason for this is that the figures under-record crime because the police are lax in sticking to the nationally agreed standards when recording crimes. So the apparent decrease in crime rates may be exaggerated.

As a result of the PASC enquiry, the UK Statistics Authority decided in January 2014 to strip police-recorded crime data of its 'National Statistics' quality Kitemark.

1 What was the purpose of the PASC enquiry?
2 According to the PASC report, can we count on crime statistics?
3 Why do the figures under-record crime?

The social construction of crime statistics

Police-recorded crime statistics may appear to provide a factual account of the extent of crime. However, when sociologists examine how these statistics are actually collected, they question how far such data provide a valid or true picture of the level of crime.

Interpretivist sociologists argue that crime statistics are a **social construct** (see Chapter 2 Topic 18). In other words, they are the end product of a series of choices and decisions made by the various people involved, such as victims, witnesses and police.

Constructing crime statistics

The diagram below shows the series of decisions made by witnesses, victims and police officers in the process of constructing statistics on police-recorded crime.

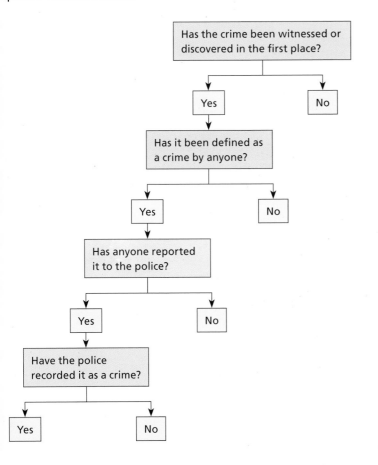

Labelling theorists argue that behaviour only becomes deviant when people such as police officers define it as such. In this case, police-recorded crime statistics will reflect police officers' reactions and their power to define and label behaviour as deviant. The police, for example, may clamp down on drink driving around Christmas in order to meet their targets.

Marxist sociologists see the statistics as reflecting the class-based nature of capitalist society. White-collar and corporate crime is not policed effectively and so is under-represented in the statistics.

Feminist sociologists argue that the statistics under-record incidents of violence against women including domestic and sexual violence.

Check your understanding: Exam practice

Discuss how far sociologists agree that police-recorded crime statistics provide an accurate measure of crime. (12 marks)

What is the relationship between social class and crime?

Objective
- Explain the relationship between social class, crime and deviance

According to official statistics, there is a relationship between people's involvement in crime and their social characteristics such as their social class, gender, ethnicity and age. Maguire (2007) notes that there are many more males, young people, black people, poor people and poorly educated people in the prison population relative to the general population. However, self-report studies suggest that between 40 and almost 100 per cent of respondents admit to having committed at least one criminal offence during their lifetime.

Glossary terms

corporate crime, invisible crime

Explanations for the link between social class, crime and deviance

There is evidence that working-class people are over-represented in the prison population in proportion to their numbers in the general population. Sociologists are interested in exploring how social class is linked to criminal and deviant behaviour. They have put forward a number of explanations for this.

- Merton uses anomie theory to explain different types of deviance including crime (see Topic 7). In his view, everyone shares the 'American dream' of becoming rich and successful, regardless of their background. Crime results from unequal opportunities in society to get rich via legal means. When legal avenues are closed to working-class people, some may turn to criminal methods to become successful.

- Working-class subcultures may stress deviant or criminal behaviour, which can bring status within particular peer groups. Albert Cohen (1955) uses subcultural theory to explain juvenile delinquency among working-class boys (see Topic 21). He linked delinquency such as vandalism and violence to status frustration at school. Working-class boys fail to meet middle-class expectations at school. They respond by joining gangs in which delinquency is already the 'thing to do'. Being part of a delinquent subculture allows the boys to gain status within the gang.

- Other approaches view the statistics as reflecting bias within the criminal justice system, including the police and courts. Marxists focus on law enforcement and argue that the agencies of social control target certain groups (such as working-class people) and certain crimes (such as street crime). By contrast, crimes such as business fraud committed by members of powerful groups are under-recorded in the official statistics.

Making connections

Cohen's subcultural theory links delinquency to a range of factors including social class, gender and age.

Is it useful to see class, gender and age as completely separate from each other or is it more useful to see them as linked together?

White-collar crime

The term 'white-collar crime' refers broadly to crimes committed by people in relatively high-status positions (such as managers in business, accountants or lawyers) during the course of their work. Examples include tax evasion, fraud and misuse of expense accounts. These crimes are conducted within the context of everyday business and workplace activity rather than, for instance, on the streets. This helps to prevent white-collar crime from being discovered.

Nelken (2007) argues that with white-collar crimes, the problem is to discover whether there has actually been an offence rather than to identify the culprit. Fraud, for example, is frequently undetected if there is no obvious victim. Furthermore, the police are often not called upon when an offence has been committed. Consequently, much white-collar crime is likely to be undiscovered, unreported and unrecorded. It is an example of an **invisible crime**.

FOCUS ON SKILLS: DISCUSSION ACTIVITY

Invisible crime

1 In a small group, discuss why it might be difficult to discover whether, with white-collar crime, there has actually been an offence.

2 Can you think of other examples of invisible crimes?

Note down the key points arising from your discussion.

Corporate crime

Corporate crime refers to crimes committed by employees on behalf of the organisation or company they work for. It includes offences against consumers such as the manufacture and sale of unsafe products or unfit foods. It also includes environmental offences involving, for instance, pollution of water and air.

Tombs (2005) notes that there is little effort by governments to keep statistics on corporate crime. It can be difficult to successfully prosecute crimes carried out by big corporations, because they can access huge resources to employ skilled lawyers, who will fight their cases in court.

Stretch and challenge

How do you think Marxist sociologists might explain the over-representation of working-class people within prisons?

Write a paragraph to summarise their approach.

Corporate crime includes environmental offences involving pollution of water and air.

Key point

Official statistics suggest that criminal activity is more commonly found in particular social groups. However, studies of white-collar and corporate crime paint a more complex picture.

Check your understanding: Exam practice

Identify and explain one reason why corporate crime may be under-represented in crime statistics. (4 marks)

What is the relationship between gender and involvement in crime?

Objectives
- Describe the relationship between gender and involvement in crime
- Explain this relationship

Official statistics such as those from the Ministry of Justice suggest that females are less likely to offend than males and are less likely to commit serious offences. Females are also less likely to reoffend than males.

Glossary term

indictable offences

- In 2014, women made up just 5 per cent of the prison population in England and Wales.
- In 2015, 58 780 females and 304 870 males were found guilty of, or cautioned for, **indictable offences** (serious crimes) in England and Wales. In other words, around 20 per cent of these offenders were female and 80 per cent were male.
- The number of females found guilty of, or cautioned for, indictable offences (serious crimes) in England and Wales was lower among those aged 10 to 20 years in 2015 than in 2005. However, it was higher among women aged 21 years and over in 2015 than in 2005.
- In 2013, around 45 per cent of all indictable convictions for females and 22 per cent of all indictable convictions for males in England and Wales were for shoplifting. The second largest number of indictable convictions for females was for violence against the person (for example, physically assaulting someone).

FOCUS ON SKILLS: WRITTEN ACTIVITY

Official statistics

Read through the information above and answer the following questions.

1 What percentage of the prison population did men make up in England and Wales in 2014?
2 Among which age group did the number of females found guilty of, or cautioned for, indictable offences in England and Wales increase between 2005 and 2015?
3 Which serious offences were most common for women in England and Wales in 2013?

FOCUS ON SKILLS: DISCUSSION ACTIVITY

Gender and serious crime

In a small group, discuss the possible reasons why females commit fewer serious crimes than males. How might feminist approaches explain this?

Note down your ideas.

Explanations for women's lesser involvement in crime

Females tend to be less involved in crime than males because of gender socialisation. From early childhood, we have different expectations of children's behaviour according to their gender. In general, girls are expected to be more passive and boys more active. If boys and men conform to society's views of masculinity, they may be under pressure to be macho and 'tough'. These expectations may lead males into conflict with the police and into criminal activity such as alcohol-related crime.

Girls and boys are often socialised differently.

Feminists such as Heidensohn (see Topic 9) argue that females have fewer opportunities than males to commit criminal offences because their behaviour is more closely monitored and controlled. Young girls, for example, tend to be supervised more carefully by their parents than young boys. Similarly, greater restrictions are often placed on the freedom of teenage girls compared to boys. As adults, women often have more domestic and caring responsibilities than men and so have less opportunity to commit serious crimes.

Female offenders may be treated differently from male offenders within the criminal justice system. One view is that they are treated more leniently because those in authority within law enforcement hold stereotyped beliefs about women and men. For example, female offenders are seen as 'sad' rather than 'bad' and in need of help rather than punishment. Consequently, female offenders, particularly those who conform to gender stereotypes, may receive more lenient treatment. This could apply at every stage: during reporting of a crime, police response, trial and sentencing. A related view is that women are treated more leniently because society sees them as though they are children who are not fully responsible for their actions. This type of explanation is sometimes known as the 'chivalry' thesis (see Topic 9).

Other approaches, however, argue that female offenders are treated more harshly than males because their offending behaviour is seen not just as illegal but also as unfeminine. This is referred to as the double deviance theory (see Topic 9).

Stretch and challenge
What do the traditional birthday cards tell us about expectations surrounding femininity and masculinity?

Making connections
Which other topic areas is the concept of socialisation relevant to?

Key points
- Official statistics such as court records suggest that more men commit crime than women.

- Possible explanations for this include gender socialisation, constraints on women and the chivalry thesis.

Check your understanding: Exam practice
Identify and explain one reason why there are far fewer women than men in prisons in England and Wales. **(4 marks)**

How do sociologists explain women's increasing involvement in crime?

Objective
- Explain the increasing involvement of women in crime

Why are women increasingly involved in crime in the UK?

Glossary term

social problem

Although females are less likely to offend than males, recent statistics suggest that the gender gap is narrowing. The number of female offenders aged 21 years and over in the UK is increasing and more women are being arrested for violence. Some explanations for this increase focus on the changing position of women in society. While becoming more independent and gaining equality in the workplace, women have lost many of the constraints or controls that kept them away from crime. So they now have similar legal and illegal opportunities to men. Some commentators link the rise in female offenders over the last 40 years to the liberation of women brought about by feminism.

An alternative explanation argues that the majority of women have not benefited greatly from equality in the workplace or in the professions. On the contrary, women are more likely than men to be unemployed or employed in low paid, unskilled, part-time jobs. As a result, more women than men live in relative poverty. According to this view, women's increased involvement in crime is related to their economic situation and their experiences of poverty. This helps to explain why female offenders tend to be poor and why they often engage in crimes such as shoplifting.

It is also argued that the female crime rate has increased because more women are now being arrested, charged and convicted – rather than because more women are actually committing offences such as violent crimes. According to this view, changing attitudes towards gender and crime mean that the more lenient treatment of women within the criminal justice system (the 'chivalry effect' – see page 216) is now less common. Joan Garrod (2007), for example, notes that the increase in the number of women in prisons over the last 10 years is almost entirely due to harsher sentencing rather than because women have started to commit more serious crimes.

Stretch and challenge

1 What is meant by the 'chivalry effect'?
2 What evidence is there to suggest that the chivalry effect is becoming less significant?

FOCUS ON SKILLS: WRITTEN ACTIVITY

Girls in gangs

Read through the information below and answer the questions that follow.

> During the 1960s and 1970s, most girls did not take part in activities associated with working-class, male youth subcultures such as drug use, football hooliganism and street fighting. They were more likely to hang out in the privacy of their bedrooms with their friends. Since then, however, young women's participation in youth subcultures and gangs has changed. They are now more likely to get involved in the types of crime and violence that occur in gangs.
>
> Some newspaper reports suggest not only that many girls are now joining criminal gangs but also that the number of girls involved in all-girl gangs is on the rise.

1 According to this information, how did many girls spend their time in the 1960s and 1970s?

2 Identify one aspect of girls' involvement in crime that has changed recently.

One view is that girls used to spend time indoors with friends rather than in street-based youth subcultures.

FOCUS ON RESEARCH: DISCUSSION ACTIVITY

Researching girls in gangs

Young people's involvement in gangs is considered a serious **social problem**, generating a lot of media coverage and public debate in recent years. Imagine that you are putting together a research proposal to get funding for a project on young females in gangs.

In a small group, put together a research proposal for a study of young females' involvement in gangs. Ensure that you discuss and make notes on the following:

1 the title of your proposed research study

2 your research questions, aims and/or hypotheses

3 at least one primary research method that you plan to use in your investigation and an explanation of how and why you would use it

4 at least one secondary source of data, explaining how you would use it

5 a discussion of at least two ethical issues that may arise during the process of doing your research and how you plan to deal with them.

Key points

- Recent statistics suggest that the number of female offenders in the UK is increasing.

- Possible explanations for this include the changing position of women in society, the impact of feminism, changing attitudes to gender and crime, and poverty.

Check your understanding: Exam practice

Discuss how far sociologists agree that feminism has led to an increase in the number of female offenders in the UK over the last 40 years.

(12 marks)

Is there a link between gender, crime and poverty?

Objective
- Describe the ideas of Pat Carlen on female offenders

FOCUS ON KEY THINKERS

Pat Carlen on women, crime and poverty

Pat Carlen (1988) focuses on both gender and social class when studying crime from a feminist perspective. She carried out detailed, unstructured, taped interviews with 39 female offenders. The women were aged 15 to 46 years and most of them were working class. They had been convicted of offences including assault, burglary, shoplifting, fraud and prostitution. Twenty of the interviews took place in Bullwood Hall, a prison and youth custody centre. Most of the other interviews took place in the women's homes.

Among her aims, Carlen wanted to find out what the women themselves saw as:

- the main influences on their criminal careers

- the major turning points in their criminal careers.

She describes the women's accounts as oral histories of their criminal careers.

FOCUS ON RESEARCH: WRITTEN ACTIVITY

Drawing on the information above, answer the following questions.

1 Describe the method used by Pat Carlen in her research.
2 Identify and explain one advantage of using this method.
3 How far is the sample likely to be representative or typical of all female offenders?
4 How far is it possible to generalise from this sample?

Glossary terms

class deal, gender deal

The class deal and the gender deal

In her analysis, Carlen draws on control theory (see Topic 9), which examines why most people conform to the rules. Control theory argues that people behave rationally and that they are controlled through a 'deal' that offers them rewards for conforming. They are more likely to conform when they feel the rewards (for example, material possessions and emotional support) are worth it.

For working-class women, the workplace and the family are both major mechanisms of social control. They are controlled through the promise of rewards at work and in the family in return for conforming. They are expected to make the '**class deal**' and the

Making connections

1 Which other sociologist whose work you have studied was interested in how deviant careers develop over time?

2 Which other feminist sociologist drew on control theory in her explanation of women and crime?

'gender deal' in return for rewards. The class deal offers them material rewards such as consumer goods if they work for a wage. The gender deal offers them material and emotional rewards if they live with a male breadwinner within the family.

However, when these rewards are not available or they turn out not to be worth it, the gender deal and the class deal break down. At this point in the women's lives, crime becomes a possibility.

Carlen explores the circumstances at specific points in the 39 women's criminal careers when they felt they had nothing to lose by breaking the law. The women identified four major factors as linked to their law breaking. These were: poverty, living in residential care, drug or alcohol addiction, and the search for excitement. Poverty and being in care led to them rejecting the class and gender deals.

FOCUS ON SKILLS: DISCUSSION ACTIVITY

Factors linked to law breaking

In a small group, discuss how the experience of poverty and the problems associated with living in residential care might lead some women to crime.

Make a note of your ideas.

Refusing the class deal

Most of the women in Carlen's study had not found any legitimate ways of earning a decent living. They had little experience of the rewards of the class deal such as consumer goods. They had more to gain than to lose by offending. For them, crime was a way of trying to solve the problems of poverty.

Refusing the gender deal

By signing up for the gender deal, women are supposed to be rewarded with happiness and fulfilment from family life. However, many of the women in Carlen's study had not experienced the rewards that the gender deal is supposed to offer. Many had lived in residential care and did not have bonds with family and friends. Some had been abused by partners or fathers. The women had nothing to lose by committing crime and everything to gain.

Key points

- Pat Carlen explores the links between poverty and law breaking among a sample of 39 female offenders.

- Working-class women are expected to sign up for the class deal and the gender deal in return for material and emotional rewards. When these rewards are not forthcoming, women reject the deals. They commit crimes because they have more to gain than to lose by offending.

Check your understanding: Exam practice

1 Describe what sociologists mean by 'the gender deal'. (3 marks)

2 Describe what sociologists mean by 'the class deal'. (3 marks)

Is there a link between gender, crime and poverty? **233**

What is the relationship between ethnicity and crime?

Objective
- Describe the patterns in the relationship between ethnicity and crime as shown in official statistics

Statistics from the Ministry of Justice (2015) show that members of some ethnic groups are over-represented in the prison population relative to their proportion in the general population. Black people, for example, are around four times more likely than white people to be in prison.

Glossary term

legislation

FOCUS ON SKILLS: WRITTEN ACTIVITY

The prison population

The bar chart shows that there were around 14 white prisoners for every 10 000 white people in England and Wales in 2014.

Examine this information, then answer the questions that follow.

British nationals in the prison population by ethnicity per 10 000 people aged 15 years or over; 2014, England and Wales

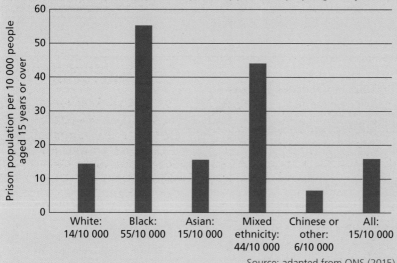

Source: adapted from ONS (2015)

1 How many prisoners were there for every 10 000 people in England and Wales?
2 How many prisoners of Asian heritage were there for every 10 000 people of Asian heritage in England and Wales?
3 Which minority ethnic group had the lowest proportion of prisoners relative to their number in the population?
4 Members of which minority ethnic group are most over-represented in prison?

Statistics from the Ministry of Justice (2014) show that black people were around four and a half times more likely than white people to be stopped and searched by the police in 2013/14. They were also more likely to be arrested after being stopped and searched.

Victims of crime

Walklate (2007) notes that some people are more likely than others to become victims of crime. The likelihood of becoming a crime victim is higher among some sections of society than others. She identifies four key factors: ethnicity, class, gender and age.

Those at high risk from crime

Class	The poor, living in private rented housing
Gender	Males
Age	The young
Ethnicity	Minority ethnic groups

Data from the Crime Survey for England and Wales (CSEW) in 2014/15 indicates that the risk of being a victim of personal crime once or more varies according to ethnicity. For example, 4 per cent of white adults were victims of a personal crime once or more in the previous 12 months, compared to around 11 per cent of adults of mixed heritage.

These CSEW results also show variations in the proportion of people from different ethnic groups who see the criminal justice system as fair. For example, a higher proportion of adults from Asian or Asian British ethnic groups than white adults are confident that the criminal justice system is fair.

FOCUS ON SKILLS: DISCUSSION ACTIVITY

Routine harassment in everyday life

In a small group, read through the information below and discuss the questions that follow.

> Researchers such as Walklate (2007) argue that police-recorded crime statistics are likely to underestimate the extent to which routine harassment is part of the everyday lives of people from minority ethnic groups in Britain.

1 What do you think researchers mean by 'routine harassment'?
2 Why do you think police-recorded crime statistics might underestimate this?
3 In the UK, there are laws to tackle hate crime and racially motivated crime. How effective do you think **legislation** can be in tackling these crimes? Can you think of other ways of addressing these social problems?

Note down the main points made during your discussion.

Check your understanding: Exam practice

Identify one ethical issue that you would need to take into consideration when researching hate crime and explain how you would address this issue. (4 marks)

FOCUS ON RESEARCH: WRITTEN ACTIVITY

Researching people's views on the criminal justice system

Imagine that you are investigating people's view on the effectiveness of the criminal justice system in the UK and their confidence in the system. Your main aim is to compare people's responses according to their ethnicity, age and gender.

1 Identify one method that you could use in your research and explain why you would use this particular method.
2 Identify one disadvantage of using your chosen method to investigate this issue.

Making connections

Institutional racism

In Chapter 2 Topic 22, we looked at the concept of institutional racism. How might this concept be applied to the criminal justice system?

Key points

- Members of some ethnic groups are over-represented, while others are under-represented, in the prison population relative to their proportion in the general population.
- Some ethnic groups are more likely to be victims of crime than others.

How do sociologists explain the patterns in the statistics on ethnicity and crime?

Objective
- Explain the relationship between ethnicity and involvement in crime as shown in statistical data

Explaining the statistics on ethnicity and crime

We could take the statistics at face value and see them as reflecting the level of crime within each ethnic group. This would involve arguing, for example, that there are more black people in prison relative to their proportion in the general population because they commit more crime than members of other ethnic groups. If we assume for the moment that this is actually the case, then one possible explanation is that higher proportions of black people experience unemployment. So the level of crime may be linked to poverty and deprivation.

An alternative approach, however, rejects the idea that the statistics reflect the actual levels of crime in society and argues instead that the statistics exaggerate crime among particular ethnic groups. Crime statistics can be seen as reflecting the way policing is carried out and bias within the criminal justice system. A number of sociologists have argued that black people are more likely to be targeted, prosecuted, convicted and sentenced for longer periods of time than people from other ethnic groups. The Macpherson Report of 1999 also identified institutional racism (see Chapter 2, Topic 22) within the Metropolitan Police.

Making connections

How have the concepts of poverty and deprivation been used to explain the underachievement of some groups of students at school? Make a note of your ideas.

FOCUS ON THEORY: DISCUSSION ACTIVITY

Theoretical approaches

1 In a small group, discuss how you might explain crime among some minority ethnic groups using Merton's ideas (see Topic 7).

2 How might you explain the over-representation of some minority ethnic groups in prison using Becker's ideas (see Topic 10)?

3 How might Marxist sociologists (see Topic 8) explain this over-representation?

Note down three points arising from your discussion.

FOCUS ON SKILLS: WRITTEN ACTIVITY

Is policing fair?

The following extract is from an article that explores whether policing focuses more on some disadvantaged groups (such as young black men), while other individuals or groups avoid attention from the police. Read the article, then answer the questions that follow.

'A view often expressed by sociologists and criminologists is that some people are "criminalised" while other (often more serious) offenders avoid police attention.

Since catching offenders "in the act" is actually rare, police officers tend to focus their attention on individuals they think are "likely" to be offenders. They do this by developing a profile of a "typical" offender. These informal profiles are largely based on two sources of information.

- First, officers' own views and previous encounters with offenders. However, these encounters are problematic because they are rarely systematic. Most offenders are never caught and those who are caught are either unlucky or slow (thus not necessarily representative of offenders in general).
- Second, information from the public. However, accounts of offenders given by victims or witnesses usually involve no more than descriptions of age, ethnicity and gender – presumably because these are often the characteristics most obvious to onlookers.

The central problem, therefore, is that police have to operate with profiles that rely on such characteristics (young, black males, etc.) rather than on anything that is clearly linked with offending. If the criteria usually used to select individuals for police attention are characteristics that someone can have little or no control over (e.g. their ethnicity, age, gender and social class) then only a narrow group of people becomes subject to police attention, on grounds that are often not justifiable.'

Source: adapted from Townsley, M. and Marshall, B. (2006) 'Is Policing Fair?' in *Sociology Review* 16(2), pp. 19–21.

1 In the first sentence, the article refers to the view that some offenders avoid police attention. Identify two examples of crime that appear to avoid police attention.
2 According to the authors of this article, what two sources of information are profiles of 'typical' offenders based on?
3 On what grounds might the quality of each of these two sources of information be questioned?

Stretch and challenge

Drawing on this article, write a paragraph to explain why the policing of young black men can be seen as unfair.

FOCUS ON SKILLS: WRITTEN ACTIVITY

Researching policing in urban zones

Identify one disadvantage of using non-participant observation to investigate policing in urban zones of cities.

Key points

- Crime among some members of minority ethnic groups has been linked to poverty and deprivation.
- Other approaches argue that official statistics of crime reflect institutional racism, policing methods and bias within the criminal justice system.

Check your understanding: Exam practice

Discuss how far sociologists agree that police-recorded crime statistics exaggerate the true level of crime among some ethnic groups. (12 marks)

What is the relationship between age and involvement in crime?

Official statistics suggest a link between age and offending behaviour, with younger people (particularly males) being more likely to engage in criminal activity than older people. For instance, in 2015, a higher proportion of males aged 15 to 20 years in England and Wales were found guilty of, or given a **police caution** for, indictable offences (serious crimes) than men aged 21 years and over.

Glossary term

police caution

FOCUS ON SKILLS: WRITTEN ACTIVITY

Offenders' age and gender

Study the information in the table and then answer the questions that follow.

The number of people who were found guilty or cautioned for indictable (serious) offences per 100 000 population, by gender and age group in 2005 and 2015 in England and Wales

2005	Males aged 10–11	Males aged 12–14	Males aged 15–17	Males aged 18–20	Males aged 21 and over
	320	1684	4489	4707	1104
	Females aged 10–11	Females aged 12–14	Females aged 15–17	Females aged 18–20	Females aged 21 and over
	27	371	780	639	187
2015	Males aged 10–11	Males aged 12–14	Males aged 15–17	Males aged 18–20	Males aged 21 and over
	44	573	2000	3031	1171
	Females aged 10–11	Females aged 12–14	Females aged 15–17	Females aged 18–20	Females aged 21 and over
	5	125	325	421	226

Source: Ministry of Justice (2016)

1 According to these figures, what was the peak offending age for males in England and Wales in both 2005 and 2015?
2 What was the peak offending age for females in 2015?
3 Do these statistics tend to suggest that people are more likely or less likely to offend when aged 21 years and over?

Findings from self-report studies suggest that the majority of young people do not engage in crime. Additionally, young people who do engage in crime tend to commit relatively minor offences. Data from the 2004 Offending, Crime and Justice Survey, for example, indicate that 74 per cent of younger interviewees (that is, around three-quarters of the 5000 young people aged 10 to 25) said that they had not committed any of the offences they were asked about during the previous year. Of those who said they had committed one of these offences, many had committed relatively minor offences or had only offended occasionally.

Stretch and challenge

The statistics on page 238 tell us about the age and gender of convicted or *known* offenders. Identify one group that the statistics do not tell us about.

FOCUS ON SKILLS: DISCUSSION ACTIVITY
Age and offending
In a small group, discuss possible reasons why:
a some young people are more likely to offend than others
b young people are generally more likely to offend than people in their parents' or grandparents' age groups.

Make a note of four points arising from your discussion.

Young offenders aged over 15 years may be held in a young offender institution.

FOCUS ON RESEARCH: WRITTEN ACTIVITY
Older people in prisons
Read through the information and then answer the question below.

Older people are much less likely than younger adults or teenagers to be arrested and convicted of a criminal offence. However, according to the Prison Reform Trust, people aged over 60 years are the fastest growing age group in prisons in England and Wales. Some of these prisoners are 'lifers' who received long sentences when they were younger and are now growing old in prison. Some are repeat offenders who have been in prison several times over the course of their lives while others offended for the first time when they were in their fifties or sixties.

The increase in the number of older prisoners is partly linked to demographic changes (see Chapter 3, Topic 18). People are living longer in the UK and, as a result, there are now more older people in the population to commit crime.

Identify and explain one advantage of using structured interviews to investigate the experiences of older people in prisons.

Making connections

The information on older people in prison is linked to the material you studied in Chapter 3 Topic 18 on the increase in life expectancy. Write a sentence to show how they are connected.

Check your understanding: Exam practice
1 Identify one ethical issue you might experience when researching young people's involvement in crime and explain how you would address this issue. (4 marks)
2 Identify and explain one problem that an adult researcher might experience when investigating young people's involvement in crime using semi-structured interviews. (4 marks)

Key point

Official statistics from the Ministry of Justice indicate that criminal activity is more commonly found in particular social groups such as young males.

How do sociologists explain the links between age and crime and deviance?

Objectives
- Explain young people's involvement in criminal and deviant behaviour
- Describe the ideas of Albert Cohen on delinquent subcultures
- Criticise Cohen's approach

Official statistics indicate that young people, particularly males, are more likely than other groups to engage in crime and deviance. One explanation for this is that young people may seek excitement, which leads them into trouble with the police. The experience of rule breaking in itself has attractions when it generates feelings of excitement and an adrenaline rush.

Inadequate socialisation

Functionalist theories stress the importance of the primary socialisation process within families. One function of the nuclear family is socialisation of children into society's norms and values. If children fail to learn the norms and values, they may engage in crime and deviance from a young age.

Some commentators suggest that children from homes where parents do not take responsibility for their upbringing tend to be more prone to crime. Such explanations focus on what they see as ineffective socialisation practices. They highlight poor parenting and lack of supervision of children – particularly in fatherless families – which lead to delinquency. Delinquent teenagers are seen as inadequately socialised into society's norms and values.

Other agencies of socialisation, such as schools, religions and the mass media, are also seen as failing to socialise children into society's norms and values. For example, the apparent lack of discipline in schools and the decline in the influence of religious values are also linked to inadequate socialisation. These approaches suggest that the mass media (including the film and music industry) have a negative impact by glamorising gun crime and violence. Such explanations identify a breakdown in the social control of some young people, both at home and at school.

Subcultural theory

Some sociologists explain both juvenile delinquency and adult crime in terms of the values of a particular subculture. This type of explanation is referred to as subcultural theory.

Glossary terms

status frustration, urban

The proud parents? Children who are not adequately socialised in families may engage in crime.

Making connections

How does this explanation (inadequate socialisation) link to the theme of the quality of parenting in Chapter 3?

FOCUS ON KEY THINKERS

Albert Cohen: Subcultural theory and delinquent subcultures

Albert Cohen (1955) studied juvenile delinquency among working-class boys in North America. He argued that individuals do not carry out delinquent acts such as vandalism or violence on their own. Cohen sees juvenile delinquency as a group phenomenon. Young males learn to become delinquents by becoming members of groups or gangs in which delinquent behaviour already exists as 'the done thing'. Delinquency is to do with being part of a delinquent subculture or a way of life among boys' gangs in **urban** neighbourhoods of large cities.

Delinquency is seen as part of a group subculture within urban neighbourhoods. But do you see a delinquent or an artist at work here?

FOCUS ON THEORY: DISCUSSION ACTIVITY

Delinquency as a group phenomenon

In a small group, discuss how far you agree with Albert Cohen's view that delinquency among young people is a group response rather than an individual activity. Do some children learn to be delinquent by joining delinquent groups or is delinquency linked to personality?

Note down three points arising from your discussion.

Cohen linked juvenile delinquency to the education system in the United States (See Chapter 5 Topic 14). He argued that schools are based on middle-class values and expectations. As a result, working-class boys cannot compete on the same terms as middle-class boys to get status and qualifications through education.

Working-class boys experience **status frustration** in trying but failing to meet middle-class expectations at school. Being part of a delinquent subculture enables these boys to gain status within their group, flout (disobey) the school rules and hit back at the school system that has branded them as failures.

Criticisms of Albert Cohen

- Cohen's work shows a middle-class bias. He assumes that working-class delinquents start out by accepting middle-class values and aspirations such as educational success.
- Cohen focuses on delinquent boys in gangs. Feminists point out that he ignores girls and question how far his explanation applies to girls.

Making connections

The lads' anti-school culture

Deviancy has been linked to school subcultures in Britain. From a Marxist perspective, Paul Willis (1977) focuses on 'the lads' in a secondary school in the Midlands (see Chapter 4 Topic 20). How does he explain the lads' anti-school culture?

Key points

- Functionalism stresses the importance of primary socialisation in nuclear families.
- Some commentators explain crime and deviance among young people in terms of inadequate socialisation and poor parenting.
- Subcultural theories explain crime and deviance in terms of the values of a particular subculture and the influence of the peer group.

Check your understanding: Exam practice

Describe one example of a delinquent subculture.   (3 marks)

What is the role of the mass media in the process of deviancy amplification?

Objective
- Explain the terms 'moral panic' and 'deviancy amplification'

Stan Cohen (1972) argues that the media are involved in the creation of **moral panics**. A moral panic involves exaggerating the extent and significance of a social problem. One important aspect of a moral panic is that a particular group is cast as a **folk devil**. In other words, it becomes defined as a threat to society's values. The group is portrayed in stereotypical terms by the mass media.

> **Glossary terms**
>
> asylum seekers, benefit cheats, case study, deviancy amplification, folk devil, image, moral panic

FOCUS ON SKILLS: DISCUSSION ACTIVITY

Folk devils

'Hoodies' have been cast as folk devils by the media. Working in pairs, can you think of examples of other groups who have been cast as folk devils?

Make a note of your ideas.

Stan Cohen undertook a **case study** of the moral panic surrounding mods and rockers during the 1960s. Events in 1964 in Clacton, a small holiday resort on the east coast of England, were the starting point. Easter Sunday in 1964 was the coldest for 80 years. A few groups of bored young people started scuffling on pavements and throwing stones at each other. The mods and rockers factions started separating out. Cohen describes what happened next:

> 'Those on bikes and scooters roared up and down, windows were broken, some beach huts were wrecked and one boy fired a starting pistol in the air. The vast number of people crowding into the streets, the noise, everyone's general irritation and the actions of an unprepared and undermanned police force had the effect of making the two days unpleasant, oppressive and sometimes frightening.'
>
> Source: Cohen, S. (1972) *Folk Devils and Moral Panics: The Creation of the Mods and Rockers.* London: MacGibbon and Kee, p. 29

Mods and rockers – the folk devils of the 1960s

The incidents described by Cohen were reported in most national newspapers the next day. Reports included sensationalist headlines about what happened. In this way, the mods and rockers were cast as folk devils.

Stan Cohen argues that the media exaggerated the seriousness of the events in terms of:

- the numbers of young people taking part
- the numbers involved in violence
- the amount and effects of any damage or violence.

The media and deviancy amplification

In Stan Cohen's view, the media distorted the events and incidents and created a false **image** of young people and their activities. Cohen describes this process as **deviancy amplification**, which involves exaggerating and distorting what actually happened. Such amplification, Cohen suggests, encouraged other young people to behave in the way portrayed by the media. This resulted in further disturbances and led to the public outcry, which Cohen calls a moral panic.

People reading newspapers and watching scenes on television began to see the mods and rockers as a threat to law and order. The police, responding to the public outcry, acted harshly and this led to further arrests. Cohen's point is that the media can actually amplify deviance or provoke more deviant behaviour.

Cohen is aware that many readers may not have heard of mods and rockers. He points out, however, that the processes that bring about moral panics remain important. He highlights the more recent moral panics that have surrounded school violence, bullying and shootouts; **benefit cheats** and single mothers; refugees and **asylum seekers**.

FOCUS ON SKILLS: WRITTEN ACTIVITY
The internet and moral panics
Read through the information below, then answer the questions that follow.

Public debates and concerns have focused on the internet. McQuail (2003) views the anxieties over the internet as an example of a moral panic. Concerns about the internet include the ease with which undesirable content (including sexually explicit content) can enter people's homes and be accessed even by children. McQuail identifies other worries about the internet including:

- invasion of privacy
- defamation (attacking a person's character)
- fraud and other cybercrime
- facilitating crime and terrorism.

1 Identify one area of concern about the internet that focuses specifically on children.
2 Identify two other worries associated with the internet.

Check your understanding: Exam practice
1 Describe what sociologists mean by a 'moral panic'. (3 marks)
2 Identify and explain one advantage of using content analysis to investigate the way the popular (or tabloid) press cover crime. (4 marks)

Key points
- The media can exaggerate and distort crime and deviance. In doing so, they can amplify or provoke more of it. Such amplification can lead to a public outcry or a moral panic.
- Some sociologists see public anxieties over the internet as a moral panic.

What sort of crime-related issues cause public debates?

Objective
- Identify and describe some of the public debates over criminal and deviant behaviour

Issues related to crime and deviance are controversial and can generate heated debate among politicians and within the media. These debates focus on issues such as media coverage of crime, violent crime, sentencing, the treatment of young offenders, and the prison system.

Glossary terms

agenda setting, community, gatekeepers, media amplification, news values, official crime statistics, scapegoat, youth crime

Media coverage of crime

Crime is a major area of public concern and debate. The media reflect public concern about crime but their coverage can also fuel it (see Topic 22). The media play a role in **agenda setting** by deciding on the focus of public debates and discussions about crime and deviance. TV news broadcasts do this, for example, by focusing on some items, stories and views and excluding others. In this way, the public come to see particular issues as social problems.

The media operate with a set of values about what is considered 'newsworthy'; that is, what issues, events and personalities they think audiences will find interesting. Media **gatekeepers** (programme controllers, editors, journalists and owners) decide what to cover and how to present it. Editors allocate staff, space and time to topics according to their **news values**. Crime is considered by editors to be newsworthy.

One view is that the media intensify public concerns about law and order. Reiner (2007) notes that various studies of news reports have found that violent crimes are over-represented compared with their incidence in **official crime statistics**. The term **'media amplification'** is used to describe the way the media exaggerate the importance of an issue by over-reporting it. Reiner also argues that news stories exaggerate the crime risks faced by particular groups such as white people of higher status. They also over-represent women, children and older people as victims of crime.

FOCUS ON SKILLS: WRITTEN ACTIVITY
Researching public concerns over violent crime
Identify and explain one disadvantage of using focus group interviews to explore people's concerns about violent crime.

Concerns about youth crime

Anti-social behaviour among teenagers is seen as a problem partly because it generates fear that damages **community** life. Incidents of vandalism and graffiti are seen as costly in economic terms. More serious incidents of violence and teenage knife crime are seen as costly in terms of the young lives lost and the devastation caused within victims' families.

Youth crime and anti-social behaviour among teenagers are issues of particular concern to British politicians and policy makers. They are also considered newsworthy within the media. Pitts (2005) notes that youth crime is often front-page news in the UK and, as a result, it is a source of public anxiety. Anti-social behaviour, drug taking, binge drinking, gangs and violent crime (including gun and knife crimes) in British cities cause particular concern.

To what extent do the media scapegoat young people?

Newburn (2007) argues that young offenders have the position of society's number one 'folk devil'. The media portrayal of young people as folk devils can result in the creation of a 'moral panic' or a public outcry about their behaviour. Minor acts of vandalism committed by young people, for example, are regarded as typical of all young people and as a threat to social order. A moral panic also involves a process in which young people become **scapegoats** who are blamed for society's problems.

FOCUS ON SKILLS: DISCUSSION ACTIVITY

Policies to tackle knife crime

Read through the information and, in a small group, discuss the questions that follow.

> A ban on the sale of so-called 'zombie killer knives' came into force in England and Wales in 2016. These knives are inspired by horror films, but police say they are increasingly being carried by criminals. In 2015, a North London teenager was killed with one of them. Sarah Newton, Minister for Vulnerability, Safeguarding and Countering Extremism, said the knives glamorise violence, cause devastating damage and have no place in society. Anyone caught carrying one of them could now serve up to four years in prison.

1 How effective do you think a ban on carrying knives is likely to be as a way to tackle knife crime?

2 What other ways of tackling violent crime could you suggest?

Make a note of your ideas.

Key points

- Crime is a major focus of concern and debate among politicians, the media and the public.

- Public concerns focus on issues such as violent crime including gun and knife crime.

- Some sociologists argue that the media portray young people as folk devils, which can lead to a moral panic.

Check your understanding: Exam practice

1 Describe what sociologists mean by 'agenda setting'. (3 marks)

2 Describe what is meant by 'news values'. (3 marks)

What other crime-related issues cause public concern?

Objective
- Describe public concerns over sentencing, the prison system, the treatment of young offenders and anti-social behaviour

Sentencing

When someone is tried and found guilty of a crime, the magistrate or judge imposes a sentence. The purposes of a sentence include: punishing the offender, protecting the public, changing an offender's behaviour and reducing crime.

Different types of sentence are available, depending on how serious the crime is. The main types include a discharge for a minor offence, a fine for a less serious offence, a community sentence and a prison sentence.

- A discharge is given for minor crimes where the court decides that further punishment would not be appropriate.
- A fine of up to £5000 may be imposed by the Magistrates' Court. An unlimited fine may be imposed by the Crown Court.
- A community sentence might involve an offender having to avoid particular activities such as going to football matches or pubs. They may have to wear an electronic tag and stick to a curfew, do unpaid **community service** and have regular meetings with their probation officer.
- A prison sentence is given for the most serious offences and to protect the public from the offender.

A community sentence might involve doing unpaid work in the community.

One area of public concern lies in the lack of clarity about sentencing policy. For example, some prisoners are released before the end of their prison term and members of the public do not necessarily understand how this early release works. Others oppose the principle of early release and believe all prisoners should serve the full term of their prison sentence behind bars. A related view is that the prison regime and sentencing are not tough enough. Some people believe that prison sentences do not punish prisoners effectively or repair the harm caused to the victims of crime.

Another concern is whether particular groups who have not committed serious or violent offences should be imprisoned at all. These groups include vulnerable people, young people and people with mental health issues.

The prison system and the treatment of young offenders

- Major issues facing prisons include overcrowding, cuts in the number of prison staff, and the levels of suicide and self-harm among prisoners.

- There is concern about how young offenders are treated within the criminal justice system. A number of young adults have died while held in custody. Other concerns include the levels of suicide, self-harm and violence among young adult offenders held in young offender institutions.

FOCUS ON SKILLS: WRITTEN ACTIVITY

Sentencing

In a small group, discuss the following information. Consider the questions below and note down your ideas.

> One view is that women suffer more in prison and are damaged more by imprisonment than men. For example, there are fewer prisons for women so they are more likely to be imprisoned further from their homes and families than male prisoners. This could, for example, make it more difficult for their family members (including any children) to visit them, and leave them feeling isolated.

1 a How far do you agree that women are likely to suffer more while in prison than men?
  b Should factors like this be taken into account before the courts impose prison sentences on female offenders?

2 a Do you think vulnerable people should be imprisoned if they have not committed serious offences?
  b Would it make a difference to your views if such people have previous convictions?

Antisocial behaviour orders (ASBOs)

Governments in Britain have tried to reduce anti-social behaviour among adults and young people aged 10 years and over by anti-social behaviour orders (ASBOs.) Such policies, however, can be counterproductive. For example, ASBOs can be a status symbol or badge of honour among young people.

Stretch and challenge

Why do you think having an ASBO might be a source of status? How might subcultural theorists view ASBOs?

FOCUS ON SKILLS: WRITTEN ACTIVITY

Policies to deal with crime

Read through the information below and answer the question that follows.

> One policy to deal with violence and drug dealing among suspected gang members is gang injunctions. The police or a local authority in England and Wales have the power to apply to court for an injunction (an order to stop an individual from doing something) against a named person to prevent gang-related violence and drug dealing.

How might sociologists inform policy makers on policies and issues related to crime and deviance?

Key point

Public debates over criminal behaviour include concerns about lack of clarity in sentencing, the fate of some young offenders in young offender institutions and problems associated with prisons.

Check your understanding: Exam practice

Identify and describe one public debate over criminal behaviour. (3 marks)

What methods are used to research crime and deviance?

Objectives
- Describe some of the methods used to research crime and deviance
- Evaluate these methods

FOCUS ON RESEARCH: WRITTEN ACTIVITY

Researching women and crime

Read through the following information and answer the questions below.

Frances Heidensohn, a feminist researcher, explored women's experiences of crime and their reactions to their experiences (see Topic 9). Her book *Women and Crime* (1985) draws on a wide range of data including secondary sources from the UK and North America. She presents personal accounts by women criminals taken from their autobiographies and from authorised biographies. She draws on data from her own study of 77 delinquent girls and from studies by other researchers that include personal accounts from female offenders. She also draws on official crime statistics for England and Wales from the Home Office.

1 Describe one of the methods that Heidensohn used.
2 Identify one disadvantage of this method.

FOCUS ON RESEARCH: WRITTEN ACTIVITY

Researching women, crime and poverty

Pat Carlen (1988) carried out research on female offenders (see Topic 17). In the following extract from her book, she discusses an aspect of her research.

Read through this extract and then answer the questions below.

'Each woman was told (though in a variety of words and ways) that I wanted her to describe her progress through law-breaking, police stations, courts and custodial institutions and to start her narrative from the point where she thought it had all begun... Either at the beginning, during, or at the end of each interview, I checked out a list of questions relating to factual details that I wanted to collect, e.g. demographic details, age of first criminal contact with the police, age of first conscious law-breaking, etc.'

Source: Carlen, P. (1988) *Women, Crime and Poverty*. Milton Keynes: Open University Press, p. 175.

1 Is this type of interview likely to generate quantitative or qualitative data? Write a sentence to explain your answer.
2 How far would it be possible to replicate this type of interview?

FOCUS ON RESEARCH: DISCUSSION ACTIVITY

Gaining access

Many researchers experience difficulties in gaining access to, and being accepted by, people who are involved in criminal subcultures.

In a small group, discuss why some offenders might be reluctant to participate in research on crime and deviance.

Make a note of your ideas.

FOCUS ON RESEARCH: WRITTEN ACTIVITY
Researching marijuana users

Read through the following information and then answer the questions below.

In his book *Outsiders*, Howard Becker (1997) studied marijuana use. In the following extract from his book, he discusses some aspects of his methods.

> 'I conducted fifty interviews with marijuana users. I had been a professional dance musician for some years when I conducted this study and my first interviews were with people I had met in the music business. I asked them to put me in contact with other users who would be willing to discuss their experiences with me.'
>
> Source: Becker, H. (1997) *Outsiders: Studies in the Sociology of Deviance*. London: Free Press, p. 45.

1 Identify and describe the sampling technique used by Becker in his study.
2 Explain one advantage of using this sampling method.
3 Explain one disadvantage of this sampling technique.

FOCUS ON RESEARCH: WRITTEN ACTIVITY
Researching the media and violence

Read through this extract about studies of the influence of violence shown in the media and then answer the questions that follow.

> 'Careful sociological studies of media influences require a lot of time and money. Consequently they are heavily outnumbered by simpler studies, which often put their subjects into artificial situations (but then pretend they are studying the everyday world).
>
> Experiments involve forcing participants to watch a particular programme which they would not have chosen if left to their own devices and – just as artificially – observing them in a particular setting afterwards.
>
> Here, behaviour of children towards an object is often taken (artificially) to represent how they would behave towards a real person. Furthermore, this all rests on the mistaken belief that children's behaviour will not be affected by the fact that they know they are being tested and/or observed.'
>
> Source: adapted from Gauntlett, D. (2001) 'The Worrying Influence of "Media Effect" Studies', in M. Barker and J. Petley (eds). *Ill Effects: The Media/Violence Debate*. London: Routledge, p. 56.

1 Why are there relatively few careful sociological studies of media influences?
2 What term do sociologists use to describe people's behaviour being affected because they know they are being observed as part of a study?

Stretch and challenge
Drawing on the information in the extract above, identify two problems with studies of media influences based on experiments.

Check your understanding: Exam practice
Identify and explain one reason why researchers might find it difficult to obtain a representative sample of offenders.   (4 marks)

Focus on skills

Making connections: Written activity

Linking crime and deviance to education

As you study and revise the different areas and topics within sociology, remember to look out for connections or links between them. There are lots of links between the topics of crime and deviance and education. For instance, schools are an example of a key agency of social control.

Study the spider diagram and answer the question below.

Choose three of the links in the spider diagram and, in each case, explain briefly how it connects the topic of crime and deviance to education.

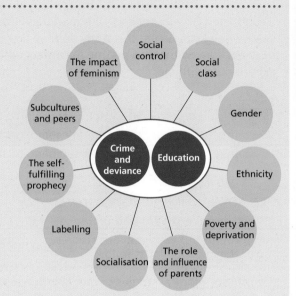

Making connections: Discussion activity

Criticisms of the criminal justice system

One important area to focus on in your revision is the views of the different perspectives, such as feminism and Marxism, on crime and deviance. For example, how would the feminist and Marxist approaches criticise the criminal justice system (including the police and the courts)?

Spider diagrams can be useful ways of organising your ideas or revising topics. An example is shown here.

In pairs, choose two of these links and discuss how each one can be used to criticise the criminal justice system.

Then team up with another pair, who have selected different links, and share your ideas.

Make a note of your ideas.

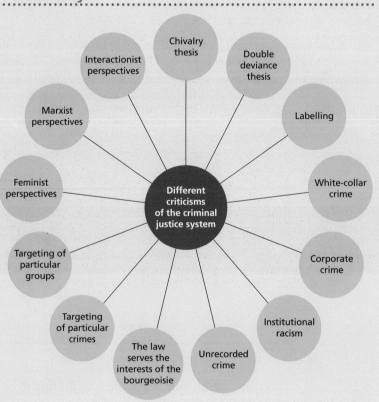

Similarities and differences between the perspectives

The various perspectives that you studied in this chapter have similarities and differences. For example, both Marxism and feminism can be seen as examples of conflict approaches because they see society as based on conflicting interests between different groups. Beyond this, however, their approaches differ. Feminists focus on gender conflict and some feminists link gender inequalities to the workings of patriarchal society. Marxists focus on class conflict and link class inequalities to the workings of capitalist society.

Drawing on what you have learned in this chapter, answer the following questions. If you are not sure about a particular answer, check back through the chapter.

1 Identify two sociological perspectives or approaches that:
   a are both structural approaches
   b refer to aspects of socialisation in their explanations.

2 Identify one sociological perspective that:
   a sees society as based on value consensus or agreement over shared values
   b rejects the idea that society is based on shared values.

3 Identify one criticism of:
   a Durkheim's work from a Marxist perspective
   b Albert Cohen's subcultural theory from a feminist perspective
   c Interactionism from a structural approach.

4 Identify one criticism of the:
   a Marxist perspective from a functionalist approach
   b Marxist perspective from a feminist approach
   c feminist perspective from a Marxist approach.

Stretch and challenge

Work your way through each of the other links in the first spider diagram on the previous page, making brief notes to explain each one.

Stretch and challenge

Work your way through the different criticisms of the criminal justice system, making brief notes to explain each one. You can skip the criticisms that you covered in the discussion activity.

Stretch and challenge

Linking families to crime and deviance

What links can you identify between the topics of crime and deviance and families?

For example:

- How does the process of social control link them together?
- Which approach connects the process of primary socialisation in families to shared norms and values?
- How is the 'gender deal' linked to families?

Crime and deviance (Paper 2)

In this section we look at what the Crime and deviance section of Paper 2 will look like, with some possible questions and marked candidate responses.*

*Please be aware that marks are advisory, based on sample AQA materials. Examination grade boundaries and marking guidance change annually – please visit the official AQA website for more information.

01 What type of sociological research asks people about crimes they have experienced? **[1 mark]**

A Self-report surveys ◯

B Victim surveys ☑ 1/1

C Police reports ◯

D Official statistics ◯

> Tip: Read these questions carefully! Often in the hurry to get started, candidates can misread the question and lose what is essentially an easy mark.

> Tip: In the exam, you simply need to tick whichever you think is the correct answer.

02 Identify and describe one formal agency of social control. **[3 marks]**

Formal social control refers to written rules and the law in society. Agencies of social control seek to enforce these laws and rules. One formal agency of social control would be the police, who investigate crimes and ensure that the people who break the laws are sent to prison, which means that people will obey the rules, as they do not want to be punished.

> Examiner comment: This is a good example of a concise response which scores full marks. This candidate has shown a clear understanding of what formal social control is and described the role the police have in enforcing social control and how fear of punishment ensures that people follow the rules. 3/3

03 Describe one example of deviant behaviour. **[3 marks]**

Deviant behaviour is behaviour that goes against the norms and values of society. For example, if you were to go outside naked this would not be seen as normal.

> Examiner comment: This candidate has demonstrated some understanding of what deviant behaviour is. This candidate needed to develop their explanation of what sociologists mean by 'norms and values' to score the extra mark. 2/3

Item A

Worry about crime

The British Crime Survey (BCS) asked approximately 50 000 people aged 16 and over about the crimes they had experienced in the last year. Respondents had to be a resident in a private household.

BSC respondents were questioned on their worry about crime. The following information shows changes in the proportion of people who answered that they were 'very worried' about burglary, violent crime and car crime.

Percentages of respondents who answered 'very worried' when asked how worried they were about particular crimes (England and Wales)

	2000	2006/07
Burglary	19	13
Violent crime	24	17
Car crime	21	13

Source: adapted from *Social Trends* (2008)

> Tip: Be sure to study items carefully. Pay extra attention to things such as dates and who conducted the research, as this is crucial to answering the next question, which tests how well you have read the item. You could be asked about the type of research methods that the researcher used, strengths or weaknesses of the research, or even to identify trends, patterns or make observations.

> Tip: The three questions that follow in the actual exam will expect you to have the 'context' of this item in mind. Try to refer to it whenever you can!

04 From **Item A**, examine **one** weakness of the research. **[2 marks]**

Tip: This question is testing how well you can read and analyse Item A!

One weakness of the research in Item A is that it only asked people who were residents in private households. This may mean it does not give you a true picture of 'worry about crime'.

Examiner comment: This candidate has identified a weakness with the sampling frame for the research (private households), which is enough to score them 1 mark. The development of why this is a weakness, implying that the sample may mean the researcher's findings are not a 'true picture', scores the second mark for this question. 2/2

05 Identify and explain **one** disadvantage of using covert observation to investigate criminal behaviour. **[4 marks]**

Covert observation is when you observe people without their knowledge. One disadvantage of using covert observation to investigate criminal behaviour would be that it could be dangerous to the researcher. The researcher will have to keep their real identity a secret otherwise the research may not be valid, but this might mean they have to do things like lie and hide cameras. If the researcher was discovered the criminals may hurt them; if the researcher used overt observation they would not be at risk as everyone would know who they are.

Examiner comment: The candidate shows a clear understanding of what covert observation is and explains a weakness of using it in the context of research into criminal activity. The comparison with overt observation as a safer method makes this a very strong answer. 4/4

06 Identify and describe **one** way the government has tried to reduce anti-social behaviour in recent years. **[4 marks]**

Tip: When a question says 'recent' years, examiners are looking for examples from the last 20 years or so. Try not to write about policies older than this.

The government introduced criminal behaviour orders (CBOs) in 2014; these orders meant that the police could put restrictions on what people convicted of anti-social behaviour offences could do. The police can tell people with CBOs that they are not allowed to do certain things or meet certain people; they can also tell them to go to things such as rehab if they need to. If people break their CBO they can go to prison (which is not the case if they break ASBOs), so these acts stop them from committing more anti-social behaviour.

Examiner comment: This is a good response where the candidate has shown a strong understanding of a recent government policy. They have explained what CBOs are and why they might reduce anti-social behaviour. Although only briefly, they compare them to ASBOs, implying they may be more effective. 4/4

07 Discuss how far sociologists agree that the middle class is less likely to commit crime than other social classes. **[12 marks]**

Sociologists would have different ideas about whether the middle class is less likely to commit crime than other classes.

Some sociologists would agree that the middle class is less likely to commit crime as they do not need the money or anything. Working class people may be poor and want things that others have and so commit crime, whereas the middle class have these things already.

Other sociologists may disagree and say that the middle class do commit lots of crime but they do things like tax evasion and stealing pens from work, so it is not that they commit less crime it is just different.

Tip: In the essays, you are being assessed on four things: 1. Sociological knowledge (AO1: 4 marks); 2. Your ability to apply knowledge of theories, research and methods (AO2: 4 marks); 3. Your ability to evaluate sociological theories and concepts (AO3: 4 marks); 4. Your ability to write clearly and coherently, spelling well and using specialist terms accurately will affect the total mark you receive. If your response is not well structured (for example, in bullet points), even if you have demonstrated knowledge, application and evaluation, you will be unable to go beyond 7–9 marks.

Examiner comment: The candidate has shown only a very limited understanding of sociological arguments about class and crime, making only two real points. This candidate would have scored more marks if they had explained their sociological terms more and given more points to support agreement/disagreement with the statement. 3/12

Social stratification

What is social stratification?

Social stratification is a key concept in sociology. It describes the way society is structured in a hierarchy of strata or layers that are unequally ranked one above another. A social hierarchy is shaped like a pyramid and each layer is smaller but more powerful than the one below it. The most privileged group in society forms the top layer and the least favoured group forms the bottom layer.

FOCUS ON SKILLS: WRITTEN ACTIVITY

Social hierarchy

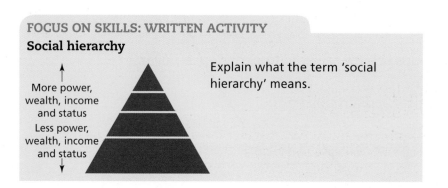

More power, wealth, income and status

Less power, wealth, income and status

Explain what the term 'social hierarchy' means.

Social inequality

Social inequality is another key concept in sociology. It refers to the uneven distribution of:

- resources such as money and power
- life chances or opportunities related to, for example, education, employment and health.

Focusing on social inequality highlights important differences between individuals and groups in their access to, and share of, these resources and opportunities. Studies of inequality explore:

- the nature of inequality
- how much inequality there is and who gets what
- why some people get more than others.

Social class, gender, ethnicity and age are all sources of inequality in the UK. In other words, resources and opportunities are distributed unequally between individuals and groups based on their class, gender, ethnicity and age. Piachaud (2009) argues that the causes of inequality within the UK include large differences between people in terms of inherited **wealth**, education and access to the labour market.

FOCUS ON SKILLS: DISCUSSION ACTIVITY

Social inequality

In a small group, discuss why some people have more opportunities than others. How far is social inequality bound to exist in all societies? How far do you think it is possible to reduce social inequality?

Make a note of three points raised during your discussion.

Social stratification and inequality

Stratification involves inequality between social groups in the distribution of economic and social resources such as wealth, **income**, status and power. These inequalities persist or carry on over time.

- **Wealth** refers to ownership of assets such as property, land and works of art. It also includes money held in savings accounts and shares in companies.
- **Income** may be received in cash (for example, wages) or in kind (for instance, use of a company car).
- **Status** refers to social standing or the prestige that an individual in a particular social position is given by other members of the community or society.
- **Power** concerns the ability of an individual or group to get what they want, despite any opposition from other people.

The group in the top rank of the social hierarchy is likely to have much more wealth, income, status or power than the one at the bottom.

Social stratification based on social class

In modern industrial societies such as Britain, social class is seen as the main form of stratification. Social class is based on economic factors such as occupation and income (how people earn a living). This form of stratification is said to be an open one, in that class position can be achieved and **social mobility** (movement up or down between the different classes) is possible.

Social class-based strata

Upper class (a minority: 10%)
Middle class (50%)
Working class (40%)

More power, wealth, income and status

Less power, wealth, income and status

In class-based societies, gender, ethnicity and age are also sources of inequality. For example, men and women in the same class may have very different life chances or opportunities in relation to pay and promotion at work. Women from different social classes may have more in common with each other than with men from their own class. Marxist approaches see social class as the key division in society. Feminist approaches see gender as a more significant source of inequality than social class.

Check your understanding: Exam practice

Describe what sociologists mean by the term 'social stratification'.
(3 marks)

Stretch and challenge

How far do you think that wealth necessarily brings status in Britain today? Note down your ideas.

Key points

- Social stratification describes the way that society is structured in a hierarchy of unequal layers.

- In Britain today, social class is seen as the main form of stratification.

- Social inequality refers to the unequal distribution of resources and opportunities.

What other forms of social stratification are there?

Forms of stratification can vary between different societies at one point in time. They can also change within one particular society over time. **Slavery**, for example, existed as a form of stratification in Ancient Greece and Rome and in the southern states of the United States in the 19th century. Under slavery, one group claims the right to own another group and treats them as property.

Stratification systems differ according to whether status is ascribed or achieved. With **ascribed status**, social positions are fixed at birth and unchanging over time. With **achieved status**, they are earned on the basis of personal talents or merit. Promotion at work, for example, can be earned through experience, ability or effort.

Stratification systems also differ according to how open or closed they are; that is, how easily an individual can move up or down between the strata. In an open society, movement up or down between the different strata is possible. In a closed society, such movement is much less likely to occur. The term 'social mobility' refers to movement between the layers or strata. In societies where status is ascribed, there is little social mobility. However, in achievement-based societies, there is movement between the layers.

> ### Glossary terms
>
> achieved status, apartheid, ascribed status, caste, feudalism, slavery

Social position may be ascribed at birth.

Feudalism

The feudal system operated, for example, in medieval Europe. In **feudalism**, there were four layers in society called estates. All subjects swore allegiance to the king, whose authority was seen as God-given. The king rewarded nobles with land. The nobles, in turn, gave some of this land to the knights, who swore allegiance to them. At the bottom of the hierarchy, peasants or serfs were given the use of small pieces of land in exchange for some of their produce and for military service.

An individual's position in society was ascribed and there was little or no chance of moving up into the next estate. As with some other forms of stratification, marriage between people from different strata was unthinkable.

The feudal system.

The caste system in traditional India

The **caste** system in India is another form of stratification. Here, people are born into a particular caste and their social position is ascribed at birth. The system is closed, so there is little movement between the different layers. Each caste was traditionally associated with particular occupations.

Main castes	Types of occupation	Status
Brahmin	Priests, teachers	Higher status
Kshatriyas	Soldiers, land owners	↑
Vaishyas	Merchants, traders	Lower status
Shudras	Servants, manual workers	↓
Dalits ('Untouchables')	Do the worst jobs in society	Social outcasts

The caste system is linked to the Hindu religion. Hindus believe that they are born into a particular caste and deserve to be there as a result of their behaviour in their previous life. By living according to the rules now, Hindus can ensure that they will be reborn into a higher caste in the next life. In this way, they can progress through the ranks of the caste system. Inequality between different groups was justified as stemming from religious belief.

Apartheid

Apartheid in South Africa (1948–1994) was based on a government policy of racial segregation, and ethnicity was used as the basis for stratification. Apartheid applied to all aspects of society and so access to health, education, housing and employment was segregated according to whether a person was black, white or coloured.

Under apartheid, a person's position in society was ascribed at birth. Black people were denied the citizenship rights, and educational and employment opportunities available to white people, so their life chances were much worse, with little scope for social mobility.

Apartheid in South Africa.

FOCUS ON SKILLS: WRITTEN ACTIVITY

Comparing different forms of stratification
Copy out and complete this table comparing caste, apartheid and class.

	Caste	Apartheid	Social class
What is stratification based on?			
Is social position ascribed or achieved?			
Is the system open or closed?			
Is social mobility possible?			

Check your understanding: Exam practice

Identify and describe one example of social stratification.

(3 marks)

Stretch and challenge

Why might it be unfair to base status on ascription rather than on achievement?

Key point

Different forms of stratification have existed in different societies over time. Examples include slavery, caste, apartheid and feudalism as well as social class.

How does the functionalist approach view stratification?

Objectives
- Describe the key ideas of Davis and Moore
- Criticise Davis and Moore's account

FOCUS ON KEY THINKERS

Davis and Moore: The functionalist theory of stratification

Davis and Moore (1945) were American sociologists who argued that all societies are stratified and they all have social inequality. In their view, stratification is necessary to the working of society because it fulfils certain vital needs.

Glossary term

functionally important roles

Stratification as functionally necessary

- Davis and Moore argue that all societies need some way of placing individuals into the different social positions or roles that must be filled.
- Some of these positions are functionally more important for society than others. For example, they provide essential services and ensure society's survival over time.
- These **functionally important roles** are difficult to fill and require people with exceptional talent, skills and abilities. Only a minority have the natural talents and the potential to fill them. They must undertake lengthy and costly education and training, which involves making sacrifices.

Davis and Moore argue that these positions must rank highly in the social scale. They must have status, a high salary and so on in order to attract the right people to fill them.

In their view, social inequality is a means by which a society ensures that the most important positions are filled by the most talented, trained and qualified individuals. All societies must treat people differently in terms of their status. As a result, all societies must have some degree of inequality built into them. This is functional, however, because people accept that it is fair.

FOCUS ON SKILLS: WRITTEN ACTIVITY

The functionalist theory of stratification

For each issue below, decide which option fits the functionalist approach to stratification. For example, does functionalism see status as ascribed or achieved? Then copy out the table with the correct answer.

Status	ascribed / achieved
Talent is distributed equally	yes / no
Positions are earned on the basis of talent	yes / no
Social mobility is possible and desirable	yes / no
Social inequality is inevitable	yes / no

FOCUS ON SKILLS: DISCUSSION ACTIVITY

Jobs, talent and pay

In a small group, read through this list of jobs:

- city banker
- English teacher
- heart surgeon
- high court judge
- boy band member
- midwife

- member of parliament
- professional footballer
- reality TV star
- refuse collector
- vicar
- TV chat show host.

1 In your group, discuss and note down which three jobs fit each of the following criteria:

   a require the highest levels of talent or education

   b the most important in terms of the contribution they make to society

   c deserve the highest earnings

   d are usually very highly paid.

Did the same three jobs come up each time?

2 Write down the two most significant points that were made during your discussion.

Criticisms of Davis and Moore

- Many jobs that are vital to society have relatively low pay (in the case of nurses) or low status (in the case of refuse collectors).
- A group's pay and status may be linked to how much power they have rather than to the functional importance of their position.
- Critics reject the idea that society is meritocratic, that equal opportunities exist and that social mobility is widespread. Social stratification can be dysfunctional when it limits the discovery of talent because of inequality of opportunity.
- Talented people do not necessarily make sacrifices during their training. In reality, they can earn back any income lost during the training period in the first 10 years of their work. They also have access to leisure and freedom, unlike their peers, who are already at work.
- Rather than seeing stratification as functional, Marxists view it as a means by which a privileged minority exploit others. Neither inequality nor stratification is inevitable.
- Marxist and feminist approaches both see stratification as a system in which some groups in society (such as the bourgeoisie or men) gain at the expense of others.

Key points

- Davis and Moore argue that some roles are more functionally important than others. Most people lack the talent to fill these posts or the motivation to train for them.

- To attract the best-qualified people, top positions must provide access to desirable rewards such as high pay and status.

- Stratification is functional for society because it ensures that the most talented and qualified people fill the most important jobs.

Check your understanding: Exam practice

Identify and explain what sociologists mean by functionally important roles.   (4 marks)

How does the Marxist approach explain social class?

Objectives
- Describe the key ideas of Karl Marx on social class
- Criticise Marx's ideas

Marxist views of social class

Social class is a key concept in sociology but there is no agreed definition of this term among sociologists. The ideas of Karl Marx (and Max Weber – see Topic 5) have been central in developing sociological views on social class. In fact, they continue to shape debates on class in the early 21st century (Crompton, 2008).

Glossary terms

alienation, distribution of power and wealth, elite, false class consciousness, oligarchy, ruling-class ideology

FOCUS ON KEY THINKERS

Karl Marx writing on class in the 19th century

Karl Marx (1818–1883) argued that in order to understand the capitalist mode of production, it is necessary to focus on the social relations of production (social classes) and the means of production (property, big businesses, land, factories and machinery).

He identified two main classes in capitalist society: the bourgeoisie (the ruling class) and the proletariat (the subject class). Membership of these classes was determined by economic factors – that is, by ownership and non-ownership of the means of production. The wealthy bourgeoisie owned the means of production through their ownership of property, big businesses and so on. The proletariat did not own any property and, as wage labourers, were forced to sell their labour to the bourgeoisie in order to survive. The workers experienced **alienation** under capitalism because they lacked control over production and over the products of their labour.

Other classes included the lumpenproletariat (such as the 'drop-outs' and criminals of society) and the petty bourgeoisie (such as the owners of small businesses).

The two main classes had very different interests. For example, while the bourgeoisie aimed for ever-increasing profits, the proletariat sought higher wages. Marx saw the bourgeoisie as exploiting the proletariat and this situation led to class struggle or conflict between them.

Marx highlighted the link between social class and power. Due to their economic power, the bourgeoisie also held political power. They used this to further their own interests. The bourgeoisie's position was justified by **ruling-class ideology**; for example, values and ideas about freedom such as the free market serve to disguise exploitation and oppression. This ruling-class ideology led to **false class consciousness**. The proletariat, for example, was not aware of the true nature of social relationships under capitalism.

FOCUS ON THEORY: WRITTEN ACTIVITY

Marx on social class

Copy and complete this table to summarise Marx's views on the differences between the bourgeoisie and proletariat.

	Bourgeoisie	**Proletariat**
Ownership	•	•
Interests	•	•

Marx believed that the bourgeoisie would shrink in size and get much richer. Fierce competition would result in members of the petty bourgeoisie sinking into the proletariat. Over time, the proletariat would get bigger and increasingly poor.

Eventually, the proletariat would rebel, leading to a revolution or radical change in society. As a result, the means of production would be communally owned and the social class system would disappear.

Criticisms of Marx

- A social revolution has not occurred in Britain, partly as a result of increased standards of living and the development of the welfare state.
- The development of a large middle class and opportunities for social mobility challenge Marxist approaches to the class structure.
- Feminists argue that Marx and Marxists focus on class at the expense of gender divisions in society, while others argue that they neglect ethnicity.

However, sociologists drawing on Marxist approaches highlight the vast differences in the **distribution of power and wealth** between property owners and workers in contemporary society. Contemporary Marxists see this as the key social division in society.

Global capitalism in the 21st century

Karl Marx developed his theories during the 19th century. Contemporary Marxists have updated his ideas on class relations and applied them to the workings of global capitalism in the 21st century.

Graham Scambler (2016) argues that we are now in the era of financial capitalism and a tiny minority (less than 1 per cent) has true wealth and/or power. He identifies a small hard core of global capitalists including chief executives and financiers. This class has increased its influence over the power **elite** who head the state. Together, these capitalists and members of the power elite make up a ruling **oligarchy**. Although they now rule us, they are barely accountable to us.

Many commentators agree that giant multinational corporations (MNCs) have too much power. Critics of MNCs argue that they are able to influence government policies and avoid paying tax by exploiting loopholes in different countries' tax systems.

The Occupy Movement opposes the global power of the richest 1 per cent.

Key points

- Marx identified two main classes under capitalism: the bourgeoisie and the proletariat. Class membership was determined by economic factors (ownership and non-ownership of the means of production).
- More recent Marxist approaches focus on the workings of global financial capitalism.

Check your understanding: Exam practice

Identify and explain one advantage of using unstructured interviews when investigating the attitudes and values of powerful groups in British society. (4 marks)

How does Weber view social class?

Objective
- Describe the key ideas of Weber on class, status and power

Glossary terms

aristocracy, market situation

FOCUS ON KEY THINKERS

Weber writing on class in the late 19th and early 20th centuries

Max Weber (1864–1920) argued that classes were formed in marketplaces such as the labour market. In the labour market, one class of people hired labour and another class sold their labour. Weber (1947) saw the processes of hiring labour and the rewards (or life chances) that arose from this as crucial in explaining class.

Weber argued that a class is a group of people who have similar access to life chances; that is, chances of being successful (or otherwise) in life and opportunities in education, health and so on. Weber identified four main social classes:

- property owners
- professionals

- the petty bourgeoisie (for example, shopkeepers)
- the working class.

These different class situations reflected different **market situations** or different life chances in the labour market. Working-class people, for example, shared similar life chances in the labour market. However, they had different life chances from property owners.

Like Marx, Weber saw class as based on the distribution of economic resources such as wealth. However, Weber also stressed the importance of non-economic factors such as status (prestige) and power (political influence) in determining life chances and in shaping patterns of stratification.

Weber distinguished between class and status. While classes were formed in marketplaces, status groups could be identified by the prestige or honour attached to their styles of life. Weber argued that each of the four classes had a different amount of status, wealth and power.

In Marx's view, ownership was the most significant division in society. Other inequalities (such as status) arose from class divisions. Weber, however, saw class and status as two separate aspects of stratification. In Weber's view, a person's status may differ from their class (or economic) position. For instance:

- members of the **aristocracy** (such as a Lord or Lady) may have no savings but their title gives them status
- nurses or religious leaders may have relatively low incomes and no wealth but high status
- National Lottery millionaires may be very wealthy but lack status.

FOCUS ON THEORY: WRITTEN ACTIVITY

Weber on class

Copy out and complete this table to summarise what Weber meant by class, status and power.

Class	
Status	
Power	

Stretch and challenge

Identify one similarity and one difference between Marx and Weber's views on social class.

Celebrity status

Some sociologists argue that celebrity status is now one of the most important forms of status in society.

In a small group, discuss how far you agree with this view. Does celebrity bring economic, legal or political power?

Note down three points arising from your discussion.

Determining someone's social class

In 2014, a YouGov survey asked 3245 adults in Britain about the factors that determine social class. Respondents were asked: 'Which two or three of these, if any, do you regard as the most important in determining someone's social class?'

The survey results are listed below. Examine this information and answer the questions that follow.

How they look/the kind of clothes they wear	9%
How well off they are financially	30%
The kind of music, books and TV programmes they enjoy most	8%
The social class of their parents	22%
The sort of local area in which they live	24%
Their accent	9%
Their occupation	35%
Their views on politics and social issues	15%
Whether or not they went to university	6%
Whether they rent or own their home	8%
Whether they went to a state or private school	22%
None of these	18%
Don't know	10%

Source: adapted from YouGov/Prospect Survey Results, p. 1.

1 Which factor did the highest percentage of respondents see as most important in determining someone's social class?
2 Which factor did the lowest proportion see as most important?
3 What percentage saw parents' social class as most important?
4 What percentage of respondents did not know?
5 Explain one advantage of using a social survey to investigate people's views on social class.
6 Explain one disadvantage of using a social survey to investigate people's views on social class.

Key points

- Weber identified four main classes, reflecting different life chances.
- He saw class, status and power as important factors in determining life chances.

Check your understanding: Exam practice

Identify and explain what Weber meant by the term 'social class'. (4 marks)

How is social class measured?

Occupation is often used to measure social class because it is related to factors such as levels of pay, social status and life chances.

The Registrar General's classification

The Registrar General's social class scale was the UK's official government class scale between 1911 and 1998. It distinguishes between manual and non-manual occupations. Manual occupations are jobs that involve some physical effort. They can be skilled, semi-skilled or unskilled, and are seen as working class. Non-manual occupations require no physical effort. Skilled non-manual, intermediate and professional occupations are seen as middle class.

The Registrar General's social class scale identifies five social classes. Classes I, II and III (Non-manual) were seen as middle class and III (Manual), IV and V were seen as working class.

I	Professional occupations such as solicitors and surgeons
II	Managerial and technical occupations such as teachers, nurses and aircraft pilots
III (N)	Skilled non-manual occupations such as clerical workers, secretaries and receptionists
III (M)	Skilled manual occupations such as bus drivers, electricians and hairdressers
IV	Partly skilled occupations such as postal delivery workers, bar tenders and caretakers
V	Unskilled occupations such as labourers and cleaners

Source: Office of Population, Censuses and Surveys (1980) *Classification of Occupations*. HMSO: London.

Problems with the Registrar General's scale

- Classifications based on occupation cannot accommodate jobless people (such as retired or unemployed people). In practice, retired and unemployed people were allocated to a class based on their most recent occupation. However, people who had never worked were difficult to place.
- Men and unmarried women were allocated to a class on the basis of their own occupations. When more married women went into paid employment in the 1970s, the practice of assessing the class position of a family or couple on the basis of the man's occupation was challenged.
- Occupational class scales tell us nothing about an individual's wealth and property. It was not clear where the wealthy **upper class** or National Lottery millionaires should be placed.

- The same job title, such as doctor, lecturer or farmer, may hide significant differences. The title 'farmer', for example, could hide huge differences in wealth, income and status depending on the size and type of farm involved.

The National Statistics Socio-economic Classification (NS-SEC)

The NS-SEC has replaced the Registrar General's scale as the UK's official classification. The NS-SEC is also based on occupation, but one advantage is that it covers the whole adult population including, for example, unemployed people. The NS-SEC groups together occupations that have similar:

- rewards from work such as pay and fringe benefits (including, for example, health insurance and a company car), career prospects and job security
- employment status (whether an employer, self-employed or an employee)
- levels of authority and control (for example, how far people are responsible for other workers).

To cover the full population, three other categories ('Students', 'Occupations not stated or inadequately described' and 'Not classifiable for other reasons') are included under 'Not classified'.

The NS-SEC class scale

1	Higher managerial, administrative and professional occupations: • 1.1 Employers in large organisations and higher managerial and administrative occupations, e.g. senior sales managers • 1.2 Higher professional occupations, e.g. solicitors
2	Lower managerial, administrative and professional occupations, e.g. social workers, teachers
3	Intermediate occupations, e.g. clerks, secretaries, computer operators
4	Employers in small businesses and own account workers (the self-employed), e.g. farmers
5	Lower supervisory and technical occupations, e.g. maintenance engineers, car mechanics
6	Semi-routine occupations, e.g. cooks, bus drivers, sales assistants, teaching assistants
7	Routine occupations, e.g. waiters, cleaners, labourers
8	Never worked and long-term unemployed

Source: *SOC2010 vol. 3: The National Statistics Socio-economic Classification;* adapted from Table 1.

Check your understanding: Exam practice

Identify one way of measuring social class and explain why this measure might be used. (4 marks)

Stretch and challenge

Assessing class position based on men's occupations

On what grounds do you think people challenged the practice of assessing the class position of a couple or family on the man's occupation?

Key points

- Occupation is often used to measure social class because it is related to factors such as status and life chances.
- The NS-SEC is seen as overcoming many of the problems with the Registrar General's scale.

What are life chances?

Objectives
- Explain the term 'life chances'
- Describe the relationship between life chances and social factors such as class, gender and ethnicity
- Describe inequalities in health

Life chances are a key concept in studying social inequality and stratification. Life chances refer to people's chances of achieving positive or negative outcomes (such as being healthy or ill, wealthy or poor) as they progress through life. These outcomes relate to many aspects of life including health, life expectancy, education, working conditions, housing, wealth and income.

Life chances or opportunities are not distributed equally between different individuals or groups. Those in higher social classes, for example, have access to more of the things considered desirable in life (such as good healthcare and decent housing) than those in other social classes. Life chances are also shaped by inequalities in wealth, income, power and status.

Researchers have identified marked inequalities between different social classes in relation to:

- life expectancy at birth (see Chapter 3 Topic 18)
- infant mortality
- morbidity (having an illness or a disease)
- educational outcomes (see Chapter 4 Topic 15)
- income and wealth
- poverty
- housing
- work conditions
- employment prospects.

The picture becomes more complicated when we examine the links between life chances and other social factors. For example, the chances of experiencing poverty are linked to gender, ethnicity, age and disability as well as to social class. The Child Poverty Action Group (2016) argues that income and material deprivation have a significant effect on schooling outcomes. Low income is 'a direct cause of reduced life chances'.

> **Glossary term**
>
> life chances

Social class

Religion and belief

Gender

Life chances are affected by factors such as:

Disability

Ethnicity

Age

Sexuality

Poverty and life chances

Read through the information below and answer the questions that follow.

In 2010, the coalition government under David Cameron commissioned the Independent Review on Poverty and Life Chances. Researchers at Bristol University drew on information from the Millennium Cohort Study (see Chapter 2 Topic 13) in order to identify a set of Life Chances Indicators that could predict future outcomes. By tracking people over time, it is possible to identify the factors involved in inequality, social mobility and outcomes over the life course.

The report published by the review suggested that children's development during their first five years had the strongest impact on their life chances. Of particular importance was the family background including the parents' level of education, good parenting and the opportunities for learning in the home during these early years.

1 What term do sociologists use to describe a study that tracks people over time?
2 According to this information, what are the advantages of tracking people over time?
3 Identify two of the social factors that have a strong impact on children's life chances.

Inequalities in health

The Marmot Review (2010) linked life chances to socio-economic position and income. People in higher socio-economic positions have better life chances, more opportunities and better health. The more advantages people have in social and economic terms, the better their health. For example, people with university degrees enjoy better health and live longer than those without. Each year, people die prematurely in England due to serious health inequalities. The Marmot Review argued that health inequalities are a result of avoidable inequalities in society, for example in education, housing, working conditions, income and standards of living.

Making connections

Outline one link between the information on the importance of good parenting and the material you studied in Chapter 3.

Reducing health inequalities

Some commentators suggest that spending more money on healthcare could reduce inequalities in health. For example, if people paid more tax, and this extra government income was spent on healthcare, this could fund a reduction in health inequalities.

1 Devise a draft opinion poll to find out whether people would be prepared to pay higher taxes in order to reduce inequalities in health. Remember to ask fixed-choice questions and include all possible answers (for example, 'don't know').
2 Pilot your opinion poll on a sample of 10 respondents. Try to ask equal numbers of men and women, younger and older people.
3 Write a short paragraph outlining the results of your pilot opinion poll.

Sociologists do not agree on how significant the different social divisions are in affecting life chances. Marxist approaches argue that social class in capitalist societies is more significant than factors such as gender or ethnicity. Feminist approaches see gender inequalities in patriarchal societies as more important.

Key point

Life chances refer to people's chances of having positive or negative outcomes (such as being healthy or ill) over their life. They are distributed unequally and are influenced by factors such as social class, gender and ethnicity.

Check your understanding: Exam practice

Describe what sociologists mean by the term 'life chances'. (3 marks)

How have sociologists studied social class?

The embourgeoisement thesis

In the late 1950s and early 1960s, some sociologists argued that a process of embourgeoisement was taking place. The **embourgeoisement thesis** suggested that working-class families were becoming middle class in their norms and values as their incomes and standards of living improved. Their **affluence** led them to adopt privatised lifestyles centred on home and family and to have aspirations based on consumerism. According to this hypothesis, traditional working-class values of solidarity and community had disappeared.

The affluent worker study

Goldthorpe and his colleagues carried out a study to test the embourgeoisement thesis in the early 1960s. This study was based in Luton, a prosperous town in southeast England. If embourgeoisement was taking place anywhere, they were likely to find it among Luton's affluent manual workers. The researchers used structured interviews to question affluent workers from three companies (including Vauxhall Motors) and their wives about their attitudes to work, lifestyles, aspirations and political views.

Based on their findings, Goldthorpe and his colleagues rejected the embourgeoisement thesis. However, they argued that affluent workers might be part of an emerging, 'new' working class. The new working class was similar to the middle class in terms of their privatised, home-centred lifestyles. They were also similar in terms of their instrumental collectivism. In other words, they joined in collective action through trade unions (collectivism) but only in a calculating (instrumental) way to further their own individual interests. For example, they wanted to improve their own pay rather than change society for the benefit of everybody. The term **instrumentalism** refers to seeing something as a means to an end rather than as an end in itself. For instance, the affluent workers viewed paid work as a means to a comfortable lifestyle rather than in terms of job satisfaction.

Glossary terms

affluence, embourgeoisement thesis, instrumentalism, privatised nuclear family

FOCUS ON SKILLS: WRITTEN ACTIVITY

Affluent workers and the privatised nuclear family

From this photograph, identify and explain one feature of the **privatised nuclear family**.

Affluent workers' privatised lifestyles centred on immediate family in the home.

Making connections

Which feminist sociologists drew on this study of affluent workers in Luton as a secondary source in their own research on families? What were their findings?

FOCUS ON KEY THINKERS

Fiona Devine: Affluent workers revisited

Fiona Devine (1992) revisited Luton two decades after Goldthorpe and his colleagues had completed their study. However, since the early 1960s, the town had experienced a recession. Her main aim was to explore how far 'working-class lifestyles centre on the immediate family in the home' in the 1980s.

Devine carried out intensive interviews with 62 Luton residents. The men all worked in shop-floor jobs at the Vauxhall car factory. Six of the women also worked at the car factory and eight had worked there previously.

Devine compared her own findings with those of the earlier study.

Goldthorpe and colleagues: the affluent worker	Devine: affluent workers revisited
Affluent workers were geographically mobile. They moved to Luton to find highly paid manual jobs and an improved standard of living. They had an **instrumental attitude to paid work**. In other words, their work was a means to an end rather than an end in itself. They worked to earn money to improve their standard of living rather than to get job satisfaction or to make friends.	The interviewees and their families were geographically mobile. However, there was little clear evidence that their move was motivated solely to improve their living standards. Many were forced to move to escape unemployment and job insecurity and to find affordable private housing. They were not purely instrumental in their motives for geographical mobility.
Affluent workers were like the traditional working class in that their friends were drawn from their working-class neighbours and kin. However, like the lower middle class, their lives and social relationships were **privatised and home-centred**. For example, they spent leisure time watching TV and socialising with immediate family members.	In general, families had not moved to Luton on their own but joined kin and friends there. They helped each other move by providing information on job opportunities and housing in Luton. Geographical mobility did not necessarily lead to separation from kin and a home-centred and family-centred lifestyle. They did not have purely privatised lifestyles.
Affluent workers had **individualistic** social and political attitudes. They supported the Labour Party for individual gain and their attitude to trade unions was instrumental. Unlike the traditional working class, these affluent workers were not motivated by working-class solidarity and the idea of 'sticking together'.	Their aspirations and their social and political values were not solely individualistic. There was plenty of evidence of **solidarity** among the interviewees rather than individualism.

Devine's own findings were different to those of the Luton team in important respects. She argued that working-class lifestyles, norms and values have not changed as much as Goldthorpe's affluent worker study suggested.

Key points

- Goldthorpe argued that affluent workers may be part of a new working class that resembled the middle class in terms of their privatism, instrumentalism and individualism.

- Devine revisited Luton and re-examined these conclusions but found little evidence of change in working-class lifestyles, norms and values.

Check your understanding: Exam practice

Identify and explain one disadvantage of using overt observation when investigating people's attitudes, lifestyles and aspirations.

(4 marks)

What is social mobility?

Objectives
- Explain the term 'social mobility'
- Discuss the extent of social mobility in Britain
- Identify problems in measuring social mobility

The term 'social mobility' refers to people's movement up or down a society's strata. In the UK, it refers to movement between social classes. Social mobility is of interest to sociologists, politicians and policy makers because it is an important measure of how open society is. High rates of upward and downward mobility can be used to argue that:

- Status is achieved rather than ascribed. Society provides equal opportunities and operates as a meritocracy.
- Individuals are rewarded on the basis of personal qualities rather than inherited wealth or personal connections (Crompton, 2008).

There are two types of social mobility:

1 **Intra-generational social mobility** refers to the movement of an individual between social classes over their lifetime as a result, for example, of promotion.
2 **Inter-generational social mobility** refers to movement between the generations of a family and occurs when a child enters a different social class from his or her parents.

Routes to mobility include:

- educational achievements and credentials
- marriage – although most people marry partners who have similar educational and occupational profiles to themselves
- windfalls such as an inheritance or a huge National Lottery win
- changes in the occupational structure; for example, a growth in white-collar work and a reduction in manual work may result in more chances of upward mobility and fewer chances of downward mobility.

Barriers to upward social mobility include discrimination based on ethnicity or gender, and lack of skills and educational credentials.

> ## Social mobility in the UK

Mobility research indicates that a working-class child's chances of getting a professional or managerial job are a quarter of those of a child from the professional class. Goldthorpe's 1972–1974 mobility study showed that although working-class children could and did end up in middle-class occupations, they were much less likely than middle-class children to do so. The relative chances of working-class and middle-class children of getting professional jobs had changed very little.

Evidence suggests that social mobility fell towards the end of the 20th century in the UK. Children born into manual working-class families in 1958 had a better chance of moving into higher

Glossary term

inter-generational

occupations than children born into similar families in the 1970s. Crompton (2008) notes that in Britain, social mobility is in decline. This is partly a result of changes in the occupational structure. Skilled manual jobs have declined and the growth in professional and manual jobs has slowed down.

FOCUS ON SKILLS: WRITTEN ACTIVITY

Class matters

Read the information below and then answer the questions that follow.

> Scott (2005) argues that education does not seem to matter very much when determining occupational success and improvements in income. Overall, it seems that class structures are self-reproducing. So the chances of a person rising or falling in the social hierarchy depend on their class background far more than on their individual educational achievement. The influence of class is weaker than in the past, but it remains the strongest influence.

1 How significant is education in influencing occupational success?
2 Does mobility depend more on an individual's educational achievements or their social origins?

FOCUS ON SKILLS: DISCUSSION ACTIVITY

Assessing people on their 'polish'

In a small group, discuss reasons for and against assessing candidates' suitability for high-flying jobs in terms of their 'polish'.

Note down your ideas.

The Social Mobility Commission (2016) found that people from more privileged backgrounds are over-represented in investment banking. These banks recruit from a small number of elite universities (such as Oxford, Cambridge and Warwick). A candidate's suitability may be assessed in relation to their educational background and also to their 'polish'. This is linked to their confidence, dress, speech, accent and behaviour. It advantages people who have been socialised in a middle-class or upper-class environment (for example, those from elite public schools such as Eton).

Should we include temporary jobs when measuring mobility?

Problems in measuring social mobility

- Some studies of inter-generational mobility focus only on males, so these results tell us nothing about women's mobility experiences.
- Studies that ask participants to remember their employment histories, or those of their parents, are likely to be based on unreliable data.
- Mobility studies record movement at two (or more) points in time. Researchers have to decide which age and point in a person's career to measure mobility from. Such decisions can be problematic. A young person, for example, might be in a temporary job (such as in a call centre) while awaiting a suitable opening in a city bank.

Check your understanding: Exam practice

Identify and describe one problem that sociologists might encounter when investigating social mobility. (3 marks)

Key points

- Social mobility refers to people's movement between society's strata. High rates of mobility suggest a meritocratic society.

- Although possible, children from working-class backgrounds have less chance of moving into professional occupations than children from professional backgrounds.

- There are problems in measuring mobility.

Does social class still matter?

Objective
- Examine the view that social class is less relevant today than in the past

How relevant is social class today?

There are hot debates within sociology about whether 'class' is still a useful concept. One approach suggests that social class is less relevant in the UK today and that class divisions and identities are no longer significant. Others suggest that the links between class and voting behaviour have weakened since the 1970s. In the past, working-class people tended to vote Labour and middle-class people tended to vote Conservative. This is known as **class alignment**. More recently, however, class is no longer seen as such a strong predictor of voting behaviour. This is referred to as **class dealignment**.

> **Glossary terms**
>
> class alignment, class dealignment, objective class, subjective class

FOCUS ON SKILLS: DISCUSSION ACTIVITY

Them and us!

One view is that social class divisions are now less clear cut than in the 1950s.

'Class was a staple part of the British way of life. Each class had unique characteristics. The upper class had stately homes, aristocratic backgrounds and posh accents; the middle class, semi-detached houses, suits and bowler hats; the working class, common accents, fish and chips and council flats. This produced a society divided between "Us" (the workers) and "Them" (the rich and the bosses). Pubs always had a public bar and a lounge. Even railway carriages were divided into First, Second and Third class compartments.'

Source: McDonough, F. (2002) 'Class and Politics', in M. Storry and P Childs (eds) *British Cultural Identities*. London: Routledge, pp. 175–207.

Discuss how far social class divisions have changed. Note down three changes.

The working class has shrunk in size due to changes in the occupational structure, a decline in manufacturing industries, mining and shipbuilding. These changes in working-class employment are linked to a decline in working-class communities centred on heavy industry, coal mining and shipbuilding. There has also been a sharp decline in trade union membership since the 1970s.

One view is that class identities have weakened over time. In the 1950s, surveys indicated that most manual workers in England identified themselves as working class and most non-manual workers (professionals, managers and clerical workers) identified as middle class (Butler and Watt, 2007). During the last 20 years, however, class identity has become less important. Class is now only one social identity alongside others (such as gender and ethnicity) that people pick and choose from.

On the other hand, the 2016 British Social Attitudes survey found that 60 per cent of people identify as working class and 40 per cent identify as middle class. Although the proportion of people doing a working-class job has fallen, the proportion who say they are working class is the same as in 1983. The results suggest that people's class identity is influenced by their family background and educational attainments. For example, many people in middle-class jobs who did not go to university or who are from working-class backgrounds see themselves as working class.

One view is that economic changes since 2005 (for example, recession and zero-hours contracts) have made people more aware of class differences.

Stretch and challenge

Some sociologists distinguish between 'objective class' and 'subjective class'. What do you think the difference between these two is?

FOCUS ON SKILLS: WRITTEN ACTIVITY

Young people and social class

One version of the view that social class is declining focuses on young people.

'Young people's experiences in education and work were once stratified in visible ways and were predictable on the basis of social class.

The majority of young people in Britain now experience further education and soon one in two will enter higher education. They combine education and work and take longer to establish their careers. As a result, their work contexts are more likely to be socially mixed. In call centres, for example, students often work, temporarily, next to same-age peers who lack advanced qualifications and who are likely to spend a large part of their lives in routine employment.'

Source: adapted from Furlong, A., Cartmel, F., Biggart, A., Sweeting, H. and West, P. (2006) 'Social Class in an "Individualised" Society'. *Sociology Review* 15(4), pp. 28–32.

Explain one way in which the experiences of young people from different social classes are becoming more blurred.

Saunders (1996) argues that class origins and the supposed advantages (such as private education) enjoyed by children born to relatively affluent parents are not particularly significant in shaping outcomes in modern Britain. In Saunders' view, social background and social identities can influence where people end up in the occupational hierarchy. He argues that the following social factors all count:

- parents (their social class, level of education and interest in their children's schooling)
- gender
- type of school attended (private education helps)
- conditions at home (overcrowding hinders success).

However, Saunders emphasises the importance of an individual's ability and motivation rather than their social class origins on the occupation they achieve. The key factors influencing occupational class destinations are mental ability, motivation to succeed and qualifications. Furthermore, Britain is, to a large extent, a meritocracy in which people are allocated to occupational class positions mainly on the basis of ability and effort.

Key point

Some sociologists argue that class is now less important as a social division. For example, class identity has declined, young people's experiences are increasingly similar regardless of class backgrounds, and people are allocated to jobs on meritocratic grounds.

Check your understanding: Exam practice

Identify and explain one reason why the importance of class may have declined over the last 50 years.   (4 marks)

What is gender?

Sex and gender

The term 'sex' refers to whether a person is considered male or female. It concerns biological differences between men and women, for example in relation to their bodies and roles in reproduction. These physical characteristics are ascribed at birth and are usually fixed throughout life.

Gender describes the different social practices, expectations and ideas that are associated with masculinity and femininity.

Families often socialise their sons and daughters differently and so children develop a gender identity – that is, they come to see themselves as masculine or feminine. Virtually from birth, we differentiate between girls and boys in their names and their clothes. As children get older, we often continue to differentiate between them, for example by giving them different books and toys (such as action figures for boys and dolls for girls) according to their gender.

Many sociologists conclude that the process of socialisation is highly gendered. By this, they mean that socialisation prepares us for social roles related to our gender, such as breadwinner or housewife.

Feminist approaches

Feminist sociologists explore the ways that gender is socially constructed or shaped by social processes such as socialisation. Agencies of socialisation including families, schools and the mass media are central in how we learn masculinity and femininity. For example, they may teach us that girls and boys should behave in different ways: while girls should be kind and caring, boys should be independent and strong.

Gender and power

Feminists see gender inequality as the most important source of division in society today. Holmes (2009) argues that society is still organised in ways that tend to benefit men more than women. This is because we live in a patriarchal society. In other words:

- society is controlled mainly by men, who have considerable power within politics and the workplace
- men generally have a bigger share of the available rewards such as wealth and social status.

Women are under-represented among holders of political power and decision-makers. For example, membership of the House of Commons is mainly male, white and elite. After the 2015 General Election, there

Sex

Male   Female

Gender

Masculine   Feminine

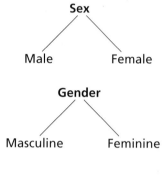

His or hers? What do you think?

were 459 male MPs and 191 female MPs. However, in 2016, Theresa May became the second ever female prime minister. In September 2016, six of the political parties represented in Westminster had female leaders.

Women are also under-represented within the judiciary in England and Wales. In April 2016, women made up 21 per cent of Court of Appeal judges, 21 per cent of High Court judges and 28 per cent of judges in the courts. However, the statistics show a different picture among those aged under 40. For example, there are slightly more female than male court judges under the age of 40.

Making connections

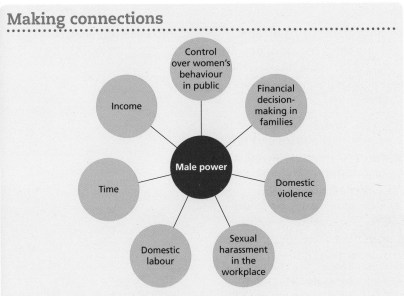

Identify and describe one aspect of male power that you have studied in other chapters such as Families, Education or Crime and deviance.

The crisis of masculinity

Some commentators suggest that currently there is a **crisis of masculinity** among many young men. This is seen as arising from:

- the underachievement of boys compared to girls in schools
- the decline of paid work in manufacturing and heavy industries
- women's increased participation in paid employment.

Boys and men see their traditional masculine identity as under threat today because they are likely to get low-paid insecure jobs in the service sector (for example, in shops) or to experience long-term unemployment. However, critics point out that many young women are in a similar position in the job market.

Check your understanding: Exam practice

1   Identify one way in which men have more power than women in society and explain why this situation continues today.   (4 marks)

2   Describe what sociologists mean by the term 'gender'.
                                                       (3 marks)

Key points

- The term 'gender' describes the different social practices and ideas that are associated with masculinity and femininity.

- Sociologists argue that gender is based on social rather than biological differences and is learned through socialisation.

- Many feminists see society as patriarchal; that is, based on male power over women.

What inequalities are based on gender?

Objectives
- Identify inequalities linked to gender
- Explain gender inequalities in employment

Many changes have taken place over the last 45 years to achieve **gender equality** in areas such as education and employment. These changes are partly linked to the introduction of equality and anti-discrimination laws.

Following the Equal Pay Act (1970), employers must pay men and women the same salary when they are doing the same work or work of equal value. The Sex Discrimination Act (1975) made it unlawful to discriminate or treat someone less favourably (for example, at work or school) because of their sex.

Some researchers argue that young women are now well positioned to benefit fully from feminist struggles for equality in the 1960s and 1970s. Others argue that gender inequalities persist. The term **sexism** refers to discrimination on the basis of sex. Historically, most sexism was directed at women, but the term also applies to **sex discrimination** against men.

> **Glossary terms**
>
> gender equality, gender pay gap, glass ceiling, sex discrimination, sexism

Gender inequalities at work

Feminist approaches explore the links between gender, life chances and social inequality. It is important to examine gender in the workplace because work is a source of status and power as well as income. Women's participation in the labour market has increased over the last 40 years.

FOCUS ON SKILLS: WRITTEN ACTIVITY

Participation in the labour market

Men's and women's employment rates: 1971 and 2013 (percentages, UK)

	Working-age men	Working-age women
1971	92	53
2013	76	67

Source: ONS (2013).

1 By how many percentage points did:
   a men's employment rate fall over this period?
   b women's employment rate rise?

2 Are men's and women's employment rates becoming increasingly similar or dissimilar? Explain your thinking.

> **Stretch and challenge**
>
> Identify one possible reason why the male rate of employment declined over this period.

Despite legislation passed nearly 50 years ago, gender inequalities in the labour market remain. Often, men and women do not work together in the same occupations. For example, fire fighting is male dominated and nursery nursing is female dominated. In 2013, 82 per cent of workers in caring, leisure and other services and 10 per cent of workers in skilled trades were female. Some sociologists use the image of invisible walls to illustrate this divide between female and male occupations.

When women and men work in the same occupation, they tend to be found in jobs at different levels. Women are more likely to be in lower or middle-level jobs while men tend to hold the higher-grade and senior management posts. It is argued that women are held back by a **glass ceiling** that acts as an invisible barrier to promotion.

The gender pay gap

Women, on average, still earn significantly less than men. This is referred to as the **gender pay gap**. Research by the Institute for Fiscal Studies (2016) found that women earned around one-fifth less than men per hour on average in 2015. The average hourly wage gap has narrowed since 1993, when women earned 28 per cent less than men. This narrowing is partly due to the fact that, in general, women are now more highly educated than men.

In terms of age, the average hourly wage gap opens up from the late twenties (when women often have their first child) and gets wider over the next 20 years. This is linked to changes in women's working patterns after they have children. For example, women with young children are more likely to work part time.

Explanations for the persistence of gender inequalities at work

- **Sex discrimination within the workplace**. Despite legislation, some women continue to be treated less favourably than men simply because they are women.
- **Women's triple shift**. Dunscombe and Marsden (1995) argue that many women in paid employment bear the burden of working a triple shift. This involves paid employment, domestic labour (housework and childcare) and 'emotion work' (making children and partners feel good). Scott and Clery (2013) argue that gender inequalities in the home make it difficult to achieve equality in the workplace.

  Women often have the main caring responsibilities for any family members who have disabilities or who are elderly or frail. So women are more likely than men to work in part-time jobs that tend to be low paid with few promotion opportunities. This means that women face obstacles that equality legislation alone cannot tackle.

- **Childcare provision**. Critics argue that Britain has inadequate or expensive childcare provision for the under-5s. This may act as a barrier, preventing women with young children from participating in full-time, paid employment or from staying in employment long enough to develop their career.

Check your understanding: Exam practice

Identify and explain one reason for the gender pay gap. (4 marks)

FOCUS ON RESEARCH: WRITTEN ACTIVITY

The Equality Act 2010

Carry out research on the internet into the Equality Act 2010.

- Which groups are covered by this Act?
- What protection does the law offer these groups?

Key point

Despite legislation, women still experience inequality in employment in relation to pay, for example. Possible reasons include the impact of women's triple shift and discrimination.

What is ethnicity?

Objectives
- Explain what sociologists mean by ethnicity
- Describe initiatives to address inequalities based on ethnicity

Some sociologists argue that in societies such as the UK and the USA, inequalities between different ethnic groups arise from discrimination. As a result, ethnicity, as with social divisions based on class and gender, affects the life chances of individuals and groups and their access to power.

An ethnic group is a social group whose members share an identity based on their cultural traditions, religion or language. The term 'ethnic minority' describes a group of people who are from a different ethnic group from the general population, who, in turn, may be described as the 'ethnic majority'. The UK is a culturally diverse society and is home to a rich mix of minority ethnic groups including those of Irish, Polish, Greek Cypriot, Indian and African-Caribbean heritage.

> **Glossary terms**
>
> assimilation, prejudice, racial discrimination

FOCUS ON SKILLS: DISCUSSION ACTIVITY

Assimilation

One view, the **assimilation** model, originated in the USA and suggests that immigrants should abandon their own culture in favour of that of the majority.

How far do you agree with this view?

The term 'race' is used in different ways. It has been used to refer to the idea that humankind could be divided into different 'racial groups' on the basis of natural, physical characteristics. Some 'races' were thought to be superior to others and some groups used this belief to justify the oppression of other groups; the colonisation of parts of Africa and Asia in the 19th century by Europeans, for example, was justified in this way. More recent scientific evidence, however, has led scientists to reject the idea of different biological 'races'.

Sociologists do not accept the idea that humankind can be divided into different racial groups. Instead, they argue that racial differences, like gender differences, are created by society rather than rooted in biology. However, sociologists (as well as many politicians and policy makers) recognise that prejudice and racism (or racial discrimination) exist. Prejudice occurs when people prejudge an individual or group, while racism occurs when people are treated differently and less favourably on the basis of their ethnicity.

> **Stretch and challenge**
>
> Explain one difference between prejudice and discrimination.

Ethnicity and power

Data from the ONS indicates that 13 per cent of the UK population were from minority ethnic backgrounds in 2015. However, they are under-represented among the holders of political power and the decision-makers. After the 2015 General Election, there were 41 MPs from minority ethnic backgrounds (21 men and 20 women). Although this was an increase of 14 MPs, only 6.3 per cent of all MPs are from minority ethnic backgrounds.

In 2015, 7 per cent of senior civil servants and 3.4 per cent of senior police officers (chief inspectors or above) were from minority ethnic backgrounds. People from minority ethnic backgrounds are also under-represented among teachers and the armed forces, particularly at the higher levels. However, over 40 per cent of NHS doctors in England were from minority ethnic backgrounds in 2015.

People from minority ethnic groups are also under-represented within the judiciary in England and Wales. In April 2016, for example, of court judges who declared their identity, 5 per cent declared their background as Black, Asian or Minority Ethnic (BAME). However, 8 per cent of court judges aged under 40 years are BAME compared with just 3 per cent aged 60 years and over.

Initiatives to address inequality based on ethnicity

Changes have taken place over the last 40 years to address inequality based on ethnicity in areas such as education, employment and criminal justice. These changes are partly linked to the following:

- **Equality and anti-discrimination legislation**: the 1976 Race Relations Act, for example, outlawed direct discrimination, indirect discrimination and victimisation. The Equality Act 2010 combined over 100 pieces of legislation into one Act. It aims to protect people from unfair treatment and to promote a fair and more equal society.
- The establishment of the Commission for Racial Equality: this later merged with the Equal Opportunities Commission to become the **Equality and Human Rights Commission**. It is Britain's national equality body and it aims to make Britain a fairer place by tackling discrimination and promoting equal opportunities.
- The recognition that **institutional racism** existed within organisations such as the Metropolitan Police and must be addressed (see Chapter 2 Topic 22).
- **Equal opportunities policies** or statements supporting diversity in the workplace and in education (see Topic 11).

Some commentators argue that inequalities based on ethnicity are much less significant today than they were 40 or 50 years ago. For example, BAME people are making inroads into the worlds of politics, the media, the arts and literature. As a result, ethnicity is no longer seen as such a major social division compared with the situation in the past.

BAME people are making inroads into politics.

FOCUS ON SKILLS: DISCUSSION ACTIVITY

Making inroads

In a small group, discuss what evidence you might need in order to establish whether and how far BAME people are making inroads into the worlds of politics, the media, the arts and literature.

Make a note of your ideas.

Key point

One view is that legislation and changes in attitudes and practices have addressed inequalities based on ethnicity to some extent. As a result, ethnicity is a less significant social division than in the past.

Check your understanding: Exam practice

Identify and explain one way in which British governments have tried to reduce social inequalities based on ethnicity over the last 40 years. (4 marks)

What inequalities are based on ethnicity?

Objectives
* Identify links between ethnicity and inequality
* Explain the persistence of inequality in paid employment

Some commentators believe that inequalities based on ethnicity are now much less significant than in the past. However, others argue that in some of the most crucial areas – such as employment, education (see Chapter 4) and the criminal justice system (see Chapter 5) – little has changed.

Glossary term

New Right

Ethnicity and unemployment

Unemployment is an important indicator of inequality. It can be linked to social problems such as poverty and homelessness, and to ill health.

FOCUS ON SKILLS: WRITTEN ACTIVITY

Unemployment and ethnicity

The table below shows unemployment rates (the proportion of the economically active population who are unemployed) among different ethnic groups and by gender. Study this information and answer the questions that follow.

Unemployment rates by ethnicity and gender: UK, 2015. (percentages)

	Men	Women
White	4.9	4.5
Black	12.2	11.5
Asian	7.5	9.8
Other ethnic background	9.5	8.8
All ethnic backgrounds	5.4	5.1

Source: adapted from Delebarre, J. (2016) House of Commons Library Briefing Paper, no. 6385. 27 April, 'Unemployment by Ethnic Background', section 1.2, p. 4.

Unemployment rates in each ethnic group were higher among young people aged 16–24 years than in older age groups.

1 What percentage of black women was unemployed in 2015?
2 What percentage of white men was unemployed?
3 Among which ethnic group was male unemployment the highest?
4 Among which ethnic group was female unemployment the lowest?

Ethnicity and paid employment

Li and colleagues (2008) examined the position of different ethnic groups in relation to paid employment in 2004/5. They focused on whether minority ethnic groups have the same employment chances as their white British peers of the same age and educational level. They found that people from Indian and Chinese minority ethnic

Stretch and challenge

Drawing on the information in the table above, write a paragraph to summarise the links between ethnicity, gender and unemployment.

groups had the same chances of getting professional and managerial jobs as their white British peers. However, men of black Caribbean ethnicity had 'much worse' chances. Weekly earnings were 'much worse' for men and 'somewhat worse' for women of Pakistani/Bangladeshi ethnicity than their white peers.

FOCUS ON SKILLS: DISCUSSION ACTIVITY

Shared experiences

In pairs, discuss how far the evidence suggests that people from different minority ethnic groups have similar experiences in relation to employment.

Note down your ideas.

Explanations for the persistence of inequality at work

Discrimination in the labour market

Having educational qualifications improves the life chances and quality of life of all ethnic groups (Li et al., 2008). However, prejudice and discrimination in the labour market persist and equality laws are difficult to enforce. As a result, the life chances and quality of life of some ethnic groups are negatively affected.

Minority ethnic groups and the underclass

New Right approaches suggest that some people from minority ethnic groups form part of an underclass. Charles Murray (1984) argued that the welfare system led to the development of an underclass – a hard core of unemployed young people who had no interest in finding jobs and working hard. He associated the underclass in the USA with African-American and Hispanic people.

Marxist approaches

Marxists see racism (and sexism) as built into the workings of capitalism. Some groups (including people from minority ethnic backgrounds and working-class women) form part of a reserve army of labour. They can be hired to work during economic booms when capitalism needs them, and fired during recessions. The reserve army of labour also keeps down wages because workers know they can be easily replaced if they demand increases in pay.

Making connections

Ethnicity and education

How far does the evidence suggest that students from different minority ethnic groups have similar experiences in relation to education?

Stretch and challenge

Why do you think some sociologists argue that women, in particular, form part of a reserve army of labour?

Key points

- Evidence suggests that discrimination based on ethnicity persists in the labour market.

- However, members of some ethnic groups (such as those of Indian heritage) are better placed than others (such as those of Pakistani/Bangladeshi heritage) in terms of employment, so it is difficult to generalise.

- Gender and social class can also have an impact.

Check your understanding: Exam practice

1 Identify and explain one advantage of using group interviews to study minority ethnic groups' experiences of unemployment. (4 marks)

2 Identify and explain one reason why people from some minority ethnic groups might experience unemployment. (4 marks)

What is age?

Chronological age

One way of looking at an individual's age is simply in terms of how long they have been alive. Someone born in 2000, for example, would be 16 years old in 2016. This is known as a person's chronological age. Your chronological age determines your rights and responsibilities in a range of areas such as buying alcohol, driving a car, voting and criminal responsibility.

Biological age

Another way of looking at age is in biological terms. In this case, a person's age may be related to the physical changes taking place in their bodies. For example, puberty begins at a relatively early point in life, while grey hair and wrinkles generally appear much later. Biological changes are usually linked to chronological age.

Age as a social category

Sociologists are interested in exploring how age is seen in social terms. For instance, we may have different expectations of people and treat them differently according to how old we think they are. We might be surprised to learn that a 78-year-old's hobbies included skateboarding or that a 4-year-old collected antiques.

Social expectations about age may influence how we view behaviour.

FOCUS ON SKILLS: DISCUSSION ACTIVITY

Attitudes to age

Discuss and note down what the following expressions tell us about society's attitudes to age. Could any of them be seen as offensive?

Act your age!

Mutton dressed as lamb.

You're as old as you feel.

Toy boy.

Pester power.

You can't teach an old dog new tricks.

Sociologists argue that age (like gender and ethnicity) is socially constructed. Expectations surrounding age vary historically (over time) and cross-culturally (from society to society).

Childhood

Research suggests that the experience of childhood in the UK has changed over time. For example, Ariès (1962) indicates that in medieval times, children over the age of 5 were seen as small adults who participated in the adult world of work and leisure. In the 19th century, child labour was the norm among working-class families (see Chapter 3 Topic 17). Poverty forced children to work long hours, for example in cotton mills or factories, to help support their families. Children were seen as particularly suited to jobs such as pulling coal sledges through narrow passages in coal mines. In contrast, child labour is considered unacceptable and is illegal in the UK today.

Since Victorian times, there have been many legal changes relating to the education and employment of children (see Chapter 3 Topic 17). In this way, the status of British children has changed historically, with children today clearly having a different status from adults. Some commentators, however, suggest that childhood may now be changing in important respects. Many children, for example, resemble adults in being active consumers of fashion, brands and technologies.

In many contemporary societies, childhood is seen as a separate stage to youth and adulthood. Children are regarded as dependent and vulnerable, and are protected by laws against exploitation in the workplace. However, in other cultures, the separation of childhood and adulthood is less marked. Some children are expected to fend for themselves or play an adult role at work. In this way, expectations surrounding childhood vary between cultures.

Power relationships in childhood

Families operate as agencies of social control and parents or guardians are authority figures in families. They are expected to exercise authority over their children and to discipline them when necessary. Parents exercise power when they try to influence their children's behaviour against their will.

Traditionally, parents (particularly fathers) were powerful figures in families and children had few rights. Since the 1950s, however, there has been a shift of power and attention towards children in working-class families (Cunningham, 2007). Parents have more democratic or equal relationships with their children. It is now recognised that children have rights within families (see Chapter 3 Topic 17).

Attitudes towards child labour have changed over time.

> **FOCUS ON SKILLS: DISCUSSION ACTIVITY**
>
> **Should smacking be banned?**
>
> In a small group, discuss the following questions and note down your ideas.
>
> - Should parents be allowed to exercise power over their children by smacking them?
>
> - Should smacking children be a criminal offence?

Key point

Age can be seen as a biological and a social category. Sociologists explore how expectations surrounding age (like those surrounding gender) vary cross-culturally and historically.

Check your understanding: Exam practice

Identify and explain one way in which expectations surrounding childhood have changed in recent years.   (4 marks)

How is youth linked to inequality?

Objectives
- Explain youth as a stage in the transition from childhood to adulthood
- Describe power relationships during youth

In contemporary Britain, youth is regarded as an important stage of development during which individuals 'grow up' and move from the status of child to adult. The transition between childhood and adulthood may involve:

- increasing independence from families
- moving from the family home to another household
- finishing full-time education
- moving into full-time paid employment
- gaining more power and status in society.

Researchers see 'youth' as a 20th-century product in Britain. One view is that 'teenagers' emerged as a social category in the 1950s. Different **youth subcultures** could be identified by their clothes, hair and taste in music.

Factors affecting the transition into adulthood

Many young people continue to be financially dependent on their parents or relatives into their twenties and beyond (see Chapter 3 Topic 17). Full-time students or unemployed young people may live at home because they cannot afford to live independently. So the transition from childhood to adulthood in Britain is not necessarily clear-cut.

It is important to bear in mind that young people are not a uniform group. For example, they are divided according to gender, ethnicity, social class and location. Some are from more privileged backgrounds than others. These factors will influence their transitions into adulthood and their life chances.

- The unemployment rate for young people aged 16 to 24 years is higher than for older groups. Young people from some minority ethnic backgrounds are more likely than others to experience unemployment.
- Between April and June 2016, 843 000 young people in the UK aged 16 to 24 years were not in education, employment or training (NEETs). This was 11.7 per cent of all 16-to-24-year-olds. Between July and September 2011, the proportion was higher, at 16.9 per cent.
- Some young people's access to secure employment or to higher education is limited by their lack of educational qualifications. Many young people without qualifications are likely to find work only in low-paid, insecure jobs or zero-hours contract work.
- Some young people may receive financial help from their families when going to university or to fund them through

Glossary term

youth subculture

Youth is a 20th-century product.

FOCUS ON SKILLS: DISCUSSION ACTIVITY

When does 'youth' begin and end?

Mizen (2002) notes that there is no obvious agreement among politicians, policy makers and youth researchers about the age at which 'youth' begins or ends.

In a small group, discuss when you think 'youth' begins and ends in the UK today. Is the transition into adulthood celebrated or marked in any way?

Note down your ideas.

unpaid work experience or internships. They may also be able to draw on social contacts in setting up internships. Others may not be able to afford to undertake unpaid work experience.

- Some young people benefit from an expensive elite education.
- Young people's entry into the labour market may be affected by global recessions.

Young people and power

In everyday relationships, individuals exercise power over others. In a school setting, for instance, teachers have the power to enforce school rules and exercise authority over students based on their position within the school structure. For example, they can legitimately tell students to form an orderly queue in the canteen for health and safety reasons. Their authority, however, is limited to particular school contexts and their status as a teacher would not authorise them to tell adults to form queues at bus stops or airport check-in desks.

Teachers may also exercise a form of authority based on their charisma. Such teachers can be seen as exceptional individuals who inspire their students. We should bear in mind, however, that some students do not necessarily conform to the school rules or authority structure. They may belong to a deviant subculture that resists teachers' authority.

Relationships between teachers and their students have changed over time. In general, they have become more informal and democratic. During the 1960s, for example, many schools routinely used physical punishment (or exercised coercive power) as a last resort to discipline students. Today, while schools still operate as an agency of social control and enforce adult authority, legal changes mean that teachers no longer have the power to use corporal (physical) punishment.

Recent educational policies can be seen as reflecting a shift in thinking about the balance of power between teachers and students. For example, by law, schools must now take students' views into account when deciding on policies that affect them.

Making connections

In Chapter 4, Education, you saw that Paul Willis studied a group of schoolboys who rejected their teachers' authority. What conclusions did he reach about the counter-school sub culture?

Key points

- The transition from childhood to adulthood is not necessarily clear-cut. Young people's experiences of education and employment and their life chances vary according to social factors such as social class, gender and ethnicity.

- Young people now have more power than in the past.

Check your understanding: Exam practice

1 Identify and explain one factor that might affect young people's life chances. (4 marks)

2 Identify and explain one reason why young people have more power over their lives today than 50 years ago. (4 marks)

How is older age linked to inequality?

Many aspects of older age that we take for granted in contemporary Britain, such as retirement or pensions, are actually relatively recent developments. Before the introduction of state retirement pensions in 1908, older people worked until they were physically unable to continue. Retirement has only been the norm in Britain since the mid-20th century.

The status of older people can vary between different cultures. In contemporary Britain, getting old is often seen as something to be avoided. Some people try to combat the ageing process by resorting to hair dye, plastic surgery or Botox injections. In other cultures, however, older age is viewed as something to look forward to, with older people enjoying high status in society.

Glossary terms

age discrimination, ageism

The ageing process is sometimes viewed as something to combat or defy.

Inequalities based on age

The term **ageism** (or **age discrimination**) is used to describe a situation in which a person is treated differently and less favourably on the basis of their age. Young people and older people tend to be more vulnerable to ageism than other groups – for example, they may experience negative stereotyping on the basis of their age. People in their fifties and sixties may find it difficult to get a job because some employers hold stereotyped ideas about their ability to learn new skills.

As a result of the Employment Equality (Age) Regulations, which came into force in 2006, there are now regulations against age discrimination in employment and training. The Equality Act 2010 protects people from age discrimination, for example at work or when accessing services in places such as banks, hotels or gyms.

In the year ending 31 March 2011, 6800 claims were filed with Employment Tribunals in Britain for age discrimination, and in the year ending 31 March 2012, 3700 cases were filed.

FOCUS ON SKILLS: DISCUSSION ACTIVITY

Defying age or growing old gracefully?

In a small group, discuss the possible reasons why people might want to look younger. What does this tell us about the status of older people in society?

Note down three points arising from your discussion.

Age, gender and TV presenters

In 2013, Harriet Harman MP revealed research findings showing that the vast majority of TV presenters aged over 50 in the UK are men. Only 18 per cent of presenters on our TV screens aged over 50 are female.

1 In a small group, discuss the possible reasons why women aged over 50 are under-represented among TV presenters.

2 Note down two possible reasons.

How far do you agree that ageism is as much a social problem as sexism and racism?

It is important to appreciate that, like youth, older people cannot be seen (or lumped together) as a uniform group. Older people's position and experiences differ according to whether they are 'young old' (65–75 years) or 'old old' (in their mid-eighties, nineties or older).

The social position of older people varies between individuals and groups. Many experience poverty, while others enjoy an affluent lifestyle and have a high-status position in society. For example, many judges, MPs, world statesmen and women and wealthy company directors are in their sixties, seventies and eighties. It is also important to recognise that age may be linked to other social divisions based on gender, ethnicity and class. The life chances of an elderly, working-class, widowed black woman, for example, may be much worse than those of a newly retired, middle-class, married white man.

Older people and poverty

Many pensioners are likely to live on a low income over time. There are, however, differences between older people in their risk of experiencing poverty. People who retire with an occupational pension are likely to enjoy a relatively good standard of living. Those who rely on the state retirement pension are more vulnerable to poverty. The likelihood of experiencing poverty is linked to social class, gender and ethnicity. Middle-class men, for example, are more likely than other groups to have built up an occupational pension.

Key points

- Age discrimination is increasingly recognised as a social problem in Britain, and legislation has been introduced to tackle this.

- The position of older people varies according to their social class, gender and ethnicity.

Check your understanding: Exam practice

1 Describe what is meant by 'age discrimination'.   (3 marks)

2 Identify and describe one way in which governments have tried to reduce age discrimination in Britain over the last 15 years.   (3 marks)

What other factors affect life chances?

The Equality Act 2010 protects people from discrimination based on characteristics such as disability, religion or belief, and sexuality. People are protected from discrimination by employers, for example, as well as by schools and colleges, banks, hospitals and local authorities. However, life chances can still be influenced by sexuality, disability, and religion and belief.

People's sexuality can affect their life chances when they experience homophobia within education or the workplace. Homophobia refers to fear or negative attitudes towards gay men or lesbian women. People's life chances can also be affected when they experience discrimination based on their religion and beliefs. The term 'Islamophobia' is used to describe fear or negative attitudes towards Muslims.

Disability, participation and poverty

Sociologists focus on the social barriers that make it difficult for people with disabilities to participate fully in society. Barriers include not only the prejudiced attitudes and stereotypes held by some people but also discriminatory practices.

The life chances of people with disabilities are affected when they experience disablism within education or the workplace. This term refers to prejudice and discrimination against people with disabilities.

People with disabilities are at risk of poverty. Lister (2008) argues that the additional needs associated with many forms of disability create extra expenses that other people on low incomes do not face. Such extra costs include, for instance, special diet, equipment and transport costs. People with disabilities may also have relatively low incomes because they are in a disadvantaged position in the labour market. For example, they are more likely not to be employed or to work in low-paid jobs.

Stephanie Millward MBE: Rio 2016 gold medal winner.

FOCUS ON SKILLS: DISCUSSION ACTIVITY

The Paralympic Games

In a small group, discuss how far the Paralympic games have changed public attitudes to disability and disability sports.

- Do the Paralympics have a positive impact on the public's perceptions of disability?
- Would the event send out a different message if the Paralympic and Olympic games took place alongside each other?

Make a note of your ideas.

Hate crime

Some people experience hate crime. In other words, they are the victim of a crime that is motivated by hostility or prejudice related to factors such as their sexual orientation, disability or religion. Legislation now protects people such as disabled women, gay men and Muslim youths against hate crime.

Hate crime is linked to the negative stereotyping of some social groups. It is also seen as an example of the use of power or coercion to try and control some groups. The victims of hate crime can be seen as scapegoats who are blamed for the social and economic problems facing society. In this view, social inequality generates resentment.

FOCUS ON SKILLS: WRITTEN ACTIVITY

Hate crime and the Brexit referendum

Read through the information and then answer the questions that follow.

The United Nations Committee on the Elimination of Racial Discrimination (2016) reported on the sharp increase in the number of hate crimes directed at ethnic and ethno-religious (such as Jews and Sikhs) minority communities around the time of the UK referendum on EU membership in June 2016. The referendum campaign was marked by anti-immigrant language. Rather than condemning this, many politicians themselves created prejudices. This emboldened (or encouraged) people to carry out acts of intimidation and hate towards ethnic or ethno-religious communities.

The UN Committee reported on the negative portrayal of people from ethnic or ethno-religious communities, immigrants, asylum seekers and refugees in the media, particularly after terrorist attacks.

The Committee was also concerned that counter terrorism measures created an atmosphere of suspicion towards Muslims.

1 Identify one example of an ethno-religious group.
2 What role did many politicians play during the Brexit campaign?
3 Identify three groups who are portrayed negatively in the media after terrorist attacks.
4 What effect did anti-terrorism measures have on Muslims?

Check your understanding: Exam practice

1 Identify and explain one factor that might limit the opportunities of people with disabilities to find secure employment. (4 marks)

2 Identify and explain one disadvantage of using content analysis to investigate the way the media portray asylum seekers and refugees. (4 marks)

Making connections

Look out for links between the material on hate crime and the media in this topic and similar issues raised in Chapter 5. For example, how might the concepts of stereotyping, labelling, folk devils and scapegoating be applied to material in this topic?

Stretch and challenge

The UN Committee reported on the sharp increase in the number of hate crimes. How far is it possible to tell whether this is due to more hate crimes being committed or to more being reported? Write a sentence to explain your answer.

Key points

- Factors such as sexuality, disability, and religion and belief, can have an impact on people's life chances due to discrimination in education and the workplace.

- People with disabilities are vulnerable to poverty.

- Some groups may experience hate crime that is motivated by hostility or prejudice related to their sexual orientation, disability or religion.

How are wealth and income distributed in the UK?

Wealth and income influence life chances. For example, many people with high annual incomes can choose between NHS and private healthcare or between state and private education. However, most people in low income households do not have these choices.

Wealth refers to the ownership of assets (things that people own) that are valued at a particular point in time. Marketable assets are things that can be sold, such as houses, land, works of art and jewellery. Wealth also includes money in savings accounts and shares in companies. Wealth is often passed down the generations through inheritance in families. It may also be built up by saving or by the value of assets such as houses or land going up.

Income refers to the flow of resources that individuals and households receive over a specific period of time. Income may be received in cash (for example, from wages) or in kind (for instance, a petrol allowance). Other sources of income include salaries, welfare benefits and pensions.

Glossary term

overclass

The distribution of wealth

In Britain, there are vast inequalities in the distribution of both wealth and income (Roberts, 2001). However, wealth is distributed more unevenly than income. The most important element of household wealth is residential buildings (such as houses and flats).

Between July 2012 and June 2014, the wealthiest 10 per cent of households in Britain owned 45 per cent of overall wealth. By contrast, the bottom 50 per cent owned only 9 per cent of overall wealth.

In the UK, we can identify a number of people, sometimes referred to as the super-rich, who are multimillionaires. The super-rich comprise:

- those who own wealth in the form of shares in industry, finance and commerce
- upper-class landowners who inherited their wealth.

Stretch and challenge

Britain's super-rich

The Sunday Times Rich List is undated every year; search the internet for the latest version.

1 Who are the top three richest people in the current list?

2 What is their wealth based on?

3 How has their position changed since last year?

FOCUS ON SKILLS: WRITTEN ACTIVITY

The 'overclass'

Read through the information below, then answer the questions that follow.

The New Right approach focuses on the underclass, a group of people whose behaviour and values are seen as threatening the moral fabric of society. However, Peter Beresford (2013) identifies an emerging 'overclass' – the very rich and powerful, known as the 'fat cats' and the 'super-rich'. He argues that this new group seems to be profiting from current economic problems. The key representatives of the overclass can be found, for example, among the leaders of huge corporations that avoid paying tax and in corporations that damage the environment. Although the overclass is small, it holds power and influence in political and economic terms.

Beresford highlights the increasing links between the overclass and politicians and government. Members of the coalition government (2010–15), for example, were separated from the rest of the people by their elite education and wealth. Beresford argues that the very rich and powerful overclass appears to show little commitment to traditional values and is more of a threat to society than the poor and powerless underclass.

1 Write a brief definition of the 'overclass'.
2 Describe one difference between the underclass and the overclass.
3 Why do you think the underclass is generally seen as more of a danger to society than the overclass?

UK Uncut takes action against tax avoidance by members of the overclass and protests against government cuts to public services.

The distribution of income

Income is linked to life chances, life expectancy and access to education, housing and health services. Income is distributed unevenly between households in the UK. During the 2014/15 financial year, for example, the average income of the richest fifth of UK households before benefits and taxes was 14 times greater than that of the poorest fifth. One way of redistributing income is through taxes (such as income tax and council tax) and benefits (such as state pensions and income support). After taxes and benefits, the average income of the richest fifth of UK households was four times greater than that of the poorest fifth.

Key points

- Life chances are influenced by wealth and income.

- There are huge inequalities in the distribution of wealth and income in Britain.

- Some researchers identify a new overclass – a small group of very rich and powerful people who have links to governments.

Check your understanding: Exam practice

1 Identify and explain one difference between wealth and income. **(4 marks)**

2 Identify and describe one way in which having a high income may improve life chances. **(3 marks)**

What is poverty?

Poverty is a controversial issue and there is no single agreed way of defining it. However, the question of how we define poverty is important. This is because our definition will influence how we measure poverty, the number of people said to be in poverty and our views on how poverty should be tackled.

FOCUS ON SKILLS: DISCUSSION ACTIVITY

What is poverty?

Poverty is:

> ...starving
>
> ...existing rather than living
>
> ...buying secondhand clothes
>
> ...homeless people sleeping on the street
>
> ...being in debt
>
> ...using a food bank
>
> ...having no money for a social life
>
> ...living in an over crowded, damp house.

1 In a small group, discuss these statements and decide which is the most satisfactory, and which is the least satisfactory, description of poverty. Be prepared to justify your choices.

2 Write your own group definition of poverty.

Absolute and relative poverty

There are two broad approaches to defining poverty – the absolute and relative approaches.

People experience **absolute poverty** when their income is insufficient to obtain the minimum they need to survive. People in absolute poverty do not have access to even the basic necessities of life such as food, clean water, shelter, heating and clothes. Their income is so low that they can barely survive.

The absolute definition is useful in that it allows researchers to measure trends over time. It is criticised, however, because in practice it is very difficult to determine what the 'minimum needed to survive' is. For example, is the minimum dietary requirement just bread and water, or should we include fresh fruit and vegetables?

People experience **relative poverty** when they cannot afford to meet the general standard of living of most other people in their

Absolute and relative poverty.

society. The income of people in relative poverty is much less than the average for society as a whole, so they are poor compared with others in their society. In relatively affluent or rich societies such as the UK and the USA, even those experiencing poverty are well off compared to people in many other countries. Most researchers in the UK today use the relative definition of poverty.

This approach recognises that what is considered to be poverty is relative to place and time. Using the relative approach means that we will always find poverty in a society in so far as we will find some people who have much less than the average income, unless incomes are distributed almost equally.

Walker and Walker (1997) argue that the definition of poverty chosen by the state is crucial. This is because it determines how far the government accepts that poverty exists, what policies are adopted to tackle poverty and how those experiencing poverty are treated. If an absolute definition of poverty were used, the role of government and the number of resources needed to address it would be much more limited than if a relative definition were used.

FOCUS ON KEY THINKERS

Peter Townsend: defining poverty

Peter Townsend has made a major contribution to the study of poverty in the UK (see Topic 21). Many sociologists have drawn on his definition of poverty in their own work:

'Individuals, families and groups in the population can be said to be in poverty when they lack the resources to obtain the types of diet, participate in the activities and have the living conditions and amenities which are customary, or at least widely encouraged or approved, in the societies to which they belong. Their resources are so seriously below those commanded by the average individual or family that they are, in effect, excluded from ordinary living patterns and activities.'

Source: Townsend, P. (1979) *Poverty in the United Kingdom*. London: Allen Lane and Penguin Books, p. 31.

FOCUS ON SKILLS: WRITTEN ACTIVITY

Townsend's definition of poverty

Read through Townsend's definition of poverty and then answer the following questions.

1 Does Townsend define poverty in absolute or relative terms?

2 How far does this definition focus simply on income?

3 What do you think Townsend meant by 'excluded from ordinary living patterns and activities'?

Social exclusion refers to being shut out or excluded from participation in society's social, economic, political and cultural life. Socially excluded people are those who would like to participate but who are prevented from doing so by factors beyond their control.

Key points

- Poverty has been defined in absolute and relative terms.

- The definition adopted by the state is important because it determines how far government accepts that poverty exists, the policies to address poverty and the way people experiencing poverty will be treated.

Check your understanding: Exam practice

1 Describe what sociologists mean by the term 'absolute poverty'. (3 marks)

2 Describe what sociologists mean by the term 'relative poverty'. (3 marks)

How do sociologists measure poverty?

Objectives
- Explain the different ways of measuring poverty
- Describe Townsend's approach to measuring poverty
- Identify reasons why poverty and inequality have increased

There are several ways of measuring poverty. The main official UK government measure is in terms of low incomes. The low income threshold is fixed at 60 per cent of the median (middle point) income of the population after housing costs (which vary between regions). In other words, low incomes are those below 60 per cent of this average. Measures of **subjective poverty** are based on whether people see themselves as living in poverty. **Environmental poverty** measures deprivation in terms of conditions such as inadequate housing, lack of a garden, inadequate outdoor play facilities and air pollution.

Glossary terms

environmental poverty, relative deprivation, relative income standard of poverty, state standard of poverty, subjective poverty

FOCUS ON KEY THINKERS

Peter Townsend: Poverty in the UK

Townsend (1979) aimed to find out how many people were living in poverty in the UK and to discover their characteristics and problems. His deprivation index was designed to measure **relative deprivation**. Examine the 12 items on the index and then answer the questions that follow.

The deprivation index

Characteristic	% of population
1 Has not had a week's holiday away from home in the last 12 months	53.6
2 *Adults only*. Has not had a relative or friend to the home for a meal or snack in the last 4 weeks	33.4
3 *Adults only*. Has not been out in the last 4 weeks to a relative or friend for a meal or snack	45.1
4 *Children only* (under 15). Has not had a friend to play or to tea in the last 4 weeks	36.3
5 *Children only*. Did not have party on last birthday	56.6
6 Has not had an afternoon or evening out for entertainment in the last 2 weeks	47.0
7 Does not have fresh meat (including meals out) as many as 4 days a week	19.3
8 Has gone through one or more days in the past fortnight without a cooked meal	7.0
9 Has not had a cooked breakfast most days of the week	67.3
10 Household does not have a refrigerator	45.1
11 Household does not usually have a Sunday joint (3 in 4 times)	25.9
12 Household does not have sole use of 4 amenities indoors (flush WC; sink or washbasin and cold-water tap; fixed bath or shower; and gas or electric cooker)	21.4

Source: adapted from Townsend, P. (1979) *Poverty in the UK*. London: Allen Lane and Penguin Books, p. 250, Table 6.3.

1 What percentage of the population had not had an afternoon or evening out for entertainment in the last two weeks?

2 Item 9 indicates that almost 7 out of 10 people did not have a cooked breakfast most days of the week. To what extent can we see this as evidence of deprivation?

3 To what extent are items 7 and 11 necessarily measures of deprivation?

4 To what extent can we see not having a fridge as indicating deprivation?

Townsend calculated that almost 23 per cent of the population were in poverty. This proportion was much higher than that based on the **state standard of poverty** (6.1 per cent of people in poverty) and the **relative income standard of poverty** (9 per cent in poverty). Townsend also identified particular groups of people who were at risk of poverty. These included elderly people who had worked in unskilled manual jobs, and children in families of young unskilled manual workers or in one-parent families.

Criticisms of Townsend's deprivation index

Critics question some of the 12 items in Townsend's index (for example, a cooked breakfast or a Sunday joint) and how they were selected. Not eating meat regularly may be linked to vegetarianism or religious belief rather than to deprivation.

If the index is inadequate, this means the statistics based on it will also be questionable.

Butler and Watt: explaining increases in poverty and inequality

When poverty grows among some groups while other people become richer, this results in greater inequality. Butler and Watt (2007) identify several factors that explain the increase in poverty and inequality. These include:

- an increase in the proportion of workless households
- an increase in the pay gap between low-skilled and high-skilled workers
- changes in taxation, such as reductions in the rate of income tax, which benefit the better off
- demographic changes that result in an increase in groups with low incomes such as pensioners and lone-parent families.

Check your understanding: Exam practice

1 Describe what sociologists mean by the term 'relative deprivation'. (3 marks)

2 Identify one way in which sociologists might measure poverty and explain one disadvantage of using this measure. (4 marks)

FOCUS ON SKILLS: DISCUSSION ACTIVITY

Groups at risk of poverty

In a small group, discuss why some groups (such as elderly people or children in one-parent families) might be at risk of poverty.

Note down your ideas.

FOCUS ON SKILLS: WRITTEN ACTIVITY

Measuring relative deprivation in the 21st century

Townsend devised his deprivation index in the 1960s.

Make a list of six indicators that would be more relevant to a study of poverty today.

Key points

- There are different measures of poverty, including subjective measures.

- The official UK government measure is in terms of low income.

- Townsend's deprivation index measured relative deprivation and he found that almost 23 per cent of people were living in poverty in the UK.

Which social groups are more likely to experience poverty?

Objectives
- Identify the social groups that are more likely to experience poverty
- Explain why these groups are at risk of poverty
- Describe the life cycle of poverty

We have seen that many older people and people with disabilities are at risk of poverty. The proportion of people in poverty is also relatively high among:
- people from some minority ethnic groups
- women
- families with children including lone-parent families.

Glossary terms

life-cycle of poverty, situational poverty, welfare state

Ethnicity and poverty

People in UK households headed by someone from a minority ethnic group are at risk of living in low income households. This is particularly the case for people of Pakistani or Bangladeshi heritage. Lister (2004) notes that most explanations for these patterns of poverty identify racism and discrimination as key factors. Minority ethnic groups, for example, are generally disadvantaged in terms of unemployment, pay and the quality of their jobs. They also tend to be disadvantaged within the **welfare state** through, for example, low take up of state assistance.

Gender and poverty

In general, women are more at risk of poverty than men. There are a number of reasons for this.
- Women have longer life expectancy than men, so there are more older female pensioners living alone than males. They are less likely to have an income from an occupational pension.
- Women are more likely than men to head lone-parent families. Many lone-parent households in the UK have low incomes.
- There is a gender pay gap between the hourly earnings of men and women. Many female-dominated jobs in sales and customer service, for example, are relatively poorly paid.
- Women are more likely than men to work in part-time paid employment.

Child poverty

Children are particularly vulnerable to poverty if they live in a family:
- with four or more children
- where the head of the household is a lone parent or from a minority ethnic group
- with no paid workers.

Poverty has a negative impact on children's life chances including their health, housing, educational attainments and job prospects.

FOCUS ON SKILLS: WRITTEN ACTIVITY

Children in poverty

Examine the table and then answer the questions below.

Poverty levels in UK, 2014/15: children in households with income below 60 per cent of the median after housing costs

Number of children	Change on year	Percentage of all children
3.9 million	Up 200 000	29

Source: adapted from McGuinness, F. (2016). *Poverty in the UK: Statistics*. House of Commons Library. Briefing Paper no. 7096, 30 June 2016, p. 3.

1 How many children were living in low-income households in 2014/15?
2 What measure of poverty is used here?
3 Using this measure, have poverty levels increased or decreased?

The life-cycle of poverty

Official statistics provide us with a snapshot of the proportion of households below average income at a particular point in time. By looking at the **life-cycle of poverty**, we get more of a moving picture over time. It highlights an individual's movement into and out of poverty over their life and suggests that people may move into and out of poverty at different stages during the course of their lives.

The life-cycle of poverty

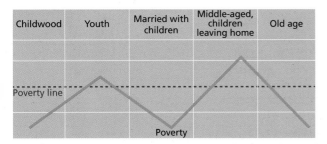

People may experience a period of **situational poverty** due to a particular situation they find themselves in such as losing their job during an economic recession, divorce or illness.

Check your understanding: Exam practice

Identify and explain one reason why women are more likely than men to experience poverty in the UK. (4 marks)

FOCUS ON SKILLS: DISCUSSION ACTIVITY

Is poverty history?

Some politicians have suggested that poverty no longer really exists in the UK. Discuss the possible arguments and evidence for and against this view. To what extent do you agree with this view?

Make a note of your conclusion with your reasons.

Stretch and challenge

Examine the illustration of the life-cycle of poverty and write a short definition of the term 'poverty line.'

Key points

- The chances of experiencing poverty are not distributed equally.

- Poverty is linked to age, with children and pensioners more at risk of poverty than other age groups. This is illustrated in the idea of the life-cycle of poverty.

- People with disabilities are also more at risk of poverty.

- The chances of experiencing poverty are also linked to factors such as gender and ethnicity.

How do sociologists explain poverty?

There are several explanations of poverty. Some focus on individuals and others focus on the structures of society. Individual accounts highlight the behaviour of individuals or groups who experience poverty, and imply that they are responsible for their position in some way. Structural accounts focus on how economic, social and political structures create and perpetuate poverty (Lister, 2004).

The culture of poverty

During the 1950s and 1960s, the persistence of poverty among some groups was explained in terms of their culture or way of life. According to this view, people from the poorest section of society were socialised within the subculture of poverty. As a result, they were unable to take up opportunities to break free from poverty.

Individuals in poverty developed a way of life and a set of values to cope with their position, including the following beliefs/attitudes:

- people can do little to change their situation so they may as well accept it
- live for today and do not worry what tomorrow may bring
- there is no point saving up or planning for the future.

These values helped those in poverty to adapt to their situation. However, they also discouraged them from taking action to escape poverty such as staying on at school or saving money for the future.

Through socialisation within families, these values were passed on from parents to their children. In this way, poverty persisted over time between generations. The policy to remove poverty consists of educating and training children to compensate for their home values.

This explanation of poverty focuses on individuals. It can be criticised as follows:

- It shows how people might adapt to poverty but it does not explain what actually causes poverty in the first place.
- By focusing on individuals and their culture, it blames those in poverty for their situation; it ignores structural factors such as unemployment levels or the impact of global economic recessions.

FOCUS ON SKILLS: WRITTEN ACTIVITY

Blaming the victims?

How far does the 'culture of poverty' explanation blame people for their poverty?

The cycle of deprivation

Supporters of the **culture of poverty** approach argued that poverty persisted from one generation to the next, locking people into a **cycle of deprivation**. During the 1970s, several versions of the cycle of deprivation were developed in the UK to explain the inter-generational persistence of poverty.

The cycle of deprivation

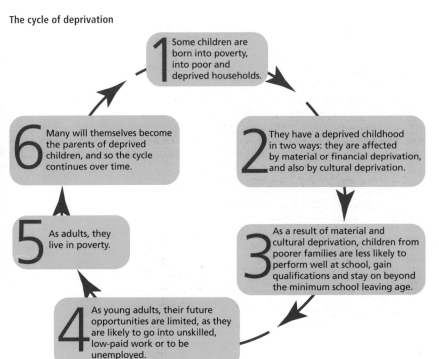

1 Some children are born into poverty, into poor and deprived households.

2 They have a deprived childhood in two ways: they are affected by material or financial deprivation, and also by cultural deprivation.

3 As a result of material and cultural deprivation, children from poorer families are less likely to perform well at school, gain qualifications and stay on beyond the minimum school leaving age.

4 As young adults, their future opportunities are limited, as they are likely to go into unskilled, low-paid work or to be unemployed.

5 As adults, they live in poverty.

6 Many will themselves become the parents of deprived children, and so the cycle continues over time.

Material deprivation involves having insufficient money to be able to afford goods and services. As a result, people may not have a balanced diet. Poverty may lead to ill health during childhood. Housing may also be inadequate and, in some cases, families may live in temporary accommodation such as hostels.

Cultural deprivation means that the children's backgrounds do not provide them with the resources to perform well at school. They have less parental encouragement and a poorer educational experience than children from more affluent backgrounds.

According to this explanation, the policy to remove poverty involves employing social workers and using local authority provision to help children break out of the cycle of deprivation.

Critics argue that, while this explanation may describe how poverty persists between generations, it fails to explain why some groups fall into poverty in the first place. Critics also argue that poverty should be explained in terms of the way society is structured and organised rather than in terms of the behaviour of individuals or families.

Making connections

How does this link to material you studied in Chapter 4 on educational achievement?

Key points

- The culture of poverty shows how the way people adapt to poverty (particularly in their subcultural values) can keep them in poverty.

- The cycle of deprivation shows how poverty is passed between the generations of a family.

Check your understanding: Exam practice

1 Describe what sociologists mean by the term 'material deprivation'. (3 marks)

2 Discuss how far sociologists agree that children who are born into poor families in Britain will go on to experience poverty over the course of their lives. (12 marks)

How do different sociological perspectives view poverty?

Objective
- Explain the functionalist, Marxist and feminist approaches to poverty

Some explanations of poverty focus on what are seen as the individual's inadequacies or the problems faced by people such as material or cultural deprivation. Structural approaches such as Marxism and functionalism, however, reject the focus on individuals and groups in explaining poverty. Instead, they examine the way in which society itself is structured or organised.

Functionalism and poverty

Davis and Moore's explanation of stratification suggests that social inequality is necessary so that functionally important positions can be filled (see Topic 3). Other functionalist accounts focus on the positive functions of poverty for some groups in industrial society. For example, poverty is useful because it helps to make sure that menial, dirty and dangerous work gets done cheaply; without poor people, there would be nobody to do these undesirable jobs. Poverty also creates jobs for groups who deal with the poor such as the police, social workers, probation officers and charity workers. The poor also have a function in reinforcing mainstream norms by providing examples of deviance such as the 'lazy' and the 'dishonest'. Critics argue, however, that functionalism tries to justify and defend the existence of poverty rather than explaining it.

Marxism and poverty

The Marxist approach argues that poverty results from class-based inequalities that are built into capitalist society. Capitalism as an economic system generates extreme wealth for the bourgeoisie (the owners of the means of production). It also produces poverty among sections of the proletariat.

Capitalist society is based on inequalities of wealth between classes, and a small group makes a profit out of the rest of the people. It is therefore inevitable that some people will be poor under capitalism. The proletariat are not paid much above subsistence levels so that the bourgeoisie can increase their profits. Poverty serves the interests of the bourgeoisie, who can hire and fire workers as needed. For example, if workers demand higher wages, then employers can threaten to replace them with workers from among the unemployed. In this way, the fear of poverty can be used to discipline the workers, keeping wages down and profits up.

FOCUS ON SKILLS: DISCUSSION ACTIVITY

Wealth as a social problem

Although poverty is generally seen as a social problem, wealth is not recognised as a problem in capitalist society.

How far do you agree that wealth is a social problem? Note down your ideas.

Marxists argue that inequality is not inevitable. The only way to remove poverty is to have revolutionary change in society, and to replace private ownership of factories, land and capital with communal ownership (in other words, they are owned by everybody rather a minority). This would end exploitation and poverty.

Critics of Marxist approaches argue, however, that societies that have undergone such social change still have poverty, inequality and differences in the distribution of income and wealth.

FOCUS ON THEORY: WRITTEN ACTIVITY

Two sociological perspectives on poverty

Copy and complete the following table by summarising each explanation and providing at least one criticism of it.

Marxist approaches	Functionalist approaches
Explanation of poverty: Criticism:	Explanation of poverty: Criticism:

Stretch and challenge

Identify one similarity and one difference between the Marxist and functionalist perspectives on poverty.

Feminism and poverty

Feminists point out that women face a greater risk of poverty than men. The two groups with the highest risk and the longest durations of poverty are lone mothers and older women living alone (Millar, 1997). Possible reasons for women's greater risk of poverty include the gender pay gap and inequality in the division of caring responsibilities (see Chapter 3 Topic 18).

Feminists argue that female poverty may be hidden in some couple households. For example, women may be poor when their male partners are relatively well off. Women may also experience poverty more intensely than their partners (Lister, 2004). Research in the UK shows that income is not always shared fairly within families (see Chapter 3 Topic 15). Mothers often go without food, clothing and warmth to protect other family members, particularly children, from the full impact of a low income. In this sense, mothers tend to act as 'shock absorbers' of poverty when managing money in low income families (Lister, 2004).

Making connections

How does this material on gender and poverty link to topics you studied in Chapter 3, Families?

How does it link to Pat Carlen's work on gender, crime and poverty in Chapter 5?

Key points

- Functionalist approaches argue that poverty performs positive functions for some groups in industrial society.

- Marxist approaches see poverty as an outcome of class-based divisions in capitalist society.

- Feminist approaches focus on the impact of poverty on women, who are more likely to experience poverty than men.

Check your understanding: Exam practice

Identify and describe one difference between individual and structural explanations of poverty. **(3 marks)**

What other explanations of poverty are there?

New Right explanations of poverty

New Right explanations of poverty are similar to the culture of poverty and cycle of deprivation in that they focus on individuals' behaviour rather than structural causes of poverty. New Right supporters stress the importance of traditional values and self-reliance. They want a reduced role for the state, especially its welfare provision. They argue that family members should provide for each other and look after sick or elderly relatives. **Welfare dependency** and the '**underclass**' are key ideas within this approach.

Glossary terms

culture of dependency, globalisation, underclass, welfare dependency

FOCUS ON KEY THINKERS

Charles Murray on the underclass

Charles Murray (1996), an American political scientist and New Right thinker, reflects on his own childhood experiences in the USA, and describes the underclass as follows:

'Their homes were littered and unkempt. The men in the family were unable to hold a job for more than a few weeks at a time. Drunkenness was common. The children grew up ill-schooled and ill-behaved and contributed a disproportionate share of the local juvenile delinquents.'

Source: Murray, C. (1996) 'The Emerging British Underclass'. In R. Lister (ed.) *Charles Murray and the Underclass: The Developing debate*. London: IEA, p. 24.

Murray (1984) examined US governments' social policy and welfare programmes since the late 1960s that aimed to help the poor and reduce poverty. He focused on the impact of these policies on the behaviour of members of the underclass. In his view, the policies actually produced poverty and encouraged more people to become dependent on welfare benefits. For example, they led to an increase in families with unmarried young mothers and encouraged a hard core of unemployed young people to have no interest in finding jobs, working hard and taking responsibility.

The underclass, in Murray's view, was associated with poor African-American and Hispanic people. He argues that the underclass is growing and poses a threat to the well being of society. This is because its members are responsible for the increase in the crime rates and they are a burden to taxpayers.

The underclass in the UK

In 1989, Charles Murray (1996) visited the UK and identified an underclass here. Four years later, he argued that the situation was getting worse.

Drawing on trends shown in official statistics, Murray argued that the UK's underclass is growing rapidly. He focused on the behaviour of the 'undeserving poor' and examined three measures of the underclass:

- rising crime rates
- an increase in the number of illegitimate or extra marital births
- drop out from the labour force among working-age men.

Making connections

Charles Murray argues that 'illegitimate children' are allowed to run wild because they have no father figure in authority over them.

Which family type do you think would work best according to New Right supporters?

He argued that welfare reform encouraged crime, single parenthood and unemployment and took away the incentive to work.

Other New Right approaches agree that Britain has an underclass of 'undeserving poor' whose cultural values and morals differ from the mainstream. They argue that generous state provision has worsened the problem of poverty by creating a **culture of dependency**. The underclass remains in poverty because the welfare state encourages them to depend on benefits. Some politicians blamed the underclass and its materialism for incidents of looting during the 2011 riots.

Criticisms of the New Right approach

* Some critics reject the idea that an underclass with different attitudes and aspirations actually exists. Others argue that the term was not developed to describe something that exists but as a label that 'blames the victims' for their misfortunes (Crompton, 2008). Labels such as the 'underclass' stigmatise people and distance them from the rest of society.
* Critics argue that sociologists should focus on the structure of society when explaining poverty. They should also focus more on the 'overclass' – the rich and powerful groups in society.

Unemployment and the inadequacies of the welfare state

While New Right approaches focus on behaviour, other explanations of poverty focus on structural factors. Piachaud (2009) sees unemployment as a central issue in understanding the causes of poverty. For example, during economic recessions, unemployment increases. Poverty also increases, through no fault of unemployed people themselves.

Some sociologists believe that the benefits system often fails to meet people's needs. For instance, many people who are entitled to benefits do not claim them. One view is that benefits are simply too low. It is argued that the solution to ending poverty is to provide people in poverty with more money (Shaw, 2002) by increasing the value of pensions and welfare benefits.

The impact of globalisation on poverty in the UK

The downturn in the global economy led to a financial crisis and recession in the UK between 2008 and 2010. This resulted in increased job insecurity, job losses, redundancies and unemployment. At the same time, the rising costs of fuel and food led to increases in the costs of living. This particularly affects people on low incomes. Some commentators argue that **globalisation** has increased inequality, not only between countries but also within them.

Check your understanding: Exam practice

Discuss how far sociologists agree that the behaviour and culture of individuals is one of the most important reasons for poverty in modern Britain.

(12 marks)

Stretch and challenge

New Right theorists see female-headed, lone-parent families as a key characteristic of an underclass whose members engage in crime.

Critics argue that the New Right scapegoat some groups. What do you think they mean by this?

FOCUS ON RESEARCH: WRITTEN ACTIVITY

Not claiming benefits

Identify and explain one advantage of using unstructured interviews to investigate why people do not claim benefits to which they are entitled.

Key points

* New Right approaches argue that welfare state provision is too generous and creates 'welfare dependency' and an underclass.
* Other approaches to explaining poverty focus on unemployment, welfare state inadequacies and globalisation.

What is the welfare state?

Objectives
- Explain the term 'welfare state'
- Describe government attempts to address poverty

The term 'welfare state' describes a system in which the state takes responsibility for protecting the health and welfare of its citizens, and for meeting their social needs. The state does this by providing services and benefits. In the UK, the welfare state was established as a safety net to protect the most vulnerable members of society and to guarantee them an adequate level of income, healthcare, education and housing.

> **Glossary terms**
>
> means testing, poverty trap, selective benefits, universal benefits, welfare benefits

Services provided by the welfare state

Today, the welfare state provides services related to, for example, health, education and **welfare benefits**, and social services such as child protection.

The National Health Service

The National Health Service (NHS) provides various healthcare-related services such as general practitioners (GPs), hospitals, opticians and dentists. These are funded by central government from national taxation.

Welfare benefits

- **National insurance (NI) benefits** are contributory benefits. To qualify for them, people must have paid sufficient contributions into the NI scheme. For example, people in paid employment pay part of their earnings into the NI scheme. If they become unemployed, they are entitled to claim NI benefits provided they have paid enough contributions. Current examples of NI benefits include contribution-based Jobseeker's Allowance and the state retirement pension.
- **Non-contributory benefits** are designed for people in financial need who have not paid enough NI contributions to qualify for NI benefits. Current examples include Income Support and Child Tax Credit.
- **Local benefits** are the responsibility of local councils, for example Lambeth or Oldham councils. They include housing benefit and education benefits such as free school meals.

POVERTY LINE

WELFARE STATE

The welfare state works as a safety net.

Government attempts to address poverty

Welfare issues provoke heated debates, not only because they involve important questions about how society tackles poverty and inequality but also because welfare provision is funded by income from taxation.

> **Stretch and challenge**
>
> One major area of debate concerns how far the state should be responsible for welfare provision.
>
> How do you think the New Right would address this issue?

One way that governments try to reduce the number of people in poverty is by state provision of financial support through **selective benefits**. Selective benefits target those in greatest financial need on the basis of a means test. **Means testing** establishes that a person is in need before they receive financial help from public funds. Whether or not a claimant qualifies for means-tested benefits, and how much they receive, depends on their income and savings.

However, critics of means testing argue that it may trap people in poverty. This is because an increase in income may reduce the benefits to which people are entitled. For example, an employed person who is receiving means-tested benefits could get a wage rise but be no better off, or even worse off, if they now earn too much to qualify for benefits. This is sometimes called the '**poverty trap**'.

Those in need may not actually claim the benefits to which they are entitled because the claims process is too complex and intrusive. Also, means testing may discourage people from saving.

Universal benefits are not means tested and are less likely than selective benefits to stigmatise recipients. In the past, child benefit was available to anyone who was responsible for a child regardless of their income or savings. Now, people on a high income (currently over £50 000) may have to pay a tax charge. As a result, some people have opted out of getting child benefit.

Another way of addressing poverty is through the introduction of a national minimum wage and a national living wage (for those aged over 25 years). Employers who break the law by not paying the correct hourly rates are named and shamed. In August 2016, the government published a list of 197 companies that did not pay the minimum wage.

JobCentre Plus deals with benefit claims and helps people to find jobs.

What is power?

Power is a key concept in sociology and sociologists study the way power relationships work in society. They focus on inequalities in power between different individuals and groups.

FOCUS ON KEY THINKERS

Max Weber writing on power in the late 19th and early 20th century

There are several ways of defining power. Max Weber (1947) was one of the most influential early sociologists to study power. He argued that an individual or group has power when they are able to get what they want, despite any opposition from other people. In Weber's view, we exercise power when we influence someone, even against his or her will.

What are the sources of power?

According to Weber, power may be based on either **coercion** or **authority**. Coercion involves the use of force. We obey an individual or group because we feel that we have no choice; we are forced into obeying against our will. Coercive power includes the threat, or use, of physical violence or torture. Kidnappers, for example, exercise coercive power when they demand a ransom and receive payment in exchange for the release of hostages.

Authority is exercised over us when we willingly obey an individual or group because we think it is the right thing to do. In this case, force is unnecessary because we agree to obey. A teacher, for example, exercises authority over students in the classroom when they willingly complete homework and hand it in on time.

What are the sources of authority?

Max Weber identified three types of authority:
- **traditional authority**
- **rational legal authority**
- **charismatic authority**.

In each of these cases, the people who are subjected to authority (such as students in classrooms) accept the exercise of power (in this case by the teacher) as legitimate. They consent to power being exercised over them.

Rational legal authority in action.

Traditional authority

Traditional authority is based on custom and tradition. We accept the authority of an individual or group because it is customary for us to do so. In the UK, for example, the authority of the **monarchy** is based on tradition.

Rational legal authority

Rational legal authority is based on people accepting a set of laws or rules. We obey an individual or group because we agree with (or recognise) the laws or rules on which their power rests. In the workplace, for example, employees accept their manager's authority to supervise their work because this is laid out in their contracts. Rational legal authority operates within a **bureaucracy**, that is, an organisation with a hierarchy and a clear set of rules.

Charismatic authority

In the case of charismatic authority, we obey a leader because we believe that he or she has extraordinary personal qualities or powers that inspire us. Charismatic leaders are seen as exceptional people. The authority of some religious leaders, for instance, is based on their charisma. Before the move to democracy in South Africa, Nelson Mandela (1918–2013), a charismatic political leader, led a large popular movement against apartheid. Such examples show that charismatic leaders can bring about social change.

Weber recognised that, in practice, an individual's authority may be based on a mix of two types of authority. For example, teachers exercise rational legal authority but a gifted teacher may also exercise charismatic authority and act as an inspiration to students.

Marxist approaches to power

Other sociologists are influenced by the work of Karl Marx (1818–1883). They see power as closely linked to social class relationships. Members of the bourgeoisie hold power and it is based on their ownership of the means of production. Marxist approaches argue that the bourgeoisie use their power to exploit the proletariat – the working class. They also argue that political power comes from economic power. This means that the bourgeoisie, by virtue of their economic power, also have political power.

Charismatic leaders can be a force for social change.

FOCUS ON SKILLS: WRITTEN ACTIVITY

Sources of power

Authority and coercion are both sources of power. Identify one difference between them.

FOCUS ON SKILLS: DISCUSSION ACTIVITY

Types of authority

In a small group, discuss which type or types of authority are involved in the following examples:

a a police officer

b a 'lollipop' lady or man

c the pope

d a village elder.

Note down your ideas.

Stretch and challenge

Explain how a religious leader or an office manager could exercise more than one type of authority.

Key point

According to Weber, people exercise power when they get what they want, despite opposition. He argued that power may be based on either coercion (the use of force) or authority (consent or agreement). He identified three types of authority: traditional, rational legal and charismatic.

Check your understanding: Exam practice

Describe what sociologists mean by 'rational legal authority'.   (3 marks)

How do feminist perspectives view power relationships?

Feminist perspectives on power

Marxist approaches see ownership of the means of production as the basis of power in capitalist society. The bourgeoisie own the means of production and this gives them power over the proletariat. In Weber's view, power can be based on either authority or coercion. We enter into power relationships when we influence someone, even against their will, or when someone influences us. This means that power relationships are found everywhere in daily life: in a home, a classroom, a workplace, a police station and a prison. Power relationships also operate when we are with our parents, teachers, friends, peer groups, bosses, partners, spouses and so on.

Feminist approaches argue that Marxist and Weberian accounts of power tend not to pay enough attention to gender. Many feminist approaches to the study of power and power relationships focus on patriarchy.

FOCUS ON KEY THINKERS

Sylvia Walby on patriarchy

Sylvia Walby (1990) is a feminist sociologist who focuses on gender inequalities and women's subordination (inferior position) in society. She uses the concept of patriarchy in her book and defines patriarchy as a 'system of social structures and practices' in which men 'dominate, oppress and exploit' women. She examines six patriarchal structures: paid work, housework, culture, sexuality, violence and the state.

- **Paid employment**: women typically earn less than men and are excluded from better types of paid work. The labour market segregates occupations by gender, and women are in the worst jobs. The labour market is more important than the family in influencing women's decisions about whether to work in paid employment. Women's lesser participation in the labour force results from material constraints, for example their wages are so low that paid work is not worthwhile.
- **The household**: husbands and partners exploit women by benefiting from their unpaid labour in the home.
- **Culture**: culture differentiates between masculinity and femininity. In society today, femininity is defined in terms of being sexually attractive to men.
- **Sexuality**: the operation of **double standards** is one aspect of male dominance. For example, sexually active young women may still be viewed as 'slags' while sexually active men are often admired.
- **Male violence against women**: male violence affects women's actions and is a form of power over them. The state refuses to intervene against it except in exceptional cases.
- **The state**: state policies and actions relating to gender have changed since the 19th century. For example, it is now easier to divorce. Nonetheless, state policies are biased towards patriarchal interests and there has been little effort to improve women's position in the public sphere, for example in the workplace.

Walby argues that there have been changes in the degree of patriarchy in Britain over the last century, such as the reduction in the gender pay gap and the qualifications gap. There has also been a shift over time from a private form of patriarchy to a public form. With private patriarchy, the household is the main site of female oppression. Public patriarchy is based mainly in public sites such as paid employment. Although women now have access to public spheres, they are often in subordinate positions; for example, they are exploited in the workplace.

Stretch and challenge

How far do you agree that the double standard as Walby describes it still operates today?

FOCUS ON SKILLS: DISCUSSION ACTIVITY

Control or coercion in intimate or family relationships

Read through the information below, then discuss the questions that follow.

Under the Serious Crime Act 2015, controlling or coercive behaviour between intimate partners or family members is now a criminal offence. For the law to apply, this behaviour must take place repeatedly or continuously. Convicted offenders may be sentenced to a maximum of five years in prison, a fine or both.

Examples of controlling or coercive behaviour include:

- isolating a partner or family member from their friends or family
- monitoring how they spend their time
- monitoring them by social media or phone
- controlling what they wear
- controlling their finances
- threatening to hurt or kill them.

1 How far would sociologists agree that each of these six examples show one person exerting power over another?
2 Why might some victims of this crime not report it to the police?
3 Note down your ideas.

FOCUS ON RESEARCH: WRITTEN ACTIVITY

Researching controlling and coercive behaviour

Identify one ethical problem you might face if you were researching controlling or coercive behaviour in family relationships and explain how you would address this issue.

FOCUS ON THEORY: WRITTEN ACTIVITY

Marxism and feminism

Identify one difference between Marxist and feminist views on which groups hold power in society.

Key points

- Some feminist approaches to power relationships focus on the workings of patriarchy.

- Sylvia Walby argues that, through patriarchal structures and practices, men dominate and exploit women.

Check your understanding: Exam practice

Discuss how far sociologists agree that gender is the most significant division in British society today.   (12 marks)

How is power exercised in the political process?

Objectives
- Explain the term 'democracy'
- Describe the pluralist and conflict approaches to the state
- Describe the pluralist and conflict approaches to pressure groups

Politics involves the exercise of power and power relationships. In many nations, including the UK, the political system is based on democracy. The term 'democracy' means 'government by the people'. In a democratic society, power is distributed widely and the government's power is based on consent rather than on coercion. In a **dictatorship**, however, political power is concentrated in the hands of a dictator who rules by force. **Censorship** of the media – that is, tight governmental control of the contents of, for example, newspapers and television news broadcasts – occurs under a dictatorship. **Propaganda** campaigns are used to further the political aims of the dictatorship, promote particular views and win people's loyalty.

In a representative democracy, citizens elect representatives who make political decisions on their behalf. In UK general elections, voters in a **constituency** each cast one vote. Most candidates belong to a **political party** such as the Labour or Conservative party. The candidate with the most votes becomes the **Member of Parliament** (MP) for that constituency and sits in the House of Commons. This type of electoral system is known as '**first-past-the-post**' or winner takes all. By contrast, under a **proportional representation (PR)** system, seats are allocated according to the total number of votes that each party receives. PR is used to elect Members of the European Parliament (MEPs).

The state is a central part of the political process and refers to the various institutions (such as the police, armed forces, civil service and judiciary) that organise and regulate society. The role of state institutions is to make, implement and enforce laws. In the UK, the state exercises authority over England, Northern Ireland, Scotland and Wales. Some state powers, however, have been passed to the Welsh Assembly, the Scottish Parliament and the Northern Irish Assembly.

The 'government' of the UK refers to MPs who are ministers, selected by the **prime minister**, who is the leader of the governing political party. In a democratic system, the government's power is based on rational legal authority rather than on coercion. Although the legal system, the military and the police force are all part of the state, they are independent of the government of the day.

Contrasting views of the role of the state

There are two broad approaches to the study of power and the state: **pluralism** and the conflict approach. They differ in their views on who holds power in society, how it is distributed and used.

Glossary terms

censorship, constituency, dictatorship, direct action, first-past-the-post, interest group, Member of Parliament, new social movement, pluralism, political party, pressure group, prime minister, propaganda, proportional representation (PR), protest movement

Stretch and challenge

Critics argue that in the 'first-past-the- post' voting system many votes are wasted. What do you think they mean by this?

Making connections

Look out for links with the material you studied in Chapter 5, Crime and deviance. For example, how are state institutions such as the police and judiciary linked to social control?

The pluralist approach argues that a range of competing interests and pressure groups exists in society. Political power is shared between these groups. No single group dominates decision-making or always gets its own way. The state's role is to act as a neutral referee rather than to take sides. It regulates the different interests and serves the needs of all citizens.

Sociologists from the Marxist or conflict approach argue that those in powerful positions within the state (such as top judges and senior civil servants) tend to come from privileged backgrounds. Many have been educated in private schools and Oxford or Cambridge university.

Marxists argue that it is the owners of the means of production who have power in capitalist society. The state's role is to protect the interests of the bourgeoisie. Those in powerful positions within the state are either drawn from – or serve the interests of – the bourgeoisie. This group's economic dominance gives it political power, so state policies generally benefit its members.

Contrasting views on the role of pressure groups and social movements

Pluralists argue that **pressure groups** (or **interest groups**), trade unions, **new social movements** and **protest movements** are crucial to democracy. Pressure groups, for example, allow like-minded citizens to join together and put forward their views. New social movements (such as environmentalism, anti-racism, feminism and civil rights movements) emerged in societies such as the USA and the UK in the 1960s and 1970s. These movements challenge the status quo (the current situation) and aim to bring about social change. Protest movements organise **direct action** to protect the environment, for instance, or to focus attention on companies that dodge taxes. In this way, all opinions and interests can be represented and heard. Such groups provide opportunities for citizens to participate in the political process.

The conflict view argues that society is based on conflicting interests between different groups. Some key groups, such as big business, have enough power, staff and financial resources to be able to influence government policies. Some groups' power is based on their ownership of property, wealth and resources. This gives them status and they can exert more influence on policy makers and dominate decision-making.

A high-profile protest.

Key points

- The state consists of institutions that make, implement and enforce laws.

- The pluralist approach sees the state as refereeing between pressure groups, while the conflict approach sees it as serving the interests of a privileged minority.

Check your understanding: Exam practice

Describe what sociologists mean by the term 'democracy'.

(3 marks)

What methods are used to research social stratification?

Objectives
- Describe some of the methods used to research social stratification
- Evaluate these methods

FOCUS ON RESEARCH: WRITTEN ACTIVITY

Fiona Devine: Researching affluent workers

Read through the extract from a book written by the sociologist Fiona Devine (1992) and answer the questions that follow.

'The research is based on intensive interviews with sixty-two Luton residents, either Vauxhall workers or their wives. Interviewed separately at home, the men and women were asked to discuss different facets of their daily lives. Topics of conversation included geographical mobility, work histories, sociability with kin, neighbours and fellow workers, conjugal roles, leisure patterns, consumer aspirations, class identities, and industrial and political attitudes and behaviour.'

Source: Devine, F. (1992) *Affluent Workers Revisited: Privatism and the Working Class.* Edinburgh: Edinburgh University Press, p. 5.

1 Identify and describe the type of interviews used by Fiona Devine.
2 Explain one advantage of using this method to investigate people's daily lives.
3 Explain one disadvantage of using this method to research people's daily lives.
4 Why do you think Devine interviewed the men and women separately rather than together?

FOCUS ON RESEARCH: WRITTEN ACTIVITY

Peter Townsend: Researching poverty in the UK

Read through this information about the research that the sociologist Peter Townsend (1979) carried out and answer the questions that follow.

Peter Townsend's main research method was a large-scale questionnaire survey that ran for 12 months during 1968/9 in 51 constituencies in the UK. He collected data on 2052 households and 6098 individuals. The national questionnaire survey covered household resources and standards of living. It was 39 pages long and contained 9 sections including housing and living facilities, employment, income, savings, health and style of living.

Four local surveys were also undertaken in Salford, Glasgow, Belfast and Neath (chosen because they all had high proportions of low income households), which collected data on 1208 households and 3950 individuals.

Trained interviewers delivered the surveys. Over 80 per cent of the interviews were carried out by a core group of around 25 interviewers.

1 Why do you think Townsend had to employ a large team of over 25 interviewers to deliver the survey?
2 Identify one disadvantage of employing so many interviewers to deliver the survey.
3 Identify one advantage and one disadvantage of using a long survey.
4 Townsend did not ask respondents whether they lacked a particular item because they did not want it or because they could not afford it. How might this affect his results?
5 Is this method designed to generate quantitative or qualitative data? Briefly explain your answer.
6 How far would it be possible to replicate this method? Write a short paragraph to explain your answer.

Fiona Devine notes that the sample of people she interviewed was not a randomly selected sample. Is this necessarily a problem in qualitative research? Write a couple of sentences to explain your answer.

Stretch and challenge

Why is it important to have a randomly selected sample in quantitative research? Write a couple of sentences to explain your answer.

FOCUS ON RESEARCH: WRITTEN ACTIVITY

Charles Murray: Researching the 'underclass'

In his book *Losing Ground: American Social Policy, 1950–1980 (1984)*, Charles Murray, an American political scientist, draws on secondary sources of quantitative data from the USA. These include official statistics from censuses, unemployment rates, crime rates and illegitimate birth rates.

His research on the underclass in Britain was also based on official statistics. He drew on trends shown in official statistics on crime rates, unemployment rates and births outside marriage to identify an emerging underclass.

1 Describe one strength of using official statistics as a source of data in research.
2 Identify and describe one problem with using police-recorded crime statistics as a measure of the level of criminal behaviour in different social groups.

FOCUS ON SKILLS: WRITTEN ACTIVITY

Secondary sources on poverty

Official statistics are one secondary source of data that researchers might use to investigate the extent of poverty. Examine the table and then answer the questions that follow.

Poverty levels in UK, 2014/15: all individuals

		Number of people	Change on year	Percentage of the population
Relative low income – living in households with income below 60 per cent of the median in 2014/15	Before housing costs	10.1 million	Up 500 000	16
	After housing costs	13.5 million	Up 300 000	21

Source: adapted from McGuinness, F. (2016). *Poverty in the UK: Statistics*. House of Commons Library, Briefing Paper no. 7096, 30 June, p. 3.

1 How many people were living in households with relatively low incomes before housing costs in 2014/15?
2 What percentage of the population was living in households with relatively low incomes after housing costs in 2014/15?
3 How many more people were living in poverty after housing costs were taken into account?

Check your understanding: Exam practice

Identify and explain one disadvantage of using social surveys to investigate people's experiences of poverty. (4 marks)

Making connections

Glossary term

proletarianisation

Making connections: Written activity

Linking social stratification to families

Remember to look out for connections or links between the different topics and areas of sociology. There are plenty of links to be found between the topics of social stratification and families. For instance, power relationships operate between different family members such as parents and children.

Study the spider diagram and answer the question below.

Choose three of the links in the spider diagram and, in each case, explain briefly how it connects the topic of social stratification with families.

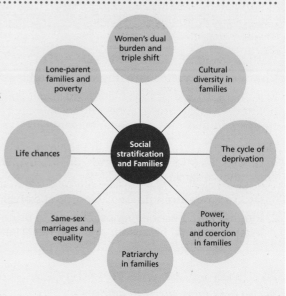

Making connections: Discussion activity

Linking social stratification to education

There are lots of links between social stratification and education. For instance, power relationships operate within schools and colleges.

Study the spider diagram and answer the question below.

In pairs, choose two of these links and, in each case, discuss how it connects the topics of social stratification and education.

Then team up with another pair, who have selected different links, and share your ideas.

Make a note of your ideas.

Making connections: Written activity

Linking social stratification to crime and deviance

The spider diagram highlights some of the links between social stratification and crime and deviance. Study the diagram and answer the question below.

Choose three of the links in the spider diagram and, in each case, explain briefly how it connects the topic of social stratification with crime and deviance.

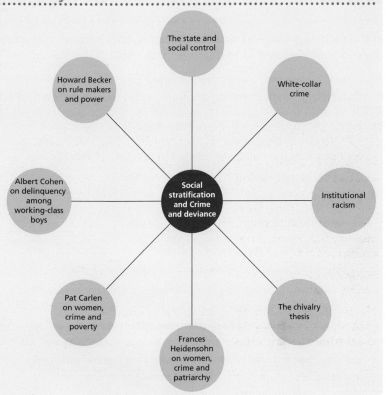

FOCUS ON THEORY: WRITTEN ACTIVITY

Similarities and differences between the perspectives

Drawing on what you have learned in this chapter, answer the following questions.

1 Identify two sociological perspectives or approaches that:

  a see society as based on conflicting interests between different groups

  b are both structural approaches.

2 Identify one sociological perspective that:

  a sees social stratification as necessary to the working of modern society

  b rejects the idea that social stratification is inevitable (bound to occur).

3 Identify one approach that:

  a focuses on welfare dependency and the underclass in their account of poverty

  b sees poverty as having positive functions for some groups.

4 Identify one criticism of the functionalist theory of stratification from:

  a a Marxist perspective

  b a feminist perspective.

5 ~~Identify~~ one difference between the pluralist and conflict
~~...~~ to:
~~...~~ te
~~...~~ups.

Stretch and challenge

Some Marxists argue that a process of **proletarianisation** of clerical workers is occurring. Office workers have joined the working class in that their work has become more routine and less skilled.

What evidence would you need in order to assess this view?

Social stratification (Paper 2)

In this section we look at what the Social stratification section of Paper 2 will look like, with some possible questions and marked candidate responses.*

*Please be aware that marks are advisory, based on sample AQA materials. Examination grade boundaries and marking guidance change annually – please visit the official AQA website for more information.

01 Which of the following is a term commonly used by sociologists to describe a state of poverty where individuals cannot afford the minimum needed to survive? **[1 mark]**

A   Material deprivation   ◯

B   Relative poverty   ◯

C   Situational poverty   ◯

D   Absolute poverty   ✓   1/1

> Tip: Read these questions carefully! Often, in the hurry to get started, candidates can misread the question and lose what is essentially an easy mark.

> Tip: In the exam you will simply need to tick whichever you think is the correct answer.

02 Describe one example of charismatic authority. **[3 marks]**

Charismatic authority is when someone is followed because of their personality or character. One example could be Barack Obama; lots of people like him and vote for him because of his personality when he does things like sing and dance as well as making inspiring speeches. Weber said this type of authority is unstable though, Barack Obama sometimes says or does things and some people will no longer vote for him.

> Examiner comment: The candidate has shown a good understanding of charismatic authority by defining it and giving a relevant example. Their use of Weber is excellent. If you can mention a key thinker in your answer, be sure to do so! 3/3

03 Identify and describe **one** example of achieved status **[3 marks]**

Achieved status is when people earn social positions through hard work, like Alan Sugar.

> Examiner comment: The candidate has shown a fragment of knowledge about what achieved status is with a relevant, but under developed example (Alan Sugar). To score higher marks, the candidate needed to describe what status Alan Sugar has achieved and how he did this. 1/3

Item A

The chart shows participation in voluntary activities (percentages in England, 2005) at least once a month in the previous year by socioeconomic classification.

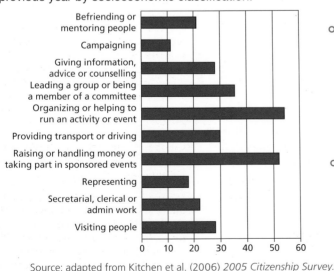

Source: adapted from Kitchen et al. (2006) *2005 Citizenship Survey.*

> Tip: Be sure to study items carefully. Pay extra attention to things such as dates and who conducted the research, as this will be crucial to answering the next couple of questions, which will test how well you have read the item. You could be asked about the type of research methods that the researcher has used, strengths or weaknesses of the research or even to identify trends, patterns or make observations.

> Tip: The two questions that follow expect you to have the 'context' of this item in mind. Try to refer to it whenever you can!

04 From **Item A**, examine **one** weakness of the research. **[2 marks]**

The research in item A was conducted by a survey. It is possible that the people who responded did not answer honestly.

Tip: This question is testing how well you can read and analyse Item A!

Examiner comment: The candidate has identified a possible weakness, but they have not examined it in the context of Item A. To score the extra mark, they might have considered why people might not be honest – for example, they could be bored when filling the survey in, or not understand the questions. 1/2

05 Identify and explain **one** factor that may prevent people taking part in the formal volunteering activities referred to in **Item A**. **[4 marks]**

Social class might prevent some people from taking part in formal volunteering. For example, someone from the working class might feel like politics is for rich people and not take part.

Examiner comment: The candidate has identified one factor (social class) that might prevent people from taking part, but they have only briefly described why this factor might affect participation. To score more marks, the candidate would need to explain in detail why being working class might affect participation – for example, feeling under-represented in politics, so seeing no point in participating. 2/4

06 Identify and describe **one** way the government has tried to reduce youth unemployment in recent years. **[4 marks]**

One way the government has tried to reduce unemployment in recent years is by making it much harder to claim benefits, for example people now have to do work experience and prove they have been looking for work. This makes it much harder for people to stay unemployed so they get back into work quicker.

Examiner comment: The candidate has described actions taken by recent governments, but the actions are not specific to reducing youth unemployment and so cannot be credited. Examiners would be looking for reference to policies such as apprenticeships that were specifically aimed at helping young people get into work. 0/4

Tip: Examiners will be expecting you to write about policies from the last 25 years or so if the question uses the phrase 'recent years'. Notice that this question specifically says 'youth' unemployment.

07 Discuss how far sociologists agree that there is an underclass in modern British society. **[12 marks]**

The underclass is a group of people in society who are below even the working class. These people may be very poor and unemployed. Some sociologists would agree that there is an underclass as programmes like 'Benefits Britain' show there are people who exist on benefits and do not work.

Tip: In the essays, you are being assessed on four things: 1. Sociological knowledge (A01: 4 marks); 2. Your ability to apply knowledge of theories, research and methods (AO2: 4 marks); 3. Your ability to evaluate sociological theories and concepts (AO3: 4 marks); 4. Your ability to write clearly and coherently, spelling well and using specialist terms accurately will affect the total mark you receive. If your response is not well structured (for example, in bullet points), you will be unable to go beyond 7–9 marks.

Examiner comment: The candidate has shown a limited understanding of what the underclass is. 2/12

08 Discuss how far sociologists agree that Britain today is a patriarchal society. **[12 marks]**

A patriarchal society is one where the men in society control all of the power. Some sociologists, like feminists, would agree that society in Britain today is still patriarchal but others would say that it is not.

Some sociologists say that there are now so many laws in society to make women equal that men do not control it anymore. It is now illegal to discriminate against women for jobs and promotions and there are lots of successful women, like Kim Kardashian.

Other sociologists argue that society is still not equal, and although women do work more now they do the triple shift and end up doing the childcare and housework as well. They are also less likely to get into top jobs because of the glass ceiling.

In conclusion women still have less power than men, so Britain is patriarchal.

Examiner comment: The candidate has made a 'basic attempt at analysis'. If the candidate had developed their points more, for example by naming specific laws that have reduced inequality between men and women, they would have scored more marks. This answer also fails to reference any sociological views which examiners would expect to see in higher mark answers. 5/12

Examination preparation and practice

Inside the exam paper

This section explains the different *question types* you can expect to see in each paper and gives some general advice on how to approach them. Remember: there are model marked responses in the Exam focus section of each chapter of this book.

1 **Multiple choice** '1-mark' questions (4% of total marks) – allow 1 minute for each of these.

   At the start of each section, there will be two multiple-choice questions (similar to the one below).

Which term is commonly used by sociologists to describe behaviour that is different to the values and expectations of society? **[1 mark]**   A   Crime   B   Deviance   C   Socialisation   D   Anomie

   > Be sure to read the question carefully and tick the appropriate response. These questions are designed only to test your *knowledge* (AO1). In total, there will be four of these question types on each paper.

2 **Describe** '3-mark' questions (12% of total marks) – allow 3 minutes for each of these.

   These follow on from the multiple-choice questions and again test your *knowledge* (A01). There will be four of these question types in each paper. An example is given below.

Describe what is meant by anomie. **[3 marks]**   _____   _____   _____

   > These questions expect relatively short (5–6 lines or so, depending on your handwriting size) descriptions of key sociological terms or concepts. **Describe** questions require less detail than **Explain** questions. Try to keep to the space given to you in the exam booklet.

3 **Items**

   You can expect to see four Items in total in each paper. Items could be extracts from research, graphs, tables or something else entirely; they could also be extracts from the work of key thinkers you will study in this book. You can see examples of items in the Exam focus sections throughout this book. Be sure to read them carefully and look out for dates and the type of research methods that might have been used. Items are used to test your ability to *read and interpret information correctly*.

4   **Examine** '2-mark' questions (4% of total marks) – allow 2 minutes to answer each of these.

These will follow the first item in each section of the paper, so there will be two of these question types in each paper you sit.

> From Item A, examine one weakness of the research. **[2 marks]**
>
> _____
>
> _____
>
> _____

These questions are testing your ability to correctly _read and interpret_ the item (AO3). **Examine** means you need to pick out the correct information from the item and comment on it. Always mention the type of research/research method used in the item before commenting on it.

5   **Identify and explain** '4-mark' questions (32% of total marks) – allow 4 minutes for each of these.

There will be eight of these question types in each paper. Sometimes they will require you to use items and other times they will be asking you to explain sociological concepts, the theories of key thinkers covered in this book or sociological research methods. These questions always ask you to identify **one** thing and develop/explain what you have identified in more depth. Note that **one** is in bold font – there is no point identifying more than **one** factor; examiners will not award you any extra marks.

> Identify and explain **one** advantage of using structured interviews to investigate relationships between family members. **[4 marks]**
>
> _____
>
> _____
>
> _____

These questions assess both your _knowledge_ (AO1) and _ability to apply your knowledge to the context of the question_ (AO2). It's also worth remembering that these questions are marked almost in two parts: 1 mark is awarded for the identification, and up to 3 marks for the explanation. You can see how these responses are marked in the Exam focus sections of this book. It is possible to score 1 mark for explanation if you identify the wrong thing. Try to stick to the space in the booklet.

6   **Discuss how far** '12-mark' questions (48% of total marks) – allow 12 minutes for each of these.

There will be four of these in each paper; you will not be able to choose between possible questions and will have to answer all four. These questions require you to critically analyse and evaluate the sociological theories of key thinkers or sociological concepts. You are being marked on your _sociological knowledge_ (AO1), _your ability to apply your knowledge to the context of the question_ (AO2) _and your ability to analyse and evaluate_ (AO3). **_Your ability to express yourself clearly in written English will also be assessed in these questions_**.

Tip: Don't forget about the items – they might be useful to refer to in your responses.

In these questions, be sure to always present two sociological points of view, to write in full sentences and to use (and explain/define) relevant key terms as often as possible. In the exam booklet, you are given about one and a half pages to write responses to these questions; it is about **quality** and **not quantity**, so try to stick to this space where possible – don't feel you _have_ to fill it. First and foremost, examiners are looking for coherent, two-sided responses which use sociological terms correctly – they know you only have 12 minutes to answer each one.

Tip: Notice that most of your marks are for answering the 12-mark and 4-mark questions. Be sure to practise these as much as possible in class and revision. Candidates who achieve high grades do so normally by producing consistent 3- or 4- mark responses to **identify and explain** questions and achieving around 8–12 marks on average for **discuss how far questions**.

Families

The 'Sociology of Families' will be assessed in Paper 1, along with the 'Sociology of Education'. You should answer all questions in this section and allow yourself around 50 minutes (so around 1 mark per minute).

In this section, there are some further sample questions with some advice on how to approach them. These are ideal to use for revision – you can either ask your teacher to mark them or attempt to mark them yourself following the model marked examples in the Exam focus sections of this book.

01 Which term is commonly used by sociologists to describe a family household that includes children, parents and grandparents? **[1 mark]**

A Nuclear family   ◯

B Beanpole family   ◯

C Reconstituted family ◯

D Extended family   ◯

02 Which term is commonly used by sociologists to describe household tasks such as cooking and cleaning? **[1 mark]**

A Conjugal roles   ◯

B Domestic labour   ◯

C Dual burden   ◯

D Triple shift   ◯

Tip: Both these questions highlight the importance of really knowing your key sociological terms – if you don't, you will really struggle to score these easy marks.

03 Describe the role families play in an individual's socialisation. **[3 marks]**

Tip: When responding to this question, it is relevant to describe how the role of the family is different to other agents of socialisation.

04 Describe what sociologists mean by family diversity. **[3 marks]**

Item A

Divorce, separation, birth outside marriage and one-parent families as well as cohabitation and sex outside marriage have increased rapidly. Children whose parents do not follow the traditional norm (i.e. taking on personal, active and long-term responsibility for their children's social upbringing) are thereby disadvantaged. On the evidence available, such children tend to die earlier, to have more illness, to do less well at school, to suffer more unemployment, to be more prone to crime, and finally to repeat the cycle of unstable parenting from which they themselves have suffered.

Dennis and Erdos highlight one consequence of family breakdown – the emergence of a new type of young male, who is weakly socialised regarding the responsibilities of being a husband and father. He no longer feels the pressure felt by previous generations of males to be a responsible adult in a functioning community.

Source: adapted from Halsey (1993).

Tip: As you read the item, consider:

- What group of sociologists would agree with Halsey's assertions in this item?
- How could you criticise or challenge his observations?
- What groups of sociologists would disagree with him?

05 From **Item A**, examine **one** consequence of families not following the traditional norm. [**2 marks**]

Tip: always read questions carefully. Note here that it says to think of a cause *other* than the one referred to in the item here.

06 Identify and explain **one** factor, other than family breakdown, that may have led to the emergence of weakly socialised young males referred to in **Item A**. [**4 marks**]

07 Identify and explain **one** disadvantage of using structured interviews to investigate family types in the UK. [**4 marks**]

Item B

> Researchers examined trends in child and adolescent rates of overweight and obesity using electronic GP records from 1994 to 2013. The data shows there was a significant increase in child and adolescent overweight and obesity rates every year during the first decade from 1994 to 2003.
>
> Overall, annual rates did not increase significantly during the second decade, 2004 to 2013. However, when split by age category, the results showed there was still a significant upward trend in overweight and obesity rates for the oldest age group (11 to 15 years) – albeit with less of an increase than there was in the first decade. At its maximum in recent years, overweight and obesity has affected almost two-fifths of adolescents in this age group.
>
> As the researchers used GP records, it is possible children who have problems with their weight and were assessed by their GP are over-represented. This could then lead to an overestimate of prevalence. However, it is hard to think of another method of analysis that would provide a more reliable estimate.
>
> Source: adapted from NHS Choices website www.nhs.uk/news/2015/01January/Pages/Child-obesity-rates-are-stabilising.aspx

08 From **Item B**, identify and describe the research method used by the researchers. [**4 marks**]

Tip: Always pay attention to the research method you have to use – in this question you have to use questionnaires. How would that limit your investigation? (For example, could you easily research how relationships have changed over the last 200 years?)

09 Identify **one** way family relationships have changed over time. Explain how you would investigate this using questionnaires. [**4 marks**]

10 Discuss how far sociologists would agree that marriage is no longer regarded as important in the UK. [**12 marks**]

11 Discuss how far sociologists would agree that gender roles in the family have changed significantly in the past 50 years. [**12 marks**]

Tip: Be sure to argue why sociologists might agree and disagree with these statements in both questions. Remember to use relevant key terms whenever you can and refer to sociological theories and concepts.

Education

01 Which term is commonly used by sociologists to describe the grouping of students for a particular academic subject that is not based on their ability in that subject? **[1 mark]**

A   Class

B   Streaming

C   Set ability

D   Mixed ability

02 Which term is commonly used by sociologists to describe a study of the same group of people over a long period of time? **[1 mark]**

A   Longitudinal

B   Mixed

C   Qualitative

D   Quantitative

Tip: While the 1-mark questions could test your knowledge of sociological terms relevant to the unit (in this case education), they could also test your understanding of key terms used to describe sociological research.

03 Describe what is meant by a faith school. **[3 marks]**

Tip: When responding to this question, it's relevant to describe how faith schools may be different to other schools.

04 Describe what sociologists mean by marketisation in education. **[3 marks]**

Item A

Parental choice in education

Tip: As you read the item think about strengths or weaknesses in Gewirtz's research, it might help to look at the next questions, in case there is something in the item that will help you to answer them.

> The researchers have identified parents as belonging to broad categories of choice-making:
>
> • Privileged/skilled choosers were generally middle class…These parents arrange for their children to attend the correct primaries and then use negotiating skills and training of their children to ensure that they are accepted by the selected schools.
>
> • Semi-skilled choosers were a mixed-class group of aspirant working-class parents. They were highly motivated for their children, but were less aware of some of the…insider knowledge of the system necessary in order to privilege their children. They were more open to media reports of the schools and they relied on the judgments of others. Many did not fully understand the significance of the open evenings and brochures and so they relied on reputation and rumour in their selection processes.
>
> • Disconnected choosers, who were less able to make choices, often viewed parental choice as being of little significance and viewed all schools as being 'much the same'. They usually made their selections on geography or on the current 'happiness' of the child rather than in terms of job prospects…
>
> Source: adapted from Gewirtz et al (1995).

05   From **Item A**, examine **one** weakness in the research. **[2 marks]**

06 Identify and explain **one** factor that may lead to a parent being a 'disconnected chooser' as described in **Item A**. **[4 marks]**

Tip: Be sure that you explain what Gewirtz means by a 'disconnected chooser' in the item. It is acceptable (and helpful) to quote the item, but do not use long quotes.

07 Identify and explain **one** disadvantage of using random samples in research that investigates parental attitudes towards education. **[4 marks]**

Tip: Always read questions carefully. This question asks for weaknesses of using a random sampling frame when investigating parental attitudes towards education. Think about what random sampling is and try to give an example.

Item B

Social class and pre-school children

Research for the Department for Education and Skills conducted in 2002 by Leon Feinstein of University College London claimed that, even by 2 years of age, pre-school children showed different aptitudes for completing simple 'educational' tasks and that the differences depended on income and class background. He estimated that a rise in home income of £100 a week was equal to a 3% improvement in the tests. Poorer parents, Feinstein noted, tended to be more passive and less engaged with the world around them – and to use a narrower vocabulary with their pre-school children. Children who do badly at pre-school level are least likely to have school success.

Source: Williams (2003).

08 From Item B, identify **one** reason children from poorer families might do badly at pre-school and explain why Feinstein thought this might be the case. **[4 marks]**

Tip: Note in this question that you are asked to explain why Feinstein thought this might be the case. Candidates who explain their own ideas, or those of other sociologists, will not be awarded marks.

09 Identify **one** possible label that might be attached to students who have special educational needs and explain the possible impact that label might have on their school career. **[4 marks]**

10 Discuss how far sociologists would agree that students who attend independent schools have better life chances than those who attend other types of school. **[12 marks]**

11 Discuss how far sociologists would agree that the main purpose of schools is to prepare students for life in the workplace. **[12 marks]**

Crime and deviance

. . . .

01 Which term is commonly used by sociologists to describe crime committed in the workplace? **[1 mark]**

    A Middle class

    B White collar

    C Blue collar

    D Organised

02 Which term is commonly used by sociologists to describe research interviews where the questions are pre-prepared and followed? **[1 mark]**

    A Structured interviews

    B Unstructured interviews

    C Semi-structured interviews

    D Face-to-face interviews

03 Describe what sociologists mean by anomie. **[3 marks]** ○————

> Tip: Candidates often fail to answer questions on anomie well. Although it is one of the more difficult areas of the specification, you are required to know it. Strong answers may refer to Merton's sociological research.

04 Describe one example of a folk devil. **[3 marks]** ○———

> Tip: Note in this question you are being asked to describe an example of a folk devil, not to simply explain what they are. A strong answer might describe the process that leads to their example becoming seen as a 'folk devil'.

Item A

Offenders' age and gender

This table provides information on the proportion of males and females aged 10, 15, 17 and 20 years and the proportion in older age groups who were found guilty of, or cautioned for, indictable (serious) offences in England and Wales in 2006.

> Tip: Be sure to read the text above the item as well as study the graph.

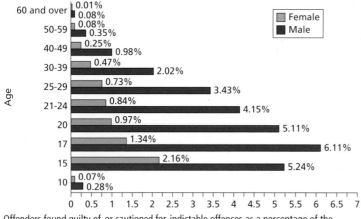

Offenders found guilty of, or cautioned for, indictable offences as a percentage of the population in England and Wales, by age and sex, 2006.

Source: adapted from Criminal Statistics 2006, England and Wales (Ministry of Justice, 2007) p. 79.

05 From **Item A**, examine **one** weakness of research using official statistics on crime. **[2 marks]** ○

> Tip: Unlike some of the other Examine questions where you are asked to specifically examine a strength or weakness of the item, in this case you are asked to examine the weakness of other researchers using such information (in this case official statistics on crime) in their own research.

06 Identify and explain **one** possible reason for the differences in the number of criminal convictions between men and women shown in **Item A**. **[4 marks]**

Tip: When answering this question, be sure to explain what the differences in the numbers of convictions between men and women are (from **Item A**).

07 Identify and explain **one** advantage of using snowball samples when carrying out research into criminal behaviour. **[4 marks]**

Item B

Is policing fair?

A view often expressed by sociologists and criminologists is that some people are 'criminalised' while other (often more serious) offenders avoid police attention.

Since catching offenders 'in the act' is actually rare, police officers tend to focus their attention on individuals they think are 'likely' to be offenders. They do this by developing a profile of a 'typical' offender. These informal profiles are largely based on two sources of information.

- First, officers' own views and previous encounters with offenders. However, these encounters are problematic because they are rarely systematic. Most offenders are never caught and those who are caught are either unlucky or slow (thus not necessarily representative of offenders in general).

- Second, information from the public. However, accounts of offenders given by victims or witnesses usually involve no more than descriptions of age, ethnicity and gender – presumably because these are often the characteristics most obvious to onlookers.

The central problem, therefore, is that police have to operate with profiles that rely on such characteristics (young, black males, etc.) rather than on anything that is clearly linked with offending. If the criteria usually used to select individuals for police attention are characteristics that someone can have little or no control over (e.g. their ethnicity, age, gender and social class), then only a narrow group of people becomes subject to police attention, on grounds that are often not justifiable.

Source: adapted from Townsley, M. and Marshall, B. (2006) 'Is Policing Fair?' in *Sociology Review* 16(2), pp. 19–21.

08 From **Item B**, identify and explain one reason why people from ethnic minority backgrounds may be more likely to receive police attention. **[4 marks]**

09 Identify **one** ethical issue you would need to consider when investigating ethnicity and criminal behaviour and explain how you would deal with this issue in your investigation. **[4 marks]**

10 Discuss how far sociologists would agree that official crime statistics give an accurate representation of crime in society. **[12 marks]**

11 Discuss how far sociologists would agree that peer pressure leads to deviant behaviour in young people. **[12 marks]**

Tip: Read questions carefully. Some candidates would write about how peer pressure may lead to criminal behaviour. Although this is linked to deviance, the question asks specifically about deviant and not criminal behaviour.

Social stratification

01 Which term do sociologists commonly use to describe a state of poverty where individuals cannot afford the average standard of living in society? **[1 mark]**

    A Material deprivation

    B Relative poverty

    C Situational poverty

    D Absolute poverty

02 Which term do sociologists commonly use to describe observation where the participant(s) are unaware they are being observed? **[1 mark]**

    A Overt observation

    B Covert observation

    C Informal observation

    D Formal observation

03 Describe what sociologists mean by the poverty trap. **[3 marks]**

> Tip: Examiners love to see real examples in responses, if you know any.

04 Describe one example of censorship. **[3 marks]**

Item A

The life expectancy gap

> In the mid-1990s, the life expectancy gap between those in professional occupations and those in unskilled manual jobs was 6.4 years for women and 9.5 years for men.
>
> There is overwhelming evidence that poverty and inequalities in material wellbeing underlie inequalities in health. Poverty and poor health are closely linked. Over the past 20 years, the number of people living in poverty grew significantly. There were also growing income inequalities in Britain, driven by factors such as the increase in 'work rich' families (with two adults in paid work) and 'work poor' families (with no adults in paid work).
>
> Source: adapted from Shaw (2002).

05 From Item A, examine **one** weakness of the research. **[2 marks]**

06 Identify and explain **one** possible reason for the differences in average life expectancies of men in professional jobs and unskilled manual jobs, shown in **Item A**. **[4 marks]**

> Tip: In your answer to this question, be sure to identify what the difference in life expectancies between men in these two groups are (from **Item A**). Note that this question only asks for a possible reason for the differences between **men** in these groups. Candidates who give reasons for the differences in women's life expectancies will not be awarded marks.

07 Identify and explain **one** advantage of using postal questionnaires when carrying out research into poverty. **[4 marks]**

Item B

Gender in everyday life

> Girls and boys are dressed in different kinds of clothes, do different school subjects, usually end up in different jobs and are portrayed differently in everything from magazines to movies to television shows. From birth, girl children and boy children are treated differently, and every day of our lives involves interacting with other people according to their gender. We talk to girls/women differently about different things, assuming they are more delicate and will be interested in, say, clothes or children or cooking. Meanwhile, boys/men are treated as though they are tough and likely to be interested in sport or cars.
>
> Source: adapted from Holmes (2009).

08 From **Item B**, identify one difference in the social expectations of boys and girls and explain how this difference impacts on the gender socialisation process. **[4 marks]**

Tip: Be sure to make it clear to the examiner that you know what 'gender socialisation' means in your response.

09 Identify **one** ethical issue you would need to consider when investigating poverty and explain how you would deal with this issue in your investigation. **[4 marks]**

10 Discuss how far sociologists would agree that Britain today is a meritocracy. **[12 marks]**

11 Discuss how far sociologists would agree that, in Britain today, gender is a more important cause of inequality than any other factor. **[12 marks]**

Tip: Candidates often 'list' or explain lots of different factors in questions like this, but notice that you are asked to what extent they would agree that gender is the **most important** factor. Be sure to refer to gender in every paragraph.

Glossary

11-plus exam: a national IQ test introduced by the 1944 Education Act to be used as a method of allocating students to one of three types of school in the tripartite system.

Absolute poverty: people in absolute poverty have incomes that are insufficient to obtain the minimum needed to survive.

Academy: a failed school, taken over by central government, in partnership with private sponsors such as businesses or churches. The aim of their creation was to raise achievement.

Academy: schools that have left local authority control and whose funding is provided directly by government. All schools have been encouraged to convert to academy status since 2010.

Achieved status: social positions that are earned on the basis of personal talents or merit.

Adolescence: the period of time in an individual's life between childhood and adulthood.

Affluence: having a lot of money and material possessions.

Age discrimination: treating someone differently and less favourably on the basis of their age.

Ageing population: in an ageing population, the proportion of the population over retirement age is gradually increasing.

Ageism: discrimination based on age.

Agencies (or agents) of social control: the groups and organisations in society that control or constrain people's behaviour and actions.

Agency (or agent) of socialisation: a social group or institution responsible for undertaking socialisation, such as a family, peer group, school, workplace, religion and the mass media.

Agenda setting: the ability of the media to focus public attention on particular topics and thereby direct public discussion and debate onto these topics.

Alienation: under capitalism, the workers feel estranged or cut off from their work because they have no control over production or the products of their labour.

Analysis: the process of examining data, highlighting significant findings and results.

Anomie: a situation of normlessness in which the norms that regulate people's behaviour break down.

Anonymity of research participants: individuals participating in research are not required to provide their name or, if they give their name, it will not appear in any reports arising from the research.

Anti-school subculture: the values shared by a group of pupils that run counter to the values of the school as a whole.

Anti-social behaviour: behaviour that causes harassment, distress or alarm to other people.

Apartheid: in South Africa (1948–94), this government policy of racial segregation was used as the basis for stratification.

Aristocracy: a class of privileged people who have hereditary titles such as Duke or Lady and who are usually wealthy landowners.

Arranged marriage: a marriage in which the family or relatives of the prospective spouses take the leading role in finding a suitable partner for them. However, the prospective spouses have the right to choose whether to accept the arrangement.

Ascribed status: social positions that are fixed at birth and unchanging over time including a hereditary title linked to family background (Princess or Lord, for example).

Assimilation: the process by which immigrants abandon their own culture and adapt their behaviour to fit the norms and values of the dominant culture. (See also multiculturalism).

Asylum seekers: people who have left their country of origin and moved to another country in order to seek protection from persecution.

Attitude survey: a social survey that measures respondents' views and thoughts on particular issues.

Authority: the exercise of power based on consent or agreement.

Beanpole families: multigenerational families that are long and thin in shape.

Benefit cheats: people who claim benefits that they are not entitled to.

Bias: being one-sided rather than neutral or open-minded. Bias can operate either in favour of or against an idea, group or point of view.

Bigamy: the offence of getting married to someone while already married to someone else.

Birth rate: the number of live births per 1000 of the population per year.

Blended (or reconstituted) family: a family in which one or both partners have a child or children from a previous relationship.

Boomerang children: young adults who have left the parental home and who later return to live at home possibly due to unemployment or the high cost of housing.

Bourgeois: relating to or belonging to the bourgeoisie.

Bourgeoisie: the ruling class who own the means of production (for example, the factories, big businesses or land) and exploit the proletariat in order to make huge profits.

Bureaucracy: an organisation (such as a government department) that operates as a hierarchy with a clear set of rules.

Bureaucratic authority: authority based on a set of rules that operate within a bureaucracy.

Canalisation: the way parents channel their children's interests into toys, games and other activities that are seen as gender appropriate.

Capitalism: an economic system that generates extreme wealth for the bourgeoisie.

Capitalist: this term can refer to capitalism as an economic system. It can also refer to members of the bourgeoisie – the capitalists who form the ruling class.

Case study: a detailed study of a particular institution (such as a school or hospital) or a series of related events (such as the moral panic surrounding mods and rockers).

Caste: an example of a stratification system linked to Hinduism and operating in India. People are born into a particular caste or strata and their social position is ascribed at birth.

Censorship: the control of information and ideas in a society often via governmental control of the press, television and other means of communication.

Census: a questionnaire survey conducted every 10 years in the UK to collect information on the whole population.

Charismatic authority: obedience based on a person's charisma or exceptional personal qualities.

Childhood: the period of time in a person's life between birth and becoming an adult. The term 'child' usually refers to younger children.

Childrearing: bringing up children.

Chivalry thesis: the idea that the criminal justice system treats female offenders, particularly those who conform to gender stereotypes, more leniently than male offenders.

Civil partnership: a relationship between two people of the same sex who register as civil partners and thereby have their relationship legally recognised.

Class alignment: strong links between class and voting behaviour with working-class people voting Labour and middle-class people voting Conservative.

Class deal: a 'deal' that offers women material rewards such as consumer goods in return for working for a wage.

Class dealignment: weakening of the links between social class and voting behaviour.

Class struggle: in capitalist society, class conflict occurs between the bourgeoisie (the owners of the means of production) and the proletariat (the working class), who have competing interests.

Classless society: a society in which there is no private ownership of property and so no social classes.

Closed question: a fixed-choice question that requires the respondent to choose between a number of given answers.

Coercion: obedience based on the threat or use of force.

Cohabitation: living with a partner outside marriage or civil partnership.

Cohort: a group of people who share a particular characteristic or experience. For example, they were all born in the same week or they all got married on the same day.

Cohort study: a longitudinal study of an entire cohort of people or a random sample of them.

Commune: a group of people who live together and share possessions, wealth and property.

Communism: a system involving communal ownership rather than individual ownership of private property.

Community: a particular area and its residents (for example, the local community) or a group of people who share a sense of identity (for example, Manchester's Irish community).

Community service: a sentence that involves an offender having to do unpaid work in the community.

Comprehensive system: introduced from 1965, this is a non-selective education system. all children attend the same type of secondary school regardless of ability.

Computer-assisted personal interviewing (CAPI): in a structured interview, the interviewer reads the questions from, and enters the answers into, a computer.

Computer-assisted self-interviewing: in a structured interview, the interviewer gives the computer to the respondent so they can input their own answers to potentially sensitive or embarrassing questions.

Computer-assisted telephone interviewing (CATI): in a structured interview over the telephone, the interviewer reads the questions from, and enters the answers into, a computer.

Confidentiality: an agreement that all information (for example, from research participants) will only be accessed by those who have the authority to access it.

Conformity: behaviour that complies with or follows society's norms and values.

Conjugal relationship: the relationship between a married or cohabiting couple.

Conjugal roles: the domestic roles of married or cohabiting partners.

Consensus: broad agreement on norms and values.

Constituency: a specific area in which the constituents elect an MP to represent them in parliament.

Content analysis: the analysis of documents and images (for example, media products) by constructing a set of categories, coding sections of the content according to these categories and then counting the number of times a theme appears.

Continuity: lack of social change; social structures, values, norms, attitudes, behaviour and so on remain the same over time.

Control theory: an approach that focuses on why most people conform. People are seen as behaving rationally and they are controlled through a deal that offers them rewards for conforming. They are likely to conform when they think the rewards are worth it.

Conventional family: a traditional nuclear family containing a married couple and their children who live together.

Corporate crime: crimes committed by employees on behalf of the company or organisation they work for. Examples include the manufacture and sale of unsafe products.

Correspondence principle: the way in which what is learned in school through the hidden curriculum mirrors what is required when in the workplace. For example, how schools are organised and how control is exerted will mirror that of the workplace in a capitalist society.

Counter-school subculture: a group within a school that rejects the values and norms of the school and replaces them with anti-school values and norms.

Covert participant observation: the researcher joins a group, observes and participates in its activities in order to study it but without informing its members about his or her research activities.

Crime: an illegal act (such as shoplifting or murder) that is punishable by law.

Crime rate: a measure of crime in terms of the number of incidents of a particular crime per specified number of adults over a given period. For example, 6 robberies per 1000 adults in a particular year.

Criminal justice system: the various agencies involved in law enforcement such as the police, the courts, the prison service and the probation service.

Criminal subculture: a social group whose members' values and behaviour involve breaking the law.

Criminality: criminal acts; involvement in behaviour that breaks the criminal law.

Crisis of masculinity: the idea that males see their traditional masculine identity as under threat today. For example, they no longer have a clear-cut role in society.

Cross-cultural studies: studies that explore similarities and differences between societies or cultures.

Cross-sectional study: a one-off or one-shot study that questions a sample of the population on the relevant issues on one occasion.

Cultural capital: the knowledge, attitudes and values that the middle class provide for their children that gives them an advantage in the education system.

Cultural deprivation: a theory that suggests that working-class and ethnic minority students lack the 'correct' values and attitudes from socialisation to succeed in education.

Cultural diversity: culturally based differences between people in a society in terms of religion, ethnicity, social class and so on.

Culture: the whole way of life of a particular society or social group. Culture includes the values, norms, customs, beliefs, knowledge, skills and language of the group or society.

Culture of dependency: a way of life that is centred on dependence on welfare benefits.

Culture of poverty: a subculture or way of life among poor people with norms and values that prevent them from escaping poverty.

Curriculum: the subject content to be taught in state schools as decided by government.

Cycle of deprivation: the idea that deprivation and poverty are passed on from parents to their children.

'Dark' figure of crime: hidden or invisible crimes (such as unreported and unrecorded crimes) that are not included within official statistics on crimes.

Data: information collected and analysed during the research process.

Data analysis: interpreting or making sense of the information collected during research and summarising the main findings or results.

Data protection: research participants who are identifiable within the data held by researchers have legal protection and, for example, can ask to see this data.

Deferential: behaving in a way that shows respect to someone such as an elder or superior.

Delinquency: minor crime and deviance usually committed by young people.

Democratic relationships: relationships between, for example, married partners or parents and children, based on equality.

Dependent children: see dependent family members.

Dependent family members: family members who depend on others within the family due to their age, for example, or lack of money. Dependent children, for instance, are those aged 0 to 15 or those aged 16 to 18 in full-time education and living with their parents.

De-schooling: the idea that the education system as it is currently organised should be abolished.

Deviance: behaviour that does not conform to society's norms and values and, if detected, is likely to lead to negative sanctions. Deviance can be – but is not necessarily – illegal.

Deviancy amplification: the process whereby public and media reaction to deviance leads to an increase in – or amplifies – deviance by provoking more of the same behaviour.

Deviant career: the process by which individuals come to see themselves as deviant and, possibly, join a deviant subculture.

Dictatorship: political power is concentrated in the hands of a dictator who rules by force.

Direct action: a campaign to raise awareness on an issue such as climate change or tax avoidance. Tactics include occupying buildings such as shop or banks.

Discrimination: less favourable or unfair treatment based, for example, on an individual's gender, ethnicity or age.

Distribution (of power and of wealth): the way in which power and wealth are shared out among different groups in society.

Division of domestic labour: see domestic division of labour.

Divorce: the legal termination (or ending) of a marriage.

Domestic division of labour: the division of tasks such as housework, childcare and DIY between men and women within the home.

Double deviance thesis: the idea that female offenders are treated more harshly than male offenders within the criminal justice system because their offending behaviour is seen not just as illegal but also as unfeminine.

Double shift: many married or cohabiting women work two shifts by doing a paid job and also most of the housework and caring for the family.

Double standards: a rule or code of behaviour that is unfairly applied to one group (such as women) and not another (such as men). For example, norms surrounding sexual behaviour allow young men more freedom than young women.

Dual-career families: a family in which two adults have careers.

Dual-earner household: a household in which two adults work in paid employment.

Dual-worker family: a family in which both adult partners work in paid employment.

Dysfunctional family: a family in which functions such as providing emotional support are not being carried out. Dysfunctional families are characterised by social problems such as domestic violence or child abuse.

Economic function (of families): from a functionalist approach, this is the function that the family carries out by providing its members with financial support, food and shelter. From a Marxist approach, the family has an economic function under capitalism because women, as housewives and mothers, carry out unpaid domestic labour (such as childrearing, cleaning and cooking) that benefits the capitalist system.

Economy: a system by which goods and services are produced, distributed and consumed in a region or country. Examples include capitalism and socialism.

Egalitarian: based on the idea that people are equal.

Elite: a group that has the most power in a society based on its wealth or privilege.

Embourgeoisement thesis: a hypothesis suggesting that working-class families are becoming middle class in their norms and values as their incomes and standards of living improve.

Emigration: the act of leaving one country to live in another.

Empty nest family: a family containing a mature couple who live together after their children have left home.

Empty shell marriage: a marriage in which the couple continue to live together (for example, for the sake of their children) even though the marriage has broken down.

Environmental poverty: a way of measuring deprivation in terms of conditions such as inadequate housing, lack of a garden, inadequate outdoor play facilities and air pollution.

Established or state church: the Church of England is the established church in England. It is linked to the state and the monarch is its Supreme Governor.

Ethical considerations: issues such as informed consent and confidentiality that sociologists must consider in order to conduct morally acceptable research.

Ethnic diversity: having a range of different ethnic groups in a society.

Ethnic group: a social group whose members share an identity based on their cultural traditions or cultural characteristics such as religion or language. Britain is home to a wide range of minority ethnic groups including those of Irish, Polish, Greek Cypriot, Indian and African-Caribbean heritage.

Ethnicity: cultural traditions, norms and values that distinguish the members of a particular social group from other groups.

Ethnocentric curriculum: the curriculum is seen as judging things in a biased way from the point of view of one culture. For example, the National Curriculum may value white, Western literature, art, history and so on.

Ethnography: the study of people's culture and practices in everyday settings.

Expectations: hopes or beliefs, for example about what marriage will – or should – be like.

Expressive role: the caring, emotional and nurturing role in the family. Parsons sees this as the woman's natural role in the family.

Extended family: a group of relatives extending beyond the nuclear family. The classic extended family contains three generations who either live under the same roof or nearby. This type of extension is known as vertical extension. In horizontally extended families, two generations live together or nearby. In modified extended families, members live apart geographically but maintain regular contact and provide support.

False class consciousness: subordinate groups such as the proletariat suffer from false consciousness when they do not recognise that they are being exploited or their true interests.

Family: an important social structure that can be broadly defined as a couple whose relationship is based on marriage, civil partnership or cohabitation, with or without dependent children, or a lone parent and their child or children.

Family diversity: the different types of family such as nuclear and lone-parent families. Aspects of family diversity also include social class, culture and cohort.

Fascism: a political movement that began with Mussolini, a dictator who came to power in Italy in 1922. The term is now often used to describe right wing political ideas or a right wing political system based on racism and nationalism.

Feminism: a movement that fights for gender equality in society. Feminists want equality in the power, status and rights of women and men in society.

Feminist: a sociologist who explores how gender operates in society and wants gender equality.

Feminist perspective: a sociological approach that examines the ways that gender operates within social structures such as families and in the wider society.

Fertility: the average number of children born to women of child-bearing age (usually 15–44) in a particular society.

Fertility rate: the number of live births per 1000 women of child-bearing age (usually 15–44).

Feudalism: a stratification system in medieval Europe with the king or queen at the top, then the lords, the knights and the peasants at the bottom.

Field note diary: a daily record of a sociologist's fieldwork experiences while researching in places such as schools, factories or communities.

Fieldwork: practical research (for example, observation and interviews) that sociologists carry out in places such as schools, factories or in communities or gangs.

First-past-the-post: an electoral system based on winner takes all. The candidate with the highest number of votes wins the seat.

Focus group interview: a type of group interview that focuses on one particular topic. It explores how people interact within the group and how they respond to each other's views.

Folk devil: a group that is defined as a threat to society's values.

Forced marriage: a marriage in which one or both parties do not give their consent to the marriage but are coerced into it.

Formal and informal rules: formal rules are written down as laws or codes of conduct. They have official status and, if we are caught breaking them, some sort of punishment, penalty or negative sanction usually follows. Informal rules are taken-for-granted, unwritten guidelines on how we are expected to behave in particular social settings.

Formal learning: this refers to the subject knowledge studied in the curriculum.

Formal social control: control of people's behaviour based on written laws and rules. Formal social control is usually associated with the ways that the state regulates and controls our behaviour. The agencies of formal social control include the police force, the courts and prisons.

Free school: schools that are funded directly by the state but are set up and run by parents, teachers, businesses, faith groups.

Function: the 'job' or role that a social structure such as the family or education system fulfils for individuals or for society.

Functionalism: a sociological approach that examines society's structures (such as the family, the education system and religion) in terms of the functions they perform for the continuation of society and for individuals.

Functionally important roles: key positions in society that, for example, provide essential services and ensure society's survival over time.

Fundamentalism: belief in the literal interpretation of religious scriptures.

Gatekeepers: the media professionals (programme controllers, editors and journalists) and owners who decide what gets covered and how it is presented.

Gender: gender relates to socially constructed or cultural (rather than biological) differences between men and women that are associated with masculinity and femininity.

Gender deal: a 'deal' that offers women emotional and material rewards in return for living with a male breadwinner within a family.

Gender equality: men and women have the same opportunities and rights in society, for example in relation to employment, education and decision-making.

Gender pay gap: the difference between men and women's hourly earnings.

Gender roles: the behaviour expected of people based on their gender and associated with masculinity and femininity.

Generalisations: general statements and conclusions that apply not only to the sample studied but also to the broader population.

Geographical mobility: moving house from one area to live in another area, region or town.

Glass ceiling: an invisible barrier to promotion faced by some groups including women.

Globalisation: the process by which societies, cultures and economies become increasingly interconnected.

Group interview: an interview in which the interviewer asks the questions and the interviewees respond. It often covers a wide range of themes or topics.

Hate crime: any crime that is perceived to be motivated by prejudice based, for example, on a person's race, religion, sexual orientation or disability.

Hidden curriculum: things learned in school that are not formally taught, such as valuing punctuality or conformity and obedience.

Home education: also called home schooling or home learning, this refers to teaching children at home rather than at school, usually by parents or private tutors.

Household: a household comprises either one person who lives alone or a group of people who live at the same address and who share at least one meal a day or facilities such as a living room.

Hypothesis: a supposition, hunch or informed guess, usually written as a statement that can be tested and then either supported by the evidence or proved wrong.

Idealisation: the representation of the traditional nuclear family as the ideal type of family.

Identity: how we see ourselves (our self-identity) and how others see us. Sources of identity include our gender, age, ethnicity, social class, religion and sexuality. 'Identity' can also refer to a person's personal details such as their name and address.

Identity theft: a crime in which the perpetrator gets hold of, or steals, personal information from a victim and uses it for personal gain.

Image: a representation or picture of a particular social group as presented, for example, in the mass media. Media images of some groups are often distorted.

Immigrant: a person who has migrated to another country in order to live and work there.

Immigration: the process of moving to another country in order to live and work there.

Income: the flow of resources that individuals and households receive over a specific period of time. Income may be received in cash (for example, from earnings) or in kind (for instance, a petrol allowance).

Independent sector: this is made up of schools that charge fees and/or are not subject to the same rules as the state sector.

In-depth interview: an unstructured or loosely structured interview that gathers rich and detailed qualitative data rather than statistics.

Indictable offence: a serious criminal offence such as murder and robbery that is tried in the Crown Court before a judge and jury.

Industrial dispute: a disagreement or conflict between employers and employees over issues such as hours, pay and work conditions.

Inequalities: differences in the distribution of resources (such as income) or outcomes (such as educational achievement).

Informal learning: this refers to the other things learned in education – the values and attitudes transmitted by the hidden curriculum.

Informal social control: control of people's behaviour based on social processes such as the approval and disapproval of others. Informal social control is enforced via social pressure. The agencies of informal social control include peer groups and families.

Informed consent: the research participant agrees to take part in the research once the sociologist has explained fully what the research is about and why it is being carried out.

Institutional racism: this occurs when an organisation (such as a police force or hospital) fails to provide an appropriate service to people because of their ethnic origin, culture or colour. Institutional racism can be seen in organisational attitudes or behaviour that discriminates, even when individuals themselves act without intending this.

Instrumental role: the breadwinner role in the family. Parsons sees this as the male's role in the family.

Instrumentalism: an attitude or approach to something (such as paid work) where it is a means to an end (for example, the wages provide a comfortable lifestyle) rather than an end in itself (for example, job satisfaction).

Integrated conjugal roles: roles that are shared equally between married or cohabiting partners.

Interactionism: a perspective that focuses on how people interact on a daily basis. Interactionists describe social reality by interpreting the feelings and actions of the people involved.

Interest group: see pressure group.

Inter-generational: between the generations.

Interpretivism: an approach in sociology that tries to understand people's lived experiences and the meanings they attach to their behaviour.

Interview: a method used to collect data in a study. In general, the interviewer asks questions and the interviewee responds.

Interview bias: this occurs when the interview situation itself influences interviewees' responses. Interviewees may give answers that they think are socially acceptable or which show them in a positive light. It is also referred to as the interview effect.

Interview schedule: the pre-set list of questions delivered by an interviewer in a structured interview.

Interviewer bias or effect: this occurs when the interviewer influences the interviewee's responses. It may be linked to the interviewer's style of interviewing (for example, asking leading questions), dress, age, gender, ethnicity, appearance or accent.

Invisible crime: crimes such as fraud and white-collar crime that are difficult to detect.

Islamophobia: hostility towards Islam and Muslims.

Isolation: the idea that the nuclear family has become more isolated or separated from the wider family.

Joint conjugal roles: domestic roles that are divided or shared in an equal way between married or cohabiting partners.

Judiciary: judges and magistrates (or Justices of the Peace – JPs – as they are also known) who sit in courts and apply the law.

Kibbutz: a group of people who live communally in settlements in Israel and who value equality and cooperation between kibbutz members.

Kin: relatives.

Kinship relationships: relationships between people based on ties of blood, marriage or adoption.

Labelling: the process of attaching a label (a sticky tag), characteristic or definition to individuals or groups.

Law: a formal rule, usually passed by the government and enforced by the state, that regulates people's behaviour.

Leading question: a question worded in such a way as to suggest a desired answer.

League table: tables of school and college results published annually to allow parents and others to make comparisons based on achievement levels.

Left and right wing: terms used to describe political parties, ideas and movements. The left wing includes socialists and communists, while the right wing includes conservatives and fascists.

Legislation: this can refer to a law or a set of laws that the government makes; it can also refer to the process of making laws.

Legislative process: the process of making laws.

Legislature: the body in a country or state that has the authority to make or change the laws. In the UK, for example, parliament has authority to make laws.

Liberal democratic values: a set of values (such as valuing freedom of speech, movement and information) associated with representative democracies.

Life chances: an individual's chances of achieving positive or negative outcomes (relating, for example, to health, education, housing) as they progress through life.

Life course: this can refer to the sequence of stages that an individual passes through over their lifetime (for example, from childhood to adolescence and beyond) or the course of a family's life over time (for example, from a nuclear to an empty nest family).

Life-cycle of poverty: movement into and out of poverty at different stages during the course of a person's life.

Life expectancy at birth: the average number of years a new born baby may be expected to live.

Lifestyles: the way in which people live including their leisure and work patterns. Lifestyle is influenced by factors such as religion, age, income and social class.

Literature review: a review of the academic literature (for example, books and journal articles) in a particular subject or field.

Lone-parent family: a family consisting of one parent and a child or children who live together.

Longitudinal study: a study of the same group of people conducted over a period of time. After the initial survey or interview has taken place, follow-up surveys or interviews are carried out at intervals over a number of years.

Lumpenproletariat: a social class made up of the 'drop outs' and criminals of society.

Magistrate: a volunteer (Justice of the Peace) who sits in the Magistrates' Court and deals with less serious crime.

Male-breadwinner household: a household in which the adult male works in paid employment and earns the bulk of the household income.

Male domination: the exercise of power and control by men over women in society.

Market situation: people's position (for example, their skills) in relation to the labour market. Weber saw class situation in terms of market situation.

Marketisation: the policy of bringing market forces (such as competition, supply and demand) into education and other areas.

Marriage: the legal union between two people.

Marxism: a sociological approach that draws on the ideas of Karl Marx and applies them to modern capitalist societies.

Marxist: sociologists who draw on the ideas of Karl Marx and apply them to contemporary capitalist societies.

Mass media: forms of communication (media) that reach large (mass) audiences, including newspapers, magazines, books, television, cinema and the internet.

Glossary

Master status: a status such as 'junkie' or 'thief' that over-rides all of an individual's other statuses such as daughter, sister, friend or employee.

Material deprivation: a lack of resources related to financial situation or poverty. In education this might include poor housing or an inability to afford educational aids.

Matriarch: a woman who holds power and authority.

Matriarchal family: a family in which a woman holds power and authority.

Means of production: the raw materials and tools used in the production process. Under capitalism, these include property, factories and machinery.

Means testing: a means test is used to establish that a claimant is in financial need before they receive financial help from the state.

Media amplification: media exaggeration of the significance of a social issue or problem by over-reporting it.

Member of Parliament (MP): a politician who has been elected to represent their constituents in the House of Commons.

Meritocracy (or meritocratic system): a system in which individuals' achievements are based on their own talents and efforts rather than their social origins and backgrounds.

Methods of social control: the processes by which individuals are encouraged or persuaded to conform to the rules and the ways in which social groups or societies deal with behaviour that breaks these rules. Social control methods may involve sanctions or other social reactions to deviance that aim to limit or reduce the frequency of deviant acts.

Middle class: a social class made up of people who work in non-manual, managerial and professional occupations.

Migration: the movement of people either nationally, from one region of a country to another, or internationally, from one country to another.

Miscarriage of justice: this occurs when a court fails to administer justice by, for example, finding an innocent person guilty of a crime.

Mixed ability: where children are taught in classes that are not organised based on ability or through setting or streaming.

Mixed methods approach: the use of different methods within one project to generate both quantitative and qualitative data

Monarchy: a system with a queen or king as the head of state.

Monogamy: the practice of being married to only one person at a time.

Moral panic: a media-fuelled over-reaction to social groups (such as 'hoodies'). This process involves the media exaggerating the extent and significance of a social problem. A particular group is cast as a folk devil and becomes defined as a threat to society's values.

Multiculturalism: the view that the cultural differences between, and identities of, the various groups in a culturally diverse society should be respected and maintained. (See also assimilation.)

National Curriculum: the subject content to be taught in state schools as decided by government.

Nature: the idea that intelligence is inherited or genetic. Educational success is thus determined by the abilities we are born with.

Negative sanctions: in the processes of social control and socialisation, negative sanctions punish those who do not conform to the group's expectations, for example by ignoring them.

Neo-conservatism: a political perspective that believes in traditional values and aims to change the moral and cultural fabric of society.

New man: a caring, sharing man who rejects sexist attitudes, believes in gender equality and puts this into practice by, for example, sharing domestic tasks and childcare.

New Right: a political perspective that believes that the influence of the state in society should be reduced and that the market should have more of a role, for example the marketisation of education. It also stresses the importance of traditional values such as self-reliance rather than relying on the welfare state.

New social movements: loosely organised groups that aim to bring about social change. Examples include animal rights, environmental and gay rights groups. Many are global rather than national movements.

News values: media professionals' ideas about what issues and personalities are seen as newsworthy, topical or important.

Non-official statistics: statistics compiled by non-governmental bodies such as banks, trade associations, professional associations, charities and market research organisations.

Non-participant observation: a research method in which a sociologist observes the community or group being studied but does not take part in any of its activities.

Non-probability sampling: a technique used to generate a non-random sample when a sampling frame is not available. Examples include snowball and quota sampling.

Non-response rate: the number of questionnaires that are not returned in proportion to the total number of questionnaires distributed.

Norms: the rules that define appropriate and expected behaviour in particular social settings such as in cinemas or aeroplanes.

Nuclear family: a family containing a father, mother and their child or children. It contains two generations, and family members live together in the same household. The parents may be married or cohabiting outside marriage.

Nurture: the idea that educational success is linked to the social environment and factors such as social class, gender, ethnicity and peer groups.

Objective class: a person's class position according to a classification such as the National Statistics Socio-economic Classification (NS-SEC).

Observation: a research method in which a sociologist gathers data by observing the community or group being studied.

Observation schedule: a structured schedule used during non-participant observation that sets out the categories of behaviour to be observed.

Observer effect: in a study based on observation, this occurs when the researcher's known presence influences and changes the behaviour of the group under study.

Official crime statistics: existing sources of quantitative data on crime compiled, for example, by government departments such as the Home Office.

Official curriculum: the formal learning that takes place in schools. This includes subjects and courses studied.

Official statistics: existing sources of quantitative data compiled, for example, by government agencies such as the Office for National Statistics.

Oligarchy: a small group of powerful individuals who control an organisation or a country usually to further their own interests.

Open-ended question: a question that allows respondents to put forward their own answers rather than choose a response from several pre-set answers.

Overclass: a small group of the very rich and powerful, known as the 'fat cats', who have political and economic power and influence.

Over-involvement: this occurs when a researcher becomes too involved with the group being studied and its activities.

Overt participant observation: in a study based on overt PO, the researcher informs participants that they are being observed as part of a research study.

Panel study: a longitudinal study in which a sample (usually randomly selected from the full population) is surveyed on two (or more) occasions.

Participant observation (PO): a qualitative research method in which the researcher joins a group and takes part in its daily activities in order to study it.

Particularistic standards: in the family, children are judged against the standards and rules of their particular family and its values.

Patriarchal families: families in which men hold power and authority.

Patriarchy: male power, authority and dominance over women.

Peer review: journal articles and conference papers are assessed (reviewed) by experienced sociologists (peers) before publication. Peer review works as a form of quality control.

Permission: agreement or consent.

Petty bourgeoisie: a social class made up of owners of small businesses.

Pilot study: a feasibility study or small-scale trial run carried out before the main research.

Pluralism: an approach which argues that a range of views, interests and opinions exists in society and no one group dominates the political process.

Police caution: a warning given to someone who has committed a minor crime such as graffiti.

Political party: an organisation such as the Labour or Conservative Party that has policies on a range of issues (such as education and crime), seeks to win an election and form a government.

Political socialisation: the process by which people acquire their political beliefs, values and preferences. Agencies include the media, families and workplaces.

Polyandry: a type of polygamy in which a woman has more than one husband at the same time.

Polygamy: a form of marriage in which an individual has more than one husband or wife at the same time.

Polygyny: a type of polygamy in which a man has more than one wife at the same time.

Popular press: the daily tabloid newspapers or 'red tops' that get large readerships.

Population: the particular group under study from which the sample is selected. The population may consist of people such as higher education students or institutions such as schools depending on the aims of the research.

Positive sanctions: in the processes of social control and socialisation, positive sanctions reward those who behave according to the group's expectations, for example through praise.

Positivism: an approach that argues that the methods of the natural sciences should be used to study society.

Poverty: There are two broad approaches to defining poverty: absolute poverty and relative poverty. (See absolute poverty; relative poverty.)

Poverty trap: people can be trapped in poverty if an increase in income reduces the benefits they are entitled to. For example, an employed person receiving means-tested benefits could be worse off after a wage rise if they now earn too much to qualify for benefits.

Power: in social relationships between individuals (for example, between spouses or parents and children) or groups, power usually refers to the dominance and control of one individual or group over others.

Prejudice: a prejudgment in favour of, or against, a person, group or issue. Prejudice involves opinions and beliefs rather than action.

Pressure group: a group of people who share an interest and try to persuade the government to adopt a particular policy or to influence public opinion on an issue.

Primary data: information that is generated and collected firsthand by doing research using techniques such as questionnaires, interviews or observation.

Primary socialisation: the process of early childhood learning, usually in families, during which babies and children acquire the basic behaviour patterns, language and skills they need in later life.

Prime minister: a politician who is head of the UK government.

Principle of stratified diffusion: the idea that social changes start at the top of the social stratification system and spread downwards. Changes in family life, for instance, spread from the middle class into the working class.

Prison service: a part of the criminal justice system that detains convicted offenders who have been given a prison sentence.

Prison system: see prison service.

Private schools: schools that charge fees.

Privatised nuclear family: a nuclear family that is cut off from the extended family. The lifestyle tends to focus on the home.

Probability (or random) sample: a sample (sub group) in which each member of the population has a known chance of being selected for inclusion. Examples include simple random samples and stratified random samples.

Probation service: a part of the criminal justice system that is responsible for supervising high-risk offenders who have been released into the community.

Probation system: see probation service.

Proletarianisation: the idea that clerical workers have experienced downward mobility into the working class. Their work has become less skilled and more routine, and now resembles factory work.

Proletariat: wage labourers who do not own any means of production and live by selling their labour to the bourgeoisie for wages.

Propaganda: information (often biased or false) that is used to promote, for example, a particular viewpoint, cause or government.

Proportional representation (PR): under a PR electoral system, seats are allocated according to the total number of votes that each party receives.

Protest movement: a movement that aims to create political change. Tactics include demonstrations, gatherings and marches possibly in many cities across the world at one time.

Public school: the older and more famous independent schools, such as Eton and Harrow.

Purposive sampling: a sampling technique in which the sample is selected according to a known characteristic (such as being a GP or a sixth form student).

Qualitative data: information presented in visual or verbal form, for example as words or quotations rather than numbers.

Qualitative interview: an unstructured or loosely structured interview that gathers rich and detailed data rather than statistics.

Qualitative methods: research methods designed to collect and analyse data in the form of words rather than numbers.

Quality press: newspapers that cover serious news issues such as UK politics, world news, the global economy and business.

Quantitative data: information presented in numerical form, for example as graphs, bar charts, pie charts or tables of statistics.

Quantitative methods: research methods designed to collect and analyse statistical data.

Questionnaire: a set of structured, standardised questions delivered to respondents.

Quota sampling: a sampling technique in which an interviewer must question an exact quota (number) of people from categories such as females or teenagers, in proportion to their numbers in the wider population.

Race: the term 'race' has been used in different ways. It has been used to refer to the idea that humankind could be divided up into different 'racial groups' on the basis of natural, physical characteristics. More recent scientific evidence, however, rejects the idea of different biological 'races'. Sociologists point to the socially constructed division of social groups according to their 'race'. Like gender differences, racial differences are created by society.

Racial discrimination: see racism.

Racism: racism or racial discrimination occurs when people are treated differently and less favourably on the basis of their ethnicity.

Radical feminist: a feminist who sees the oppression of women as based on patriarchy.

Random sample: a sample (subgroup) in which each member of the population has a known chance of being selected for inclusion in the sample.

Rational legal authority: a type of authority in which obedience is based on the operation of a set of rules or laws.

Reconstituted (or blended) family: a family in which one or both partners have a child or children from a previous relationship.

Recorded crime: crime that is recorded by the police and appears in police recorded crime statistics.

Relative deprivation: lacking material resources compared to other people in society.

Relative income standard of poverty: a measure of poverty based on how much income a household has compared to other households. One way, for example, would be to put households in rank order according to their income and then identify 10 per cent of households with the lowest incomes.

Relative poverty: people in relative poverty cannot afford to meet the general standard of living of most other people in their society.

Reliability: reliability refers to consistency. Research findings are reliable if the same or consistent results are obtained a second time using the same methods.

Religion: broad definitions see religion as any set of beliefs and practices that aim to give meaning to human life. Narrow definitions see religion as beliefs and practices related to a god or gods.

Replication: standardised methods such as questionnaires can be replicated or repeated by other researchers to check the reliability of the research findings. Getting the same or similar results a second time round confirms reliability.

Reported crime: crime that is reported to the police.

Representative sample: a sample is a subgroup of the wider population. A representative sample is one that reflects the characteristics of its population. It is just like the population but a smaller version of it.

Representativeness: sociologists usually want the organisation or people they study to represent a larger group so that the findings are typical of the wider group. To achieve representativeness, a random sample is necessary.

Research: the collection of data in an organised way by methods such as questionnaires or interviews.

Research aim: a statement that sets out what a researcher plans to investigate and provides the study with a focus.

Research design: the combination of techniques and sources (such as individual interviews, observation, questionnaires and official statistics) used in a particular study.

Research ethics: ethics relate to morals and, in the context of sociological research, raise questions about how to conduct morally acceptable research that protects the rights and interests of research participants and safeguards their well being.

Research process: the process of carrying out sociological research involving the following broad stages: literature review; research aims or hypotheses; choice of methods; pilot study; sample selection; data collection; data analysis; and evaluation.

Research techniques: systematic methods of collecting data, such as questionnaires, interviews and observation.

Respondent: the person from whom information is sought.

Response rate: the number of replies received in proportion to the total number of questionnaires distributed.

Right to appeal: a person who is found guilty of a criminal offence has the right to appeal against (or challenge) this verdict.

Role: the pattern of expected and acceptable behaviour of people who occupy a particular status or social position. The role of 'teacher', for instance, defines how we expect a teacher to behave during the working day.

Role conflict: this occurs when the demands of one of our roles (for example, student) conflict or clash with those of another (for example, friend or part-time employee).

Ruling class ideology: a set of dominant ideas in society that distort reality and serve the interests of the bourgeoisie.

Rural: relating to country as opposed to urban – life. Rural areas are more sparsely populated than cities.

Same-sex family: a family in which a same-sex couple live together with their child or children.

Sample: a subgroup of the population selected for study.

Sampling frame: a complete list of all members of the population from which a sample is drawn. Examples include membership lists, school registers and the Royal Mail's list of postcode addresses.

Sampling procedures: the techniques used in order to obtain a sample such as probability (or random) sampling and non-probability sampling.

Sanctions: rewards or punishments to those who conform to or break the rules.

Sandwich generation: the generation that is sandwiched between younger family generations (children and grandchildren) and older generations (parents). People in the sandwich generation may provide care not only for their parents but also for their grandchildren.

Scapegoat: an individual or a group that is blamed for something that is not their fault.

Secondary data: information that already exists and has previously been generated or collected by other people. Sources include official statistics, the mass media, autobiographies and studies by other sociologists.

Secondary socialisation: through this process, which begins during later childhood and continues throughout our adult lives, we learn society's norms and values. Agencies of secondary socialisation include peer groups, religions and the mass media.

Secularisation: the process whereby the influence of religion in a society declines.

Segregated conjugal roles: this term describes domestic roles of married or cohabiting partners which are separated out or divided in an unequal way.

Selective benefits: means-tested welfare benefits that are targeted at those in greatest financial need rather than available to everyone, regardless of income and savings.

Selective schooling: where schools have some form of criteria that need to be met in order for someone to go to that school.

Self-fulfilling prophecy: this occurs when a person who has been labelled comes to fit the image people have of them – the prediction comes true.

Self-report study: a study that ask respondents whether they have committed particular offences during a specified time period such as the last year. It provides information on offenders and offences that are not necessarily dealt with by the police or courts.

Separate spheres (in relation to the role of women): the split between the private world of home and the public world of work.

Serial monogamy: the practice of divorcing, remarrying, divorcing, remarrying and so on.

Sex discrimination: treating someone differently and less favourably on the basis of their sex (or gender).

Sex equality: see gender equality.

Sexism: discrimination based on sex (or gender).

Sexual division of labour: in the functionalist account, this refers to the division of work and occupations between men and women based on their biological differences.

Sexuality: the way an individual expresses themselves and behaves as a sexual being. It also refers to sexual orientation (for example, being heterosexual, bisexual, lesbian or gay).

Simple random sampling: a sampling technique in which each member of the population has an equal chance of being included in the sample.

Situational poverty: poverty experienced by people due to a particular situation they find themselves in such as redundancy, death of a partner, divorce, illness or flooding.

Slavery: a form of stratification in which one group claims the right to own another group and treat them as property.

Snowball sampling: a sampling technique in which the researcher contacts one member of the population and through them identifies others in the same population.

Social change: an alteration in social structures, attitudes, behaviour, relationships, norms, values and so on.

Social class: a form of social stratification based on economic factors such as occupation and income (how people earn a living).

Social cohesion: the idea that people in society should have a shared set of values and attitudes that help to unite society and to bring people together.

Social construct: a product of society or culture. Crime statistics are a social product in that they are the end product of a series of interactions, choices and decisions of the people involved.

Social construction: this term is often used in relation to age, gender and race and reflects the idea that, rather than being rooted in biology or nature, these are created by society or culture.

Social control: control or constraints over people's actions and behaviour from society or groups. (See also formal social control and informal social control.)

Social conventions: the norms or accepted ways to behave in particular situations.

Social exclusion: being shut out or excluded from participation in society's social, economic, political and cultural life.

Social inequality: the uneven distribution of resources such as money and power or of opportunities related to education and health.

Social issues: issues that affect groups, communities, societies and people's lives. Examples include the quality of parenting and care of the elderly.

Social mobility: movement up or down between the layers or strata of society. Inter-generational social mobility refers to movement up or down between the layers as measured between the generations of a family. Intra-generational social mobility refers to movement of an individual over the course of their life up or down from one occupational classification to another.

Social network: a network of relatives and friends.

Social order: social order occurs when society is stable, ordered and runs smoothly without continual disruption.

Social policies: sets of plans and actions put into place by governments, local authorities or other organisations in order to address particular social problems, for example, in the fields of education, criminal justice or welfare.

Social problem: a problem facing society such as racism, discrimination, youth crime, poverty, unemployment and domestic violence. Social problems are seen as damaging or harmful to society and therefore require tackling or solving through social policies.

Social processes: processes in society that involve interaction between individuals, groups and social structures. The process of socialisation, for example, involves interaction between individuals and social structures such as families and education.

Social stigma: the shame or disgrace attached to something. In the past, for example, having an illegitimate child (a child born outside marriage) was seen as a source of shame for women.

Social stratification: the way that society is structured or divided into hierarchical strata – or layers – with the most privileged at the top and the least favoured at the bottom. Social class is an example of a stratification system.

Social structures: the 'parts' or institutions that make up society, such as families, education and stratification systems.

Social surveys: research based on self-administered questionnaires or structured interviews. Questions are standardised so respondents answer an identical set of questions.

Socialisation: the process through which people learn the culture, norms and values of the group or society they were born into.

Socialism: a system in which capital, land, factories and so on are not owned and controlled by a few private individuals but are owned by the community as a whole.

Society: a group of people who share a culture or a way of life.

Socially defined behaviour: behaviour (such as deviance) that is defined according to the social setting in which it occurs. What we consider as 'deviant behaviour', for example, does not depend on the behaviour or act itself but on the social setting and how others label it.

Specialist schools: centres of excellence in particular subject areas, such as languages or technology. They are intended to raise standards of teaching and learning in these areas.

State standard of poverty: a measure of poverty based on the rates paid by the state, the level at which people are entitled to claim state benefits.

Status: status can refer to social positions linked, for example, to occupations (such as teacher or train driver) and families (such as child or parent). It can also refer to the amount of prestige or social standing that members of a group or society give an individual in a particular social position.

Status frustration: Cohen argued that working-class boys experience this when they try but fail to meet middle-class expectations at school.

Step-family: a reconstituted family in which one or both partners have a child or children from a previous relationship living with them.

Step-parent: someone who is the social parent of their partner's child or children but not their biological parent.

Stereotype: a fixed, standardised and distorted view of the characteristics of particular groups such as women. Stereotypes are often based on prejudice.

Stigma: the social shame or disgrace attached to something. In the past, for example, having an illegitimate child (a child born outside marriage) was seen as a source of shame for women.

Stratified random sampling: a sampling technique used when a sociologist wants the sample to reflect particular characteristics of the population such as age and gender. The population is divided into strata (subgroups) for example according to age and gender, and a random sample is drawn from each subgroup in proportion to their numbers in the population.

Streaming: where students are separated into different ability groups and then taught in these separate groups for all of their subjects.

Structural approach: an approach that focuses on the structure and culture of society in its explanations rather than on interaction between people.

Structural theory: a theory that considers the structure and culture of society in its explanations rather than how people interact with each other.

Structured or systematic observation: a type of non-participant observation in which the observer uses a schedule to observe and record behaviour and interaction between people as it unfolds.

Subject setting: where students are placed into ability groups for each specific subject.

Subjective class: how people see or identify themselves in class terms.

Subjective poverty: when people see themselves as being poor.

Surveillance: monitoring people and gathering information on them in order to prevent crime.

Surveys: see social surveys.

Symmetrical family: a family form in which spouses carry out different tasks but each makes a similar contribution within the home.

Systematic sampling: a sampling technique that involves taking every 'nth' item from the sampling frame, for example every 10th name from a college register to generate the required sample size.

Technological change: developments in technology (such as computers, IVF or test tube babies, mobile phones).

Terrorism: the use of violence or intimidation in order to achieve a set of political aims.

Theoretical perspective: an approach such as functionalism, Marxism or feminism that provides a set of ideas to explain the social world.

Theory: a set of ideas to explain something.

Time budget diaries: diaries in which people record how they use their time. For example, they might record the sequence, times and duration of their daily activities.

Time budget study: a study that asks people to record how they use their time during a specific period.

Trade union: an organisation of employees or workers that protects and promotes its members' interests in the workplace.

Traditional authority: a type of authority in which obedience is based on custom and tradition.

Traditional family roles: conventional gender roles within the nuclear family such as the male breadwinner and female homemaker.

Transcript: a written copy of the full contents of an interview.

Trend: the general direction in which statistics on something (such as the divorce rate) move or change over time. For example, the divorce rate may increase or decrease over time.

Triangulation: cross-checking the findings from a qualitative method against the findings from a quantitative method.

Tri-partite system: created by the 1944 Education Act, this system used the 11-plus test to identify students' ability levels. Students were then allocated to one of three types of school based on their tested abilities (grammar, secondary modern or technical).

Underclass: this term can refer to a group whose norms and values are different from those of mainstream society. It can also refer to people who experience long-term poverty and who are unable to earn a living.

Underemployment: a situation in which workers are employed at less than full time, and are willing and available to work more hours than they currently do.

Unemployment: a situation in which people do not have jobs but are actively seeking work and available to start work.

Universal benefits: welfare benefits that are available to everyone, regardless of their income and savings, rather than targeted at those in most financial need.

Universalistic standards: where people are judged by the standards of the wider society, which are applied in the same way to everyone. In school, each student is judged against the same standards, for example in terms of rules and exam criteria.

Unrepresentative sample: a sample (subgroup) that does not reflect the characteristics of its population.

Unstructured interviews: informal interviews that are like guided conversations based around a set of themes or points rather than a standardised interview schedule. The aim is to gather rich and detailed qualitative data.

Unwritten rules: informal or 'taken-for-granted' guidelines on how we are expected to behave in particular social settings.

Upper class: a social class made up of the rich and powerful, particularly those who have inherited wealth.

Urban: associated with cities.

Validity: findings are valid if they truly measure or capture what they are supposed to be studying.

Value consensus: broad agreement on values.

Values: beliefs and ideas about what is seen as desirable or worth striving for in a society. Values such as privacy and respect for life provide general guidelines for behaviour.

Victim survey: a survey that asks respondents about their experiences of crime, whether they have been victims of particular offences during a specified time period and, if so, whether they reported the crimes to the police.

Vocational education: work or career-related education.

Wage: a daily, weekly or monthly income that an employee earns from paid work.

Wealth: ownership of assets such as property, land and works of art as well as money held in savings accounts and shares in companies.

Welfare benefits: financial support such as Income Support provided by the state to help those in need.

Welfare dependency: the idea that some groups remain in poverty because the welfare state encourages them to depend on overly generous state provision.

Welfare reform: changes to the way the welfare system operates, for instance cutting or replacing state benefits.

Welfare state: a system in which the state takes responsibility for protecting the health and welfare of its citizens and meeting their social needs. The state does this by providing services (for example, the NHS) and benefits (for example, Income Support).

White-collar crime: this refers broadly to crimes committed by people in relatively high status positions, such as accountants, doctors or solicitors, during their work. Examples include tax evasion and 'fiddling' expense accounts at work.

White-collar workers: people in clerical, administrative or managerial jobs.

Worklife balance: getting the priorities right between career (for example, hours spent at the office, ambitions) and lifestyle (for example, having time for family, leisure and health).

Working class: a social class made up of people engaged in manual occupations.

Worldview: a perspective on, or way of seeing, society and the social world.

Youth crime: criminal offences committed by young people.

Youth culture: a group of young people, such as emos and punks, who share a culture and style of dress which differs from that of older generations.

Bibliography

Chapter 1: The sociological approach

British Social Attitudes 32,
http://www.bsa.natcen.ac.uk/media/38917/
bsa32_highereducation.pdf

British Social Attitudes 33,
http://www.bsa.natcen.ac.uk/media/39058/
bsa33_welfare.pdf

Child Poverty Action Group
http://www.cpag.org.uk/sites/default/files/
Child%20Poverty%20Action%20Group%20-%20
Child%20poverty%20in%20the%20UK%20-%20
A%20few%20facts.pdf

Lips, H.M. (2013) *Gender: The Basics.* Abingdon:
Routledge.

McLellan, D. (2000) *Karl Marx: Selected Writings.*
2nd edition.Oxford: OUP.

ONS https://www.ons.gov.uk/
peoplepopulationandcommunity/
birthsdeathsandmarriages/livebirths/datasets/
birthsummarytables

http://www.sheffield.ac.uk/polopoly_
fs/1.550495!/file/Int-Living-in-Shef-16.pdf

Taylor, C.F. (1996) *Native American Life.* London:
Salamander Books.

Weber, M. (1947) *The Theory of Social and
Economic Organization.* New York: OUP.

Chapter 2: Sociological research methods

Bagguley, P. and Hussain, Y. (2007) *The Role of
Higher Education in Providing Opportunities for
South Asian Women.* Bristol: Policy Press.

Bryman, A. (2016) *Social Research Methods.* 5th
edition. Oxford: Oxford University Press.

BSA (2002). Statement of Ethical Practice. www.
britsoc.co.uk.

Charles, N., Aull Davies, C. and Harris, C. (2008)
*Families in Transition: Social Change, Family
Formation and Kin Relationships.* Bristol: Policy
Press.

Eden, K. and Roker, D. (2002) *'...Doing
Something': Young People as Social Actors.*
Leicester: National Youth Agency.

Hatterton, P. and Hollands, R. (2003) *Urban
Nightscapes: Youth Cultures, Pleasure Spaces and
Corporate Power.* London: Routledge.

Heath, S. and Cleaver, E. (2003) *Young, Free
and Single? Twenty-Somethings and Household
Change.* Basingstoke: Palgrave Macmillan.

Korczynski, M. (2014) *Songs of the Factory: Pop
Music, Culture, and Resistance.* New York: Cornell
University Press.

May, T. (2001) *Social Research: Issues, Methods
and Process.* Buckingham: Open University Press.

McNeill, P. and Chapman, S. (2005) *Research
Methods.* Abingdon: Routledge.

NSPCC
https://www.nspcc.org.uk/globalassets/
documents/annual-reports/childline-annual-
review-always-there-2014-2015.pdf Accessed:
07/07/2016

Oakley, A. (1974) *Sociology of Housework.*
London: Robertson.

ONS (2005) Census 2001 Quality Report for
England and Wales. Basingstoke: Palgrave
Macmillan.

ONS (2012) http://www.ons.gov.uk/
peoplepopulationandcommunity/culturalidentity/
ethnicity/articles/ethnicityandnationalidentityin
englandandwales/2012-12-11

ONS (2015) http://www.ons.gov.uk/peoplepopulationandcommunity/birthsdeathsandmarriages/divorce/bulletins/divorcesinenglandandwales/2013#divorce-rates

O'Reilly, K. (2000) *The British on the Costa del Sol: Transnational Identities and Local Communities*. London: Routledge.

Papapolydorou, M. (2013) 'Direct, indirect and relational: social class manifestations in teenage students' accounts'. In: *Youth and Policy*. No: 111, October 2013.

Pilcher, J. (2004) 'The uses of sociology', *Sociology Review* 14(1), 2–4.

Reay, D., David, M.E. and Ball, S. (2005) *Degrees of Choice: Social Class, Race and Gender in Higher Education*. Stoke on Trent: Trentham Books.

Robson, E. (2001) 'The routes project: disadvantaged young people interviewing their peers'. In: J. Clark et al., *Young People as Researchers: Possibilities, Problems and Politics*. Leicester: National Youth Agency.

Roseneil, S. (2016) 'Couples who live apart', *Sociology Review*, 25(3), 18–21.

Sapsford, R. (2007) *Survey Research*. London: SAGE Publications Ltd.

Shildrick, T. (2002) 'Young people, illicit drug use and the question of normalization', *Journal of Youth Studies*, 5(1), 35–48.

Ward, J. (2008). 'Researching drug sellers: an "experiential" account from "the field"', *Sociological Research Online*, 13(1). http://www.socresonline.org.uk/13/1/14.html

Williams, J., Dunning, E. and Murphy, P. (1989) *Hooligans Abroad*. 2nd edition. London: Routledge.

Winlow, S. and Hall, S. (2006). *Violent Night: Urban Leisure and Contemporary Culture*. Oxford: BERG.

Zebiri, K. (2008) *British Muslim Converts*. Oxford: Oneworld Publications.

Zempi, I. and Chakraborti, N. (2014) *Islamophobia, Victimisation and the Veil*. Basingstoke: Palgrave Macmillan.

https://www.gov.uk/government/uploads/system/uploads/attachment_data/file/531243/family-resources-survey-background-note-and-methodology-2014-15.pdf. Accessed: 29/06/2016

Chapter 3: Families

Allan, G. and Crow, G. (2001) *Families, Households and Society*. Basingstoke: Palgrave.

Anderson, M. (1971) *Family Structure in Nineteenth Century Lancashire*. Cambridge: Cambridge University Press.

Aries, P. (1973) *Centuries of Childhood*. London: Peregrine.

Bott, E. (1971) *Family and Social Network*. 2nd edition. London: Tavistock.

Brannen, J. (2003) 'The age of beanpole families', *Sociology Review*, 13 (1), 6–9.

Case, J. and Taylor, R.C.R. (eds) (1979) *Co-ops, Communes and Collectives*. New York: Pantheon Books.

Charles, N., Aull Davies, C. and Harris, C. (2008a) *Families in Transition: Social Change, Family Formation and Kin Relationships*. Bristol: Policy Press.

Charles, N., Davies, C. and Harris, C. (2008b) 'The family: continuity and change', *Sociology Review*, 18(2), 2–5.

Clarke, J. (1997) 'Domestic violence revisited', *Sociology Review*, 6(4), 32–33.

Charter, D. (2007) 'You won't see New Man for dust when the cleaning needs doing', *The Times*, 17 March.

Delphy, C. and Leonard, D. (1992) *Familiar Exploitation: A New Analysis of Marriage in Contemporary Western Societies*. Cambridge: Polity Press.

Bibliography

Denscombe, M. (1997) Sociology Update series.

Duncan, S. (2006). 'What's the problem with teenage parents?', *Sociology Review*, 16(1), 2–5.

Garrod, J. (2005) 'Forced marriages', *Sociology Review*, 14(4), 14–15.

Gatrell, C. (2008) 'Involved fatherhood?', *Sociology Review*, 18(1), 2–5.

Ginn, J. and Arber, S. (1992) 'Gender and resources in later life', *Sociology Review*, 2(2), 6-10.

Halsey, A.H. (1993) Foreword. In: N. Dennis and G. Erdos, *Families Without Fatherhood*.

Jewson, N. (1994) 'Family values and relationships', *Sociology Review*, 3(3).

Joseph Rowntree Foundation (2007) Parenting and the different ways it can affect children's lives: research evidence. https://www.jrf.org.uk/sites/default/files/jrf/migrated/files/2132-parenting-literature-reviews.pdf. Accessed: 04/08/16.

Kanter, R.M. (1979) 'Communes in cities'. In: J. Case and R.C.R. Taylor (eds) *Co-ops, Communes and Collectives*. New York: Pantheon Books.

Kephart, W.M. and Zeller W.W. (1991). *Extraordinary Groups*. New York: St. Martin's Press, Inc.

Laslett, P.K. (1965). *The World We Have Lost*. London: Methuen.

Leach, E. (1967) *A Runaway World?* London: BBC Publications.

Murdock, G.P. (1949) *Social Structure*. New York: Macmillan.

Oakley, A. (1974). *The Sociology of Housework*. Oxford: Martin Robertson.

Oakley, A. (1986) *From Here to Maternity*. Harmondsworth: Penguin.

Oakley, A. (1982) 'Conventional families'. In: R.N. Rapoport, M.P. Fogarty and R. Rapoport (eds) *Families in Britain*. London: Routledge and Kegan Paul, pp. 123–137.

ONS (2015) Statistical Bulletin: Families and Households.

http://www.ons.gov.uk/peoplepopulationandcommunity/birthsdeathsandmarriages/families/bulletins/familiesandhouseholds/2015-11-05#families Accessed: 21/07/2016.

ONS (2014) http://webarchive.nationalarchives.gov.uk/20160105160709/http://www.ons.gov.uk/ons/rel/family-demography/stepfamilies/2011/stepfamilies-rpt.html Accessed: 01/08/2016

ONS (2015) http://www.ons.gov.uk/peoplepopulationandcommunity/birthsdeathsandmarriages/divorce/bulletins/divorcesinenglandandwales/2013#number-of-divorces Accessed 15/07/16.

ONS (2015) Statistical Bulletin Families and Households

http://www.ons.gov.uk/peoplepopulationandcommunity/birthsdeathsandmarriages/families/bulletins/familiesandhouseholds/2015-11-05#living-alone Accessed: 21/07/16.

ONS (2014) http://web.ons.gov.uk/ons/rel/census/2011-census-analysis/do-the-demographic-and-socio-economic-characteristics-of-those-living-alone-in-england-and-wales-differ-from-the-general-population-/sty-living-alone-in-the-uk.html Accessed: 22/07/2016.

Pahl, J. (1989). *Money and Marriage*. Basingstoke: Macmillan.

Parsons, T. (1959) 'The social structure of the family'. In: R.N. Anshen. (ed.) *The Family: Its Function and Destiny*. New York: Harper and brothers, Publishers. pp. 241–274.

Parsons, T. and Bales, R.F. (1956) *Family, Socialization and Interaction Process*.

London: Routledge and Kegan Paul.

Pryor, J. and Trinder, L. (2004) 'Children, families, and divorce'. In J. Scott, J. Treas and M. Richards (eds) *The Blackwell Companion to the Sociology of Families*. Oxford: Blackwell Publishing.

Qureshi, K., Charsley, K. and Shaw, A. (2015) 'British Asians and family structure', *Sociology Review*, 25(2), 18–21.

Rapoport, R.N., Fogarty M.P. and Rapoport, R. (eds) (1982) *Families in Britain*. London: Routledge and Kegan Paul.

Refuge
http://www.refuge.org.uk/about-domestic-violence/ Accessed 31/07/2016.

Roseneil, S. and Budgeon, S. (2006) 'Beyond "the family": personal life and social change', *Sociology Review*, 16(1), 14–16.

Scott, J. (2004) 'Children's families'. In J. Scott, J. Treas and M. Richards (eds) *The Blackwell Companion to the Sociology of Families*. Oxford: Blackwell Publishing.

Scott, J. and Clery, E. (2013) *British Social Attitudes* 30

Westwood, S. and Bhachu, P. (1988) 'Images and Reality', *New Society*, 6 May 1988, 20–22.

Williams, J. (2008) 'In focus: households', *Sociology Review*, 18(1), 34.

Winstanley, M. (ed.) (1995) *Working Children in Nineteenth-Century Lancashire*. Preston: Lancashire County Books.

Young, M. and Willmott, P. (1957) *Family and Kinship in East London*. London: Routledge and Kegan Paul.

Young, M. and Willmott, P. (1973) *The Symmetrical Family*. London: Routledge and Kegan Paul.

Zadeh, S. (2014) 'Fatherless families: are they the future?', *Sociology Review*, 24(2), 6–9.

Zaretsky, E. (1976) *Capitalism, the Family and Personal Life*. London: Pluto Press.

Chapter 4: Education

Asthana, A. (2006) 'Single-sex schools no benefit for girls', *Observer*, 25/6/06.

Ball S.J. (1981) *Beachside Comprehensive. A Case Study of Secondary Schooling*, Cambridge: Cambridge University Press.

Ball, S. (2003) 'It's not what you know – education and social capital', *Sociology Review*, 13(2), November 2003.

Ball, S.J., Bowe, R. and Gewirtz, S. (1994) 'Market forces and parental choice'. In S. Tomlinson (ed). *Education Reform and its Consequences*. London: IPPR/Rivers Oram Press.

Bhatti, G. (1999) *Asian Children at Home and at School*. London: Routledge.

Bowles, S. and Gintis, H. (1976) *Schooling in Capitalist America*. London: Routledge and Kegan Paul.

Burgess-Macey, C. (1992) 'Tackling racism in the classroom'. In D. Gill, B. Mayor and M. Blair (eds) *Racism and Education – Structures and strategies*. London: Sage.

Clarke, J. (1997) 'Ethnicity and education revisited', *Sociology Review,* 7(2).

Coughlan, S. (2016) *Oxford University to have most state school students for decades*, BBC News, September 2016.

Davies, C. and Born, M. (2000) 'Girl power leaves lads lagging behind', *The Telegraph,* 18 August.

Department for Children, Schools and Families (2008) Education and training statistics.

Department for Education *Revised GCSE and equivalent results in England, 2014 to 2015,* January 2016.

Department for Education and Skills (2006) 'Ethnicity and education: the evidence on minority ethnic pupils aged 5–16'. Research paper.

Bibliography

Douglas, J.W.B. et al. (1967) *The Home and the School.* London: Panther.

Durkheim, E. (1925) *Moral Education.* Glencoe: Free Press.

Fuller, C. (2011) *Sociology, gender and educational aspirations,* Continuum.

Gewirtz, S. et al (1995) *Markets, Choice and Equity in Education,* Oxford: OUP

Gillborn, D. and Youdell, D. (2000) *Rationing Education: policy, practice, reform and equity,* Oxford: OUP.

Halsey, Heath and Ridge (1980) *Origins and Destinations.* Oxford: Clarendon Press

Hargreaves, D. (1967) *Social Relations in a Secondary School.* London: Routledge and Kegan Paul.

Harris, S. et al. (1993) 'Schoolwork, homework and gender', *Gender and Education,* 5(1).

Higher Education Policy Institute, reported in BBC Education, 12/5/16

JCQ: GCE A-level results 2016

Kelly, A. (1981) *The Missing Half: Girls and Science Education.* Manchester: Manchester University Press.

Lacey, D. (1970) *Hightown Grammar: The School as a Social System.* Manchester: Manchester University Press.

Macbeath, J. and Mortimore, P. (2001) *Improving School Effectiveness,* Oxford: OUP.

Mac an Ghaill, M. (1992) 'Coming of age in 1980s England'. In D. Gill, B. Mayor and M. Blair (eds), *Racism and Education – Structures and Strategies.* London: Sage.

Mirza, H.S. (1997) *Black British Feminism.* London: Routledge.

Mitsos, E. and Browne, K. (1998) 'Gender and Education', *Sociology Review.*

Moir, A. and Moir, B. (1998) *Why men don't iron: the real science of gender studies.* London: HarperCollins.

Murphy, P. and Elwood, J. (1998) 'Gendered learning outside and inside school'. In: D. Epstein et al (ed) *Failing Boys?* Oxford University Press

Newschoolsnetwork.org

Parsons, T. (1961) 'The School class as a social system'. In: Halsey et al, *Education, Economy and Society.* New York: The Free Press.

Pryce, K. (1979) *Endless Pressure.* Harmondsworth: Penguin.

Reid, I. (1996) 'Education and Inequality', *Sociology Review,* 6(2).

Rosenthal, R. and Jacobson, L. *Pygmalion in the Classroom*

Holt, Rinehart and Winston (1968), New York Schools Week, 17/9/16

Sharpe, S. (1994) *Just Like a Girl.* Harmondsworth: Penguin.

Smith, D. and Tomlinson, S. (1989) *The School Effect: A Study of Multi-Racial Comprehensives,* Policy Studies Institute.

Sutton Trust, *Leading People Report* 2016.

Wilkinson, H. (1994) 'No turning back: generations and genderquake', *Weekend Guardian,* October.

Williams, J. (2003) 'Schooling and educational performance', *Sociology Review,* 13(2), November.

Willis, P. (1977) *Learning to Labour.* Farnborough: Saxon House.

Wragg, T. (2003) 'Education – bouncing back', *Sociology Review,* 13(2), November.

Wright, C. (1992) 'Multi-racial primary school classrooms'. In D. Gill, B. Mayor and M. Blair (eds), *Racism and Education – Structures and Strategies.* London: Sage.

Chapter 5: Crime and deviance

Becker, H. (1997) *Outsiders: Studies in the Sociology of Deviance*. London: Free Press. New edition.

Carlen, P. (1988) *Women, Crime and Poverty*. Milton Keynes: Open University Press.

Carrington, K. (2013) 'Girls and violence: the case for a feminist theory of female violence'. www.crimejusticejournal.com IJCJ 2013 2(2): 63–79. Accessed: 12/08/2016.

Chambliss, W. (1978) *On the Take*. Bloomington: IUP.

Cohen, A.K. (1955) *Delinquent Boys: The Culture of the Gang*. New York: Free Press.

Cohen, S. (1972) *Folk Devils and Moral Panics: the creation of the mods and rockers*. London: MacGibbon and Kee.

Garrod, J. (2007) 'Women in Prison'. *Sociology Review*, 16(3) 26–27.

Gauntlett, D. (2001) 'The worrying influence of "media effects" studies.' In M. Barker and J. Petley (eds) *Ill Effects: The Media / Violence Debate*. London: Routledge.

Goode, E. (2008) 'Introduction: the significance of extreme deviance'. In E. Goode and D.A. Vail. *Extreme Deviance*. London: Sage Publications Ltd.

Hedderman, C (2015) 'Gender and criminal justice', *Sociology Review*. 24(3), 30–33.

Heidensohn, F. (1985) *Women and Crime*. Basingstoke: Macmillan Press Ltd.

Heidensohn, F. (1996). *Women and Crime*. 2nd edition. Basingstoke: Macmillan Press Ltd.

Kelling, G.L. and Coles, C.M. (1996) *Fixing Broken Windows: Restoring Order and Reducing Crime in our Communities*. New York: The Free Press.

Maguire, M. (2007) 'Crime data and statistics'. In M. Maguire, R. Morgan and R. Reiner (eds) *The Oxford Handbook of Criminology*. Oxford: Oxford University Press, pp. 241–301.

Marsh, I. (2006) (ed.) *Theories of Crime*. Abingdon: Routledge.

McQuail, D. (2003) *Media Accountability and Freedom of Publication*. Oxford: Oxford University Press.

Merton, R.K. (1938a) 'Social Structure and Anomie', *American Sociological Review*. 3(5), 672–682.

Merton, R.K. (1938b) *Social Theory and Social Structure*. New York: The Free Press.

Ministry of Justice (2016). Table A3.1b. Persons found guilty at all courts or cautioned for indictable offences per 100 000 population, by sex and age group, 2005 to 2015.

Overview tables: https://www.gov.uk/government/statistics/criminal-justice-system-statistics-quarterly-december-2015, Accessed: 1/8/16.

Murray, C. (1996) 'The emerging British underclass'. In *Charles Murray and the Underclass: the Developing Debate*. London: IEA Health and Welfare Unit.

Nelken, D. (2007) 'White-collar and corporate crime'. In M. Maguire, R. Morgan and R. Reiner (eds). The *Oxford Handbook of Criminology*. Oxford: Oxford University Press, pp. 733–770.

Newburn, T. (2007) 'Youth crime and youth culture'. In M. Maguire, R. Morgan and R. Reiner (eds) *The Oxford Handbook of Criminology*. Oxford: Oxford University Press, pp. 575–601.

ONS (2016) Statistical Bulletin Crime in England and Wales: Year ending December 2015 (Release date: 21 April)

http://www.ons.gov.uk/peoplepopulationandcommunity/crimeandjustice/bulletins/crimeinenglandandwales/yearendingdecember2015

ONS (2015) Figure 7.01. Page 69. British nationals in the prison population by ethnicity per 10, 000 people aged 15 years old or more, 2014 Accessed 12/08/16

https://www.gov.uk/government/uploads/system/uploads/attachment_data/file/480250/bulletin.pdf

Phillips, C. and Bowling, B. (2007) 'Ethnicities, racism, crime and criminal justice'. In M. Maguire, R. Morgan and R. Reiner (eds) *The Oxford Handbook of Criminology*. Oxford: Oxford University Press, pp. 421–460.

Pitts, J. (2005) 'New Labour, the media and youth justice', *Sociology Review*, 14(3), 8–10.

Tombs, S. (2005) 'Corporate crime', *Sociology Review*, 14(4) 2–5.

Townsley, M. and Marshall, B. (2006) 'Is policing fair?' *Sociology Review*, 16(2) 19–21.

Walklate, S. (2007) *Imagining the Victim of Crime*. Maidenhead: Open University Press.

Willis, P. (1977) *Learning to Labour: How Working-class Kids Get Working- Jobs*. Farnborough: Saxon House.

Wilson, J.Q. and Kelling, G.L. (1982) 'The police and neighborhood safety', *The Atlantic*, March, 29–38. http://www.theatlantic.com/magazine/archive/1982/03/broken-windows/304465/ Accessed: 12/08/2016.

Chapter 6: Social stratification

Ariès, P. (1962) *Centuries of Childhood*. London: Jonathan Cape.

Beresford, P. (2013). 'From "underclass" to 'overclass'?' *Sociology Review*, 22(3), 12–15.

British Social Attitudes 33 (2016) http://www.bsa.natcen.ac.uk/media/39094/bsa33_social-class_v5.pdf

Butler, T. and Watt, P. (2007) *Understanding Social Inequality*. London: SAGE Publications.

Crompton, R. (2008) *Class and Stratification*. Cambridge: Polity Press.

Cunningham, H. (2007) 'Social construction of childhood', *Sociology Review*, 17(1), 12–15.

Davis, K. and Moore, W.E. (1945) 'Some principles of stratification', *American Sociological Review*, 10(2).

Delebarre, J. (2016) House of Commons Library Briefing Paper. Number 6385. 27 April 2016. Unemployment by Ethnic Background.

Devine, F. (1992) *Affluent Workers Revisited: Privatism and the Working Class*. Edinburgh: Edinburgh University Press.

Dunscombe, J. and Marsden, D. (1995) 'Women's "triple shift": paid employment, domestic labour and 'emotion work'', *Sociology Review*, 4(4), April.

Furlong, A., Cartmel, F., Biggart, A., Sweeting, H. and West, P. (2006) 'Social class in an "individualised" society', *Sociology Review*, 15(4), 28–32.

Goldthorpe, J.H. et al. (1969) *The Affluent Worker in the Class Structure*. Cambridge: Cambridge University Press.

Holmes, M. (2009) *Gender and Everyday Life*. London: Routledge.

Institute for Fiscal Studies (2016) https://www.ifs.org.uk/uploads/publications/bns/bn186.pdf

Li, Y., Devine, F. and Heath, A. (2008) *Equality Group Inequalities in Education, Employment and Earnings*. Equality and Human Rights Commission.

Lister, R. (2004) *Poverty*. Cambridge: Polity.

Lister, R. (2008) In J. Strelitz and R. Lister (eds) *Why Money Matters: Family Income, Poverty and Children's Lives*. London: Save the Children.

Marmot, M. (2010) The Marmot Review. http://www.instituteofhealthequity.org/Content/FileManager/pdf/fairsocietyhealthylives.pdf

McDonough, F. (2002) 'Class and politics'. In M. Storry and P Childs (Eds) *British Cultural Identities*. London: Routledge, pp. 175–207.

McGuinness, F. (2016) Poverty in the UK: statistics. House of Commons Library. Briefing Paper No. 7096, 30 June 2016.

McLellan, D. (2000) *Karl Marx: Selected Writings*. 2nd edition. Oxford: OUP.

Millar, J. (1997) 'Gender.' In A. Walker and C. Walker (eds) *Britain Divided*. Child Poverty Action Group.

Mizen, P. (2002) 'Putting the politics back into youth studies: Keynesianism, monetarism and the changing state of youth', *Journal of Youth Studies*, 5(1), 5–20.

Murray, C. (1984) *Losing Ground: American Social Policy, 1950–1980*. New York: Basic Books.

Murray, C. (1996) 'The emerging British underclass'. In *Charles Murray and the Underclass: The Developing Debate*. London: IEA Health and Welfare Unit.

Office of Population, Censuses and Surveys (1980) *Classification of Occupations*. HMSO: London.

ONS (2013) http://www.ons.gov.uk/ employmentandlabourmarket/peopleinwork/ employmentandemployeetypes/articles/ womeninthelabourmarket/2013-09-25 Accessed: 30/08/16

Piachaud, D. (2009) 'Making poverty history in the UK?', *Sociology Review*, 18(3), 2–5.

Roberts, K. (2001) *Class in Modern Britain*. Basingstoke: Palgrave.

Saunders, P. (1996) *Unequal but Fair? A Study of Class Barriers in Britain*. London: IEA.

Scambler, G. (2016) 'A new Marxist theory of social class?', *Sociology Review*, 25(4), 8–12.

Scott, J. (2005) 'Social mobility: occupational snakes and ladders', *Sociology Review*, 15(2),18–21.

Scott, J. and Clery, E. (2013) British Social Attitudes 30.

Shaw, M. (2002) 'A matter of life and death: how can we reduce inequalities in health?' *Sociology Review* 11(4), 10–13.

Social Mobility Commission (2016): https://www .gov.uk/government/uploads/system/uploads/ attachment_data/file/549994/Socio-economic_ diversity_in_life_sciences_and_investment_ banking.pdf

Townsend, P. (1979) *Poverty in the United Kingdom*. London: Allen Lane and Penguin Books.

Walby, S. (1990) *Theorizing Patriarchy*. Oxford: Blackwell Publishers.

Walker, C. and Walker, A. (1997) 'Poverty and social exclusion.' In *Developments in Sociology*, 13, Causeway Press.

Weber, M. (1947) *The Theory of Social and Economic Organization*. New York: OUP.

http://webarchive.nationalarchives.gov. uk/20160105160709/http://www.ons.gov.uk/ons/ guide-method/classifications/current-standard- classifications/soc2010/soc2010-volume-3-ns-sec-- rebased-on-soc2010--user-manual/index.html

Index

Acknowledgments

Every effort has been made to trace copyright holders and to obtain their permission for the use of copyright material. The publishers will gladly receive any information enabling them to rectify any error or omission at the first opportunity.

The publishers would like to thank the following for permission to reproduce copyright material:

(t = top, b = bottom, c = centre, l = left, r = right)

P10/11 Denijal photography/Shutterstock; p13 Blend Images/Alamy; Hilary Morgan/Alamy; p14 Rawpixel.com/Shutterstock; p20 Kamira/Shutterstock; p22 Pictorial Press Ltd/Alamy; p24 Keystone Pictures USA/Alamy; p27 Redorbital Photography/Alamy; p30/31 Pavel L Photo and Video; p32 Jonny White/Alamy; p35 Leonid Plotkin/Alamy; p36 David Herraez Calzada/Shutterstock; p42 Matej Kastelic/Shutterstock; p44 Robert Kneschke/Alamy; p49 Image Source Plus (RF)/Alamy; p51 PhotoAlto (RF)/Alamy; p56 Frank Schwere/Getty Images; p59 iStockphoto; p61 David Grossman/Alamy; p62 Bananastock; p65 Jo Ann Snover/Alamy; p68 © NSPCC 2016; p72 Wavebreakmedia/Shutterstock; p75James Boardman Archive/Alamy; pp78, 79 Rawpixel.com/Shutterstock; p80 Monkey Business Images/Shutterstock; p83(t) Rob Van Petten/Getty Images; p83(b) aldpmurillo/Getty Images; pp84, 89, 91 Monkey Business Images/Shutterstock; p92 Reuters/Alamy; p95 Shutterstock; p97 Image Source/Alamy; p100 Caiaimage/Lukas Olek/Getty Images; p102 George Marks/Retrofile/Hulton Archive/Getty Images; p107 Photos.com; p112 Mary Evans Picture Library/Alamy; p114 Peter Cavanagh/Alamy; p122 China Photo/Getty Images; p128 REX/Shutterstock; p131 Ocskay Bence/Shuttersetock; p138/139 Iocifa/Shutterstock; p145 John Powell/Alamy; p146 Pictorial Press Ltd/Alamy; p147 Andrew Fox/Alamy; p150 Myrleen Pearson/Alamy; p153 Maggie Murray/Photofusion Picture Library/Alamy; p156(t) Image State Media Productions Ltd-Impact Photo/Alamy; p156(b) LondonPhotos-Homer Sykes/Alamy; p159 Bjan Milinkov/Shutterstock; p161 Janine Wiedel Photolibrary/Alamy; p163 Enigma/Alamy; p164 The Photolibrary Wales/Alamy; p171 Scott Hartop/Alamy; p177 John Powell/Alamy; p179 Alex Segre/Alamy; p181 Nigel Pacquette/Alamy; p185 l Eric Raptosh Photography/Alamy; p185 r Cultura RM/Alamy; p193 Monkey Business Images/Shutterstock; p198/199 A_Leslik/Shutterstock; p200 WENN Ltd/Alamy; p203 European Press Acengy b.v/Alamy; p204 Narin Nonthaman/Shutterstock; p207 (a) European Press Agency/Alamy; p207 (b) Ullstein Bild/Getty Images; p207 (c) Peter Brooker/REX/Shutterstock; p211 Carl Court/Getty Image; p215 Janine Wiedel Photolibrary/Alamy; p217 Air Images/Shutterstock; p222 Alastair Balderstone/Alamy; p227 narvikk/iStockphoto; p231 Joakim Lloyd Raboff/Shutterstock; p241 Cleave Photography/Alamy; p242 Haynes Archive/Popperfoto/Getty Images; p245 Loop Images Ltd/Alamy; p246 Roger Bamber/Alamy; p 256/257 Thor Jorgen Udvang/Shutterstock; p259 Suretha Rous/Alamy; p261(t) Dmitry Kalinovsky/Shutterstock; p261(b) ChaNaWiT/Shutterstock; p263 Jeff Gilbert/Alamy; p270 Monkey Business Images/Shutterstock; p273 quavondo/iStockphoto; p276 (r) Beepstock/Alamy; p276(l) Stefan Solfers/Alamy; p281 Delia Batchelor/Alamy; p285 Classic Image/Alamy; p286 Keystone Features/Getty Images; p288 Juice Images/Alamy; p290 Nick Savage/Alamy; p293 Martyn Wheatley/Alamy; p294(t) Gavin Rodgers/Alamy; p294(b) Libbey Welch/Alamy; p307 LEE BEEL/Alamy; p308 Reuters/Alamy; p309 ITAR-TASS/Alamy; p313 Michael Kemp/Alamy

We are grateful to the following for permission to reproduce copyright material:

Office of National Statistics for the figure on p.8 'People aged from 16 to 24 not in education, employment or training as a percentage of all people aged from 16 to 24, seasonally adjusted UK, April to June 2011 to April to June 2016' adapted from Figure 1 in *Young people not in education, employment or training (NEET), UK: Aug 2016,* August 2016, https://www.ons.gov.uk/, © Crown copyright, 2015. All content is available under the Open Government Licence v3.0; NatCen Social Research for the table on p.15 'Attitudes to government spending on different benefits, 2002–2015', adapted from Table 1 in "Welfare, Support for government welfare reform", *NatCen's British Social Attitudes, 33,* 2016, p.5 http://www.bsa.natcen.ac.uk/media/39058/bsa33_welfare.pdf. Reproduced with permission; The University of Sheffield for an extract on p.16 adapted from *Essential Guides 2016*: http://www.sheffield.ac.uk/polopoly_fs/1.550495!/file/Int-Living-in-Shef-16.pdf, pp.17, 38. Reproduced with permission; Office of National Statistics for the table on p.28 'Live births outside marriage, England and Wales, 1970–2015 (Percentages)' adapted from Table 1 in *Birth Summary Tables - England and Wales,* July 2016, https://www.ons.gov.uk/, © Crown copyright, 2015. All content is available under the Open Government Licence v3.0; NatCen Social Research for statistics on p.29 'Views on higher education grants, England, 2014' adapted from Table 3 in *NatCen's British Social Attitudes, 32,* 2015, p.7, http://www.bsa.natcen.ac.uk/media/38917/bsa32_highereducation.pdf. Reproduced with permission; Child Poverty Action Group for an extract on p.29 adapted from 'Child poverty in the UK: A few facts' http://www.cpag.org.uk/sites/default/files/Child%20Poverty%20Action%20Group%20-%20Child%20poverty%20in%20the%20UK%20-%20A%20few%20facts.pdf. Reproduced with permission; Taylor & Francis for an extract on p.36 adapted from *The British on the Costa Del Sol: Transnational Identities and Local Communities* by Karen O'Reilly, Routledge, 2000, pp.154-155, 170, copyright © Karen O'Reilly. Reproduced with permission; Dr Maria Papapolydorou, for an extract on p.51 from 'Direct, Indirect and Relational: Social Class Manifestations in 'Teenage Students' Accounts' by Maria Papapolydorou published in *Youth and Policy,* No: 111, October 2013, p.36. Reproduced with permission; National Youth Agency for an extract on p.53 from 'The routes project: disadvantaged young people interviewing their peers' by E. Robson, in *Young People as Researchers: Possibilities, Problems and Politics* by Jill Clark et al, 2001, p.48. Reproduced with permission; Office of National Statistics for the data on p.67 'Ethnic groups, England and Wales, 2011', from Figure 1 in *Ethnicity and National Identity in England and Wales: 2011,* December 2012, https://www.ons.gov.uk/. Source: 2011 Census, © Crown copyright, 2012. All content is available under the Open Government Licence v3.0; NSPCC for the table on p.68 'How children and young people contacted Childline in 2014/15' from *Always there when I need you.* Childline Review, NSPCC, p.9 https://www.nspcc.org.uk/globalassets/documents/annual-reports/childline-annual-review-always-there-2014-2015.pdf, Accessed: 07/07/2016. Reproduced with permission; The British Sociological Association for an extract on p.73 adapted from BSA (2002) Statement of Ethical Practice, copyright © The British

Sociological Association www.britsoc.co.uk. Reproduced with permission from the British Sociological Association; Philip Allan Updates for an extract on p.75 adapted from 'The uses of sociology' by Jane Pilcher in *Sociology Review*, Vol 14 (1), September 2004, pp.2–4. Reproduced in adapted form by permission of Philip Allan (for Hodder Education); Office of National Statistics for the figure on p.77 'Number of marriages and divorces, 1933 to 2013', from Figure 1 in *Divorces in England and Wales: 2013*, November 2015, https://www.ons.gov.uk/, © Crown copyright, 2015. All content is available under the Open Government Licence v3.0; Palgrave Macmillan for an extract on p.81 adapted from *Families, Households and Society* by Graham Allan and Graham Crow, 2001, copyright © Palgrave. Reproduced with permission; Office of National Statistics for the table on p.85 'People living alone: by age group, 2005 to 2015' adapted from Figure 9 in *Families and Households: 2015*, November 2015, https://www.ons.gov.uk/; and the figure on p.88 'Percentage of the population aged 16 and over living alone by ethnic group, 2011', adapted from Figure 9 in *2011 Census Analysis, Do the Demographic and Socio-Economic Characteristics of those Living Alone in England and Wales Differ from the General Population?*, December 2014, p.18 Source: 2011 Census, http://webarchive.nationalarchives.gov.uk, © Crown copyright 2012, 2015. All content is available under the Open Government Licence v3.0; NatCen Social Research for the tables on pp.105, 106 'Attitudes to male and female roles in workplace and home, 1984–2012' and 'Average (mean) reported hours spent by men and women in couple on household work, 2002 and 2012' by Jacqueline Scott and Elizabeth Clery from Tables A.2, 5.5 in *NatCen British Social Attitudes 30*, 2013, pp.127, 137. Reproduced with permission; Refuge for information on p.109 about domestic violence, http://www.refuge.org.uk. Reproduced with permission; Office of National Statistics for the table on p.116 'Percentage of dependent children: by family type, 2005 to 2015' adapted from Figure 3 in *Families and Households: 2015*, November 2015. Source: Labour Force Survey; the statistics on pp.116, 117 from *General Lifestyle Survey in 2011 for Great Britain*, March 2013; the figure on p.120 'Dataset: Birth Summary Tables - England and Wales' adapted from Table 1 in *Summary of key live birth statistics, 1938 to 2015*, July 2016; the table of data on p.126 from the tables 'Average1,2,3 (mean) age of grooms: previous marital status, 1846 to 2013' and 'Average1,2,3 (mean) age of brides: previous marital status, 1846 to 2013' adapted from Tables 6 and 7 in *Dataset: Marriages in England and Wales, 2013*, April 2016; and the figure on p.126 'Number of marriages and divorces, 1933 to 2013' adapted from Figure 1 in *Divorces in England and Wales: 2013*, November 2015, https://www.ons.gov.uk/, © Crown copyright, 2013, 2015, 2016. All content is available under the Open Government Licence v3.0; Joseph Rowntree Foundation for an extract on p.130 adapted from *Parenting and the different ways it can affect children's lives: research evidence* by David Utting, published August 2007 by the Joseph Rowntree Foundation. Reproduced by permission; Office of National Statistics for an extract on p.136 adapted from *Families and Households: 2015*, November 2015, https://www.ons.gov.uk/, © Crown copyright, 2015. All content is available under the Open Government Licence v3.0; The Sutton Trust for an extract on p.157 adapted from 'Leading People 2016' by Dr. Philip Kirby, February 2016 www.suttontrust.com/researcharchive/leading-people-2016, copyright © The Sutton Trust 2016. Reproduced with permission; Sands School for details on p.159 about the school, www.sands-school.co.uk. Reproduced with permission; Sharon Gewirtz, Stephen J. Ball and Richard Bowe for extracts on pp.160, 162-163, 324 adapted from *Markets, Choice and Equity in Education* by Sharon Gewirtz, Stephen J. Ball and Richard Bowe, 1995. Reproduced with permission of the authors; Philip Allan Updates for an extract on p.161 from an interview with Ted Wragg in *Sociology Review*, Vol 13 (2), November 2003, p.12. Reproduced by permission of Philip Allan (for Hodder Education); Schools Week for an extract on p.167 adapted from 'Fears of 'free-for-all' as government opens up free school bid criteria' by Freddie Whittaker, *Schools Week*, 17/09/2016; http://schoolsweek.co.uk/fears-of-free-for-all-as-government-opens-up-free-school-criteria/. Reproduced with permission; Department for Education, Office of National Statistics for the tables on pp.169, 180, 186, 194 'Percentage of disadvantaged and all other pupils achieving the main attainment indicators England, state-funded schools, 2014-2015', 'Percentage achieving 5+ A*-C including English and maths by gender England, all schools, 2014-2015', 'Percentage of pupils achieving the main attainment indicators by major ethnic group England, state-funded schools, 2015' and 'Percentage of FSM eligible pupils achieving 5+ A*-C including English and maths for selected minor ethnic groups, by gender England, state-funded schools, 2015' adapted from Tables 2, 22 and Figures 11, 12 in *Revised GCSE and equivalent results in England, 2014 to 2015*, SFR 01/2016, January 2016, pp.3, 21, 23, 24, https://www.gov.uk, © Crown copyright, 2016. All content is available under the Open Government Licence v3.0; Philip Allan Updates for extracts on pp.173, 325 from 'Schooling and Educational Performance' by J. Williams, and 'Education and Social Capital' by S. Ball in *Sociology Review*, Vol 13 (2), November 2003, pp.3, 34. Reproduced by permission of Philip Allan (for Hodder Education); Cengage Learning Inc. for an extract on p.175 from *Pygmalion in the Classroom* by Robert Rosenthal PhD and Lenore Jacobson EdD, copyright © 1968 South-Western, a part of Cengage Learning, Inc. Reproduced by permission, www.cengage.com/permissions; JCQ for the tables on pp.180, 182 'Percentage achieving A*-C grades at A level by subject June 2016 (all UK candidates)' and 'Entries by subject at A level 2016' adapted from JCQ provisional results data, Summer 2016 www.jcq.org.uk; Higher Education Policy Institute for statistics on p.180 from 'Boys to Men: the underachievement of young men in higher education and how to start tackling it' by N. Hillman and N. Robinson, *HEPI Report 84*, May 2016, http://www.hepi.ac.uk/wp-content/uploads/2016/05/Boys-to-Men.pdf. Reproduced by permission; Guardian News & Media Ltd for an extract on p.183 from 'Single-sex schools no benefit for girls' by Anushka Asthana, *The Observer*, 25 June 2006, copyright © Guardian News & Media Ltd, 2006; Department for Education, Office of National Statistics for the table on p.186 'Percentage of pupils achieving 5+ A*- C GCSEs (or equivalent) grades including English and mathematics England, 2013/14 (2014 methodology)' from Figure 2 in *Statistical First Release GCSE and equivalent attainment by pupil characteristics, 2013 to 2014 (Revised)*, p.8, January 2015, https://www.gov.uk; and an extract on p.188 from *Ethnicity and Education: The Evidence on Minority Ethnic Pupils aged 5-16*. Research Topic paper 2006, p.5, http://webarchive.nationalarchives.gov.uk © Crown copyright 2006, 2016. All content is available under the Open Government Licence v3.0; The Open University for an extract on p.192 adapted from *Rationing Education: Policy, Practice, Reform and Equity* by David Gillborn and Deborah Youdell, 2000. Reproduced with permission of Open International Publishing Ltd. All rights reserved; SAGE for an extract on p.193 from 'Multi-racial primary school classrooms' by C. Wright, in *Racism and Education: Structures and Strategies* by Dawn Gill, Barbara Mayor and Maud Blair, Sage Publications Ltd, copyright © 1992, CCC Republication. Republished with permission of

Sage, permission conveyed through Copyright Clearance Center, Inc.; Office of National Statistics for table of data on p.196 from the tables 'Attainment of 5 or more GCSE grades A*-C in Year 11 (2006) by characteristics: 1988-2006' and 'Academic attainment in Year 11 (2006) by characteristics' from Tables 4.1.1, 4.1.2 in *Youth Cohort Study & Longitudinal Study of Young People in England: The Activities and Experiences of 16 year olds: England 2007*, June 2008, pp.18, 19, https://www.gov.uk; the table on p.220 'CSEW incidence rates and numbers of incidents for year ending March 2016 and percentage change' adapted from Table 1a in *Crime in England and Wales: year ending Mar 2016*, p.66, July 2016. Source: Crime Survey for England and Wales, http://www.ons.gov.uk; and the table on p.222 'Trends in overall crime for England and Wales, CSEW and police recorded crime, year ending December 1981 to year ending December 2015' adapted from Figure 1 in *Crime in England and Wales: Year ending December 2015*, April 2016, http://www.ons.gov.uk; Ministry of Justice for statistics on p.228 from *Statistics on Women and the Criminal Justice System 2013*, 2014, p.63 and *Statistics on Women and the Criminal Justice System 2015*, 2016, p.12; and Office of National Statistics for the figure on p.234 'British nationals in the prison population by ethnicity per 10,000 people aged 15 years old or more, 2014' adapted from Figure 7.01 in *Statistics on Race and the Criminal Justice System 2014*, p.69, http://www.ons.gov.uk, © Crown copyright, 2008, 2014, 2015, 2016. All content is available under the Open Government Licence v3.0; Philip Allan Updates for extracts on pp.273, 327 adapted from 'Is policing fair?' by Michael Townsley and Ben Marshall in *Sociology Review*, Vol 16 (2), November 2006, pp.19-21. Reproduced in adapted form by permission of Philip Allan (for Hodder Education); Office of National Statistics for the table on p.238 'Persons found guilty at all courts or cautioned for indictable offences per 100,000 population, by sex and age group, 2005 to 2015' from Table A3.1b in *National Statistics Criminal justice system statistics quarterly: December 2015*, May 2016, https://www.gov.uk, © Crown copyright, 2016. All content is available under the Open Government Licence v3.0; Taylor & Francis for an extract on p.249 adapted from 'The worrying influence of 'media effects' studies' by D. Gauntlett, in *Ill Effects: The media/violence debate, Second edition* eds Martin Barker and Julian Petley, Routledge, 2001, pp.55-56, copyright © 1997, 2001 Martin Barker and Julian Petley. Reproduced with permission; Office of National Statistics for the table on p.252 'Trends in worry about crime, England & Wales' adapted from Figure 9.9 in *Social Trends 38*, Crime and Justice, 2008. Source British Crime Survey, Home Office, http://webarchive.nationalarchives.gov.uk, © Crown copyright, 2009; YouGov for an extract on p.265 adapted from *YouGov/Prospect Survey Results*, p.1; https://d25d2506sfb94s.cloudfront.net/cumulus_uploads/document/kqc6u0jxq7/Prospect_Results_Social_Class_140129_website.pdf, January 2014, copyright © 2014 YouGov Plc. All Rights Reserved; HMSO for the table on p.266 'Socio-economic Group and Social Class allocations of Occupation and Employment Status Groups' from Appendix B.1 in *Classification of occupations and coding index*, 1980, p.84, http://webarchive.nationalarchives.gov.uk; and Office of National Statistics for the table on p.267 'NS-SEC Analytic classes' from Table 1 in *SOC2010 Volume 3: the National Statistics Socio-economic classification (NS-SEC rebased on SOC2010)*, http://www.ons.gov.uk, © Crown copyright, 1980, 2010; Edinburgh University Press Limited via PLSClear for extracts on pp.271, 314 from *Affluent Workers Revisited: Privatism and the Working Class* by Fiona Devine, Edinburgh University Press, 1992, pp.5, 202. Reproduced with permission; Philip Allan Updates for an extract on p.275 adapted from 'Social class in an 'individualised' society' by Andy Furlong, Fred Cartmel, Andy Biggart, Helen Sweeting and Patrick West in *Sociology Review*, Vol 15 (4), April 2006, pp.28-32. Reproduced in adapted form by permission of Philip Allan (for Hodder Education); Office of National Statistics for the table on p.278 'Employment rates for men and women aged 16-64, 1971 to 2013, UK' from *Women in the labour market: 2013*, September 2013, http://www.ons.gov.uk. Source: Labour Force Survey; and the table on p.282 'Unemployment by ethnic background and gender: UK, January to December 2015', adapted from *Unemployment by ethnic background, Briefing Paper No. 6385*, 27 April 2016 by Jeanne Delebarre, p.4. Source: ONS *Annual Population Survey 2015*, March 2016, researchbriefings.files.parliament.uk, © Crown copyright, 2013, 2016. All content is available under the Open Government Licence v3.0; Penguin Books Ltd, University of California Press and The P. B. Townsend Settlement for an extract and table on p.295 from *Poverty in the United Kingdom: A Survey of Household Resources and Standards of Living* by Peter Townsend, pp.31, 250, copyright © Peter Townsend 1979, 1980. Reproduced by permission of Penguin Books Ltd and University of California Press as publishers, and The P. B. Townsend Settlement; House of Commons for the tables on pp.299, 315 'Poverty levels in the UK, 2014/15: children' and 'Poverty levels in the UK, 2014/15: all individuals' adapted from *Poverty in the UK: statistics, Briefing Paper No. 7096*, November 2016 by Feargal McGuiness, p.3, researchbriefings.parliament.uk, © Parliamentary Copyright 2016. All content is available under the Open Parliament Licence; Department for Communities and Local Government for the table on p.318 adapted from *2005 Citizenship Survey: Active communities topic report* by Sarah Kitchen, Juliet Michaelson, Natasha Wood and Peter John, 2006 © Crown copyright 2006. All content is available under the Open Government Licence v3.0; Civitas: Institute for the Study of Civil Society for an extract on p.322, adapted from the foreword by A.H. Halsey in *Families Without Fatherhood, 2nd edition* by Norman Dennis and George Erdos, 2000, pp.xii–xiii. Reproduced with permission; NHS Choices for an extract on p.323 adapted from 'Child obesity rates are 'stabilising'', 30 January 2015, NHS Choices http://www.nhs.uk/news/2015/01January/Pages/Child-obesity-rates-are-stabilising.aspx. Reproduced with permission; Ministry of Justice for a table on p.326 adapted from *Criminal Statistics 2006, England and Wales*, 2007, p.79, © Crown copyright 2007. All content is available under the Open Government Licence v3.0; Philip Allan Updates for an extract on p.328 adapted from 'A matter of life and death' by Mary Shaw in *Sociology Review*, Vol 11 (4), April 2002, pp.10–13. Reproduced in adapted form by permission of Philip Allan (for Hodder Education); and Taylor & Francis for an extract on p.329 adapted *Gender and Everyday life (The New Sociology)* by Mary Holmes, Routledge, 2008, p.3, copyright © 2009 Mary Holmes. Reproduced with permission.